Teach

Yourself

C

Third Edition

Herbert Schildt

Osborne **McGraw-Hill**

Berkeley New York St. Louis San Francisco Auckland Bogotá Hamburg London Madrid Mexico City
Milan Montreal New Delhi Panama City Paris São Paulo Singapore Sydney Tokyo Toronto

Publisher
Brandon A. Nordin

Editor-in-Chief
Scott Rogers

Acquisitions Editor
Wendy Rinaldi

Project Editor
Heidi Poulin

Editorial Assistant
Ann Sellers

Technical Editor
Gregg Guntle

Copy Editor
Erik Van Eaton

Proofreader
Karen Mead

Indexer
Sheryl Schildt

Computer Designers
Roberta Steele
Sylvia Brown

Illustrator
Roberta Steele

Series Design
Peter Hancik

Osborne **McGraw-Hill**
2600 Tenth Street
Berkeley, California 94710
U.S.A.

For information on translations or book distributors outside the U.S.A., or to arrange bulk purchase discounts for sales promotions, premiums, or fundraisers, please contact Osborne/**McGraw-Hill** at the above address.

Teach Yourself C, Third Edition

1234567890 DOC 9987

ISBN 0-07-882311-0

About the Author

Herbert Schildt is the world's leading programming author. He is an authority on the C and C++ languages, a master Windows programmer, and an expert on Java. His programming books have sold nearly two million copies worldwide and have been translated into all major foreign languages. He is the author of numerous best-sellers, including *C: The Complete Reference*, *C++: The Complete Reference*, *C++ from the Ground Up*, *MFC Programming from the Ground Up*, *Windows 95 Programming in C and C++*, *Windows NT 4 Programming from the Ground Up*, and many others. He is also a member of both the ANSI C and C++ standardization committees.

Contents

Preface

This book teaches you how to program in what is usually regarded as the world's most important professional programming language: C.

One reason for C's success and staying power is that *programmers like it*. C combines subtlety and elegance with raw power and flexibility. It is a structured language that does not confine. It is a high-performance language that does not constrain. C is also a language that puts you, the programmer, firmly in charge. C was created by a programmer for programmers. It is not the contrived product of a committee, but rather the outcome of programmers seeking a better programming language.

C is important for another reason. It is the gateway to the world's two other professional programming languages: C++ and Java. C++ is built upon C, and Java is built upon C++. Thus, C is at the foundation of all modern programming, and knowledge of C is fundamental to the successful creation of high-performance, high-quality software. Simply put, to be a professional programmer today means that you are competent in C.

A Short History of C

C was invented and first implemented by Dennis Ritchie on a DEC PDP-11 using the UNIX operating system. C is the result of a development process that started with an older language called BCPL, developed by Martin Richards. BCPL influenced a language called B that was invented by Ken Thompson and that led to the development of C in the 1970s.

For many years, the de facto standard for C was the one described in *The C Programming Language* by Brian Kernighan and Dennis Ritchie (Prentice-Hall, 1978). However, as C grew in popularity, a committee was organized in 1983 to create an ANSI (American National Standards Institute) standard for C. The standardization process took six years (much longer than anyone reasonably expected). The ANSI C standard was finally adopted late in 1989 and the first copies became generally available in 1990. The standard was amended slightly in 1996. Today, virtually all C compilers comply with ANSI standard C and that is the version of C you will learn in this book. (That is, this book teaches ANSI standard C.)

C is often referred to as a *middle-level language*. Before C there were basically two types of languages used to program computers. One is called *assembly language*, which is the symbolic representation of the actual machine instructions executed by the computer. Assembly language is a *low-level language* because the programmer is working with (in symbolic form) the actual instructions that the computer will execute. Assembly language can be used to create very efficient programs, but it provides no built-in control structures or I/O functions. All such items must be manually constructed by the programmer. By contrast, a *high-level language* buffers the programmer from the computer. A high-level language typically supplies various control structures, input and output commands, and the like, which make programming easier and faster. However, the elements of a high-level language may not relate directly to the way that the computer ultimately carries out the program. This separation often causes programs written using a high-level language to be less efficient than those written in assembly language. Because many people find assembly language programming to be a tedious, difficult task, there was a need for a language that balanced ease-of-use with efficiency. Many programmers feel that C provides this balance. It successfully combines the structure of a high-level language with the power and efficiency of assembly language. Since it spans the gap between assembly language and high-level languages, it is called a middle-level language.

Initially, C was used primarily for creating *systems software*. Systems software consists of those programs that help run the computer. These include programs such as operating systems, compilers, and editors. However, as C gained in popularity, it began to be used for general purpose programming. Today, C is used by programmers for virtually any programming task. It is a language that has survived the test of time and proven itself to be as versatile as it is powerful.

C vs. C++

Newcomers are sometimes confused about the differences between C and C++ and how they relate to each other. In short, C++ is an extended version of C that is designed to support object-oriented programming (OOP). C++ contains and supports the entire C language in addition to a set of object-oriented extensions. (That is, C++ is a superset of C.) Because C++ is built upon the foundation of C, you cannot learn C++ without learning the basics of C. Therefore, if you think that you will someday move on to C++, your knowledge of C will not only be useful, it will be necessary.

About This Book

This book is unique because it teaches you the C language by applying mastery learning. It does so by presenting one idea at a time, followed by numerous examples and exercises to help you thoroughly understand each topic. This approach ensures that you master each topic before moving on.

The material is presented sequentially. Therefore, you should work carefully through each chapter because each chapter assumes that you know the material presented in all preceding chapters.

This book teaches ANSI standard C. This ensures that your knowledge will be applicable to the widest range of C environments. This book also uses contemporary syntax and structure, which means that you will be learning the right way to write C programs from the very beginning.

How This Book is Organized

This book is composed of 12 chapters and 4 appendices. Each chapter (except Chapter 1) begins with a Review Skills Check, which consists of questions and exercises covering the previous chapter's material. The chapters are divided into sections. Each section covers one topic. At the end of each section are examples followed by exercises that test your understanding of the topic. At the end of each chapter, you will find a Mastery Skills Check, which checks your knowledge of the material in the chapter. Finally, a Cumulative Skills Check is presented that tests how well you are integrating new material with that presented in earlier chapters.

What's New in the Third Edition

For the most part, the form and structure of this book are unchanged from the previous two editions. Since C is a stable, standardized language, there was no reason to make major revisions. The two significant changes are the inclusion of full function prototypes in all programs, beginning with Chapter 1. Since all compilers now support—indeed, nearly demand—function prototyping, initial coverage of this issue was moved to the beginning of the book. Another set of changes was prompted by the emerging dominance of 32-bit environments. This caused a number of examples to be rewritten so that they would work for both 16- and 32-bit programs. In some places, additional examples, expanded coverage, or more exercises can be found. Finally, a few changes were made simply to reflect modern coding styles.

Conventions Used in this Book

Whenever a part of a program (such as a variable name) is referenced in text, it will be shown using boldface. Whenever a generic name is referenced in text, it will be shown in italics.

Will a C++ Compiler Work With C Programs?

Today, most compilers can compile both C and C++ programs. In fact, it is common to see a compiler advertised as a "C/C++" compiler, or sometimes just as a "C++" compiler. However, any and all compilers that can compile C++ programs can also compile C programs. Therefore, if your compiler calls itself a C++ compiler, don't worry; it is also a full, ANSI-standard C compiler.

If You're Using Windows

If you use Windows, and if your goal is to write Windows-based programs, then you have chosen the right language to learn. C is the language for which Windows programming was designed, and the language in which many Windows programs are written. However, you will not be able to write Windows programs immediately. Here is why.

Windows programs are much more complex to create than non-Windows programs. Even a minimal, do-nothing Windows program makes use of several sophisticated C techniques, such as structures, pointers, and advanced function parameter types. For this reason, it is not possible to teach C programming by writing Windows programs because a Windows program assumes that you are an experienced C programmer!

If you are using Windows (rather than DOS, UNIX, etc.) on your computer, you can still learn C. However, you will need to run your programs from the DOS prompt because they will not be Windows-based programs. All modern C/C++ compilers will automatically create the correct environment to execute the programs shown in this book, so it isn't something that you will typically need to worry about.

If you will be writing Windows programs, you will want to read Appendix C after you complete this book. It contains a brief overview of Windows programming basics, and includes a Windows skeleton program that you can try. Examining this skeleton will also show you that a thorough knowledge of C is required before Windows programs can be written.

Don't Forget: Code On The Web

Remember, the source code for all of the programs in this book is available free-of-charge on the Web at **http://www.osborne.com**. Downloading this code prevents you from having to type in the examples.

For Further Study

Teach Yourself C, Third Edition is your gateway into the "Herb Schildt" series of programming books. Here is a partial list of Schildt's other programming books published by Osborne/McGraw-Hill.

If you want to learn more about C, you will find these books especially helpful.

C: The Complete Reference
The Annotated ANSI C Standard

If you will be moving on to C++ (C's object-oriented extension), then you will find that Schildt's C++ books provide excellent coverage of this important language. We recommend

Teach Yourself C++
C++: The Complete Reference
C++ from the Ground Up

If you will be developing programs for the Web, you will want to read

Java: The Complete Reference

co-authored by Herbert Schildt and Patrick Naughton.

Finally, if you want to program for Windows, we recommend

Schildt's Windows 95 Programming in C and C++
Schildt's Advanced Windows 95 Programming in C and C++
Windows NT 4 from the Ground Up
MFC Programming from the Ground Up

**When you need solid answers, fast, turn to
Herbert Schildt, the recognized authority on
programming.**

1

C Fundamentals

chapter objectives

THE individual elements of a computer language such as C do not stand alone, but rather in conjunction with one another. Therefore, it is necessary to understand several key aspects of C before examining each element of the language in detail. To this end, this chapter presents a quick overview of the C language. Its goal is to give you sufficient working knowledge of C so that you can understand the examples in later chapters.

As you work through this chapter, don't worry if a few points are not entirely clear. The main thing you need to understand is how and why the example programs execute as they do. Keep in mind that most of the topics introduced in this chapter will be discussed in greater detail later in this book. In this chapter, you will learn about the basic structure of a C program; what a C statement is; and what variables, constants, and functions are. You will learn how to display text on the screen and input information from the keyboard.

To use this book to the fullest, you must have a computer, a C compiler, and a text editor. (You may also use a C++ compiler. C++ compilers can also compile C programs.) Your compiler may include its own text editor, in which case you won't need a separate one. For the best results, you should work along with the examples and try the exercises.

1.1 UNDERSTAND THE COMPONENTS OF A C PROGRAM

All C programs share certain essential components and traits. All C programs consist of one or more *functions*, each of which contains one or more *statements*. In C, a function is a named subroutine that can be called by other parts of the program. Functions are the building blocks of C. A statement specifies an action to be performed by the program. In other words, statements are the parts of your program that actually perform operations.

All C statements end with a semicolon. C does not recognize the end of the line as a terminator. This means there are no constraints on the position of statements within a line. Also, you may place two or more statements on one line.

The general form of a C function is shown here:

```
ret-type function-name(param-list)
{
 statement sequence
}
```

Here, *ret-type* specifies the type of data returned by the function. As you will see, it is possible for a function to return a value. The *function-name* is the name of the function. Information can be passed to a function through its parameters, which are specified in the function's parameter list, *param-list*. The *statement sequence* may be one or more statements. (Technically, a function can contain no statements, but since this means the function performs no action, it is a degenerative case.) If return types and parameters are new concepts, don't worry, they will be explained later in this chapter.

With few exceptions, you can call a function by any name you like. It must be composed of only the upper- and lowercase letters of the alphabet, the digits 0-9, and the underscore. A digit cannot start a function name, however. C is *case-sensitive*, which means that C recognizes the difference between upper- and lowercase letters. Thus, as far as C is concerned, **Myfunc** and **myfunc** are entirely different names.

Although a C program may contain several functions, the only function that it *must* have is **main( )**. The **main( )** function is where execution of your program begins. That is, when your program begins running, it starts executing the statements inside **main( )**, beginning with the first statement after the opening curly brace. Your program ends when **main( )**'s closing curly brace is reached. Of course, the curly brace does not actually exist in the compiled version of your program, but it is helpful to think of it in this way.

Throughout this book, when a function is referred to in text, it will be printed in bold and followed by parentheses. This way, you can see immediately that the name refers to a function, not some other part of the program.

Another important component of all C programs is *library functions*. The ANSI C standard specifies a set of library functions to be supplied by all C compilers, which your program may use. This collection of functions is usually referred to as the *C standard library*. The standard library contains functions to perform disk I/O (input/ output), string manipulations, mathematical computations, and much more. When your program is compiled, the code for each library function used by your program is automatically included. This differs from the way some other computer languages work. For example, in BASIC or Pascal, operations such as writing to a file or computing a cosine are performed using keywords that are built into the language. The advantage C gains by having them as library functions is increased flexibility. Library functions can be enhanced and expanded as needed to accommodate changing circumstances. The C language itself does not need to change. As you will see, virtually all C programs you create will use functions from the C standard library.

One of the most common library functions is called **printf( )**. This is C's general-purpose output function. The **printf( )** function is quite versatile, allowing many variations. Its simplest form is shown here:

```
printf("string-to-output");
```

The **printf( )** function outputs the characters that are contained between the beginning and ending double quotes to the screen. (The double quotes are not displayed on the screen.) In C, one or more characters enclosed between double quotes is called a *string*. The quoted string between **printf( )**'s parentheses is said to be an *argument* to **printf( )**. In general, information passed to a function is called an argument. In C, calling a library function is a statement; therefore, it must end with a semicolon.

To call a function, you specify its name followed by a parenthesized list of arguments that you will be passing to it. If the function does not require any arguments, no arguments will be specified—and the parenthesized list will be empty. If there is more than one argument, the arguments must be separated by commas.

Another component common to most C programs is the *header file*. In C, information about the standard library functions is found in various files supplied with your compiler. These files all end with a .H extension. The C compiler uses the information in these files to handle the library functions properly. You add these files to your program using the **#include** *preprocessor directive*. All C compilers use as their first phase of compilation a *preprocessor*, which performs various manipulations on your source file before it is compiled.

Preprocessor directives are not actually part of the C language, but rather instructions from you to the compiler. The **#include** directive tells the preprocessor to read in another file and include it with your program. You will learn more about the preprocessor later in this book.

The most commonly required header file is called STDIO.H. Here is the directive that includes this file:

```
#include <stdio.h>
```

You can specify the file name in either upper- or lowercase, but lowercase is the traditional method. The STDIO.H header file contains, among other things, information related to the **printf( )** library function. Notice that the **#include** directive does not end with a semicolon. The reason for this is that **#include** is not a C keyword that can define a statement. Instead, it is an instruction to the C compiler itself.

One last point: With few exceptions, C ignores spaces. That is, it doesn't care where on a line a statement, curly brace, or function name occurs. If you like, you can even put two or more of these items on the same line. The examples you will see in this book reflect the way C code is normally written; it is a form you should follow. The actual positioning of statements, functions, and braces is a stylistic, not a programming, decision.

EXAMPLES

1. Since all C programs share certain common traits, understanding one program will help you understand many others. One of the simplest C programs is shown here:

```
#include <stdio.h>

int main(void)
{
  printf("This is a short C program.");

  return 0;
}
```

When compiled and executed, this program displays the message
This is a short C program. on the screen of your computer.

Even though this program is only six lines long, it illustrates
those aspects common to all C programs. Let's examine it line
by line.

The first line of the program is

```
#include <stdio.h>
```

It causes the file STDIO.H to be read by the C compiler and to
be included with the program. This file contains information
related to **printf( )**.

The second line,

```
int main(void)
```

begins the **main( )** function. As stated earlier, all C programs
must have a **main( )** function. This is where program execution
begins. The **int** specifies that **main( )** returns an integer value.
The **void** tells the compiler that **main( )** does not have any
parameters.

After **main( )** is an opening curly brace. This marks the
beginning of statements that make up the function.
The next line in the program is

```
printf("This is a short C program.");
```

This is a C statement. It calls the standard library function,
printf( ), which causes the string to be displayed.

The following line causes **main( )** to return the value zero. In
this case, the value is returned to the calling process, which is
usually the operating system.

```
return 0;
```

By convention, a return value of zero from **main( )** indicates
normal program termination. Any other value represents an
error. The operating system can test this value to determine
whether the program ran successfully or experienced an error.
return is one of C's keywords and is examined more closely
later in this chapter.

Finally, the program is formally concluded when **main( )**'s
closing curly brace is encountered.

2. Here is another simple C program:

```c
#include <stdio.h>

int main(void)
{
  printf("This is ");
  printf("another C ");
  printf("program.");

  return 0;
}
```

This program displays **This is another C program.** on the screen. The key point to this program is that statements are executed sequentially, beginning with the opening curly brace and ending with the closing curly brace.

1.2   CREATE AND COMPILE A PROGRAM

How you will create and compile a program is determined to a very large extent by the compiler you are using and the operating system under which it is running. If you are using a PC or compatible, you have your choice of a number of excellent compilers, such as those by Borland and Microsoft, that contain integrated program-development environments. If you are using such an environment, you can edit, compile, and run your programs directly inside this environment. This is an excellent option for beginners—just follow the instructions supplied with your compiler.

If you are using a traditional command-line compiler, then you need to follow these steps to create and compile a program:

1. Create your program using an editor.

2. Compile the program.

3. Execute your program.

The exact method to accomplish these steps will be explained in the user's manual for your compiler.

Nearly all modern C compilers are also C++ compilers. As you may know, C++ is the object-oriented extension to C. Most likely you will be using a C++ compiler to compile your C code. Don't worry. This is perfectly acceptable because all C++ compilers are capable of compiling C programs. For example, if you are using Borland C++ or Microsoft Visual C++, then everything will work just fine. However, there is one thing about which you must be very careful: the extension you give your files.

When naming your program's file, you must give it a .C—not .CPP—extension. This is important. If you are using a C++ compiler, then it will automatically assume that a file using the .C extension contains a C program and will compile it as a C program. But, if the file uses a .CPP extension, then the compiler will assume that the program is written in C++ and compile it as such. The problem is that while C is the foundation for C++, not all C programs are valid C++ programs. Trying to compile a C program *as if it were* a C++ program will cause errors in a few cases. Since the programs in this book are C programs, they should be compiled as C programs. Using the .C extension ensures this.

Remember *Your program must be compiled as a C program—not a C++ program. To ensure this, make sure that your programs use the .C, not the .CPP, extension.*

The file that contains the C program that you create is called the *source file*. The file that contains the compiled form of your program that the computer executes is called the *object file*, or, sometimes, the *executable file*.

If you enter something into your program incorrectly, the compiler will report syntax error messages when it attempts to compile it. Most C compilers attempt to make sense out of your source code no matter what you have written. For this reason, the error that gets reported may not always reflect the actual cause of the error. For example, accidentally forgetting the opening curly brace to the **main( )** function in the preceding sample programs will cause some compilers to report the **printf( )** statement as an incorrect identifier. So, when you receive a syntax error message, be prepared to look at the last few lines of code in your program before the point at which the error is reported to find its cause.

Many compilers report not only actual errors but also warning errors. The C language was designed to be very forgiving and to allow virtually anything that is syntactically correct to be compiled. However, some things, even though syntactically correct, are highly suspicious. When the compiler encounters one of these situations it prints a warning. You, as the programmer, then decide whether its suspicions are justified. Frankly, some compilers are a bit too helpful and flag warnings on perfectly correct C statements. More important, some compilers allow you to enable various options that simply report information about your program that you might like to know. Sometimes this type of information is reported in the form of a warning message, even though there is nothing to be "warned" about. The programs in this book are in compliance with the ANSI standard for C and will not generate any warning messages about which you need be concerned.

EXAMPLES

1. If you are using Borland C++, you can create and compile your program using the integrated environment. Online instructions are provided. If you are using the command-line version of Borland C++, you will use a command line such as this (assuming that the name of your program is called TEST.C) to compile the program once you have used a text editor to create it.

   BCC TEST.C

2. If you are using Microsoft Visual C++, you can use the integrated environment to create and compile your program. Online instructions are provided. When using the command line compiler, this command line will compile your program after using a text file to create it. (Again, assume that the program is called TEST.C.)

   CL TEST.C

3. If you are using another brand of compiler, refer to your user's manual for details on compiling your programs.

1. Enter into your computer the example programs from Section 1.1. Compile them and run them.

1.3 *D*ECLARE VARIABLES AND ASSIGN VALUES

A *variable* is a named memory location that can hold various values. Only the most trivial C programs do not include variables. In C, unlike some computer languages, all variables must be declared before they can be used. A variable's declaration serves one important purpose: It tells the compiler *what type of variable* is being used. C supports five different basic data types, as shown in Table 1-1 along with the C keywords that represent them. Don't be confused by **void**. This is a special-purpose data type that we will later examine closely.

A variable of type **char** is 8 bits long and is most commonly used to hold a single character. Because C is very flexible, a variable of type **char** can also be used as a "little integer" if desired.

Integer variables (**int**) may hold signed whole numbers (numbers with no fractional part). For 16-bit environments, such as DOS or Windows 3.1, integers are usually 16 bits long and may hold values in the range -32,768 to 32,767. In 32-bit environments, such as Windows NT or Windows 95, integers are typically 32 bits in length. In this case, they may store values in the range -2,147,483,648 to 2,147,483,647.

Type	Keyword
character data	char
signed whole numbers	int
floating-point numbers	float
double-precision floating-point numbers	double
valueless	void

TABLE 1-1 *C's Five Basic Data Types* ▼

Variables of types **float** and **double** hold signed floating-point values, which may have fractional components. One difference between **float** and **double** is that **double** provides about twice the precision (number of significant digits) as does **float**. Also, for most uses of C, a variable of type **double** is capable of storing values with absolute magnitudes larger than those stored by variables of type **float**. Of course, in all cases, variables of types **float** and **double** can hold very large values.

To declare a variable, use this general form:

type var-name;

where *type* is a C data type and *var-name* is the name of the variable. For example, this declares **counter** to be of type **int**:

```
int counter;
```

In C, a variable declaration is a statement and it must end in a semicolon.

There are two places where variables are declared: inside a function or outside all functions. Variables declared outside all functions are called *global variables* and they may be accessed by any function in your program. Global variables exist the entire time your program is executing.

Variables declared inside a function are called *local variables*. A local variable is known to—and may be accessed by—only the function in which it is declared. It is common practice to declare all local variables used by a function at the start of the function, after the opening curly brace. There are two important points you need to know about local variables at this time. First, the local variables in one function have no relationship to the local variables in another function. That is, if a variable called **count** is declared in one function, another variable called **count** may also be declared in a second function—the two variables are completely separate from and unrelated to each other. The second thing you need to know is that local variables are created when a function is called, and they are destroyed when the function is exited. Therefore, local variables do not maintain their values between function calls. The examples in this and the next few chapters will use only local variables. Chapter 4 discusses more thoroughly the issues and implications of global and local variables.

You can declare more than one variable of the same type by using a comma-separated list. For example, this declares three floating-point variables, **x**, **y**, and **z**:

```
float x, y, z;
```

Like function names, variable names in C can consist of the letters of the alphabet, the digits 0 through 9, and the underscore. (But a digit may not start a variable's name.) Remember, C is case-sensitive; **count** and **COUNT** are two completely different variable names.

To assign a value to a variable, put its name to the left of an equal sign. Put the value you want to give the variable to the right of the equal sign. In C, an assignment operation is a statement; therefore, it must be terminated by a semicolon. The general form of an assignment statement is:

variable-name = value;

For example, to assign an integer variable named **num** the value 100, you can use this statement:

```
num = 100;
```

In the preceding assignment, 100 is a constant. Just as there are different types of variables, there are different types of constants. A *constant* is a fixed value used in your program. Constants are often used to initialize variables at the beginning of a program's execution.

A character constant is specified by placing the character between single quotes. For example, to specify the letter "A," you would use **'A'**. Integers are specified as whole numbers. Floating-point values must include a decimal point. For example, to specify 100.1, you would use **100.1**. If the floating-point value you wish to specify does not have any digits to the right of the decimal point, then you must use 0. For example, to tell the compiler that 100 is a floating-point number, use **100.0**.

You can use **printf( )** to display values of characters, integers, and floating-point values. To do so, however, requires that you know more about the **printf( )** function. Let's look first at an example. This statement:

```
printf("This prints the number %d", 99);
```

displays **This prints the number 99** on the screen. As you can see, this call to **printf( )** contains not one, but two arguments. The first is the quoted string and the other is the constant 99. Notice that the arguments are separated from each other by a comma. In general, when there is more than one argument to a function, the arguments are separated from each other by commas. The operation of the **printf( )** function is as follows. The first argument is a quoted string that may contain either normal characters or format specifiers that begin with the percent sign. Normal characters are simply displayed as-is on the screen in the order in which they are encountered in the string (reading left to right). A format specifier, also called a format code, informs **printf( )** that a different type item is to be displayed. In this case, the **%d** means that an integer is to be output in decimal format. The value to be displayed is found in the second argument. This value is then output to the screen at the point where the format specifier is found in the string. To understand the relationship between the normal characters and the format codes, examine this statement:

```
printf("This displays %d, too", 99);
```

Now the call to **printf( )** displays **This displays 99, too**. The key point is that the value associated with a format code is displayed at the point where that format code is encountered in the string.

If you want to specify a character value, the format specifier is **%c**. To specify a floating-point value, use **%f**. The **%f** works for both **float** and **double**. As you will see, **printf( )** has many more capabilities.

Keep in mind that the values matched with the format specifier need not be constants; they may be variables, too.

EXAMPLES

1. The program shown here illustrates the three new concepts introduced in this section. First, it declares a variable named **num**. Second, it assigns this variable the value 100. Finally, it uses **printf( )** to display **The value is 100** on the screen. Examine this program closely:

```
#include <stdio.h>

int main(void)
{
  int num;

  num = 100;
  printf("The value is %d", num);

  return 0;
}
```

The statement

```
int num;
```

declares **num** to be an integer variable.

To display the value of **num**, the program uses this statement:

```
printf("The value is %d", num);
```

2. This program creates variables of types **char**, **float**, and **double**; assigns each a value; and outputs these values to the screen.

```
#include <stdio.h>

int main(void)
{
  char ch;
  float f;
  double d;

  ch = 'X';
  f = 100.123;
  d = 123.009;

  printf("ch is %c, ", ch);
  printf("f is %f, ", f);
  printf("d is %f", d);

  return 0;
}
```

EXERCISES

1. Enter, compile, and run the example programs in this section.

2. Write a program that declares one integer variable called **num**. Give this variable the value 1000 and then, using one **printf( )** statement, display the value on the screen like this:

```
1000 is the value of num
```

1.4 ▮NPUT NUMBERS FROM THE KEYBOARD

Although there are actually several ways to input numeric values from the keyboard, one of the easiest is to use another of C's standard library functions called **scanf( )**. Although it possesses considerable versatility, we will use it in this chapter to read only integers and floating-point numbers entered from the keyboard.

To use **scanf( )** to read an integer value from the keyboard, call it using the general form

```
scanf("%d", &int-var-name);
```

where *int-var-name* is the name of the integer variable you wish to receive the value. The first argument to **scanf( )** is a string that determines how the second argument will be treated. In this case, the **%d** specifies that the second argument will be receiving an integer value entered in decimal format. This fragment, for example, reads an integer entered from the keyboard.

```
int num;
scanf("%d", &num);
```

The **&** preceding the variable name is essential to the operation of **scanf( )**. Although a detailed explanation will have to wait until later, loosely, the **&** allows a function to place a value into one of its arguments.

It is important to understand one key point: When you enter a number at the keyboard, you are simply typing a string of digits. The **scanf( )** function waits until you have pressed ENTER before it converts the string into the internal binary format used by the computer.

To read a floating-point number from the keyboard, call **scanf( )** using the general form

scanf("%f", &*float-var-name*);

where *float-var-name* is the name of a variable that is declared as being of type **float**. If you want to input to a **double** variable, use the **%lf** specifier.

Notice that the format specifiers for **scanf( )** are similar to those used for **printf( )** for the corresponding data types except that **%lf** is used to read a **double**. This is no coincidence—**printf( )** and **scanf( )** are complementary functions.

EXAMPLE

1. This program asks you to input an integer and a floating-point number. It then displays the values you enter.

```c
#include <stdio.h>

int main(void)
{
  int num;
  float f;

  printf("Enter an integer: ");
  scanf("%d", &num);

  printf("Enter a floating point number: ");
  scanf("%f", &f);

  printf("%d ", num);
  printf("%f", f);

  return 0;
}
```

EXERCISES

1. Enter, compile, and run the example program.

2. Write a program that inputs two floating-point numbers (use type **float**) and then displays their sum.

1.5   *P*ERFORM CALCULATIONS USING ARITHMETIC EXPRESSIONS

In C, the expression plays a much more important role than it does in most other programming languages. Part of the reason for this is that C defines many more operators than do most other languages. An *expression* is a combination of operators and operands. C expressions follow the rules of algebra, so, for the most part, they will be familiar. In this section we will look only at arithmetic expressions.

C defines these five arithmetic operators:

Operator	Meaning
+	addition
–	subtraction
*	multiplication
/	division
%	modulus

The +, –, /, and * operators may be used with any of the basic data types. However, the **%** may be used with integer types only. The modulus operator produces the remainder of an integer division. This has no meaning when applied to floating-point types.

The – has two meanings. First, it is the subtraction operator. Second, it can be used as a unary minus to reverse the sign of a number. A unary operator uses only one operand.

An expression may appear on the right side of an assignment statement. For example, this program fragment assigns the integer variable **answer** the value of 100*31.

```
int answer;
answer = 100 * 31;
```

The *, /, and **%** are higher in precedence than the **+** and the **–**. However, you can use parentheses to alter the order of evaluation. For example, this expression produces the value zero,

   10 - 2 * 5

but this one produces the value 40.

   (10 - 2) * 5

A C expression may contain variables, constants, or both. For example, assuming that **answer** and **count** are variables, this expression is perfectly valid:

```
answer = count - 100;
```

Finally, you may use spaces liberally within an expression.

EXAMPLES

1. As stated earlier, the modulus operator returns the remainder of an integer division. The remainder of 10 % 3 equals 1, for example. This program shows the outcome of some integer divisions and their remainders:

```
#include <stdio.h>

int main(void)
{
  printf("%d", 5/2);
  printf(" %d", 5%2);
  printf(" %d", 4/2);
  printf(" %d", 4%2);

  return 0;
}
```

This program displays **2 1 2 0** on the screen.

2. In long expressions, the use of parentheses and spaces can add clarity, even if they are not necessary. For example, examine this expression:

```
count *num+88/val-19%count
```

This expression produces the same result, but is much easier to read:

```
(count * num) + (88 / val) - (19 % count)
```

3. This program computes the area of a rectangle, given its dimensions. It first prompts the user for the length and width of the rectangle and then displays the area.

```c
#include <stdio.h>

int main(void)
{
  int len, width;

  printf("Enter length: ");
  scanf("%d", &len);
  printf("Enter width: ");
  scanf("%d", &width);

  printf("Area is %d", len * width);

  return 0;
}
```

4. As stated earlier, the − can be used as a unary operator to reverse the sign of its operand. To see how this works, try this program:

```c
#include <stdio.h>

int main(void)
{
  int i;

  i = 10;
  i = -i;
  printf("This is i: %d", i);
```

```
        return 0;
    }
```

EXERCISES

1. Write a program that computes the volume of a cube. Have the program prompt the user for each dimension.

2. Write a program that computes the number of seconds in a year.

1.6   *A*DD COMMENTS TO A PROGRAM

A *comment* is a note to yourself (or others) that you put into your source code. All comments are ignored by the compiler. They exist solely for your benefit. Comments are used primarily to document the meaning and purpose of your source code, so that you can remember later how it functions and how to use it.

In C, the start of a comment is signaled by the /* character pair. A comment is ended by */. For example, this is a syntactically correct C comment:

```
/* This is a comment. */
```

Comments can extend over several lines. For example, this is completely valid in C:

```
/*
  This is a longer comment
  that extends over
  five lines.
*/
```

In C, a comment can go anywhere except in the middle of any C keyword, function name, or variable name.

You can use a comment to temporarily remove a line of code. Simply surround the line with the comment symbols.

Although not currently defined by ANSI C standard, you may see another style of comment, called a *single-line comment*. It begins with a // and stops at the end of the line. The single-line comment was created by C++. Its use in a C program is technically invalid, but most compilers will accept it. As such, many programmers have begun to use it in their C programs. Since the single-line comment is not defined by the current ANSI C standard, this book will not use it. However, don't be surprised if you see it in commercially written C programs.

One final point: In C, you can't have one comment within another comment. That is, comments may not be nested. For example, C will not accept this:

```
/* this is a comment /* this is another comment
   nested inside the first — which will cause
   a syntax error */ with a nested comment
*/
```

EXAMPLES

1. A year on Jupiter (the time it takes for Jupiter to make one full circuit around the Sun) takes about 12 Earth years. The following program allows you to convert Earth days to Jovian years. Simply specify the number of Earth days, and it computes the equivalent number of Jovian years. Notice the use of comments throughout the program.

```
/* This program converts Earth days into Jovian years. */
#include <stdio.h>

int main(void)
{
    float e_days; /* number of Earth days */
    float j_years; /* equivalent number of Jovian years */

    /* get number of Earth days */
```

```
printf("Enter number of Earth days: ");
scanf("%f", &e_days);

/* now, compute Jovian years */
j_years = e_days / (365.0 * 12.0);

/* display the answer */
printf("Equivalent Jovian years: %f", j_years);

return 0;
}
```

Notice that comments can appear on the same line as other C program statements.

Comments are often used to help describe what the program is doing. Although this program is easy to understand even without the comments, many programs are very difficult to understand even with the liberal use of comments. For more complex programs, the general approach is the same as used here: simply describe the actions of the program. Also, notice the comment at the start of the program. In general, it is a good idea to identify the purpose of a program at the top of its source file.

2. You cannot place a comment inside the name of a function or variable name. For example, this is an incorrect statement:

```
pri/* wrong */ntf("this won't work");
```

---

1. Go back and add comments to the programs developed in previous sections.

2. Is this comment correct?

```
/**/
```

3. Is this comment correct?

```
/* printf("this is a test"); */
```

1.7   **W**RITE YOUR OWN FUNCTIONS

Functions are the building blocks of C. So far, the programs you have seen included only one function: **main( )**. Most real-world programs, however, will contain many functions. In this section you will begin to learn how to write programs that contain multiple functions.

The general form of a C program that has multiple functions is shown here:

```
/* include header files here */

/* function prototypes here */

int main(void)
{
 /* ... */
}

ret-type f1(param-list)
{
 /* ... */
}

ret-type f2(param-list)
{
 /* ... */
}
   .
   .
   .
ret-type fN(param-list)
{
 /* ... */
}
```

Of course, you can call your functions by different names. Here, *ret-type* specifies the type of data returned by the function. If a function does not return a value, then its return type should be **void**. If a function does not use parameters, then its *param-list* should contain the keyword **void**.

Notice the comment about prototypes. A *function prototype* declares a function before it is used and prior to its definition. A prototype consists of a function's name, its return type, and its parameter list. It is terminated by a semicolon. The compiler needs to know this information in order for it to properly execute a call to the function. For example, given this simple function:

```
void myfunc(void)
{
  printf("This is a test.");
}
```

Its prototype is

```
void myfunc(void);
```

The only function that does not need a prototype is **main( )** since it is predefined by the C language.

Prototypes are an important part of C programming, but you will need to learn more about C before you can fully understand their purpose and value. For the next few chapters we will be using prototypes without any further explanation. They will be included as needed in all of the example programs shown in this book. You should also include them in programs that you write. A full explanation of prototypes is found in Chapter 7.

When a function is called, execution transfers to that function. When the end of that function is reached, execution returns to a point immediately after the place at which the function was called. Put differently, when a function ends, execution resumes at the point in your program immediately following the call to the function. Any function inside a program may call any other function within the same program. Traditionally, **main( )** is not called by any other function, but there is no technical restriction to this effect.

In the examples that follow, you will learn to create the simplest type of C functions: those that that do not return values and do not use parameters. The skeletal form of such a function is shown here:

```
void FuncName(void) {
  /* body of function here */
}
```

Of course, the name of the function will vary. Because the function does not return a value, its return type is **void**. Because the function does not have parameters, its parameter list is **void**.

EXAMPLES

1. The following program contains two functions: **main( )** and **func1( )**. Try to determine what it displays on the screen before reading the description that follows it.

```c
/* A program with two functions */

#include <stdio.h>

void func1(void); /* prototype for func1() */

int main(void)
{
  printf("I ");
  func1();
  printf("C.");

  return 0;
}

void func1(void)
{
  printf("like ");
}
```

This program displays **I like C.** on the screen. Here is how it works. In **main( )**, the first call to **printf( )** executes, printing the **I**. Next, **func1( )** is called. This causes the **printf( )** inside **func1( )** to execute, displaying **like**. Since this is the only statement inside **func1( )**, the function returns. This causes execution to resume inside **main( )** and the **C.** is printed. Notice that the statement that calls **func1( )** ends with a semicolon. (Remember a function call is a statement.)

A key point to understand about writing your own functions is that when the closing curly brace is reached the function will return, and execution resumes one line after the point at which the function was called.

Notice the prototype for **func1( )**. As you can see, it consists of its name, return type, and parameters list, but no body. It is terminated by a semicolon.

2. This program prints **1 2 3** on the screen:

```
/* This program has three functions. */

#include <stdio.h>

void func1(void); /* prototypes */
void func2(void);

int main(void)
{
  func2();
  printf("3");

  return 0;
}

void func2(void)
{
  func1();
  printf("2 ");
}

void func1(void)
{
  printf("1 ");
}
```

In this program, **main( )** first calls **func2( )**, which then calls **func1( )**. Next, **func1( )** displays **1** and then returns to **func2( )**, which prints **2** and then returns to **main( )**, which prints **3**.

EXERCISES

1. Enter, compile, and run the two example programs in this section.

2. Write a program that contains at least two functions and prints the message **The summer soldier, the sunshine patriot**.

3. Remove the prototype from the first example program and then compile it. What happens?

1.8   *U*SE FUNCTIONS TO RETURN VALUES

In C, a function may return a value to the calling routine. For example, another of C's standard library functions is **sqrt( )**, which returns the square root of its argument. For your program to obtain the return value, you must put the function on the right side of an assignment statement. For example, this program prints the square root of 10:

```
#include <stdio.h>
#include <math.h> /* needed by sqrt() */

int main(void)
{
  double answer;

  answer = sqrt(10.0);
  printf("%f", answer);

  return 0;
}
```

This program calls **sqrt( )** and assigns its return value to **answer**. Notice that **sqrt( )** uses the MATH.H header file.

Actually, the assignment statement in the preceding program is not technically necessary because **sqrt( )** could simply be used as an argument to **printf( )**, as shown here:

```
#include <stdio.h>
#include <math.h> /* needed by sqrt() */

int main(void)
{
  printf("%f", sqrt(10.0));

  return 0;
}
```

The reason this works is that C will automatically call **sqrt( )** and obtain its return value before calling **printf( )**. The return value then becomes the second argument to **printf( )**. If this seems strange, don't worry; you will understand this sort of situation better as you learn more about C.

The **sqrt( )** function requires a floating-point value for its argument, and the value it returns is of type **double**. You must match the type of value a function returns with the variable that the value will be assigned to. As you learn more about C, you will see why this is important. It is also important that you match the types of a function's arguments to the types it requires.

When writing your own functions, you can return a value to the calling routine using the **return** statement. The **return** statement takes the general form

    return *value*;

where *value* is the value to be returned. For example, this program prints **10** on the screen:

```
#include <stdio.h>

int func(void); /* prototype */

int main(void)
{
  int num;

  num = func();
```

```
  printf("%d", num);

  return 0;
}

int func(void)
{
  return 10;
}
```

In this example, **func( )** returns an integer value and its return type is specified as **int**. Although you can create functions that return any type of data, functions that return values of type **int** are quite common. Later in this book, you will see many examples of functions that return other types. Functions that are declared as **void** may not return values.

If a function does not explicitly specify a return type, it is assumed to return an integer by default. For example, **func( )** could have been coded like this:

```
func(void)
{
  return 10;
}
```

In this case, the **int** is implied. The use of the "default to **int**" rule is very common in older C code. However, recently there has been a move away from using the integer default. Whether this trend will continue is unknown. In any event, to avoid misunderstandings, this book will always explicitly specify **int**.

One important point: When the **return** statement is encountered, the function returns immediately. No statements after it will be executed. Thus, a **return** statement causes a function to return before its closing curly brace is reached.

The value associated with the **return** statement need not be a constant. It can be any valid C expression.

A **return** statement can also be used by itself, without a return value. This form of **return** looks like this:

```
return ;
```

It is used mostly by **void** functions (i.e., functions that have a **void** return type) to cause the function to return immediately, before the function's closing curly brace is reached. While not recommended, you can also use this form of **return** in functions that are supposed to return values. However, doing so makes the returned value undefined.

There can be more than one **return** in a function. You will see examples of this later in this book.

Even though a function returns a value, you don't necessarily have to assign that value to anything. If the return value of a function is not used, it is lost, but no harm is done.

EXAMPLES

1. This program displays the square of a number entered from the keyboard. The square is computed using the **get_sqr( )** function. Its operation should be clear.

```c
#include <stdio.h>

int get_sqr(void);

int main(void)
{
  int sqr;

  sqr = get_sqr();
  printf("Square: %d", sqr);

  return 0;
}

int get_sqr(void)
{
  int num;

  printf("Enter a number: ");
  scanf("%d", &num);
  return num*num; /* square the number */
}
```

2. As mentioned earlier, you can use **return** without specifying a value. This allows a function to return before its closing curly brace is reached. For example, in the following program, the line **This is never printed.** will not be displayed.

```c
#include <stdio.h>

void func1(void);

int main(void)
{
  func1();

  return 0;
}

void func1(void)
{
  printf("This is printed.");
  return; /* return with no value */
  printf("This is never printed.");
}
```

EXERCISES

1. Enter, compile, and run the example programs in this section.

2. Write a program that uses a function called **convert( )**, which prompts the user for an amount in dollars and returns this value converted into pounds. (Use an exchange rate of $2.00 per pound.) Display the conversion.

3. What is wrong with this program?

```c
#include <stdio.h>

int f1(void);

int main(void)
{
  double answer;

  answer = f1();
  printf("%f", answer);

  return 0;
```

```
    }

    int f1(void)
    {
      return 100;
    }
```

4. What is wrong with this function?

```
    void func(void)
    {
      int i;

      printf("Enter a number: ");
      scanf("%d", &i);

      return i;
    }
```

 1.9   ***U*SE FUNCTION ARGUMENTS**

As stated earlier, a function's argument is a value that is passed to the function when the function is called. A function in C can have from zero to several arguments. (The upper limit is determined by the compiler you are using, but the ANSI C standard specifies that a function must be able to take at least 31 arguments.) For a function to be able to take arguments, special variables to receive argument values must be declared. These are called the *formal parameters* of the function. The parameters are declared between the parentheses that follow the function's name. For example, the function listed below prints the sum of the two integer arguments used to call it.

```
void sum(int x, int y)
{
  printf("%d ", x + y);
}
```

Each time **sum( )** is called, it will sum the value passed to **x** with the value passed to **y**. Remember, however, that **x** and **y** are simply the function's operational variables, which receive the values you use when calling the function. Consider the following short program, which illustrates how to call **sum( )**.

```
/* A simple program that demonstrates sum(). */

#include <stdio.h>

void sum(int x, int y);

int main(void)
{
  sum(1, 20);
  sum(9, 6);
  sum(81, 9);

  return 0;
}

void sum(int x, int y)
{
  printf("%d ", x + y);
}
```

This program will print **21**, **15**, and **90** on the screen. When **sum( )** is called, the value of each argument is copied into its matching parameter. That is, in the first call to **sum( )**, 1 is copied into **x** and 20 is copied into **y**. In the second call, 9 is copied into **x** and 6 into **y**. In the third call, 81 is copied into **x** and 9 into **y**.

If you have never worked with a language that allows parameterized functions, the preceding process may seem strange. Don't worry—as you see more examples of C programs, the concept of arguments, parameters, and functions will become clear.

It is important to keep two terms straight. First, *argument* refers to the value that is passed to a function. The variable that receives the value of the argument inside the function is the *formal parameter* of the function. Functions that take arguments are called *parameterized functions*. Remember, if a variable is used as an argument to a function, it has nothing to do with the formal parameter that receives its value.

In C functions, arguments are always separated by commas. In this book, the term *argument list* will refer to comma-separated arguments.

All function parameters are declared in a fashion similar to that used by **sum( )**. You must specify the type and name of each parameter and, if there is more than one parameter, you must use a comma to separate them. Functions that do not have parameters should use the keyword **void** in their parameter list.

EXAMPLES

1. An argument to a function can consist of an expression. For example, it is perfectly valid to call **sum( )** as shown here:

   ```
   sum(10-2, 9*7);
   ```

2. This program uses the **outchar( )** function to output characters to the screen. The program prints **ABC**.

   ```c
   #include <stdio.h>

   void outchar(char ch);

   int main(void)
   {
     outchar('A');
     outchar('B');
     outchar('C');

     return 0;
   }

   void outchar(char ch)
   {
     printf("%c", ch);
   }
   ```

EXERCISES

1. Write a program that uses a function called **outnum( )** that takes one integer argument and displays it on the screen.

2. What is wrong with this program?

```c
#include <stdio.h>

void sqr_it(int num);

int main(void)
{
  sqr_it(10.0);

  return 0;
}

void sqr_it(int num)
{
  printf("%d", num * num);
}
```

1.10   *R*EMEMBER THE C KEYWORDS

Before concluding this chapter, you should familiarize yourself with the keywords that make up the C language. ANSI C standard has 32 *keywords* that may not be used as variable or function names. These words, combined with the formal C syntax, form the C programming language. They are listed in Table 1-2.

Many C compilers have added several additional keywords that are used to take better advantage of the environment in which the compiler is used, and that give support for interlanguage programming, interrupts, and memory organization. Some commonly used extended keywords are shown in Table 1-3.

The lowercase lettering of the keywords is significant. C requires that all keywords be in lowercase form. For example, **RETURN** will *not* be recognized as the keyword **return**. Also, no keyword may be used as a variable or function name.

auto	double	int	struct
break	else	long	switch
case	enum	register	typedef
char	extern	return	union
const	float	short	unsigned
continue	for	signed	void
default	goto	sizeof	volatile
do	if	static	while

TABLE 1-2 *The 32 Keywords as Defined by the ANSI C Standard* ▼

asm	_cs	_ds	_es
_ss	cdecl	far	huge
interrupt	near	pascal	

TABLE 1-3 *Some Common C Extended Keywords* ▼

**Mastery
Skills Check**

1. The moon's gravity is about 17 percent of Earth's. Write a program that allows you to enter your weight and computes your effective weight on the moon.

2. What is wrong with this program fragment?

   ```
   /* this inputs a number
   scanf("%d", &num);
   ```

3. There are 8 ounces in a cup. Write a program that converts ounces to cups. Use a function called **o_to_c( )** to perform the conversion. Call it with the number of ounces and have it return the number of cups.

4. What are the five basic data types in C?

5. What is wrong with each of these variable names?

   a) short-fall

   b) $balance

   c) last + name

   d) 9times

2

Introducing C's Program Control Statements

chapter objectives

2.1 Become familiar with the **if**

2.2 Add the **else**

2.3 Create blocks of code

2.4 Use the **for** loop

2.5 Substitute C's increment and decrement operators

2.6 Expand **printf( )**'s capabilities

2.7 Program with C's relational and logical operators

N this chapter you will learn about two of C's most important program control statements: **if** and **for**. In general, program control statements determine your program's flow of execution. As such, they form the backbone of your programs. In addition to these, you will also learn about blocks of code, the relational and logical operators, and more about the **printf( )** function.

**Review
Skills Check**

Before proceeding, you should be able to correctly answer these questions and do these exercises:

1. All C programs are composed of one or more functions. What is the name of the function that all programs must have? Further, what special purpose does it perform?

2. The **printf( )** function is used to output information to the screen. Write a program that displays **This is the number 100.** (Output the **100** as a number, not as a string.)

3. Header files contain information used by the standard library functions. How do you tell the compiler to include one in your program? Give an example.

4. C supports five basic types of data. Name them.

5. Which of these variable names are invalid in C?

    a. _count

    b. 123count

    c. $test

    d. This_is_a_long_name

    e. new-word

6. What is **scanf( )** used for?

7. Write a program that inputs an integer from the keyboard and displays its square.

8. How are comments entered into a C program? Give an example.

9. How does a function return a value to the routine that called it?

10. A function called **Myfunc( )** has these three parameters: an **int** called **count**, a **float** called **balance**, and a **char** called **ch**. The function does not return a value. Show how this function is prototyped.

2.1   *B*ECOME FAMILIAR WITH THE if

The **if** statement is one of C's *selection statements* (sometimes called *conditional statements*). Its operation is governed by the outcome of a conditional test that evaluates to either true or false. Simply put, selection statements make decisions based upon the outcome of some condition.

In its simplest form, the **if** statement allows your program to conditionally execute a statement. This form of the **if** is shown here:

if(*expression*) *statement* ;

The expression may be any valid C expression. If the expression evaluates as true, the statement will be executed. If it does not, the statement is bypassed, and the line of code following the **if** is executed. In C, an expression is true if it evaluates to any nonzero value. If it evaluates to zero, it is false. The statement that follows an **if** is usually referred to as the *target* of the **if** statement.

Commonly, the expression inside the **if** compares one value with another using a *relational operator*. Although you will learn about all the relational operators later in this chapter, three are introduced here so that we can create some example programs. A relational operator tests how one value relates to another. For example, to see if one value is greater than another, C uses the > relational operator. The outcome of this comparison is either true or false. For example, **10 > 9** is true, but **9 > 10** is false. Therefore, the following **if** will cause the message **true** to be displayed.

```
if(10 > 9) printf("true");
```

However, because the expression in the following statement is false, the **if** does not execute its target statement.

```
if(5 > 9) printf("this will not print");
```

C uses < as its *less than operator*. For example, **10 < 11** is true. To test for equality, C provides the **==** operator. (There can be no space between the two equal signs.) Therefore, **10 == 10** is true, but **10 == 11** is not.

Of course, the expression inside the **if** may involve variables. For example, the following program tells whether an integer entered from the keyboard is negative or non-negative.

```
#include <stdio.h>

int main(void)
{
  int num;

  printf("Enter an integer: ");
  scanf("%d", &num);

  if(num < 0) printf("Number is negative.");
  if(num > -1) printf("Number is non-negative.");

  return 0;
}
```

Remember, in C, true is any nonzero value and false is zero. Therefore, it is perfectly valid to have an **if** statement such as the one shown here:

```
if(count+1) printf("Not Zero");
```

EXAMPLES

1. This program forms the basis for an addition drill. It displays two numbers and asks the user what the answer is. The program then tells the user if the answer is right or wrong.

   ```
   #include <stdio.h>

   int main(void)
   {
     int answer;
   ```

```
printf("What is 10 + 14? ");
scanf("%d", &answer);
if(answer == 10+14) printf("Right!");

return 0;
}
```

2. This program converts either feet to meters or meters to feet, depending upon what the user requests.

```
#include <stdio.h>

int main(void)
{
  float num;
  int choice;

  printf("Enter value: ");
  scanf("%f", &num);

  printf("1: Feet to Meters, 2: Meters to Feet. ");
  printf("Enter choice: ");
  scanf("%d", &choice);

  if(choice == 1) printf("%f", num / 3.28);
  if(choice == 2) printf("%f", num * 3.28);

  return 0;
}
```

EXERCISES

1. Which of these expressions are true?

   a. 0

   b. 1

   c. 10 * 9 < 90

   d. 1==1

   e. −1

2. Write a program that asks the user for an integer and then tells the user if that number is even or odd. (Hint, use C's modulus operator %.)

ADD THE else

You can add an **else** statement to the **if**. When this is done, the **if** statement looks like this:

if(*expression*) *statement1*;
else *statement2*;

If the expression is true, then the target of the **if** will execute, and the **else** portion will be skipped. However, if the expression is false, then the target of the **if** is bypassed, and the target of the **else** will execute. Under no circumstances will both statements execute. Thus, the addition of the **else** provides a two-way decision path.

EXAMPLES

1. You can use the **else** to create more efficient code in some cases. For example, here the **else** is used in place of a second **if** in the program from the preceding section, which determines whether a number is negative or non-negative.

```
#include <stdio.h>

int main(void)
{
  int num;

  printf("Enter an integer: ");
  scanf("%d", &num);

  if(num < 0) printf("Number is negative.");
  else printf("Number is non-negative.");
```

```
      return 0;
}
```

Recall that the original version of this program explicitly tested for non-negative numbers by comparing **num** to –1 using a second **if** statement. But since there are only two possibilities— **num** is either negative or non-negative—there is no reason for this second test. Because of the way a C compiler generates code, the **else** requires far fewer machine instructions than an additional **if** and is, therefore, more efficient.

2. This program prompts the user for two numbers, divides the first by the second, and displays the result. However, division by zero is undefined, so the program uses an **if** and an **else** statement to prevent division by zero from occurring.

```c
#include <stdio.h>

int main(void)
{
  int num1, num2;

  printf("Enter first number: ");
  scanf("%d", &num1);

  printf("Enter second number: ");
  scanf("%d", &num2);

  if(num2 == 0) printf("Cannot divide by zero.");
  else printf("Answer is: %d.", num1 / num2);

  return 0;
}
```

EXERCISES

1. Write a program that requests two numbers and then displays either their sum or product, depending on what the user selects.

2. Rewrite Exercise 2 from Section 2.1 so that it uses an **else** statement.

2.3 **C**REATE BLOCKS OF CODE

In C, you can link two or more statements together. This is called a *block of code* or a *code block*. To create a block of code, you surround the statements in the block with opening and closing curly braces. Once this is done, the statements form one logical unit, which may be used anywhere that a single statement may.

For example, the general form of the **if** using blocks of code is

```
if(expression) {
  statement1;
  statement2;
  .
  .
  .
  statement N;
}
else {
  statement1;
  statement2;
  .
  .
  .
  statement N;
}
```

If the expression evaluates to true, then all the statements in the block of code associated with the **if** will be executed. If the expression is false, then all the statements in the **else** block will be executed. (Remember, the **else** is optional and need not be present.) For example, this fragment prints the message **This is an example of a code block.** if the user enters any positive number.

```
scanf("%d", &num);

if(num > 0) {
  printf("This is ");
  printf("an example of ");
  printf("a code block.");
}
```

Keep in mind that a block of code represents one indivisible logical unit. This means that under no circumstances could one of the **printf( )** statements in this fragment execute without the others also executing.

In the example shown, the statements that appear within the block of code are indented. Although C does not care where a statement appears on a line, it is common practice to indent one level at the start of a block. Indenting makes the structure of a program easier to understand. Also, the placement of the curly braces is arbitrary. However, the way they are shown in the example is a common method and will be used by the examples in this book.

In C, as you will see, you can use a block of code anywhere you can use a single statement.

EXAMPLES

1. This program is an improved version of the feet-to-meters, meters-to-feet conversion program. Notice how the use of code blocks allows the program to prompt specifically for each unit.

```
#include <stdio.h>

int main(void)
{
  float num;
  int choice;

  printf("1: Feet to Meters, 2: Meters to Feet. ");
  printf("Enter choice: ");
  scanf("%d", &choice);

  if(choice == 1) {
    printf("Enter number of feet: ");
```

48 TEACH YOURSELF
▼ *C*

```
    scanf("%f", &num);
    printf("Meters: %f", num / 3.28);
  }
  else {
    printf("Enter number of meters: ");
    scanf("%f", &num);
    printf("Feet: %f", num * 3.28);
  }

  return 0;
}
```

2. Using code blocks, we can improve the addition drill program so that it also prints the correct answer when the user makes a mistake.

```
#include <stdio.h>

int main(void)
{
  int answer;

  printf("What is 10 + 14? ");
  scanf("%d", &answer);

  if(answer == 10+14) printf("Right!");
  else {
    printf("Sorry, you're wrong. ");
    printf("The answer is 24.");
  }

  return 0;
}
```

This example illustrates an important point: it is not necessary for targets of both the **if** and the **else** statements to be blocks of code. In this case, the target of **if** is a single statement, while the target of **else** is a block. Remember, you are free to use either a single statement or a code block at either place.

EXERCISES

1. Write a program that either adds or subtracts two integers. First, prompt the user to choose an operation; then prompt for the two numbers and display the result.

2. Is this fragment correct?

```
if(count < 100)
   printf("Number is less than 100.");
   printf("Its square is %d.", count * count);
}
```

*U*SE THE for *LOOP*

The **for** loop is one of C's three loop statements. It allows one or more statements to be repeated. If you have programmed in any other computer language, such as BASIC or Pascal, you will be pleased to learn that the **for** behaves much like its equivalent in other languages.

The **for** loop is considered by many C programmers to be its most flexible loop. Although the **for** loop allows a large number of variations, we will examine only its most common form in this section.

The **for** loop is used to repeat a statement or block of statements a specified number of times. Its general form for repeating a single statement is shown here.

for(*initialization* ; *conditional-test* ; *increment*) *statement* ;

The *initialization* section is used to give an initial value to the variable that controls the loop. This variable is usually referred to as the *loop-control variable.* The initialization section is executed only once, before the loop begins. The *conditional-test* portion of the loop tests the loop-control variable against a target value. If the conditional test evaluates true, the loop repeats. If it is false, the loop stops, and program execution picks up with the next line of code that follows the loop. The conditional test is performed at the start or *top* of the loop each time the loop is repeated. The *increment* portion of the **for** is executed at the bottom of the loop. That is, the increment portion is executed after the statement or block that forms its *body* has been executed. The purpose of the increment portion is to increase (or decrease) the loop-control value by a certain amount.

As a simple first example, this program uses a **for** loop to print the numbers **1** through **10** on the screen.

```
#include <stdio.h>

int main(void)
{
  int num;

  for(num=1; num<11; num=num+1) printf("%d ", num);
  printf("terminating");

  return 0;
}
```

This program produces the following output:

1 2 3 4 5 6 7 8 9 10 terminating

The program works like this: First, the loop control variable **num** is initialized to 1. Next, the expression **num < 11** is evaluated. Since it is true, the **for** loop begins running. After the number is printed, **num** is incremented by one and the conditional test is evaluated again. This process continues until **num** equals 11. When this happens, the **for** loop stops, and **terminating** is displayed. Keep in mind that the initialization portion of the **for** loop is only executed once, when the loop is first entered.

As stated earlier, the conditional test is performed at the start of each iteration. This means that if the test is false to begin with, the loop will not execute even once. For example, this program only displays **terminating** because **num** is initialized to 11, causing the conditional test to fail.

```
#include <stdio.h>

int main(void)
{
  int num;

  /* this loop will not execute */
  for(num=11; num<11; num=num+1) printf("%d ", num);

  printf("terminating");

  return 0;
}
```

To repeat several statements, use a block of code as the target of the **for** loop. For example, this program computes the product and sum of the numbers from 1 to 5:

```
#include <stdio.h>

int main(void)
{
  int num, sum, prod;

  sum = 0;
  prod = 1;

  for(num=1; num<6; num=num+1) {
    sum = sum + num;
    prod = prod * num;
  }
  printf("product and sum: %d %d", prod, sum);

  return 0;
}
```

A **for** loop can run negatively. For example, this fragment decrements the loop-control variable.

```
for(num=20; num>0; num=num-1)...
```

Further, the loop-control variable may be incremented or decremented by more than one. For example, this program counts to 100 by fives:

```
#include <stdio.h>

int main(void)
{
  int i;

  for(i=0; i<101; i=i+5) printf("%d ", i);

  return 0;
}
```

EXAMPLES

1. The addition-drill program created earlier can be enhanced using a **for** loop. The version shown here asks for the sums of the numbers between 1 and 10. That is, it asks for 1 + 1, then 2 + 2, and so on. This program would be useful to a first grader who is learning to add.

```
#include <stdio.h>

int main(void)
{
  int answer, count;

  for(count=1; count<11; count=count+1) {
    printf("What is %d + %d? ", count, count);
    scanf("%d", &answer);

    if(answer == count+count) printf("Right! ");
    else {
      printf("Sorry, you're wrong. ");
      printf("The answer is %d. ", count+count);
    }
  }

  return 0;
}
```

Notice that this program has an **if** statement as part of the **for** block. Notice further that the target of **else** is a block of code. This is perfectly valid. In C, a code block may contain statements that create other code blocks. Notice how the indentation adds clarity to the structure of the program.

2. We can use a **for** loop to create a program that determines if a number is prime. The following program asks the user to enter a number and then checks to see if it has any factors.

```c
/* Prime number tester. */
#include <stdio.h>

int main(void)
{
  int num, i, is_prime;

  printf("Enter the number to test: ");
  scanf("%d", &num);

  /* now test for factors */
  is_prime = 1;
  for(i=2; i<=num/2; i=i+1)
    if((num%i)==0) is_prime = 0;

  if(is_prime==1) printf("The number is prime.");
  else printf("The number is not prime.");

  return 0;
}
```

EXERCISES

1. Create a program that prints the numbers from **1** to **100**.

2. Write a program that prints the numbers between **17** and **100** that can be evenly divided by 17.

3. Write a program similar to the prime-number tester, except that it displays all the factors of a number entered by the user. For example, if the user entered **8**, it would respond with **2** and **4**.

| 2.5 | **S**UBSTITUTE C'S INCREMENT AND DECREMENT OPERATORS |

When you learned about the **for** in the preceding section, the increment portion of the loop looked more or less like the one shown here:

```
for(num=0; num<some_value; num=num+1)...
```

Although not incorrect, you will almost never see a statement like **num = num + 1** in professionally written C programs because C provides a special operator that increments a variable by one. The *increment operator* is ++(two pluses with no intervening space). Using the increment operator, you can change this line of code:

```
i = i + 1;
```

into this:

```
i++;
```

Therefore, the **for** shown earlier will normally be written like this:

```
for(num=0; num<some_value; num++)...
```

In a similar fashion, to decrease a variable by one, you can use C's *decrement operator:* – –. (There must be no space between the two minus signs.) Therefore,

```
count = count - 1;
```

can be rewritten as

```
count--;
```

Aside from saving you a little typing effort, the reason you will want to use the increment and decrement operators is that, for most C compilers, they will be faster than the equivalent assignment statements. The reason for this difference is that the C compiler can often avoid separate load-and-store machine-language instructions and substitute a single increment or decrement instruction in the executable version of a program.

The increment and decrement operators do not need to follow the variable; they can precede it. Although the effect on the variable is the same, the position of the operator does affect when the operation is performed. To see how, examine this program:

```
#include <stdio.h>

int main(void)
{
  int i, j;

  i = 10;
  j = i++;

  /* this will print 11 10 */
  printf("i and j: %d %d", i, j);

  return 0;
}
```

Don't let the **j = i++** statement trouble you. The increment operator may be used as part of any valid C expression. This statement works like this. First, the current value of **i** is assigned to **j**. Then **i** is incremented. This is why **j** has the value 10, not 11. When the increment or decrement operator follows the variable, the operation is performed *after* its value has been obtained for use in the expression. Therefore, assuming that **max** has the value 1, an expression such as this:

```
count = 10 * max++;
```

assigns the value 10 to **count** and increases **max** by one.

If the variable is preceded by the increment or decrement operator, the operation is performed first, and then the value of the variable is obtained for use in the expression. For example, rewriting the previous program as follows causes **j** to be 11.

```
#include <stdio.h>

int main(void)
{
  int i, j;

  i = 10;
  j = ++i;
```

```
/* this will print 11 11 */
printf("i and j: %d %d", i, j);

return 0;
}
```

If you are simply using the increment or decrement operators to replace equivalent assignment statements, it doesn't matter if the operator precedes or follows the variable. This is a matter of your own personal style.

EXAMPLES

1. Here is the addition drill program developed in Section 2. It has been rewritten using the increment operator.

```
#include <stdio.h>

int main(void)
{
  int answer, count;

  for(count=1; count<11; count++) {
    printf("What is %d + %d? ", count, count);
    scanf("%d", &answer);

    if(answer == count+count) printf("Right! ");
    else {
      printf("Sorry, you're wrong. ");
      printf("The answer is %d. ", count+count);
    }
  }

  return 0;
}
```

2. This program illustrates the use of the increment and decrement operators:

```
#include <stdio.h>

int main(void)
```

```
{
  int i;

  i = 0;

  i++;
  printf("%d ", i); /* prints 1 */
  i--;
  printf("%d ", i); /* prints 0 */

  return 0;
}
```

EXERCISES

1. Rewrite the answer to the **for** loop exercises in the previous
   section so that they use the increment or decrement operators.

2. Change all appropriate assignment statements in this program
   to increment or decrement statements.

```
#include <stdio.h>

int main(void)
{
  int a, b;

  a = 1;

  a = a + 1;

  b = a;

  b = b - 1;

  printf("%d %d", a, b);

  return 0;
}
```

▮ 2.6 ▮ ▮ EXPAND printf( )'S CAPABILITIES

So far, we have used **printf( )** to output strings and numbers. However, you might have been wondering how to tell **printf( )** that you want the output to advance to the next line. The way to accomplish this and other actions is to use C's _backslash-character constants_. The C language defines several special character codes, shown in Table 2-1, which represent characters that cannot be entered from the keyboard, are non-printing characters, may not be found in all character sets, or that serve other unique needs. You can use the backslash codes anywhere you can use a normal character. The backslash constants are also referred to as _escape sequences_.

Code	Meaning
\b	Backspace
\f	Form feed
\n	Newline
\r	Carriage return
\t	Horizontal tab
\"	Double quote
\'	Single quote
\0	Null
\\	Backslash
\v	Vertical tab
\a	Alert
\?	Question mark
\N	Octal constant (where _N_ is an octal value)
\x_N_	Hexadecimal constant (where _N_ is a hexidecimal value)

▮ TABLE 2-1 ▮ _C's Backslash Codes_ ▼

Perhaps the single most important backslash code is **\n**, which is often referred to as the *newline character*. When the C compiler encounters **\n**, it translates it into a carriage return/linefeed combination. For example, this program:

```
#include <stdio.h>

int main(void)
{
  printf("This is line one.\n");
  printf("This is line two.\n");
  printf("This is line three.");

  return 0;
}
```

displays

> This is line one.
> This is line two.
> This is line three.

on the screen.

Remember, the backslash codes are character constants. Therefore, to assign one to a character variable, you must enclose the backslash code within single quotes, as shown in this fragment:

```
char ch;

ch = '\t'; /* assign ch the tab character */
```

EXAMPLES

1. This program sounds the bell:

   ```
   #include <stdio.h>

   int main(void)
   {
     printf("\a");
   ```

```
   return 0;
}
```

2. You can enter any special character by specifying it as an octal or hexadecimal value following the backslash. The octal number system is based on 8 and uses the digits 0 through 7. In octal, the number 10 is the same as 8 in decimal. The hexadecimal number system is based on 16 and uses the digits 0 through 9 plus the letters 'A' through 'F', which stand for 10, 11, 12, 13, 14, and 15. For example, the hexadecimal number 10 is 16 in decimal. When specifying a character in hexadecimal, you must follow the backslash with an 'x', followed by the number. The ASCII character set is defined from 0 to 127. However, many computers, including most PCs, use the values 128 to 255 for special and graphics characters. If your computer supports these extra characters, the following program will display a few of them on the screen.

```c
#include <stdio.h>

int main(void)
{
   printf("\xA0 \xA1 \xA2 \xA3");

   return 0;
}
```

3. The **\n** newline character does not have to go at the end of the string that is being output by **printf( )**; it can go anywhere in the string. Further, there can be as many newline characters in a string as you desire. The point is that there is no connection between a newline and the end of a string. For example, this program:

```c
#include <stdio.h>

int main(void)
{
   printf("one\ntwo\nthree\nfour");

   return 0;
}
```

displays

one
two
three
four

on the screen.

EXERCISES

1. Write a program that outputs a table of numbers. Each line in the table contains three entries: the number, its square, and its cube. Begin with **1** and end with **10**. Also, use a **for** loop to generate the numbers.

2. Write a program that prompts the user for an integer value. Next, using a **for** loop, make it count down from this value to 0, displaying each number on its own line. When it reaches 0, have it sound the bell.

3. Experiment on your own with the backslash codes.

2.7   *P*ROGRAM WITH C'S RELATIONAL AND LOGICAL OPERATORS

The C language contains a rich set of operators. In this section you will learn about C's relational and logical operators. As you saw earlier, the relational operators compare two values and return a true or false result based upon that comparison. The logical operators connect together true/false results. These operators are shown in Table 2-2 and Table 2-3.

Operator	Action
>	Greater than
>=	Greater than or equal
<	Less than
<=	Less than or equal
==	Equal
!=	Not equal

TABLE 2-2 *Relational Operators* ▼

The logical operators are used to support the basic logical operations of AND, OR, and NOT according to this truth table. The table uses 1 for true and 0 for false.

p	q	p&&q	p||q	!p
0	0	0	0	1
0	1	0	1	1
1	1	1	1	0
1	0	0	1	0

The relational and logical operators are both lower in precedence than the arithmetic operators. This means that an expression like

```
10 + count > a + 12
```

Operator	Action
&&	AND
||	OR
!	NOT

TABLE 2-3 *Logical Operators* ▼

is evaluated as if it were written

```
(10 + count) > (a + 12)
```

You may link any number of relational operations together using logical operators. For example, this expression joins three relational operations.

```
var > max || !(max==100) && 0 <= item
```

The table below shows the relative precedence of the relational and logical operators.

Highest	!
	> >= < <=
	== !=
	&&
Lowest	||

There is one important fact to remember about the values produced by the relational and logical operators: the result is either 0 or 1. Even though C defines true as any nonzero value, the relational and logical operators always produce the value 1 for true. Your programs may make use of this fact.

You can use the relational and logical operators in both the **if** and **for** statements. For example, the following statement reports when both **a** and **b** are positive:

```
if(a>0 && b>0) printf("Both are positive.");
```

EXAMPLES

1. In professionally written C code, it is uncommon to find a statement like this:

```
if(count != 0)...
```

The reason is that in C, true is any nonzero value and false is zero. Therefore, the preceding statement is generally written as this:

```
if(count)...
```

Further, statements like this:

```
if(count == 0)...
```

are generally written as:

```
if(!count)...
```

The expression **!count** is true only if **count** is zero.

2. It is important to remember that the outcome of a relational or logical operation is 0 when false and 1 when true. For example, the following program requests two integers, then displays the outcome of each relational and logical operation when applied to them. In all cases, the result will be a 0 or a 1.

```
#include <stdio.h>

int main(void)
{
  int i, j;

  printf("Enter first number: ");
  scanf("%d", &i);
  printf("Enter second number: ");
  scanf("%d", &j);

  /* relational operations */
  printf("i < j %d\n", i < j);
  printf("i <= j %d\n", i <= j);
  printf("i == j %d\n", i == j);
  printf("i > j %d\n", i > j);
  printf("i >= j %d\n", i >= j);

  /* logical operations */
  printf("i && j %d\n", i && j);
  printf("i || j %d\n", i || j);
  printf("!i !j %d %d\n", !i, !j);

  return 0;
}
```

3. C does not define an exclusive-OR (XOR) logical operator. However, it is easy to create a function that performs the operation. The XOR operation uses this truth table:

p	q	XOR
0	0	0
0	1	1
1	0	1
1	1	0

That is, the XOR operation produces a true result when one and only one operand is true. The following function uses the *&&* and || operators to construct an XOR operation. It compares the values of its two arguments and returns the outcome of an XOR operation.

```
int xor(int a, int b)
{
  return (a || b) && !(a && b);
}
```

The following program uses this function. It displays the result of an AND, OR, and XOR on the values you enter.

```
/* This program demonstrates the xor() function. */
#include <stdio.h>

int xor(int a, int b);

int main(void)
{
  int p, q;

  printf("enter P (0 or 1): ");
  scanf("%d", &p);
  printf("enter Q (0 or 1): ");
  scanf("%d", &q);
  printf("P AND Q: %d\n", p && q);
  printf("P OR Q: %d\n", p || q);
  printf("P XOR Q: %d\n", xor(p, q));

  return 0;
}

int xor(int a, int b)
```

```
{
    return (a || b) && !(a && b);
}
```

EXERCISES

1. What does this loop do?

   ```
   for(x=0; x<100; x++) printf("%d ", x);
   ```

2. Is this expression true?

   ```
   !(10==9)
   ```

3. Do these two expressions evaluate to the same outcome?

   a. 0 && 1 || 1

   b. 0 && (1 || 1)

4. On your own, experiment with the relational and logical operators.

Mastery Skills Check

1. Write a program that plays a computerized form of the "guess the magic number" game. It works like this: The player has ten tries to guess the magic number. If the number entered is the value you have selected for your magic number, have the program print the message "RIGHT!" and then terminate. Otherwise, have the program report whether the guess was high or low and then let the player enter another number. This process goes on until the player guesses the number or the ten tries have been used up. For fun, you might want to report the number of tries it takes to guess the number.

2. Write a program that computes the square footage of a house given the dimensions of each room. Have the program ask the user how many rooms are in the house and then request the dimensions of each room. Display the resulting total square footage.

3. What are the increment and decrement operators and what do they do?

4. Create an improved addition-drill program that keeps track of the number of right and wrong answers and displays them when the program ends.

5. Write a program that prints the numbers **1** to **100** using 5 columns. Have each number separated from the next by a tab.

3

More C Program Control Statements

chapter objectives

3.1 Input characters

3.2 Nest **if** statements

3.3 Examine **for** loop variations

3.4 Understand C's **while** loop

3.5 Use the **do** loop

3.6 Create nested loops

3.7 Use **break** to exit a loop

3.8 Know when to use the **continue** statement

3.9 Select among alternatives with the **switch** statement

3.10 Understand the **goto** statement

THIS chapter continues the discussion of C's program control statements. Before doing so, however, the chapter begins by explaining how to read characters from the keyboard. Although you know how to input numbers, it is now time for you to know how to input individual characters because several examples in this chapter will make use of them. Next, the chapter finishes the discussion of the **if** and **for** statements. Then it presents C's two other loop statements, the **while** and **do**. Next you will learn about nested loops and two more of C's control statements, the **break** and **continue**. This chapter also covers C's other selection statement, the **switch**. It ends with a short discussion of C's unconditional jump statement, **goto**.

Review
Skills Check

Before proceeding, you should be able to answer these questions and perform these exercises:

1. What are C's relational and logical operators?

2. What is a block of code? How do you make one?

3. How do you output a newline using **printf( )**?

4. Write a program that prints the numbers **-100** to **100**.

5. Write a program that prints 5 different proverbs. The program prompts the user for the number of the proverb to print and then displays it. (Use any proverbs you like.)

6. How can this statement be rewritten?

```
count = count + 1;
```

7. What values are true in C? What values are false?

3.1 ▮NPUT CHARACTERS

Although numbers are important, your programs will also need to read characters from the keyboard. In C you can do this in a variety of ways. Unfortunately, this conceptually simple task is complicated by some baggage left over from the origins of C. However, let's begin with the traditional way characters are read from the keyboard. Later you will learn an alternative.

C defines a function called **getchar( )**, which returns a single character typed on the keyboard. When called, the function waits for a key to be pressed. Then **getchar( )** echoes the keystroke to the screen and returns the value of the key to the caller. The **getchar( )** function is defined by the ANSI C standard and requires the header file STDIO.H. This program illustrates its use by reading a character and then telling you what it received. (Remember, to display a character, use the **%c** **printf( )** format specifier.)

```
#include <stdio.h>

int main(void)
{
  char ch;

  ch = getchar(); /* read a char */
  printf(" you typed: %c", ch);

  return 0;
}
```

If you try this program, it may behave differently than you expected. The trouble is this: in many C compilers, **getchar( )** is implemented in such a way that it *line buffers* input. That is, it does not immediately return as soon as you have pressed a key, but waits until you have entered an entire line, which may include several other characters. This means that even though it will read and return only one character, **getchar( )** waits until you enter a carriage return (i.e., press ENTER) before doing so. When **getchar( )** returns, it will return the first character you typed. However, any other characters that you entered, including the carriage return, will still be in the input buffer. These characters will be consumed by subsequent input requests, such as through calls to **scanf( )**. In some circumstances, this can lead to trouble. This situation is examined more closely in Chapter 8. For now, just be aware that **getchar( )** may behave differently than your intuition would suggest. Of course, the programs shown in this book behave properly.

The reason that **getchar( )** works the way it does is that the version of UNIX for which C was developed line-buffered input. When C compilers were created for other interactive environments, developers had to decide how to make **getchar( )** behave. Many C compiler developers have decided, for the sake of compatibility, to keep **getchar( )** line-buffered, even though there is no technical reason for it. (In fact, the ANSI C standard states that **getchar( )** need not be line-buffered.) When **getchar( )** is implemented in a line-buffered fashion in a modern interactive environment, its use is severely limited.

Because many compilers have implemented line-buffered versions of **getchar( )**, most C compilers supply another function to perform interactive console input. Although it is not defined by the ANSI C standard, most compilers call this function **getche( )**. You use it just like **getchar( )**, except that it will return its value immediately after a key is pressed; it does not line-buffer input. For most compilers, this function requires a header file called CONIO.H, but it might be called something different in your compiler. Thus, if you want to achieve interactive character input, you will usually need to use the **getche( )** function rather than **getchar( )**.

Since all readers will have access to the **getchar( )** function, it will be used by most of the examples in this book that require character input. However, some examples will use the **getche( )** function. If your compiler does not include this function, substitute **getchar( )**. You should feel free to experiment with **getche( )** on your own.

Note
*At the time of this writing, when using Microsoft's Visual C++ compiler, **getche( )** is not compatible with C's standard input functions, such as **scanf( )**. Instead, you must use special console versions of these of these functions, such as **cscanf( )**. This and other non-standard I/O functions are described in Chapter 8. The examples in this book that use **getche( )** work correctly with Visual C++ because they avoid the use of the standard input functions.*

Virtually all computers use the ASCII character codes when representing characters. Therefore, characters returned by either **getchar( )** or **getche( )** will be represented by their ASCII codes. This is useful because the ASCII character codes are an ordered sequence; each letter's code is one greater than the previous letter; each digit's code is one greater than the previous digit. This means that 'a' is less than 'b', '2' is less than '3', and so on. You may compare characters just like you compare numbers. For example,

```
ch = getchar();
if(ch < 'f' printf("character is less than f");
```

is a perfectly valid fragment that will display its message if the user enters any character that comes before **f**.

EXAMPLES

1. This program reads a character and displays its ASCII code. This illustrates an important feature of C: You can use a character as if it were a "little integer." The program also demonstrates the use of the **getche( )** function.

```
#include <conio.h>
#include <stdio.h>

int main(void)
{
  char ch;

  printf("Enter a character: ");
  ch = getche();
  printf("\nIts ASCII code is %d", ch);

  return 0;
}
```

Because this program uses **getche( )**, it responds as soon as you press a key. Before continuing, try substituting **getchar( )** for **getche( )** in this program and observe the results. As you will see, **getchar( )** does not return a character to your program until you press ENTER.

2. One of the most common uses of character input is to obtain a menu selection. For example, this program allows the user to add, subtract, multiply, or divide two numbers.

```
#include <stdio.h>
```

```
int main(void)
{
  int a, b;
  char ch;

  printf("Do you want to:\n");
  printf("Add, Subtract, Multiply, or Divide?\n");
  printf("Enter first letter: ");
  ch = getchar();
  printf("\n");

  printf("Enter first number: ");
  scanf("%d", &a);
  printf("Enter second number: ");
  scanf("%d", &b);

  if(ch=='A') printf("%d", a+b);
  if(ch=='S') printf("%d", a-b);
  if(ch=='M') printf("%d", a*b);
  if(ch=='D' && b!=0) printf("%d", a/b);

  return 0;
}
```

One point to keep in mind is that C makes a distinction between upper- and lowercase letters. So, if the user enters an **s**, the program will not recognize it as a request to subtract. (Later, you will learn how to convert the case of a character.)

3. Another common reason that your program will need to read a character from the keyboard is to obtain a yes/no response from the user. For example, this fragment determines if the user wants to proceed.

```
printf("Do you wish to continue? (Y/N : ");
ch = getche();
if(ch=='Y') {
  /* continue with something */
    .
    .
    .
}
```

EXERCISES

1. Write a program that reads ten letters. After the letters have been read, display the one that comes earliest in the alphabet. (Hint: The one with the smallest value comes first.)

2. Write a program that displays the ASCII codes for the characters A through Z and a through z. How do the codes differ between the upper- and lowercase characters?

3.2 *N*EST if *STATEMENTS*

When an **if** statement is the target of another **if** or **else**, it is said to be *nested* within the outer **if**. Here is a simple example of a nested **if**:

```
if(count > max) /* outer if */
  if(error) printf("Error, try again."); /* nested if */
```

Here, the **printf( )** statement will only execute if **count** is greater than **max** and if **error** is nonzero. Notice how the nested **if** is indented. This is common practice. It enables anyone reading your program to know quickly that the **if** is nested and what actions are nested. A nested **if** may also appear inside a block of statements that are the target of the outer **if**.

An ANSI-standard compiler will allow you to nest **if**s at least 15 levels deep. (However, it would be rare to find such a deep nesting.)

One confusing aspect of nested **if**s is illustrated by the following fragment:

```
if(p)
  if(q) printf("a and b are true");
else printf("To which statement does this else apply?");
```

The question suggested by the second **printf( )** is: which **if** is associated with the **else**? Fortunately, the answer is quite easy: An **else** always associates with the nearest **if** in the same block that does not already have an **else** associated with it. In this example, the **else** is associated with the second **if**.

1. It is possible to string together several **if**s and **else**s into what is sometimes called an *if-else-if ladder* or *if-else-if staircase* because of its visual appearance. In this situation a nested **if** has as its target another **if**. The general form of the if-else-if ladder is shown here:

   ```
   if(expression) statement;
   else
     if(expression) statement;
     else
       if(expression) statement;
       .
       .
       .
           else statement;
   ```

   The expressions are evaluated from the top downward. As soon as a true condition is found, the statement associated with it is executed, and the rest of the ladder is bypassed. If none of the expressions are true, the final **else** will be executed. That is, if all other conditional tests fail, the last **else** statement is performed. If the final **else** is not present, no action will take place if all expressions are false.

   Although the indentation of the general form of the if-else-if ladder just shown is technically correct, it can lead to overly deep indentation. Because of this, the if-else-if ladder is generally written like this:

   ```
   if(expression) statement;
   else if(expression) statement;
   else if(expression) statement;
   .
   .
   .
   else statement;
   ```

   We can improve the arithmetic program developed in Section 3.1 by using an if-else-if ladder, as shown here:

```
#include <stdio.h>

int main(void)
{
  int a, b;
  char ch;

  printf("Do you want to:\n");
  printf("Add, Subtract, Multiply, or Divide?\n");
  printf("Enter first letter: ");
  ch = getchar();
  printf("\n");

  printf("Enter first number: ");
  scanf("%d", &a);
  printf("Enter second number: ");
  scanf("%d", &b);

  if(ch=='A') printf("%d", a+b);
  else if(ch=='S') printf("%d", a-b);
  else if(ch=='M') printf("%d", a*b);
  else if(ch=='D' && b!=0) printf("%d", a/b);

  return 0;
}
```

This is an improvement over the original version because once a match is found, any remaining **if** statements are skipped. This means that the program isn't wasting time on needless operations. While this is not too important in this example, you will encounter situations where it will be.

2. Nested **if** statements are very common in programming. For example, here is a further improvement to the addition drill program developed in the preceding chapter. It lets the user have a second try at getting the right answer.

```
#include <stdio.h>

int main(void)
{
  int answer, count;
```

```
         int again;

         for(count=1; count<11; count++) {
           printf("What is %d + %d? ", count, count);
           scanf("%d", &answer);

           if(answer == count+count) printf("Right!\n");
           else {
             printf("Sorry, you're wrong\n");
             printf("Try again.\n ");

             printf("\nWhat is %d + %d? ", count, count);
             scanf("%d", &answer);

             /* nested if */
             if(answer == count+count) printf("Right!\n");
             else
               printf("Wrong, the answer is %d\n",
                     count+count);
           }
         }
         return 0;
       }
```

Here, the second **if** is nested within the outer **if**'s **else** block.

EXERCISES

1. To which **if** does the **else** relate to in this example?

```
if(ch=='S') { /* first if */
  printf("Enter a number: ");
  scanf("%d", &y);

  /* second if */
  if(y) printf("Its square is %d.", y*y);
}
else printf("Make next selection.");
```

2. Write a program that computes the area of either a circle,
   rectangle, or triangle. Use an if-else-if ladder.

3.3   *E*XAMINE for *LOOP VARIATIONS*

The **for** loop in C is significantly more powerful and flexible than in most other computer languages. When you were introduced to the **for** loop in Chapter 2, you were only shown the form similar to that used by other languages. However, you will see that **for** is much more flexible.

The reason that **for** is so flexible is that the expressions we called the *initialization*, *conditional-test*, and *increment* portions of the loop are not limited to these narrow roles. The **for** loop places no limits on the types of expressions that occur inside it. For example, you do not have to use the initialization section to initialize a loop-control variable. Further, there does not need to be any loop-control variable because the conditional expression may use some other means of stopping the loop. Finally, the increment portion is technically just an expression that is evaluated each time the loop iterates. It does not have to increment or decrement a variable.

Another important reason that the **for** is so flexible is that one or more of the expressions inside it may be empty. For example, if the loop-control variable has already been initialized outside the **for**, there is no need for an initialization expression.

EXAMPLES

1. This program continues to loop until a **q** is entered at the keyboard. Instead of testing a loop-control variable, the conditional test in this **for** checks the value of a character entered by the user.

```
#include <stdio.h>
#include <conio.h>

int main(void)
{
  int i;
  char ch;

  ch = 'a'; /* give ch an initial value */

  for(i=0; ch != 'q'; i++) {
    printf("pass: %d\n", i);
```

```
    ch = getche();
  }

  return 0;
}
```

Here, the condition that controls the loop has nothing to do with the loop-control variable. The reason **ch** is given an initial value is to prevent it from accidentally containing a **q** when the program begins.

2. As stated earlier, it is possible to leave an expression in a loop empty. For example, this program asks the user for a value and then counts down to zero from this number. Here, the loop-control variable is initialized by the user outside the loop, so the initialization portion of the loop is empty.

```c
#include <stdio.h>

int main(void)
{
  int i;

  printf("Enter an integer: ");
  scanf("%d", &i);

  for(; i; i--) printf("%d ", i);

  return 0;
}
```

3. Another variation to **for** is that its target may be empty. For example, this program simply keeps inputting characters until the user types **q**.

```c
#include <stdio.h>
#include <conio.h>

int main(void)
{
  char ch;

  for(ch=getche(); ch!='q'; ch=getche());
  printf("Found the q.");
```

```
    return 0;
}
```

Notice that the statements assigning **ch** a value have been moved into the loop. This means that when the loop starts, **getche( )** is called. Then, the value of **ch** is tested against **q**. Next, conceptually, the nonexistent target of the **for** is executed, and the call to **getche( )** in the increment portion of the loop is executed. This process repeats until the user enters a **q**.

The reason the target of the **for** can be empty is because C allows null statements.

4. Using the **for**, it is possible to create a loop that never stops. This type of loop is usually called an *infinite loop.* Although accidentally creating an infinite loop is a bug, you will sometimes want to create one on purpose. (Later in this chapter, you will see that there are ways to exit even an infinite loop!) To create an infinite loop, use a **for** construct like this:

```
for( ;  ; ) {
  .
  .
  .
}
```

As you can see, there are no expressions in the **for**. When there is no expression in the conditional portion, the compiler assumes that it is true. Therefore, the loop continues to run.

5. In C, unlike most other computer languages, it is perfectly valid for the loop-control variable to be altered outside the increment section. For example, the following program manually increments **i** at the bottom of the loop.

```
#include <stdio.h>

int main(void)
{
  int i;

  for(i=0; i<10; ) {
    printf("%d ", i);
    i++;
  }
```

```
    return 0;
}
```

---

1. Write a program that computes driving time when given the distance and the average speed. Let the user specify the number of drive time computations he or she wants to perform.

2. To create time-delay loops, **for** loops with empty targets are often used. Create a program that asks the user for a number and then iterates until zero is reached. Once the countdown is done, sound the bell, but don't display anything on the screen.

3. Even if a **for** loop uses a loop-control variable, it need not be incremented or decremented by a fixed amount. Instead, the amount added or subtracted may vary. Write a program that begins at 1 and runs to 1000. Have the program add the loop-control variable to itself inside the increment expression. This is an easy way to produce the arithmetic progression 1 2 4 8 16, and so on.

3.4 *U*NDERSTAND C'S while *LOOP*

Another of C's loops is **while**. It has this general form:

while(*expression*) *statement*;

Of course, the target of **while** may also be a block of code. The **while** loop works by repeating its target as long as the expression is true. When it becomes false, the loop stops. The value of the expression is checked at the top of the loop. This means that if the expression is false to begin with, the loop will not execute even once.

EXAMPLES

1. Even though the **for** is flexible enough to allow itself to be controlled by factors not related to its traditional use, you should generally select the loop that best fits the needs of the situation. For example, a better way to wait for the letter **q** to be typed is shown here using **while**. If you compare it to Example 3 in Section 3.3, you will see how much clearer this version is. (However, you will soon see that a better loop for this job exists.)

```c
#include <stdio.h>
#include <conio.h>

int main(void)
{
  char ch;

  ch = getche();

  while(ch!='q') ch = getche();
  printf("Found the q.");

  return 0;
}
```

2. The following program is a simple code machine. It translates the characters you type into a coded form by adding 1 to each letter. That is, 'A' becomes 'B,' and so forth. The program stops when you press ENTER. (The **getche( )** function returns **\r** when ENTER is pressed.)

```c
#include <stdio.h>
#include <conio.h>

int main(void)
{
  char ch;

  printf("Enter your message.\n");

  ch = getche();
  while(ch != '\r') {
```

```
        printf("%c", ch+1);
        ch = getche();
      }

      return 0;
    }
```

1. In Exercise 1 of Section 3.3, you created a program that computed driving time, given distance and average speed. You used a **for** loop to let the user compute several drive times. Rework that program so that it uses a **while** loop.

2. Write a program that will decode messages that have been encoded using the code machine program in the second example in this section.

3.5 *U*SE THE do LOOP

C's final loop is **do**, which has this general form:

```
do {
  statements
} while(expression);
```

If only one statement is being repeated, the curly braces are not necessary. Most programmers include them, however, so that they can easily recognize that the **while** that ends the **do** is part of a **do** loop, not the beginning of a **while** loop.

The **do** loop repeats the statement or statements while the expression is true. It stops when the expression becomes false. The **do** loop is unique because it will always execute the code within the loop at least once, since the expression controlling the loop is tested at the bottom of the loop.

EXAMPLES

1. The fact that **do** will always execute the body of its loop at least once makes it perfect for checking menu input. For example, this version of the arithmetic program reprompts the user until a valid response is entered.

```c
#include <stdio.h>

int main(void)
{
  int a, b;
  char ch;

  printf("Do you want to:\n");
  printf("Add, Subtract, Multiply, or Divide?\n");

  /* force user to enter a valid response */
  do {
    printf("Enter first letter: ");
    ch = getchar();
  } while(ch!='A' && ch!='S' && ch!='M' && ch!='D');
  printf("\n");

  printf("Enter first number: ");
  scanf("%d", &a);
  printf("Enter second number: ");
  scanf("%d", &b);

  if(ch=='A') printf("%d", a+b);
  else if(ch=='S') printf("%d", a-b);
  else if(ch=='M') printf("%d", a*b);
  else if(ch=='D' && b!=0) printf("%d", a/b);

  return 0;
}
```

2. The **do** loop is especially useful when your program is waiting for some event to occur. For example, this program waits for the user to type a **q**. Notice that it contains one less call to **getche( )** than the equivalent program described in the section on the **while** loop.

```c
#include <stdio.h>
#include <conio.h>
```

```
int main(void)
{
  char ch;

  do {
    ch = getche();
  } while(ch!='q');

  printf("Found the q.");

  return 0;
}
```

Since the loop condition is tested at the bottom, it is not necessary to initialize **ch** prior to entering the loop.

EXERCISES

1. Write a program that converts gallons to liters. Using a **do** loop, allow the user to repeat the conversion. (One gallon is approximately 3.7854 liters.)

2. Write a program that displays the menu below and uses a **do** loop to check for valid responses. (Your program does not need to implement the actual functions shown in the menu.)

   Mailing list menu:

   1. Enter addresses

   2. Delete address

   3. Search the list

   4. Print the list

   5. Quit

   Enter the number of your choice (1–5).

| 3.6 | | **C**REATE NESTED LOOPS |

When the body of one loop contains another, the second is said to be nested inside the first. Any of C's loops may be nested within any other loop. The ANSI C standard specifies that loops may be nested at least 15 levels deep. However, most compilers allow nesting to virtually any level. As a simple example of nested **for**s, this fragment prints the numbers **1** to **10** on the screen ten times.

```
for(i=0; i<10; i++) {
  for(j=1; j<11; j++) printf("%d ", j); /* nested loop */
  printf("\n");
}
```

EXAMPLES

1. You can use a nested **for** to make another improvement to the arithmetic drill. In the version shown below, the program will give the user three chances to get the right answer. Notice the use of the variable **right** to stop the loop early if the correct answer is given.

```
#include <stdio.h>

int main(void)
{
  int answer, count, chances, right;

  for(count=1; count<11; count++) {
    printf("What is %d + %d?", count, count);
    scanf("%d", &answer);

    if(answer == count+count) printf("Right!\n");
    else {
      printf("Sorry, you're wrong.\n");
      printf("Try again.\n");

      right = 0;
```

```
                /* nested for */
                for(chances=0; chances<3 && !right; chances++) {
                  printf("What is %d + %d? ", count, count);
                  scanf("%d", &answer);

                  if(answer == count+count) {
                    printf("Right!\n");
                    right = 1;
                  }
                }

                /* if answer still wrong, tell user */
                if(!right)
                    printf("The answer is %d.\n", count+count);
            }
        }

        return 0;
    }
```

2. This program uses three **for** loops to print the alphabet three times, each time printing each letter twice:

```
#include <stdio.h>

int main(void)
{
  int i, j, k;
  for(i=0; i<3; i++)
    for(j=0; j<26; j++)
      for(k=0; k<2; k++) printf("%c", 'A'+j);

  return 0;
}
```

The statement

```
printf("%c", 'A'+j);
```

works because ASCII codes for the letters of the alphabet are strictly ascending—each one is greater than the letter that precedes it.

EXERCISES

1. Write a program that finds all the prime numbers between **2** and **1000**.

2. Write a program that reads ten characters from the keyboard. Each time a character is read, use its ASCII code value to output a string of periods equal in number to this code. For example, given the letter 'A', whose code is 65, your program would output 65 periods.

3.7   **U**SE break *TO EXIT A LOOP*

The **break** statement allows you to exit a loop from any point within its body, bypassing its normal termination expression. When the **break** statement is encountered inside a loop, the loop is immediately stopped, and program control resumes at the next statement following the loop. For example, this loop prints only the numbers **1** to **10**:

```c
#include <stdio.h>

int main(void)
{
  int i;

  for(i=1; i<100; i++) {
    printf("%d ", i);
    if(i==10) break; /* exit the loop */
  }

  return 0;
}
```

The **break** statement can be used with all three of C's loops.

You can have as many **break** statements within a loop as you desire. However, since too many exit points from a loop tend to destructure your code, it is generally best to use the **break** for special purposes, not as your normal loop exit.

1. The **break** statement is commonly used in loops in which a special condition can cause immediate termination. Here is an example of such a situation. In this case, a keypress can stop the execution of the program.

```
#include <stdio.h>
#include <conio.h>

int main(void)
{
  int i;
  char ch;

  /* display all numbers that are multiples of 6 */
  for(i=1; i<10000; i++) {
    if(!(i%6)) {
      printf("%d, more? (Y/N)", i);
      ch = getche();
      if(ch=='N') break; /* stop the loop */
      printf("\n");
    }
  }

  return 0;
}
```

2. A **break** will cause an exit from only the innermost loop. For example, this program prints the numbers **0** to **5** five times:

```
#include <stdio.h>

int main(void)
{
  int i, j;

  for(i=0; i<5; i++) {
    for(j=0; j<100; j++) {
      printf("%d", j);
      if(j==5) break;
    }
    printf("\n");
```

```
    }

    return 0;
}
```

3. The reason C includes the **break** statement is to allow your programs to be more efficient. For example, examine this fragment:

```
do {
  printf("Load, Save, Edit, Quit?\n");
  do {
    printf("Enter your selection: ");
    ch = getchar();
  } while(ch!='L' && ch!='S' && ch!='E' && ch!='Q');

  if(ch != 'Q') {
    /* do something */
  }

  if(ch != 'Q') {
    /* do something else*/
  }
  /* etc. */
} while(ch != 'Q')
```

In this situation, several additional tests are performed on **ch** to see if it is equal to 'Q' to avoid executing certain sections of code when the **Quit** option is selected. Most C programmers would write the preceding loop as shown here:

```
for( ; ; ) { /* infinite for loop */
  printf("Load, Save, Edit, Quit?\n");
  do {
    printf ("Enter your selection: ");
    ch = getchar();
  } while(ch!='L' && ch!='S' && ch!='E' && ch!='Q');

  if(ch == 'Q') break;

  /* do something */
  /* do something else */
  /* etc. */
}
```

In this version, **ch** need only be tested once to see if it contains a 'Q'. As you can see, this implementation is more efficient because only one **if** statement is required.

1. On your own, write several short programs that use **break** to exit a loop. Be sure to try all three loop statements.

2. Write a program that prints a table showing the proper amount of tip to leave. Start the table at $1 and stop at $100, using increments of $1. Compute three tip percentages: 10%, 15%, and 20%. After each line, ask the user if he or she wants to continue. If not, use **break** to stop the loop and end the program.

3.8 ***K*NOW WHEN TO USE THE continue STATEMENT**

The **continue** statement is somewhat the opposite of the **break** statement. It forces the next iteration of the loop to take place, skipping any code in between itself and the test condition of the loop. For example, this program never displays any output:

```
#include <stdio.h>

int main(void)
{
  int x;

  for(x=0; x<100; x++) {
    continue;
    printf("%d ", x); /* this is never executed */
  }
```

```
 return 0;
}
```

Each time the **continue** statement is reached, it causes the loop to repeat, skipping the **printf( )** statement.

In **while** and **do-while** loops, a **continue** statement will cause control to go directly to the test condition and then continue the looping process. In the case of **for**, the increment part of the loop is performed, the conditional test is executed, and the loop continues.

Frankly, **continue** is seldom used, not because it is poor practice to use it, but simply because good applications for it are not common.

EXAMPLE

1. One good use for **continue** is to restart a statement sequence when an error occurs. For example, this program computes a running total of numbers entered by the user. Before adding a value to the running total, it verifies that the number was correctly entered by having the user enter it a second time. If the two numbers don't match, the program uses **continue** to restart the loop.

```
#include <stdio.h>

int main(void)
{
  int total, i, j;

  total = 0;
  do {
    printf("Enter next number (0 to stop): ");
    scanf("%d", &i);
    printf("Enter number again: ");
    scanf("%d", &j);
    if(i != j) {
      printf("Mismatch\n");
      continue;
    }
    total = total + i;
```

```
    } while(i);

    printf("Total is %d\n", total);

    return 0;
  }
```

1. Write a program that prints only the odd numbers between **1** and **100**. Use a **for** loop that looks like this:

   ```
   for(i=1; i<101; i++) . . .
   ```

   Use a **continue** statement to avoid printing even numbers.

3.9 SELECT AMONG ALTERNATIVES WITH THE switch STATEMENT

While **if** is good for choosing between two alternatives, it quickly becomes cumbersome when several alternatives are needed. C's solution to this problem is the **switch** statement. The **switch** statement is C's multiple selection statement. It is used to select one of several alternative paths in program execution and works as follows. A value is successively tested against a list of integer or character constants. When a match is found, the statement sequence associated with that match is executed. The general form of the **switch** statement is this:

```
switch(value) {
    case constant1:
        statement sequence
        break;
```

```
   case constant2:
     statement sequence
     break;
   case constant3:
     statement sequence
     break;

     .
     .
     .

   default:
     statement sequence
     break;
 }
```

The **default** statement sequence is performed if no matches are found. The **default** is optional. If all matches fail and **default** is absent, no action takes place. When a match is found, the statements associated with that **case** are executed until **break** is encountered or, in the case of **default** or the last **case**, the end of the **switch** is reached.

As a very simple example, this program recognizes the numbers 1, 2, 3, and 4 and prints the name of the one you enter. That is, if you enter **2**, the program displays **two**.

```c
#include <stdio.h>

int main(void)
{
  int i;

  printf("Enter a number between 1 and 4: ");
  scanf("%d", &i);

  switch(i) {
    case 1:
      printf("one");
      break;
    case 2:
      printf("two");
      break;
    case 3:
      printf("three");
      break;
```

```
      case 4:
        printf("four");
        break;
      default:
        printf("Unrecognized Number");
  }

  return 0;
}
```

The **switch** statement differs from **if** in that **switch** can only test for equality, whereas the **if** conditional expression can be of any type. Also, **switch** will work with only **int** or **char** types. You cannot, for example, use floating-point numbers.

The statement sequences associated with each **case** are *not* blocks; they are not enclosed by curly braces.

The ANSI C standard states that at least 257 **case** statements will be allowed. In practice, you should usually limit the amount of **case** statements to a much smaller number for efficiency reasons. Also, no two **case** constants in the same **switch** can have identical values.

It is possible to have a **switch** as part of the statement sequence of an outer **switch**. This is called a *nested switch.* If the **case** constants of the inner and outer **switch** contain common values, no conflicts will arise. For example, the following code fragment is perfectly acceptable:

```
switch(a) {
  case 1:
    switch(b) {
      case 0: printf("b is false");
              break;
      case 1: printf("b is true");
    }
    break;
  case 2:
    .
    .
    .
```

An ANSI-standard compiler will allow at least 15 levels of nesting for **switch** statements.

EXAMPLES

1. The **switch** statement is often used to process menu commands. For example, the arithmetic program can be recoded as shown here. This version reflects the way professional C code is written.

```c
#include <stdio.h>

int main(void)
{
  int a, b;
  char ch;

  printf("Do you want to:\n");
  printf("Add, Subtract, Multiply, or Divide?\n");
  /* force user to enter a valid response */
  do {
    printf("Enter first letter: ");
    ch = getchar();
  } while(ch!='A' && ch!='S' && ch!='M' && ch!='D');
  printf("\n");

  printf("Enter first number: ");
  scanf("%d", &a);
  printf("Enter second number: ");
  scanf("%d", &b);

  switch(ch) {
    case 'A': printf("%d", a+b);
      break;
    case 'S': printf("%d", a-b);
      break;
    case 'M': printf("%d", a*b);
      break;
    case 'D': if(b!=0) printf("%d", a/b);
  }

  return 0;
}
```

2. Technically, the **break** statement is optional. The **break** statement, when encountered within a **switch**, causes the program flow to exit from the entire **switch** statement and continue on to the next statement outside the **switch**. This is much the way it works when breaking out of a loop. However, if a **break** statement is omitted, execution continues into the following **case** or **default** statement (if either exists). That is, when a **break** statement is missing, execution "falls through" into the next **case** and stops only when a **break** statement or the end of the **switch** is encountered. For example, study this program carefully:

```c
#include <stdio.h>
#include <conio.h>

int main(void)
{
  char ch;

  do {
    printf("\nEnter a character, q to quit: ");
    ch = getche();
    printf("\n");

    switch(ch) {
      case 'a':
        printf("Now is ");
      case 'b':
        printf("the time ");
      case 'c':
        printf("for all good men");
        break;
      case 'd':
        printf("The summer ");
      case 'e':
        printf("soldier ");
    }
  } while(ch != 'q');

  return 0;
}
```

If the user types **a**, the entire phrase **Now is the time for all good men** is displayed. Typing **b** displays **the time for all**

good men. As you can see, once execution begins inside a **case**, it continues until a **break** statement or the end of the **switch** is encountered.

3. The statement sequence associated with a **case** may be empty. This allows two or more **case**s to share a common statement sequence without duplication of code. For example, here is a program that categorizes letters into vowels and consonants:

```c
#include <stdio.h>
#include <conio.h>

int main(void)
{
  char ch;

  printf("Enter the letter: ");
  ch = getche();

  switch(ch) {
    case 'a':
    case 'e':
    case 'i':
    case 'o':
    case 'u':
    case 'y':
      printf(" is a vowel\n");
      break;
    default:
      printf(" is a consonant");
  }

  return 0;
}
```

EXERCISES

1. What is wrong with this fragment?

```c
float f;

scanf("%f", &f);
```

```
switch(f) {
  case 10.05:
  .
  .
  .
```

2. Write a program that counts the numbers of letters, digits, and common punctuation symbols entered by the user. Stop inputting when the user presses ENTER. Use a **switch** statement to categorize the characters into punctuation, digits, and letters. When the program ends, report the number of characters in each category. (If you like, simply assume that, if a character is not a digit or punctuation, it is a letter. Also, just use the most common punctuation symbols.)

3.10 **U**NDERSTAND THE goto STATEMENT

C supports a non-conditional jump statement, called the **goto**. Because C is a replacement for assembly code, the inclusion of **goto** is necessary because it can be used to create very fast routines. However, most programmers do not use **goto** because it destructures a program and, if frequently used, can render the program virtually impossible to understand later. Also, there is no routine that requires a **goto**. For these reasons, it is not used in this book outside of this section.

The **goto** statement can perform a jump within a function. It cannot jump between functions. It works with a label. In C, a *label* is a valid identifier name followed by a colon. For example, the following **goto** jumps around the **printf( )** statement:

```
goto mylabel;
printf("This will not print.");
mylabel: printf("This will print.");
```

About the only good use for **goto** is to jump out of a deeply nested routine when a catastrophic error occurs.

EXAMPLE

1. This program uses **goto** to create the equivalent of a **for** loop
   running from **1** to **10**. (This is just an example of **goto**. In actual
   practice, you should use a real **for** loop when one is needed.)

```
#include <stdio.h>

int main(void)
{
  int i;

  i = 1;
  again:
    printf("%d ", i);
    i++;
    if(i<10) goto again;

  return 0;
}
```

EXERCISE

1. Write a program that uses **goto** to emulate a **while** loop that
   counts from **1** to **10**.

Mastery
Skills Check

At this point, you should be able to answer these questions and
perform these exercises:

1. As illustrated by Exercise 2 in Section 3.1, the ASCII codes for
   the lowercase letters are separated from the uppercase letters
   by a difference of 32. Therefore, to convert a lowercase letter to

an uppercase one, simply subtract 32 from it. Write a program that reads characters from the keyboard and displays lowercase letters as uppercase ones. Stop when ENTER is pressed.

2. Using a nested **if** statement, write a program that prompts the user for a number and then reports if the number is positive, zero, or negative.

3. Is this a valid **for** loop?

```
char ch;

ch = 'x';
for( ; ch != ' ' ; ) ch = getche();
```

4. Show the traditional way to create an infinite loop in C.

5. Using the three loop statements, show three different ways to count from 1 to 10.

6. What does the **break** statement do when used in a loop?

7. Is this **switch** statement correct?

```
switch(i) {
  case 1: printf("nickel");
    break;
  case 2: printf("dime");
    break;
  case 3: printf("quarter");
}
```

8. Is this **goto** fragment correct?

```
goto alldone;
.
.
.
alldone
```

**Cumulative
Skills Check**

This section checks how well you have integrated the material in this chapter with that from earlier chapters.

1. Using a **switch** statement, write a program that reads characters from the keyboard and watches for tabs, newlines, and backspaces. When one is received, display what it is in words. For example, when the user presses the TAB key, print **tab**. Have the user enter a **q** to stop the program.

2. While this program is not incorrect, show how it would look if written by an experienced C programmer.

```c
#include <stdio.h>

int main(void)
{
  int i, j, k;

  for(k=0; k<10; k=k+1) {
    printf("Enter first number: ");
    scanf("%d", &i);

    printf("Enter second number: ");
    scanf("%d", &j);

    if(j != 0) printf("%d\n", i/j);
    if(j == 0) printf("cannot divide by zero\n");
  }

  return 0;
}
```

4

A Closer Look at Data Types, Variables, and Expressions

chapter objectives

4.1 Use C's data-type modifiers

4.2 Learn where variables are declared

4.3 Take a closer look at constants

4.4 Initialize variables

4.5 Understand type conversions in expressions

4.6 Understand type conversions in assignments

4.7 Program with type casts

THIS chapter more fully examines several concepts presented in Chapter 1. It covers C's data-type modifiers, global and local variables, and constants. It also discusses how C handles various type conversions.

Review

Skills Check

Before proceeding, you should be able to answer these questions and perform these exercises:

1. Using C's three loop statements, show three ways to write a loop that counts from **1** to **10**.

2. Convert this series of **if**s into an equivalent **switch**.

```
if(ch=='L') load();
else if(ch=='S') save();
else if(ch=='E') enter();
else if(ch=='D') display();
else if(ch=='Q') quit();
```

3. Write a program that inputs characters until the user strikes the ENTER key.

4. What does **break** do?

5. What does **continue** do?

6. Write a program that displays this menu, performs the selected operation, and then repeats until the user selects **Quit**.

Convert
  1. feet to meters
  2. meters to feet
  3. ounces to pounds
  4. pounds to ounces
  5. Quit
Enter the number of your choice:

4.1 ▪ *U*SE C'S DATA-TYPE MODIFIERS

In Chapter 1 you learned that C has five basic data types: **void**, **char**, **int**, **float**, and **double**. These basic types, except type **void**, can be modified using C's *type modifiers* to more precisely fit your specific need. The type modifiers are

long
short
signed
unsigned

The type modifier precedes the type name. For example, this declares a **long** integer:

```
long int i;
```

The effect of each modifier is examined next.

The **long** and **short** modifiers may be applied to **int.** As a general rule, **short int**s are often smaller than **int**s and **long int**s are often larger than **int**s. For example, in most 16-bit environments, an **int** is 16 bits long and a **long int** is 32 bits in length. However, the precise meaning of **long** and **short** is implementation dependent. When the ANSI C standard was created, it specified *minimum ranges* for integers, short integers, and long integers. It did not set fixed sizes for these items. (See Table 4-1.) For example, using the minimum ranges set forth in the ANSI C standard, the smallest acceptable size for an **int** is 16 bits and the smallest acceptable size for a **short int** is also 16 bits. Thus, it is permissible for integers and short integers to be the same size! In fact, in most 16-bit environments, there is no difference between an **int** and a **short int**. Further, in many 32-bit environments, you will find that integers and long integers are the same size. Since the exact effect of **long** and **short** on integers is determined by the environment in which you are working and by the compiler you are using, you will need to check your compiler's documentation for their precise effects.

The **long** modifier may also be applied to **double**. Doing so roughly doubles the precision of a floating point variable.

The **signed** modifier is used to specify a signed integer value. (A signed number means that it can be positive or negative.) However, the use of **signed** on integers is redundant because the default integer declaration automatically creates a signed variable. The main use of the **signed** modifier is with **char**. Whether **char** is signed or unsigned by itself is implementation dependent. In some implementations **char** is unsigned by default; in others, it is signed. To ensure a signed character variable in all environments, you must declare it as **signed char**. Since most compilers implement **char** as signed, this book simply assumes that characters are **signed** and will not use the **signed** modifier.

The **unsigned** modifier can be applied to **char** and **int**. It may also be used in combination with **long** or **short**. It is used to create an unsigned integer. The difference between signed and unsigned integers is in the way the high-order bit of the integer is interpreted. If a signed integer is specified, then the C compiler will generate code that assumes the high-order bit is used as a sign flag. If the sign flag is 0, the number is positive; if it is 1, the number is negative. Negative numbers are generally represented using the *two's complement* approach. In this method, all bits in the number (except the sign flag) are reversed, and 1 is added to this number. Finally, the sign flag is set to 1. (The reason for this method of representation is that it makes it easier for the CPU to perform arithmetic operations on negative values.)

Signed integers are important for a great many algorithms, but they only have half the absolute magnitude of their unsigned relatives. For example, here is 32,767 shown in binary:

```
0 1 1 1 1 1 1 1   1 1 1 1 1 1 1 1
```

If this is a signed value and the high-order bit is set to 1, the number would then be interpreted as –1 (assuming two's complement format). However, if this is an unsigned value, then when the high-order bit is set to 1, the number becomes 65,535.

Table 4-1 shows all allowed combinations of the basic types and the type modifiers. The table also shows the most common size and minimum range for each type as specified by the ANSI C standard.

It is important to understand that the ranges shown in Table 4-1 are just the minimums that all compilers must provide. The compiler is free to exceed them, and most compilers do for at least some data types. As mentioned, an **int** in a 32-bit environment will usually have a range larger than the minimum. Also, in environments that use

Type	Typical Size in Bits	Minimal Range
char	8	–127 to 127
unsigned char	8	0 to 255
signed char	8	–127 to 127
int	16 or 32	–32,767 to 32,767
unsigned int	16 or 32	0 to 65,535
signed int	16 or 32	same as int
short int	16	same as int
unsigned short int	16	0 to 65,535
signed short int	16	same as short int
long int	32	–2,147,483,647 to 2,147,483,647
signed long int	32	same as long int
unsigned long int	32	0 to 4,294,967,295
float	32	Six digits of precision
double	64	Ten digits of precision
long double	80	Ten digits of precision

TABLE 4-1   *All Data Types Defined by the ANSI C Standard* ▼

two's complement arithmetic (which is the case for the vast majority of computers), the lower bound for signed characters and integers is one greater than the minimums shown. For instance, in most environments, a **signed char** has a range of –128 to 127 and a **short int** is typically –32,768 to 32,767. You will need to check your compiler's documentation for the specific ranges of the data types as they apply to your compiler.

C allows a shorthand notation for declaring **unsigned**, **short**, or **long** integers. You may simply use the word **unsigned**, **short**, or **long** without the **int**. The **int** is implied. For example,

```
unsigned count;
unsigned int num;
```

both declare **unsigned int** variables.

It is important to remember that variables of type **char** may be used to hold values other than just the ASCII character set. C makes little distinction between a character and an integer, except for the magnitudes of the values each may hold. Therefore, as mentioned earlier, a signed **char** variable can also be used as a "small" integer when the situation does not require larger numbers.

When outputting integers modified by **short**, **long**, or **unsigned** using **printf( )**, you cannot simply use the **%d** specifier. The reason is that **printf( )** needs to know precisely what type of data it is receiving. To use **printf( )** to output a **short**, use **%hd**. To output a **long**, use **%ld**. When outputting an **unsigned** value, use **%u**. To output an **unsigned long int**, use **%lu**. Also, to output a **long double** use **%Lf**.

The **scanf( )** function operates in a fashion similar to **printf( )**. When reading a **short int** using **scanf( )**, use **%hd**. When reading a **long int**, use **%ld**. To read an **unsigned long int**, use **%lu**. To read a **double**, use **%1f**. To read a **long double**, use **%Lf**.

EXAMPLES

1. This program shows how to input and output **short**, **long**, and **unsigned** values.

```
#include <stdio.h>

int main(void)
{
  unsigned u;
  long l;
  short s;

  printf("Enter an unsigned: ");
  scanf("%u", &u);
  printf("Enter a long: ");
  scanf("%ld", &l);
  printf("Enter a short: ");
  scanf("%hd", &s);

  printf("%u %ld %hd\n", u, l, s);

  return 0;
}
```

2. To understand the difference between the way that signed and unsigned integers are interpreted by C, run the following short program. (This program assumes that short integers are 16 bits wide.)

```
#include <stdio.h>

int main(void)
{
  short int i;   /* a signed short integer */
  unsigned short int u; /* an unsigned short integer */

  u = 33000;
  i = u;
  printf("%hd %hu", i, u);

  return 0;
}
```

When this program is run, the output is **–32536 33000**. The reason for this is that the bit pattern that 33000 represents as an **unsigned short int** is interpreted as –32536 as a **signed short int**.

3. In C, you may use a **char** variable any place you would use an **int** variable (assuming the differences in their ranges is not a factor). For example, the following program uses a **char** variable to control the loop that is summing the numbers between 1 and 100.   In some cases it takes the computer less time to access a single byte (one character) than it does to access two bytes. Therefore, many professional programmers use a character variable rather than an integer one when the range permits.

```
#include <stdio.h>

int main(void)
{
  int i;
  char j;

  i = 0;
  for(j=1; j<101; j++) i = j + i;

  printf("Total is: %d", i);

  return 0;
}
```

1. Show how to declare an **unsigned short int** called **loc_counter**.

2. Write a program that prompts the user for a distance and computes how long it takes light to travel that distance. Use an **unsigned long int** to hold the distance. (Light travels at approximately 186,000 miles per second.)

3. Write this statement another way:

```
short int i;
```

4.2 *LEARN WHERE VARIABLES ARE DECLARED*

As you learned in Chapter 1, there are two basic places where a variable will be declared: inside a function and outside all functions. These variables are called *local* variables and *global* variables, respectively. It is now time to take a closer look at these two types of variables and the *scope rules* that govern them.

Local variables (declared *inside* a function) may be referenced only by statements that are inside that function. They are not known outside their own function. One of the most important things to understand about local variables is that they exist only while the function in which they are declared is executing. That is, a local variable is created upon entry into its function and destroyed upon exit.

Since local variables are not known outside their own function, it is perfectly acceptable for local variables in different functions to have the same name. Consider the following program:

```
#include <stdio.h>

void f1(void), f2(void);

int main(void)
{
  f1();

  return 0;
}
```

```
void f1(void)
{
  int count;

  for(count=0; count<10; count++) f2();
}

void f2(void)
{
  int count;

  for(count=0; count<10; count++) printf("%d ", count);
}
```

This program prints the numbers **0** through **9** on the screen ten times. The fact that both functions use a variable called **count** has no effect upon the operation of the code. Therefore, what happens to **count** inside **f2( )** has no effect on **count** in **f1( )**.

The C language contains the keyword **auto**, which can be used to declare local variables. However, since all local variables are, by default, assumed to be **auto**, it is virtually never used. Hence, you will not see it in any of the examples in this book.

Within a function, local variables can be declared at the start of any block. They do not need to be declared only at the start of the block that defines the function. For example, the following program is perfectly valid:

```
#include <stdio.h>

int main(void)
{
  int i;

  for(i=0; i<10; i++) {
    if(i==5) {
      int j; /* declare j within the if block */

      j = i * 10;
      printf ("%d", j);
    }
  }

  return 0;
}
```

A variable declared within a block is known only to other code within that block. Thus, **j** may not be used outside of its block. Frankly, most C programmers declare all variables used by a function at the start of the function's block because it is simply more convenient to do so. This is the approach that will be used in this book.

Remember one important point: You must declare all local variables at the start of the block in which they are defined, prior to any program statements. For example, the following is incorrect:

```
#include <stdio.h>

int main(void)
{
  printf("This program won't compile.");
  int i; /* this should come first */
  i = 10;
  printf("%d", i);

  return 0;
}
```

When a function is called, its local variables are created, and upon its return, they are destroyed. This means that local variables cannot retain their values between calls.

The formal parameters to a function are also local variables. Even though these variables perform the special task of receiving the value of the arguments passed to the function, they can be used like any other local variable within that function.

Unlike local variables, global variables are known throughout the entire program and may be used by any piece of code in the program. Also, they will hold their value during the entire execution of the program. Global variables are created by declaring them outside any function. For example, consider this program:

```
#include <stdio.h>

void f1(void);

int max; /* this is a global variable */

int main(void)
{
  max = 10;
```

```
    f1();

    return 0;
}

void f1(void)
{
    int i;

    for(i=0; i<max; i++) printf("%d ", i);
}
```

Here, both **main( )** and **f1( )** use the global variable **max**. The **main( )**
function sets the value of **max** to 10, and **f1( )** uses this value to
control its **for** loop.

EXAMPLES

1. In C, a local variable and a global variable may have the same
    name. For example, this is a valid program:

```
#include <stdio.h>

void f1(void);

int count; /* global count */

int main(void)
{
    count = 10;
    f1();
    printf("count in main(): %d\n", count);

    return 0;
}

void f1(void)
{
    int count; /* local count */

    count = 100;
    printf("count in f1() : %d\n", count);
}
```

The program displays this output:

```
count in f1() : 100
count in main() : 10
```

In **main( )**, the reference to **count** is to the global variable. Inside **f1( )**, a local variable called **count** is also defined. When the assignment statement inside **f1( )** is encountered, the compiler first looks to see if there is a local variable called **count**. Since there is, the local variable is used, not the global one with the same name. That is, when local and global variables share the same name, the compiler will always use the local variable.

2. Global variables are very helpful when the same data is used by many functions in your program. However, you should always use local variables where you can because the excessive use of global variables has some negative consequences. First, global variables use memory the entire time your program is executing, not just when they are needed. In situations where memory is in short supply, this could be a problem. Second, using a global where a local variable will do makes a function less general, because it relies on something that must be defined outside itself. For example, here is a case where global variables are being used for no reason:

```c
#include <stdio.h>

int power(void);

int m, e;

int main(void)
{
  m = 2;
  e = 3;

  printf("%d raised to the %d power is %d", m, e, power());

  return 0;
}

/* Non-general version of power. */
int power(void)
```

```
{
  int temp, temp2;

  temp = 1;
  temp2 = e;
  for( ; temp2> 0; temp2--) temp = temp * m;

  return temp;
}
```

Here, the function **power( )** is created to compute the value of **m** raised to the eth power. Since **m** and **e** are global, the function cannot be used to compute the power of other values. It can only operate on those contained within **m** and **e**. However, if the program is rewritten as follows, **power( )** can be used with any two values.

```
#include <stdio.h>

int power(int m, int e);

int main(void)
{
  int m, e;
  m = 2;
  e = 3;

  printf("%d to the %d is %d\n", m, e, power(m, e));
  printf("4 to the 5th is %d\n", power(4, 5));
  printf("3 to the 3rd is %d\n", power(3, 3));

  return 0;
}

/* Parameterized version of power. */
int power(int m, int e)
{
  int temp;

  temp = 1;
  for( ; e> 0; e--) temp = temp * m;

  return temp;
}
```

By parameterizing **power( )**, you can use it to return the result of any value raised to some power, as the program now shows.

The important point is that in the non-generalized version, any program that uses **power( )** must always declare **m** and **e** as global variables and then load them with the desired values each time **power( )** is used. In the parameterized form, the function is complete within itself—no extra baggage need be carried about when it is used.

Finally, using a large number of global variables can lead to program errors because of unknown and unwanted side effects. A major problem in developing large programs is the accidental modification of a variable's value because it was used elsewhere in the program. This can happen in C if you use too many global variables in your programs.

3. Remember, local variables do not maintain their values between functions calls. For example, the following program will not work correctly:

```c
#include <stdio.h>

int series(void);

int main(void)
{
  int i;

  for(i=0; i<10; i++) printf("%d ", series());

  return 0;
}

/* This is incorrect. */
int series(void)
{
  int total;

  total = (total + 1423) % 1422;
  return total;
}
```

This program attempts to use **series( )** to generate a number series in which each number is based upon the value of the preceding one. However, the value **total** will not be maintained between function calls, and the function fails to carry out its intended task.

1. What are key differences between local and global variables?

2. Write a program that contains a function called **soundspeed( )**, which computes the number of seconds it will take sound to travel a specified distance. Write the program two ways: first, with **soundspeed( )** as a non-general function and second, with **soundspeed( )** parameterized. (For the speed of sound, use 1129 feet per second).

4.3   *T*AKE A CLOSER LOOK AT CONSTANTS

Constants refer to fixed values that may not be altered by the program. For example, the number 100 is a constant. We have been using constants in the preceding sample programs without much fanfare because, in most cases, their use is intuitive. However, the time has come to cover them formally.

Integer constants are specified as numbers without fractional components. For example, 10 and –100 are integer constants. Floating-point constants require the use of the decimal point followed by the number's fractional component. For example, 11.123 is a floating-point constant. C also allows you to use scientific notation for floating-point numbers. Constants using scientific notation must follow this general form:

number E *sign exponent*

The *sign* is optional. Although the general form is shown with spaces between the component parts for clarity, there may be no spaces between the parts in an actual number. For example, the following defines the value 1234.56 using scientific notation:

```
123.456E1
```

Character constants are enclosed between single quotes. For example 'a' and '%' are both character constants. As some of the examples have shown, this means that if you wish to assign a character to a variable of type **char**, you will use a statement similar to

```
ch = 'Z';
```

However, there is nothing in C that prevents you from assigning a character variable a value using a numeric constant. For example, the ASCII code for 'A' is 65. Therefore, these two assignment statements are equivalent.

```
char ch;

ch = 'A';
ch = 65;
```

When you enter numeric constants into your program, the compiler must decide what type of constant they are. For example, is 1000 an **int**, an **unsigned**, or a **short**? The reason we haven't worried about this earlier is that C automatically converts the type of the right side of an assignment statement to that of the variable on the left. (We will examine this process more fully later in this chapter.) So, for many situations it doesn't matter what the compiler thinks 1000 is. However, this can be important when you use a constant as an argument to a function, such as in a call to **printf( )**.

By default, the C compiler fits a numeric constant into the smallest compatible data type that will hold it. Assuming 16-bit integers, 10 is an **int** by default and 100003 is a **long**. Even though the value 10 could be fit into a **char**, the compiler will not do this because it means crossing type boundaries. The only exceptions to the smallest-type rule are floating-point constants, which are assumed to be **double**s. For virtually all programs you will write as a beginner, the compiler defaults are perfectly adequate. However, as you will see later in this book, there will come a point when you will need to specify precisely the type of constant you want.

In cases where the assumption that C makes about a numeric constant is not what you want, C allows you to specify the exact type by using a suffix. For floating-point types, if you follow the number with an 'F', the number is treated as a **float**. If you follow it with an 'L', the number becomes a **long double**. For integer types, the 'U' suffix stands for **unsigned** and the 'L' stands for **long**.

As you may know, in programming it is sometimes easier to use a number system based on 8 or 16 instead of 10. As you learned in Chapter 2, the number system based on 8 is called *octal* and it uses the digits 0 through 7. The base-16 number system is called *hexadecimal* and uses the digits 0 through 9 plus the letters 'A' through 'F', which stand for 10 through 15. C allows you to specify integer constants as hexadecimal or octal instead of decimal if you prefer. A hexadecimal constant must begin with '0x' (a zero followed by an x) then the constant in hexadecimal form. An octal constant begins with a zero. For example, **0xAB** is a hexadecimal constant, and **024** is an octal constant. You may use either upper- or lowercase letters when entering hexadecimal constants.

C supports one other type of constant in addition to those of the predefined data types: the string. A *string* is a set of characters enclosed by double quotes. You have been working with strings since Chapter 1 because both the **printf( )** and **scanf( )** functions use them. Keep in mind one important fact: although C allows you to define string constants, it does not formally have a string data type. Instead, as you will see a little later in this book, strings are supported in C as character arrays. (Arrays are discussed in Chapter 5.)

To display a string using **printf( )** you can either make it part of the control string or pass it as a separate argument and display it using the **%s** format code. For example, this program prints **Once upon a time** on the screen:

```
#include <stdio.h>

int main(void)
{
  printf("%s %s %s", "Once", "upon", "a time");

  return 0;
}
```

Here, each string is passed to **printf( )** as an argument and displayed using the **%s** specifier.

1. To see why it is important to use the correct type specifier with **printf( )**, try this program. (It assumes that short integers are 16 bits.) Instead of printing the number **42340**, it displays **−23196**, because it thinks that it is receiving a signed short integer. The problem is that 42,340 is outside the range of a **short int**. To make it work properly, you must use the **%hu** specifier.

```
#include <stdio.h>

int main(void)
{
  printf("%hd", 42340); /* this won't work right */

  return 0;
}
```

2. To see why you may need to explicitly tell the compiler what type of constant you are using, try this program. For most compilers, it will not produce the desired output. (If it does work, it is only by chance.)

```
#include <stdio.h>

int main(void)
{
  printf("%f", 2309);

  return 0;
}
```

This program is telling **printf( )** to expect a floating point value, but the compiler assumes that 2309 is simply an **int**. Hence, it does not output the correct value. To fix it, you must specify 2309 as 2309.0. Adding the decimal point forces the compiler to treat the value as a **double**.

EXERCISES

1. How do you tell the C compiler that a floating-point constant should be represented as a **float** instead of a **double**?

2. Write a program that reads and writes a **long int** value.

3. Write a program that outputs **I like C** using three separate strings.

4.4   *I̶NITIALIZE VARIABLES*

A variable may be given an initial value when it is declared. This is called *variable initialization*. The general form of variable initialization is shown here:

type var-name = constant;

For example, this statement declares **count** as an **int** and gives it an initial value of 100.

```
int count = 100;
```

The main advantage of using an initialization rather than a separate assignment statement is that the compiler may be able to produce faster code. Also, this saves some typing effort on your part.

Global variables may be initialized using only constants. Local variables can be initialized using constants, variables, or function calls as long as each is valid at the time of the initialization. However, most often both global and local variables are initialized using constants.

Global variables are initialized only once, at the start of program execution. Local variables are initialized each time a function is entered.

Global variables that are not explicitly initialized are automatically set to zero. Local variables that are not initialized should be assumed to contain unknown values. Although some C compilers automatically initialize un-initialized local variables to 0, you should not count on this.

1. This program gives **i** the initial value of –1 and then displays its value.

```
#include <stdio.h>

int main(void)
{
  int i = -1;

  printf("i is initialized to %d", i);

  return 0;
}
```

2. When you declare a list of variables, you may initialize one or more of them. For example, this fragment initializes **min** to 0 and **max** to 100. It does not initialize **count**.

```
int min=0, count, max=100;
```

3. As stated earlier, local variables are initialized each time the function is entered. For this reason, this program prints **10** three times.

```
#include <stdio.h>

void f(void);

int main(void)
{
  f();
  f();
  f();

  return 0;
}

void f(void)
{
  int i = 10;

  printf("%d ", i);
}
```

4. A local variable can be initialized by any expression valid at the time the variable is declared. For example, consider this program:

```c
#include <stdio.h>

int x = 10; /* initialize global variable */

int myfunc(int i);

int main(void)
{
  /* initialize a local variable using
     a global variable */
  int y = x;

  /* initialize a local variable using another
     local variable and a function call */
  int z = myfunc(y);

  printf("%d %d", y, z);

  return 0;
}

int myfunc(int i)
{
  return i/2;
}
```

The local variable **y** is initialized using the value of the global variable **x**. Since **x** is initialized before **main( )** is called, it is valid to use its value to initialize a local variable. The value of **z** is initialized by calling **myfunc( )** using **y** as an argument. Since **y** has already been initialized, it is entirely proper to use it as an argument to **myfunc( )** at this point.

EXERCISES

1. Write a program that gives an integer variable called **i** an initial value of **100** and then uses **i** to control a **for** loop that displays the numbers **100** down to **1**.

2. Assume that this line of code declares global variables. Is it correct?

```
int a=1, b=2, c=a;
```

3. If the preceding declaration was for local variables, would it be correct?

UNDERSTAND TYPE CONVERSIONS IN EXPRESSIONS

Unlike many other computer languages, C lets you mix different types of data together in one expression. For example, this is perfectly valid C code:

```
char ch;
int i;
float f;
double outcome;

ch = '0';
i = 10;
f = 10.2;

outcome = ch * i / f;
```

C allows the mixing of types within an expression because it has a strict set of conversion rules that dictate how type differences are resolved. Let's look closely at them in this section.

One portion of C's conversion rules is called *integral promotion*. In C, whenever a **char** or a **short int** is used in an expression, its value is automatically elevated to **int** during the evaluation of that expression. This is why you can use **char** variables as "little integers" anywhere you can use an **int** variable. Keep in mind that the integral promotion is only in effect during the evaluation of an expression. The variable does not become physically larger. (In essence, the compiler just uses a temporary copy of its value.)

After the automatic integral promotions have been applied, the C compiler will convert all operands "up" to the type of the largest operand. This is called *type promotion* and is done on an operation-by-operation basis, as described in the following type-conversion algorithm.

> IF an operand is a **long double**
> THEN the second is converted to **long double**
> ELSE IF an operand is a **double**
> THEN the second is converted to **double**
> ELSE IF an operand is a **float**
> THEN the second is converted to **float**
> ELSE IF an operand is an **unsigned long**
> THEN the second is converted to **unsigned long**
> ELSE IF an operand is **long**
> THEN the second is converted to **long**
> ELSE IF an operand is **unsigned**
> THEN the second is converted to **unsigned**

There is one additional special case: If one operand is **long** and the other is **unsigned int**, and if the value of the **unsigned int** cannot be represented by a **long**, both operands are converted to **unsigned long**.

Once these conversion rules have been applied, each pair of operands will be of the same type and the result of each operation will be the same as the type of both operands.

EXAMPLES

1. In this program, **i** is elevated to a **float** during the evaluation of the expression **i*f**. Thus, the program prints **232.5**.

```c
#include <stdio.h>

int main(void)
{
  int i;
  float f;

  i = 10;
  f = 23.25;

  printf("%f", i*f);

  return 0;
}
```

2. This program illustrates how **short int**s are automatically promoted to **int**s. The **printf( )** statement works correctly even though the **%d** modifier is used because **i** is automatically elevated to **int** when **printf( )** is called.

```
#include <stdio.h>

int main(void)
{
  short int i;

  i = -10;
  printf("%d", i);

  return 0;
}
```

3. Even though the final outcome of an expression will be of the largest type, the type conversion rules are applied on an operation-by-operation basis. For example, in this expression

```
100.0/(10/3)
```

the division of 10 by 3 produces an integer result, since both are integers. Then this value is elevated to 3.0 to divide 100.0.

EXERCISES

---

1. Given these variables,

```
char ch;
short i;
unsigned long ul;
float f;
```

what is the overall type of this expression:

```
f/ch - (i*ul)
```

2. What is the type of the subexpression **i*ul**, above?

4.6 **U***NDERSTAND TYPE CONVERSIONS IN ASSIGNMENTS*

In an assignment statement in which the type of the right side differs from that of the left, the type of the right side is converted into that of the left. When the type of the left side is larger than the type of the right side, this process causes no problems. However, when the type of the left side is smaller than the type of the right, data loss may occur. For example, this program displays **–24**:

```
#include <stdio.h>

int main(void)
{
  char ch;
  int i;

  i = 1000;
  ch = i;

  printf("%d", ch);

  return 0;
}
```

The reason for this is that only the low-order eight bits of **i** are copied into **ch**. Since this sort of assignment type conversion is not an error in C, you will receive no error message. Remember, one reason C was created was to replace assembly language, so it must allow all sorts of type conversions. For example, in some instances you may only want the low-order eight bits of **i**, and this sort of assignment is an easy way to obtain them.

When there is an integer-to-character or a longer-integer to shorter-integer type conversion across an assignment, the basic rule is that the appropriate number of high-order bits will be removed. For example, in many environments, this means 8 bits will be lost when going from an **int** to a **char**, and 16 bits will be lost when going from a **long** to an **int**.

When converting from a **long double** to a **double** or from a **double** to a **float**, precision is lost. When converting from a floating-point value to an integer value, the fractional part is lost, and if the number is too large to fit in the target type, a garbage value will result.

Remember two important points: First, the conversion of an **int** to a **float** or a **float** to **double**, and so on, will not add any precision or accuracy. These kinds of conversions will only change the form in which the value is represented. Second, some C compilers will always treat a **char** variable as an **unsigned** value. Others will treat it as a **signed** value. Thus, what will happen when a character variable holds a value greater than 127 is implementation-dependent. If this is important in a program that you write, it is best to declare the variable explicitly as either **signed** or **unsigned**.

EXAMPLES

1. As stated, when converting from a floating-point value to an integer value, the fractional portion of the number is lost. The following program illustrates this fact. It prints **1234.0098 1234**.

```
#include <stdio.h>

int main(void)
{
  int i;
  float f;

  f = 1234.0098;
  i = f; /* convert to int */
  printf("%f %d", f, i);

  return 0;
}
```

2. When converting from a larger integer type to a smaller one, it is possible to generate a garbage value, as this program illustrates. (This program assumes that short integers are 16 bits long and that long integers are 32 bits long.)

```
#include <stdio.h>

int main(void)
{
  short int si;
  long int li;
```

```
li = 100000;
si = li; /* convert to short int */

printf("%hd", si);

return 0;
}
```

Since the largest value that a short integer can hold is 32,767, it cannot hold 100,000. What the compiler does, however, is copy the lower-order 16 bits of **li** into **si**. This produces the meaningless value of **–31072** on the screen.

EXERCISES

1. What will this program display?

```
#include <stdio.h>

int main(void)
{
  int i;
  long double ld;

  ld = 10.0;
  i = ld;

  printf("%d", i);
}
```

2. What does this program display?

```
#include <stdio.h>

int main(void)
{
  float f;

  f = 10 / 3;
  printf("%f", f);

  return 0;
}
```

PROGRAM WITH TYPE CASTS

Sometimes you may want to transform the type of a variable temporarily. For example, you may want to use a floating-point value for one computation, but wish to apply the modulus operator to it elsewhere. Since the modulus operator can only be used on integer values, you have a problem. One solution is to create an integer variable for use in the modulus operation and assign the value of the floating-point variable to it when the time comes. This is a somewhat inelegant solution, however. The other way around this problem is to use a *type cast*, which causes a temporary type change.

A type cast takes this general form:

(*type*) *value*

where *type* is the name of a valid C data type. For example,

```
float f;

f = 100.2;

/* print f as an integer */
printf("%d", (int) f);
```

Here, the type cast causes the value of **f** to be converted to an **int**.

EXAMPLES

1. As you learned in Chapter 1, **sqrt( )**, one of C's library functions, returns the square root of its argument. It uses the MATH.H header file. Its single argument must be of type **double**. It also returns a **double** value. The following program prints the square roots of the numbers between **1** and **100** using a **for** loop. It also prints the whole number portion and the fractional part of each result separately. To do so, it uses a type cast to convert **sqrt( )**'s return value into an **int**.

```c
#include <stdio.h>
#include <math.h>

int main(void)
{
  double i;

  for(i=1.0; i<101.0; i++) {
    printf("The square root of %lf is %lf\n", i, sqrt(i));
    printf("Whole number part: %d ", (int)sqrt(i));
    printf("Fractional part: %lf\n", sqrt(i)-(int)sqrt(i));
    printf("\n");
  }

  return 0;
}
```

2. You cannot cast a variable that is on the left side of an assignment statement. For example, this is an invalid statement in C:

```c
int num;

(float) num = 123.23; /* this is incorrect */
```

EXERCISES

1. Write a program that uses **for** to print the numbers **1** to **10** by tenths. Use a floating-point variable to control the loop. However, use a type cast so that the conditional expression is evaluated as an integer expression in the interest of speed.

2. Since a floating point value cannot be used with the % operator, how can you fix this statement?

```c
x = 123.23 % 3; /* fix this statement */
```

Mastery
Skills Check

At this point you should be able to answer these questions and perform these exercises:

1. What are C's data-type modifiers and what function do they perform?

2. How do you explicitly define an **unsigned** constant, a **long** constant, and a **long double** constant?

3. Show how to give a **float** variable called **balance** an initial value of 0.0.

4. What are C's automatic integral promotions?

5. What is the difference between a **signed** and an **unsigned** integer?

6. Give one reason why you might want to use a global variable in your program.

7. Write a program that contains a function called **series( )**. Have this function generate a series of numbers, based upon this formula:

   next-number = (*previous-number* * 1468) % 467

   Give the number an initial value of 21. Use a global variable to hold the last value between function calls. In **main( )** demonstrate that the function works by calling it ten times and displaying the result.

8. What is a type cast? Give an example.

Cumulative Skills Check

This section checks how well you have integrated the material in this chapter with that from earlier chapters.

1. As you know from Chapter 3, no two **case**s with the same **switch** may use the same value. Therefore, is this **switch** valid or invalid? Why? (Hint: the ASCII code for 'A' is 65.)

```
switch(x) {
  case 'A' : printf("is an A");
    break;
  case 65 : printf("is the number 65");
    break;
}
```

2. Technically, for traditional reasons the **getchar( )** and **getche( )** functions are declared as returning integers, not character values. However, the character read from the keyboard is contained in the low-order byte. Can you explain why this value can be assigned to **char** variables?

3. In this fragment, will the loop ever terminate? Why? (Assume integers are 16 bits long.)

```
int i
for(i=0; i<33000; i++);
```

5

*Exploring Arrays
and Strings*

chapter objectives

5.1 Declare one-dimensional arrays

5.2 Use strings

5.3 Create multidimensional arrays

5.4 Initialize arrays

5.5 Build arrays of strings

N this chapter you will learn about arrays. An *array* is essentially a list of related variables and can be very useful in a variety of situations. Since in C strings are simply arrays of characters, you will also learn about strings and several of C's string functions.

Review
Skills Check

Before proceeding, you should be able to answer these questions and perform these exercises:

1. What is the difference between a local and a global variable?

2. What data type will a C compiler assign to these numbers? (Assume 16-bit integers.)

   a. 10

   b. 10000

   c. 123.45

   d. 123564

   e. –45099

3. Write a program that inputs a **long**, a **short**, and a **double** and then writes these values to the screen.

4. What does a type cast do?

5. To which **if** is the **else** in this fragment associated? What is the general rule?

```
if(i)
   if(j)  printf("i and j are true");
else printf("i is false");
```

6. Using the following fragment, what is the value of **a** when **i** is 1? What is **a**'s value when **i** is 4?

```
switch(i) {
  case 1: a = 1;
  case 2: a = 2;
    break;
  case 3: a = 3;
    break;
```

```
        case 4:
        case 5: a = 5;
    }
```

5.1 ▮ *D*ECLARE ONE-DIMENSIONAL ARRAYS

In C, a one-dimensional array is a list of variables that are all of the same type and are accessed through a common name. An individual variable in the array is called an *array element*. Arrays form a convenient way to handle groups of related data.

To declare a one-dimensional array, use the general form

type var_name[size];

where *type* is a valid C data type, *var_name* is the name of the array, and *size* specifies the number of elements in the array. For example, to declare an integer array with 20 elements called **myarray**, use this statement.

```
int myarray[20];
```

An array element is accessed by indexing the array using the number of the element. In C, all arrays begin at zero. This means that if you want to access the first element in an array, use zero for the index. To index an array, specify the index of the element you want inside square brackets. For example, the following refers to the second element of **myarray**:

```
myarray[1]
```

Remember, arrays start at zero, so an index of 1 references the second element.

To assign an array element a value, put the array on the left side of an assignment statement. For example, this gives the first element in **myarray** the value 100:

```
myarray[0] = 100;
```

C stores one-dimensional arrays in one contiguous memory location with the first element at the lowest address. For example, after this fragment executes,

```
int i[5];
int j;

for(j=0; j<5; j++) i[j] = j;
```

array **i** will look like this:

```
       i[0]  i[1]  i[2]  i[3]  i[4]

   i |  0  |  1  |  2  |  3  |  4  |
```

You may use the value of an array element anywhere you would use a simple variable or constant. For example, the following program loads the **sqrs** array with the squares of the numbers 1 through 10 and then displays them.

```
#include <stdio.h>

int main(void)
{
  int sqrs[10];
  int i;

  for(i=1; i<11; i++) sqrs[i-1] = i*i;

  for(i=0; i<10; i++) printf("%d ", sqrs[i]);

  return 0;
}
```

When you want to use **scanf( )** to input a numeric value into an array element, simply put the **&** in front of the array name. For example, this call to **scanf( )** reads an integer into **count[9]**.

```
scanf("%d", &count[9]);
```

C does not perform any bounds checking on array indexes. This means that it is possible to overrun the end of an array. For example, if an array called **a** is declared as having five elements, the compiler will still let you access the (nonexistent) tenth element with a statement like **a[9]**. Of course, attempting to access nonexistent elements will generally have disastrous results, often causing the program to crash. It is up to you, the programmer, to make sure that the ends of arrays are never overrun.

In C, you may not assign one entire array to another. For example, this fragment is incorrect.

```
char a1[10], a2[10];
.
.
.
a2 = a1; /* this is wrong */
```

If you wish to copy the values of all the elements of one array to another, you must do so by copying each element separately.

EXAMPLES

1. Arrays are very useful when lists of information need to be managed. For example, this program reads the noonday temperature for each day of a month and then reports the month's average temperature, as well as its hottest and coolest days.

```c
#include <stdio.h>

int main(void)
{
  int temp[31], i, min, max, avg;
  int days;

  printf("How many days in the month? ");
  scanf("%d", &days);

  for(i=0; i<days; i++) {
    printf("Enter noonday temperature for day %d: ", i+1);
    scanf("%d", &temp[i]);
  }

  /* find average */
  avg = 0;
  for(i=0; i<days; i++) avg = avg + temp[i];
```

```
      printf("Average temperature: %d\n", avg/days);

      /* find min and max */
      min = 200;   /* initialize min and max */
      max = 0;
      for(i=0; i<days; i++) {
        if(min>temp[i]) min = temp[i];
        if(max<temp[i]) max = temp[i];
      }

      printf("Minimum temperature: %d\n", min);
      printf("Maximum temperature: %d\n", max);

      return 0;
    }
```

2. As stated earlier, to copy the contents of one array to another, you must explicitly copy each element separately. For example, this program loads **a1** with the numbers 1 through 10 and then copies them into **a2**.

```c
#include <stdio.h>

int main(void)
{
  int a1[10], a2[10];
  int i;

  for(i=1; i<11; i++) a1[i-1] = i;

  for(i=0; i<10; i++) a2[i] = a1[i];

  for(i=0; i<10; i++) printf("%d ", a2[i]);

  return 0;
}
```

3. The following program is an improved version of the code-machine program developed in Chapter 3. In this version, the user first enters the message, which is stored in a character array. When the user presses ENTER, the entire message is then encoded by adding 1 to each letter.

```
#include <stdio.h>
#include <conio.h>

int main(void)
{
  char mess[80];
  int i;

  printf("Enter message (less than 80 characters)\n");
  for(i=0; i<80; i++) {
    mess[i] = getche();
    if(mess[i]=='\r') break;
  }
  printf("\n");

  for(i=0; mess[i]!='\r'; i++) printf("%c", mess[i]+1);

  return 0;
}
```

4. Arrays are especially useful when you want to sort information.
   For example, this program lets the user enter up to 100
   numbers and then sorts them. The sorting algorithm is the
   bubble sort. The bubble sort algorithm is not very efficient, but
   it is simple to understand and easy to code. The general concept
   behind the bubble sort, indeed how it got its name, is the
   repeated comparisons and, if necessary, exchanges of adjacent
   elements. This is a little like bubbles in a tank of water with
   each bubble, in turn, seeking its own level.

```
#include <stdio.h>
#include <stdlib.h>

int main(void)
{
  int item[100];
  int a, b, t;
  int count;

  /* read in numbers */
  printf("How many numbers? ");
  scanf("%d", &count);
  for(a=0; a<count; a++) scanf("%d", &item[a]);
```

```
/* now, sort them using a bubble sort */
for(a=1; a<count; ++a)
  for(b=count-1; b>=a; --b) {
    /* compare adjacent elements */
    if(item[b-1] > item[b]) {
      /* exchange elements */
      t = item[b-1];
      item[b-1] = item[b];
      item[b] = t;
    }
  }

/* display sorted list */
for(t=0; t<count; t++) printf("%d ", item[t]);

return 0;
}
```

EXERCISES

1. What is wrong with this program fragment?

```
#include <stdio.h>

int main(void)
{
  int i, count[10];

  for(i=0; i<100; i++) {
    printf("Enter a number: ");
    scanf("%d", &count[i]);
  }
  .
  .
  .
```

2. Write a program that reads ten numbers entered by the user and reports if any of them match.

3. Change the sorting program shown in the examples so that it sorts data of type **float**.

*U*SE STRINGS

The most common use of the one-dimensional array in C is the string. Unlike most other computer languages, C has no built-in string data type. Instead, a string is defined as a *null-terminated character array*. In C, a null is zero. The fact that string must be terminated by a null means that you must define the array that is going to hold a string to be one byte larger than the largest string it will be required to hold, to make room for the null. A string constant is null-terminated by the compiler automatically.

There are several ways to read a string from the keyboard. The method we will use in this chapter employs another of C's standard library functions: **gets( )**. Like the other standard I/O functions, **gets( )** also uses the STDIO.H header file. To use **gets( )**, call it using the name of a character array without any index. The **gets( )** function reads characters until you press ENTER. The ENTER key (i.e., carriage return) is not stored, but is replaced by a null, which terminates the string. For example, this program reads a string entered at the keyboard. It then displays the contents of that string one character at a time.

```
#include <stdio.h>

int main(void)
{
  char str[80];
  int i;

  printf("Enter a string (less than 80 chars): ");
  gets(str);
  for(i=0; str[i]; i++) printf("%c", str[i]);

  return 0;
}
```

Notice how the program uses the fact that a null is false to control the loop that outputs the string.

There is a potential problem with **gets( )** that you need to be aware of. The **gets( )** function performs no bounds checking, so it is possible for the user to enter more characters than the array receiving them can hold. For example, if you call **gets( )** with an array that is 20 characters long, there is no mechanism to stop you from entering more than 20 characters. If you *do* enter more than 20 characters, the array will be overrun. This can obviously lead to trouble, including a program crash. Later in this book you will learn some alternative ways to read strings, although none are as convenient as using **gets( )**. For now, just be sure to call **gets( )** with an array that is more than large enough to hold the expected input.

In the previous program, the string that was entered by the user was output to the screen a character at a time. There is, of course, a much easier way to display a string using **printf( )**, as shown in this version of the program:

```
#include <stdio.h>

int main(void)
{
  char str[80];

  printf("Enter a string (less than 80 chars): ");
  gets(str);
  printf(str); /* output the string */

  return 0;
}
```

Recall that the first argument to **printf( )** is a string. Since **str** contains a string it can be used as the first argument to **printf( )**. The contents of **str** will then be displayed.

If you wanted to output other items in addition to **str**, you could display **str** using the **%s** format code. For example, to output a newline after **str**, you could use this call to **printf( )**.

```
printf("%s\n", str);
```

This method uses the **%s** format specifier followed by the newline character and uses **str** as a second argument to be matched by the **%s** specifier.

The C standard library supplies many string-related functions. The four most important are **strcpy( )**, **strcat( )**, **strcmp( )**, and **strlen( )**. These functions require the header file STRING.H. Let's look at each now.

The **strcpy( )** function has this general form:

strcpy(*to, from*);

It copies the contents of *from* to *to*. The contents of *from* are unchanged. For example, this fragment copies the string "hello" into **str** and displays it on the screen:

```
char str[80];

strcpy(str, "hello");
printf("%s", str);
```

The **strcpy( )** function performs no bounds checking, so you must make sure that the array on the receiving end is large enough to hold what is being copied, including the null terminator.

The **strcat( )** function adds the contents of one string to another. This is called *concatenation*. Its general form is

strcat(*to, from*);

It adds the contents of *from* to the contents of *to*. It performs no bounds checking, so you must make sure that *to* is large enough to hold its current contents plus what it will be receiving. This fragment displays **hello there**.

```
char str[80];

strcpy(str, "hello");
strcat(str, " there");
printf(str);
```

The **strcmp( )** function compares two strings. It takes this general form:

strcmp(*s1, s2*);

It returns zero if the strings are the same. It returns less than zero if *s1* is less than *s2* and greater than zero if *s1* is greater than *s2*. The strings are compared lexicographically; that is, in dictionary order. Therefore, a string is less than another when it would appear before the other in a dictionary. A string is greater than another when it would appear after the other. The comparison is not based upon the length of the string. Also, the comparison is case-sensitive, lowercase characters being greater than uppercase. This fragment prints **0**, because the strings are the same:

```
printf("%d", strcmp("one", "one"));
```

The **strlen( )** function returns the length, in characters, of a string. Its general form is

strlen(_str_);

The **strlen( )** function does not count the null terminator. This means that if **strlen( )** is called using the string "test", it will return 4.

1. This program requests input of two strings, then demonstrates the four string functions with them.

```c
#include <string.h>
#include <stdio.h>

int main(void)
{
  char str1[80], str2[80];
  int i;

  printf("Enter the first string: ");
  gets(str1);
  printf("Enter the second string: ");
  gets(str2);

  /* see how long the strings are */
  printf("%s is %d chars long\n", str1, strlen(str1));
  printf("%s is %d chars long\n", str2, strlen(str2));

  /* compare the strings */
  i = strcmp(str1, str2);
  if(!i) printf("The strings are equal.\n");
  else if(i<0) printf("%s is less than %s\n", str1, str2);
  else printf("%s is greater than %s\n", str1, str2);

  /* concatenate str2 to end of str1 if
     there is enough room */
  if(strlen(str1) + strlen(str2) < 80) {
    strcat(str1, str2);
    printf("%s\n", str1);
```

```
    }

    /* copy str2 to str1 */
    strcpy(str1, str2);
    printf("%s %s\n", str1, str2);

    return 0;
}
```

2. One common use of strings is to support a *command-based interface*. Unlike a menu, which allows the user to make a selection, a command-based interface displays a prompting message, waits for the user to enter a command, and then does what the command requests. Many operating systems, such as Windows or DOS, support command-line interfaces, for example. The following program is similar to a program developed in Section 3.1. It allows the user to add, subtract, multiply, or divide, but does not use a menu. Instead, it uses a command-based interface.

```
#include <stdlib.h>
#include <stdio.h>
#include <string.h>

int main(void)
{
  char command[80], temp[80];
  int i, j;

  for( ; ; ) {
    printf("Operation? ");
    gets(command);

    /* see if user wants to stop */
    if(!strcmp(command, "quit")) break;

    printf("Enter first number: ");
    gets(temp);
    i = atoi(temp);

    printf("Enter second number: ");
    gets(temp);
    j = atoi(temp);
```

```
    /*  now, perform the operation */
    if(!strcmp(command, "add"))
      printf("%d\n", i+j);
    else if(!strcmp(command, "subtract"))
      printf("%d\n", i-j);
    else if(!strcmp(command, "divide")) {
      if(j) printf("%d\n", i/j);
    }
    else if(!strcmp(command, "multiply"))
      printf("%d\n", i*j);
    else printf("Unknown command. \n");
  }

  return 0;
}
```

Notice that this example also introduces another of C's standard library functions: **atoi( )**. The **atoi( )** function returns the integer equivalent of the number represented by its string argument. For example, **atoi("100")** returns the value 100. The reason that **scanf( )** is not used to read the numbers is because, in this context, it is incompatible with **gets( )**. (You will need to know more about C before you can understand the cause of this incompatibility.) The **atoi( )** function uses the header file STDLIB.H.

3. You can create a zero-length string using a **strcpy( )** statement like this:

```
strcpy(str, "");
```

Such a string is called a *null string*. It contains only one element: the null terminator.

EXERCISES

1. Write a program that inputs a string, then displays it backward on the screen.

2. What is wrong with this program?

```
#include <string.h>
#include <stdio.h>

int main(void)
{
  char str[5];

  strcpy(str, "this is a test");
  printf(str);

  return 0;
}
```

3. Write a program that repeatedly inputs strings. Each time a string is input, concatenate it with a second string called **bigstr**. Add newlines to the end of each string. If the user types **quit**, stop inputting and display **bigstr** (which will contain a record of all strings input). Also stop if **bigstr** will be overrun by the next concatenation.

5.3   *C*REATE MULTIDIMENSIONAL ARRAYS

In addition to one-dimensional arrays, you can create arrays of two or more dimensions. For example, to create a 10x12 two-dimensional integer array called **count**, you would use this statement:

```
int count[10][12];
```

As you can see, to add a dimension, you simply specify its size inside square brackets.

A two-dimensional array is essentially an array of one-dimensional arrays and is most easily thought of in a row, column format. For example, given a 4x5 integer array called **two_d**, you can think of it looking like that shown in Figure 5-1. Assuming this conceptual view, a two-dimensional array is accessed a row at a time, from left to right. This means that the rightmost index will change most quickly when the array is accessed sequentially from the lowest to highest memory address.

A conceptual view of a 4x5 two-dimensional array

▼

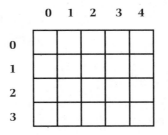

Two-dimensional arrays are used like one-dimensional ones. For example, this program loads a 4x5 array with the products of the indices, then displays the array in row, column format.

```
#include <stdio.h>

int main(void)
{
  int twod[4][5];
  int i, j;

  for(i=0; i<4; i++)
    for(j=0; j<5; j++)
      twod[i][j] = i*j;

  for(i=0; i<4; i++) {
    for(j=0; j<5; j++)
      printf("%d ", twod[i][j]);
    printf("\n");
  }

  return 0;
}
```

The program output looks like this:

```
0 0 0 0 0
0 1 2 3 4
0 2 4 6 8
0 3 6 9 12
```

To create arrays of three dimensions or greater, simply add the size of the additional dimension. For example, the following statement creates a 10x12x8 three-dimensional array.

```
float values[10][12][8];
```

A three-dimensional array is essentially an array of two-dimensional arrays.

You may create arrays of more than three dimensions, but this is seldom done because the amount of memory they consume increases exponentially with each additional dimension. For example, a 100-character one-dimensional array requires 100 bytes of memory. A 100x100 character array requires 10,000 bytes, and a 100x100x100 array requires 1,000,000 bytes. A 100x100x100x100 four-dimensional array would require 100,000,000 bytes of storage—large even by today's standards.

EXAMPLE

1. A good use of a two-dimensional array is to manage lists of numbers. For example, you could use this two-dimensional array to hold the noontime temperature for each day of the year, grouped by month.

   ```
   float yeartemp[12][31];
   ```

   In the same vein, the following program can be used to keep track of the number of points scored per quarter by each member of a basketball team.

   ```
   #include <stdio.h>

   int main(void)
   {
     int bball[4][5];
     int i, j;

     for(i=0; i<4; i++)
       for(j=0; j<5; j++) {
         printf("Quarter %d, player %d, ", i+1, j+1);
         printf("Enter number of points: ");
   ```

```
      scanf("%d", &bball[i][j]);
    }

    /* display results */
    for(i=0; i<4; i++)
      for(j=0; j<5; j++) {
        printf("Quarter %d, player %d, ", i+1, j+1);
        printf("%d\n", bball[i][j]);
      }

    return 0;
  }
```

EXERCISES

1. Write a program that defines a 3x3x3 three-dimensional array, and load it with the numbers 1 to 27.

2. Have the program from the first exercise display the sum of its elements.

5.4 *INITIALIZE ARRAYS*

Like other types of variables, you can give the elements of arrays initial values. This is accomplished by specifying a list of values the array elements will have. The general form of array initialization for one-dimensional arrays is shown here:

type array-name[size] = {*value-list*};

The *value-list* is a comma-separated list of constants that are type compatible with the base type of the array. Moving from left to right, the first constant will be placed in the first position of the array, the second constant in the second position, and so on. Note that a semicolon follows the }. In the following example, a five-element integer array is initialized with the squares of the numbers 1 through 5.

```
int i[5] = {1, 4, 9, 16, 25};
```

This means that **i[0]** will have the value 1 and **i[4]** will have the value 25.

You can initialize character arrays two ways. First, if the array is not holding a null-terminated string, you simply specify each character using a comma-separated list. For example, this initializes **a** with the letters 'A', 'B', and 'C'.

```
char a[3] = {'A', 'B', 'C'};
```

If the character array is going to hold a string, you can initialize the array using a quoted string, as shown here:

```
char name[5] = "Herb";
```

Notice that no curly braces surround the string. They are not used in this form of initialization. Because strings in C must end with a null, you must make sure that the array you declare is long enough to include the null. This is why **name** is 5 characters long, even though "Herb" is only 4. When a string constant is used, the compiler automatically supplies the null terminator.

Multidimensional arrays are initialized in the same way as one-dimensional arrays. For example, here the array **sqr** is initialized with the values 1 through 9, using row order:

```
int  sqr[3][3] = {
  1, 2, 3,
  4, 5, 6,
  7, 8, 9
};
```

This initialization causes **sqr[0][0]** to have the value 1, **sqr[0][1]** to contain 2, **sqr[0][2]** to hold 3, and so forth.

If you are initializing a one-dimensional array, you need not specify the size of the array—simply put nothing inside the square brackets. If you don't specify the size, the compiler counts the number of initializers and uses that value as the size of the array. For example,

```
int pwr[] = {1, 2, 4, 8, 16, 32, 64, 128};
```

causes the compiler to create an initialized array eight elements long. Arrays that don't have their dimensions explicitly specified are called *unsized arrays*. An unsized array is useful because the size of the array will be automatically adjusted when you change the number of its initializers. It also helps avoid counting errors on long lists, which is especially important when initializing strings. For example, here an unsized array is used to hold a prompting message.

```
char prompt[] = "Enter your name: ";
```

If, at a later date, you wanted to change the prompt to "Enter your last name:", you would not have to count the characters and then change the array size. The size of **prompt** would automatically be adjusted.

Unsized array initializations are not restricted to one-dimensional arrays. However, for multidimensional arrays you must specify all but the leftmost dimension to allow C to index the array properly. In this way you may build tables of varying lengths with the compiler allocating enough storage for them automatically. For example, the declaration of **sqr** as an unsized array is shown here:

```
int sqr[][3] = {
  1, 2, 3,
  4, 5, 6,
  7, 8, 9
};
```

The advantage to this declaration over the sized version is that tables may be lengthened or shortened without changing the array dimensions.

EXAMPLES

1. A common use of an initialized array is to create a lookup table. For example, in this program a 5x2 two-dimensional array is initialized so that the first element in each row is the number of a file server in a network and the second element contains the number of users connected to that server. The program allows a user to enter the number of a server. It then looks up the server in the table and reports the number of users.

```
#include <stdio.h>

int main(void)
{
```

```
int ServerUsers[5][2] = {
  1, 14,
  2, 28,
  3, 19,
  4, 8,
  5, 15
};

int server;
int i;

printf("Enter the server number: ");
scanf("%d", &server);

/* look it up in the table */
for(i=0; i<5; i++)
  if(server == ServerUsers[i][0]) {
    printf("There are %d users on server %d.\n",
           ServerUsers[i][1], server);
    break;
  }

/* report error if not found */
if(i==5) printf("Server not listed.\n");

return 0;
}
```

2. Even though an array has been given an initial value, its contents may be changed. For example, this program prints **hello** on the screen.

```
#include <stdio.h>
#include <string.h>

int main(void)
{
  char str[80] = "I like C";

  strcpy(str, "hello");
  printf(str);

  return 0;
}
```

As this program illustrates, in no way does an initialization fix the contents of an array.

1. Is this fragment correct?

```
int balance[] = 10.0, 122.23, 100.0;
```

2. Is this fragment correct?

```
#include <stdio.h>
#include <string.h>

int main(void)
{
  char name[] = "Tom";

  strcpy(name, "Tom Brazwell");
```

3. Write a program that initializes a 10x3 array so that the first element of each row contains a number, the second element contains its square, and the third element contains its cube. Start with 1 and stop at 10. For example, the first few rows will look like this:

   1, 1, 1,
   2, 4, 8,
   3, 9, 27,
   4, 16, 64,

   .
   .
   .

   Next, prompt the user for a cube, look up this value in the table, and report the cube's root and the root's square. Use an unsized array so that the table size may be easily changed.

5.5 # **B**UILD ARRAYS OF STRINGS

Arrays of strings, often called *string tables*, are very common in C programming. A string table is created like any other two-dimensional array. However, the way you think about it will be slightly different. For example, here is a small string table. What do you think it defines?

```
char names[10][40];
```

This statement specifies a table that can contain 10 strings, each up to 40 characters long (including the null terminator). To access a string within this table, specify only the left-most index. For example, to read a string from the keyboard into the third string in **names**, use this statement:

```
gets(names[2]);
```

By the same token, to output the first string, use this **printf( )** statement:

```
printf(names[0]);
```

The declaration that follows creates a three-dimensional table with three lists of strings. Each list is five strings long, and each string can hold 80 characters.

```
char animals[3][5][80];
```

To access a specific string in this situation, you must specify the two left-most indexes. For example, to access the second string in the third list, specify **animals[2][1]**.

EXAMPLES

1. This program lets you enter ten strings, then lets you display them, one at a time, in any order you choose. To stop the program, enter a negative number.

```
#include <stdio.h>

int main(void)
```

```
{
  char text[10][80];
  int i;

  for(i=0; i<10; i++) {
    printf("%d: ", i+1);
    gets(text[i]);
  }

  do {
    printf("Enter number of string (1-10) : ");
    scanf("%d", &i);
    i--;  /* adjust value to match array index */
    if(i>=0 && i<10) printf("%s\n", text[i]);
  } while(i>=0);

  return 0;
}
```

2. You can initialize a string table as you would any other type of array. For example, the following program uses an initialized string table to translate between German and English. Notice that curly braces are needed to surround the list. The only time they are not needed is when a single string is being initialized.

```
/* English-to-German Translator. */

#include <stdio.h>
#include <string.h>

char words[][2][40] = {
  "dog", "Hund",
  "no", "nein",
  "year", "Jahr",
  "child", "Kind",
  "I",   "Ich",
  "drive", "fahren",
  "house", "Haus",
  "to", "zu",
  "",""
};

int main(void)
{
  char english[80];
```

```
    int i;

    printf("Enter English word: ");
    gets(english);

    /* look up the word */
    i = 0;
    /* search while null string not yet encountered */
    while(strcmp(words[i][0], "")) {
      if(!strcmp(english, words[i][0])) {
        printf("German translation: %s", words[i][1]);
        break;
      }
      i++;
    }
    if(!strcmp(words[i][0], ""))
      printf("Not in dictionary\n");

    return 0;
}
```

3. You can access the individual characters that comprise a string within a string table by using the rightmost index. For example, the following program prints the strings in the table one character at a time.

```
#include <stdio.h>

int main(void)
{
  char text[][80] = {
    "When", "in", "the",
    "course", "of", "human",
    "events", ""
  };

  int i, j;

  /* now, display them */
  for(i=0; text[i][0]; i++) {
    for(j=0; text[i][j]; j++)
      printf("%c", text[i][j]);
    printf(" ");
  }
```

```
        return 0;
    }
```

1. Write a program that creates a string table containing the English words for the numbers 0 through 9. Using this table, allow the user to enter a digit (as a character) and then have your program display the word equivalent. (Hint: to obtain an index into the table, subtract '0' from the character entered.)

Mastery
Skills Check

At this point you should be able to perform these exercises and answer these questions:

1. What is an array?

2. Given the array

   ```
   int count[10];
   ```

   will this statement generate an error message?

   ```
   for(i=0; i<20; i++) count[i] = i;
   ```

3. In statistics, the *mode* of a group of numbers is the one that occurs the most often. For example, given the list 1, 2, 3, 6, 4, 7, 5, 4, 6, 9, 4, the mode is 4, because it occurs three times. Write a program that allows the user to enter a list of 20 numbers and then finds and displays the mode.

4. Show how to initialize an integer array called **items** with the values 1 through 10.

5. Write a program that repeatedly reads strings from the keyboard until the user enters **quit**.

6. Write a program that acts like an electronic dictionary. If the user enters a word in the dictionary, the program displays its

meaning. Use a three-dimensional character array to hold the words and their meanings.

Cumulative Skills Check

This section checks how well you have integrated the material in this chapter with that from earlier chapters.

1. Write a program that inputs strings from the user. If the string is less than 80 characters long, pad it with periods. Print out the string to verify that you have correctly lengthened the string.

2. Write a program that inputs a string and then encodes it by taking the characters from each end, starting with the left side and alternating, stopping when the middle of the string has been reached. For example, the string "Hi there" would be "Heir eth".

3. Write a program that counts the number of spaces, commas, and periods in a string. Use a **switch** to categorize the characters.

4. What is wrong with this fragment?

```
char str[80];
str = getchar();
```

5. Write a program that plays a computerized version of Hangman. In the game of Hangman, you are shown the length of a magic word (using hyphens) and you try to guess what the word is by entering letters. Each time you enter a letter, the magic word is checked to see if it contains that letter. If it does, that letter is shown. Keep a count on the number of letters entered to complete the word. For the sake of simplicity, a player wins when the magic word is entirely filled by characters using 15 or fewer guesses. For this exercise make the magic word "concatenation."

6

Using Pointers

chapter objectives

6.1 Understand pointer basics

6.2 Learn restrictions to pointer expressions

6.3 Use pointers with arrays

6.4 Use pointers to string constants

6.5 Create arrays of pointers

6.6 Become acquainted with multiple indirection

6.7 Use pointers as parameters

THIS chapter covers one of C's most important and sometimes most troublesome features: the *pointer*. A pointer is basically the address of an object. One reason that pointers are so important is that much of the power of the C language is derived from the unique way in which they are implemented. You will learn about the special pointer operators, pointer arithmetic, and how arrays and pointers are related. Also, you will be introduced to using pointers as parameters to functions.

Review Skills Check

Before proceeding, you should be able to answer these questions and perform these exercises:

1. Write a program that inputs 10 integers into an array. Then have the program display the sum of the even numbers and the sum of the odd numbers.

2. Write a program that simulates a log-on to a remote system. The system can be accessed only if the user knows the password, which in this case is "Tristan." Give the user three tries to enter the correct password. If the user succeeds, simply print **Log-on Successful** and exit. If the user fails after three attempts to enter the correct password, display **Access Denied** and exit.

3. What is wrong with this fragment?

   ```c
   char name[10] = "Thomas Jefferson";
   ```

4. What is a null string?

5. What does **strcpy( )** do? What does **strcmp( )** do?

6. Write a program that creates a string table consisting of names and telephone numbers. Initialize the array with some names of people you know and their phone numbers. Next, have the program request a name and print the associated telephone number. In other words, create a computerized telephone book.

*U*NDERSTAND POINTER BASICS

A pointer is a variable that holds the memory address of another object. For example, if a variable called **p** contains the address of another variable called **q**, then **p** is said to *point* to **q**. Therefore if **q** is at location 100 in memory, then **p** would have the value 100.

To declare a pointer variable, use this general form:

*type *var-name;*

Here, *type* is the *base type* of the pointer. The base type specifies the type of the object that the pointer can point to. Notice that the variable name is preceded by an asterisk. This tells the computer that a pointer variable is being created. For example, the following statement creates a pointer to an integer:

```
int *p;
```

C contains two special pointer operators: * and &. The & operator returns the address of the variable it precedes. The * operator returns the value stored at the address that it precedes. (The * pointer operator has no relationship to the multiplication operator, which uses the same symbol.) For example, examine this short program:

```
#include <stdio.h>

int main(void)
{
  int *p, q;

  q = 199; /* assign q 199 */

  p = &q; /* assign p the address of q */

  printf("%d", *p); /* display q's value using pointer */

  return 0;
}
```

This program prints **199** on the screen. Let's see why.

First, the line

```
int *p, q;
```

defines two variables: **p**, which is declared as an integer pointer, and **q**, which is an integer. Next, **q** is assigned the value 199. In the next line, **p** is assigned the *address of* **q**. You can verbalize the **&** operator as "address of." Therefore, this line can be read as "assign **p** the address of **q**." Finally, the value is displayed using the * operator applied to **p**. The * operator can be verbalized as "at address." Therefore, the **printf( )** statement can be read as "print the value at address **q**," which is 199.

When a variable's value is referenced through a pointer, the process is called *indirection*.

It is possible to use the * operator on the left side of an assignment statement in order to assign a variable a new value given a pointer to it. For example, this program assigns **q** a value indirectly using the pointer **p**:

```
#include <stdio.h>

int main(void)
{
  int *p, q;

  p = &q; /* get q's address */

  *p = 199; /* assign q a value using a pointer */

  printf("q's value is %d", q);

  return 0;
}
```

In the two simple example programs just shown, there is no reason to use a pointer. However, as you learn more about C, you will understand why pointers are important. Pointers are used to support linked lists and binary trees, for example.

The base type of a pointer is very important. Although C allows any type of pointer to point anywhere in memory, it is the base type that determines how the object pointed to will be treated. To understand the importance of this, consider the following fragment:

```
int q;
double *fp;

fp = &q;

/* what does this line do? */
*fp = 100.23;
```

Although not syntactically incorrect, this fragment is wrong. The pointer **fp** is assigned the address of an integer. This address is then used on the left side of an assignment statement to assign a floating-point value. However, **int**s are usually shorter than **double**s, and this assignment statement causes memory adjacent to **q** to be overwritten. For example, in an environment in which integers are 2 bytes and **double**s are 8 bytes, the assignment statement uses the 2 bytes allocated to **q** as well as 6 adjacent bytes, thus causing an error.

In general, the C compiler uses the base type to determine how many bytes are in the object pointed to by the pointer. This is how C knows how many bytes to copy when an indirect assignment is made, or how many bytes to compare if an indirect comparison is made. Therefore, it is very important that you always use the proper base type for a pointer. Except in special cases, never use a pointer of one type to point to an object of a different type.

If you attempt to use a pointer before it has been assigned the address of a variable, your program will probably crash. Remember, declaring a pointer variable simply creates a variable capable of holding a memory address. It does not give it any meaningful initial value. This is why the following fragment is incorrect.

```
int main(void)
{
  int *p;

  *p = 10;  /* incorrect - p is not pointing to
                anything */
```

As the comment notes, the pointer **p** is not pointing to any known object. Hence, trying to indirectly assign a value using **p** is meaningless and dangerous.

As pointers are defined in C, a pointer that contains a null value (zero) is assumed to be unused and pointing at nothing. In C, a null is, by convention, assumed to be an invalid memory address. However, the compiler will still let you use a null pointer, usually with disastrous results.

Examples

1. To graphically illustrate how indirection works, assume these declarations:

```
int *p, q;
```

Further assume that **q** is located at memory address 102 and that **p** is right before it, at location 100. After this statement

```
p = &q;
```

the pointer **p** contains the value 102. Therefore, after this assignment, memory looks like this:

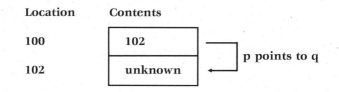

After the statement

```
*p = 1000;
```

executes, memory looks like this:

Remember, the value of **p** has nothing to do with the *value* of **q**. It simply holds **q**'s *address*, to which the indirection operator may be applied.

2. To illustrate why you must make sure that the base type of a pointer is the same as the object it points to, try this incorrect but benign program. (Some compilers may generate a warning message when you compile it, but none will issue an actual error message and stop compilation.)

```
/* This program is wrong, but harmless. */

#include <stdio.h>

int main(void)
{
  int *p;
  double q, temp;

  temp = 1234.34;

  p = &temp; /* attempt to assign q a value using */
  q = *p;    /* indirection through an integer pointer */

  printf("%f", q); /* this will not print 1234.34 */

  return 0;
}
```

Even though **p** points to **temp**, which does, indeed, hold the value 1234.34, the assignment

```
q = *p;
```

fails to copy the number because only 2 bytes (assuming 2-byte integers) will be transferred. Since **p** is an integer pointer, it cannot be used to transfer an 8-byte quantity (assuming 8-byte **double**s).

EXERCISES

1. What is a pointer?
2. What are the pointer operators and what are their effects?

3. Why is the base type of a pointer important?

4. Write a program with a **for** loop that counts from 0 to 9, displaying the numbers on the screen. Print the numbers using a pointer.

LEARN RESTRICTIONS TO POINTER EXPRESSIONS

In general, pointers may be used like other variables. However, you need to understand a few rules and restrictions.

In addition to the * and & operators, there are only four other operators that may be applied to pointer variables: the arithmetic operators +, ++, –, and – –. Further, you may add or subtract only integer quantities. You cannot, for example, add a floating-point number to a pointer.

Pointer arithmetic differs from "normal" arithmetic in one very important way: it is performed relative to the base type of the pointer. Each time a pointer is incremented, it will point to the next item, as defined by its base type, beyond the one currently pointed to. For example, assume that an integer pointer called **p** contains the address 200. After the statement

```
p++;
```

executes, **p** will have the value 202, assuming integers are two bytes long. By the same token, if **p** had been a **float** pointer (assuming 4-byte **float**s), then the resultant value contained in **p** would have been 204.

The only pointer arithmetic that appears as "normal" occurs when **char** pointers are used. Because characters are one byte long, an increment increases the pointer's value by one, and a decrement decreases its value by one.

You may add or subtract any integer quantity to or from a pointer. For example, the following is a valid fragment:

```
int *p
    .
    .
    .
p = p + 200;
```

This statement causes **p** to point to the 200th integer past the one to which **p** was previously pointing.

Aside from addition and subtraction of an integer, you may not perform any other type of arithmetic operations—you may not multiply, divide, or take the modulus of a pointer. However, you may subtract one pointer from another in order to find the number of elements separating them.

It is possible to apply the increment and decrement operators to either the pointer itself or the object to which it points. However, you must be careful when attempting to modify the object pointed to by a pointer. For example, assume that **p** points to an integer that contains the value 1. What do you think the following statement will do?

```
*p++;
```

Contrary to what you might think, this statement first increments **p** and then obtains the value at the new location. To increment what is pointed to by a pointer, you must use a form like this:

```
(*p)++;
```

The parentheses cause the value pointed to by **p** to be incremented.

You may compare two pointers using the relational operators. However, pointer comparisons make sense only if the pointers relate to each other—if they both point to the same object, for example. (Soon you will see an example of pointer comparisons.) You may also compare a pointer to zero to see if it is a null pointer.

At this point you might be wondering what use there is for pointer arithmetic. You will shortly see, however, that it is one of the most valuable components of the C language.

1. You can use **printf( )** to display the memory address contained in a pointer by using the **%p** format specifier. We can use this **printf( )** capability to illustrate several aspects of pointer arithmetic. The following program, for example, shows how all pointer arithmetic is relative to the base type of the pointer.

```
#include <stdio.h>

int main(void)
{
  char *cp, ch;
  int  *ip, i;
  float  *fp, f;
  double *dp, d;

  cp = &ch;
  ip = &i;
  fp = &f;
  dp = &d;

  /* print the current values */
  printf("%p %p %p %p\n", cp, ip, fp, dp);

  /* now increment them by one */
  cp++;
  ip++;
  fp++;
  dp++;

  /* print their new values */
  printf("%p %p %p %p\n", cp, ip, fp, dp);

  return 0;
}
```

Although the values contained in the pointer variables in this program will vary widely between compilers and even between versions of the same compiler, you will see that the address pointed to by **ch** will be incremented by one byte. The others will be incremented by the number of bytes in their base types. For example, in a 16-bit environment this will typically be 2 for **int**s, 4 for **float**s, and 8 for **double**s.

2. The following program illustrates the need for parentheses when you want to increment the object pointed to by a pointer instead of the pointer itself.

```c
#include <stdio.h>

int main(void)
{
   int *p, q;

   p = &q;

   q = 1;
   printf("%p ", p);

   *p++; /* this will not increment q */
   printf("%d %p", q, p);

   return 0;
}
```

After this program has executed, **q** still has the value 1, but **p** has been incremented. However, if the program is written like this:

```c
#include <stdio.h>

int main(void)
{
   int *p, q;

   p = &q;

   q = 1;
   printf("%p ", p);

   (*p)++; /* now q is incremented and p is unchanged */
   printf("%d %p", q, p);

   return 0;
}
```

q is incremented to 2 and **p** is unchanged.

EXERCISES

1. What is wrong with this fragment?

```
int *p, i;

p = &i;

p = p * 8;
```

2. Can you add a floating-point number to a pointer?

3. Assume that **p** is a **float** pointer that currently points to location 100 and that **float**s are 4 bytes long. What is the value of **p** after this fragment has executed?

```
p = p + 2;
```

6.3 *U*SE POINTERS WITH ARRAYS

In C, pointers and arrays are closely related. In fact, they are often interchangeable. It is this relationship between the two that makes their implementation both unique and powerful.

When you use an array name without an index, you are generating a pointer to the start of the array. This is why no indexes are used when you read a string using **gets( )**, for example. What is being passed to **gets( )** is not an array, but a pointer. In fact, you cannot pass an array to a function in C; you may only pass a pointer to the array. This important point was not mentioned in the preceding chapter on arrays because you had not yet learned about pointers. However, this fact is crucial to understanding the C language. The **gets( )** function uses the pointer to load the array it points to with the characters you enter at the keyboard. You will see how this is done later.

Since an array name without an index is a pointer to the start of the array, it stands to reason that you can assign that value to another pointer and access the array using pointer arithmetic. And, in fact, this is exactly what you can do. Consider this program:

```
#include <stdio.h>

int main(void)
{
  int a[10] = {10, 20, 30, 40, 50, 60, 70, 80, 90, 100};
  int *p;

  p = a; /* assign p the address of start of a */

  /* this prints a's first, second and third elements */
  printf("%d %d %d\n", *p, *(p+1), *(p+2));

  /* this does the same thing using a */
  printf("%d %d %d", a[0], a[1], a[2]);

  return 0;
}
```

Here, both **printf( )** statements display the same thing. The parentheses in expressions such as *$*(p+2)$* are necessary because the * has a higher precedence than the + operator.

Now you should be able to fully understand why pointer arithmetic is done relative to the base type—it allows arrays and pointers to relate to each other.

To use a pointer to access multidimensional arrays, you must manually do what the compiler does automatically. For example, in this array:

```
float balance[10][5];
```

each row is five elements long. Therefore, to access **balance[3][1]** using a pointer you must use a fragment like this:

```
float *p;

p = (float *) balance;
*(p + (3*5) + 1)
```

To reach the desired element, you must multiply the row number by the number of elements in the row and then add the number of the element within the row. Generally, with multidimensional arrays it is easier to use array indexing rather than pointer arithmetic.

In the preceding example, the cast of **balance** to **float** * was necessary. Since the array is being indexed manually, the pointer arithmetic must be relative to a **float** pointer. However, the type of pointer generated by **balance** is to a two-dimensional array of **float**s. Thus, there is need for the cast.

Pointers and arrays are linked by more than the fact that by using pointer arithmetic you can access array elements. You might be surprised to learn that you can index a pointer as if it were an array. The following program, for example, is perfectly valid:

```
#include <stdio.h>

int main(void)
{
  char str[] = "Pointers are fun";
  char *p;
  int i;

  p = str;

  /* loop until null is found */
  for(i=0; p[i]; i++)
    printf("%c", p[i]);

  return 0;
}
```

Keep one point firmly in mind: you should index a pointer only when that pointer points to an array. While the following fragment is syntactically correct, it is wrong; if you tried to execute it, you would probably crash your computer.

```
char *p, ch;
int i;

p = &ch;
for(i=0; i<10; i++) p[i] = 'A'+i;  /* wrong */
```

Since **ch** is not an array, it cannot be meaningfully indexed.

Although you can index a pointer as if it were an array, you will seldom want to do this because pointer arithmetic is usually more convenient. Also, in some cases a C compiler can generate faster executable code for an expression involving pointers than for a comparable expression using arrays.

Because an array name without an index is a pointer to the start of the array, you can, if you choose, use pointer arithmetic rather than array indexing to access elements of the array. For example, this program is perfectly valid and prints **c** on the screen:

```
#include <stdio.h>

int main(void)
{
  char str[80];

  *(str+3) = 'c';
  printf("%c", *(str+3));

  return 0;
}
```

You cannot, however, modify the value of the pointer generated by using an array name. For example, assuming the previous program, this is an invalid statement:

```
str++;
```

The pointer that is generated by **str** must be thought of as a constant that always points to the start of the array. Therefore, it is invalid to modify it and the compiler will report an error.

EXAMPLES

1. Two of C's library functions, **toupper( )** and **tolower( )**, are called using a character argument. In the case of **toupper( )**, if the character is a lowercase letter, the uppercase equivalent is returned; otherwise the character is returned unchanged. For **tolower( )**, if the character is an uppercase letter, the lowercase equivalent is returned; otherwise the character is returned unchanged. These functions use the header file CTYPE.H. The following program requests a string from the

user and then prints the string, first in uppercase letters and then in lowercase. This version uses array indexing to access the characters in the string so they can be converted into the appropriate case.

```c
#include <ctype.h>
#include <stdio.h>

int main(void)
{

  char str[80];
  int i;

  printf("Enter a string: ");
  gets(str);

  for(i=0; str[i]; i++)
    str[i] = toupper(str[i]);

  printf("%s\n", str); /* uppercase string */

  for(i=0; str[i]; i++)
    str[i] = tolower(str[i]);

  printf("%s\n", str); /* lowercase string */

  return 0;
}
```

The same program is shown below, only this time, a pointer is used to access the string. This second approach is the way you would see this program written by professional C programmers because incrementing a pointer is often faster than indexing an array.

```c
#include <ctype.h>
#include <stdio.h>

int main(void)
{
  char str[80], *p;

  printf("Enter a string: ");
```

```
  gets(str);
  p = str;

  while(*p) {
    *p = toupper(*p);
    p++;
  }

  printf("%s\n", str); /* uppercase string */

  p = str; /* reset p */

  while(*p) {
    *p = tolower(*p);
    p++;
  }

  printf("%s\n", str); /* lowercase string */

  return 0;
}
```

Before leaving this example, a small digression is in order. The routine

```
while(*p) {
  *p = toupper(*p);
  p++;
}
```

will generally be written by experienced programmers like this:

```
while(*p)
  *p++ = toupper(*p);
```

Because the **++** follows the **p**, the value pointed to by **p** is first modified and then **p** is incremented to point to the next element. Since this is the way C code is often written, this book will use the more compact form from time to time when it seems appropriate.

2. Remember that although most of the examples have been incrementing pointers, you can decrement a pointer as well. For example, the following program uses a pointer to copy the contents of one string into another in reversed order.

```
#include <stdio.h>
#include <string.h>

int main(void)
{
  char str1[] = "Pointers are fun to use";
  char str2[80], *p1, *p2;

  /* make p point to end of str1 */
  p1 = str1 + strlen(str1) - 1;

  p2 = str2;

  while(p1 >= str1)
    *p2++ = *p1--;

  /* null terminate str2 */
  *p2 = '\0';

  printf("%s %s", str1, str2);

  return 0;
}
```

This program works by setting **p1** to point to the end of **str1**, and **p2** to the start of str2. It then copies the contents of **str1** into **str2** in reverse order. Notice the pointer comparison in the **while** loop. It is used to stop the copying process when the start of **str1** is reached.

Also, notice the use of the compacted forms ***p2++** and ***p1--**. The loop is the equivalent of this one:

```
while(p1 >= str1) {
  *p2 = *p1;
  p1--;
  p2++;
}
```

Again, it is important for you to become familiar with the compact form of these types of pointer operations.

EXERCISES

1. Is this fragment correct?

   ```
   int count[10];
   .
   .
   .
   count = count + 2;
   ```

2. What value does this fragment display?

   ```
   int temp[5] = {10, 19, 23, 8, 9};
   int *p;

   p = temp;

   printf("%d", *(p+3));
   ```

3. Write a program that inputs a string. Have the program look for the first space. If it finds one, print the remainder of the string.

6.4   USE POINTERS TO STRING CONSTANTS

As you know, C allows string constants enclosed between double quotes to be used in a program. When the compiler encounters such a string, it stores it in the program's string table and generates a pointer to the string. For this reason, the following program is correct and prints **one two three** on the screen.

```c
#include <stdio.h>

int main(void)
{
  char *p;

  p = "one two three";

  printf(p);

  return 0;
}
```

Let's see how this program works. First, **p** is declared as a character pointer. This means that it may point to an array of characters. When the compiler compiles the line

```
p = "one two three";
```

it stores the string in the program's string table and assigns to **p** the address of the string in the table. Therefore, when **p** is used in the **printf( )** statement, **one two three** is displayed on the screen.

This program can be written more efficiently, as shown here:

```
#include <stdio.h>

int main(void)
{
  char *p = "one two three";

  printf(p);

  return 0;
}
```

Here, **p** is initialized to point to the string.

EXAMPLES

1. This program continues to read strings until you enter **stop**:

```
#include <stdio.h>
#include <string.h>

int main(void)
{
  char *p = "stop";
  char str[80];

  do {
   printf("Enter a string: ");
   gets(str);
  } while(strcmp(p, str));
```

```
        return 0;
    }
```

2. Using pointers to string constants can be very helpful when those constants are quite long. For example, suppose that you had a program that at various times would prompt the user to insert a diskette into drive A. To save yourself some typing, you might elect to initialize a pointer to the string and then simply use the pointer when the message needed to be displayed; for example:

```
char *InsDisk = "Insert disk into drive A, then press ENTER";
    .
    .
    .

printf(InsDisk);
    .
    .
    .

printf(InsDisk);
```

Another advantage to this approach is that to change the prompt, you only need to change it once, and all references to it will reflect the change.

EXERCISE

1. Write a program that creates three character pointers and initialize them so that one points to the string "one", the second to the string "two", and the third to the string "three". Next, have the program print all six permutations of these three strings. (For example, one permutation is "one two three", another is "two one three".)

6.5	**C**REATE ARRAYS OF POINTERS

Pointers may be arrayed like any other data type. For example, the following statement declares an integer pointer array that has 20 elements:

```
int *pa[20];
```

The address of an integer variable called **myvar** is assigned to the ninth element of the array as follows:

```
pa[8] = &myvar;
```

Because **pa** is an array of pointers, the only values that the array elements may hold are the addresses of integer variables. To assign the integer pointed to by the third element of **pa** the value 100, use the statement:

```
*pa[2] = 100;
```

EXAMPLES

1. Probably the single most common use of arrays of pointers is to create string tables in much the same way that unsized arrays were used in the previous chapter. For example, this function displays an error message based on the value of its parameter **err_num**.

```
char *p[] = {
  "Input exceeds field width",
  "Out of range",
  "Printer not turned on",
  "Paper out",
  "Disk full",
  "Disk write error"
};

void error(int err_num)
{
  printf(p[err_num]);
}
```

2. The following program uses a two-dimensional array of pointers to create a string table that links apple varieties with their colors. To use the program, enter the name of the apple, and the program will tell you its color.

```c
#include <stdio.h>
#include <string.h>

char *p[][2] = {
  "Red Delicious", "red",
  "Golden Delicious", "yellow",
  "Winesap", "red",
  "Gala", "reddish orange",
  "Lodi", "green",
  "Mutsu", "yellow",
  "Cortland", "red",
  "Jonathan", "red",
  "", "" /* terminate the table with null strings */
};

int main(void)
{
  int i;
  char apple[80];

  printf("Enter name of apple: ");
  gets(apple);

  for(i=0; *p[i][0]; i++) {
    if(!strcmp(apple, p[i][0]))
      printf("%s is %s\n", apple, p[i][1]);
  }

  return 0;
}
```

Look carefully at the condition controlling the **for** loop. The expression ***p[i][0]** gets the value of the first byte of the **i**th string. Since the list is terminated by null strings, this value will be zero (false) when the end of the table is reached. In all other cases it will be nonzero, and the loop will repeat.

EXERCISE

---

1. In this exercise, you will create an "executive decision aid." This is a program that answers yes, no, or maybe to a question entered at the keyboard. To create this program use an array of character pointers and initialize them to point to these three strings: "Yes", "No", and "Maybe. Rephrase the question". Next, input the user's question and find the length of the string. Next, use this formula to compute an index into the pointer array:

   index = length % 3

6.6 ▐ BECOME ACQUAINTED WITH MULTIPLE INDIRECTION

It is possible in C to have a pointer point to another pointer. This is called *multiple indirection* (see Figure 6-1). When a pointer points to another pointer, the first pointer contains the address of the second pointer, which points to the location containing the object.

To declare a pointer to a pointer, an additional asterisk is placed in front of the pointer's name. For example, this declaration tells the compiler that **mp** is a pointer to a character pointer:

```
char **mp;
```

It is important to understand that **mp** is not a pointer to a character, but rather a pointer to a character pointer.

FIGURE 6-1

Multiple indirection
▼

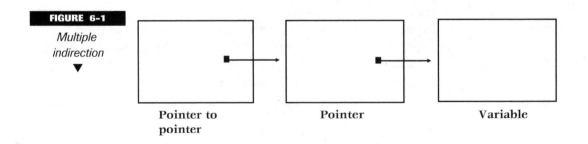

Pointer to pointer　　　　Pointer　　　　Variable

Accessing the target value indirectly pointed to by a pointer to a pointer requires that the asterisk operator be applied twice. For example,

```
char **mp, *p, ch;

p = &ch; /* get address of ch */
mp = &p; /* get address of p */
**mp = 'A'; /* assign ch the value A using multiple
                indirection */
```

As the comments suggest, **ch** is assigned a value indirectly using two pointers.

Multiple indirection is not limited to merely "a pointer to a pointer." You can apply the * as often as needed. However, multiple indirection beyond a pointer to a pointer is very difficult to follow and is not recommended.

You may not see the need for multiple indirection at this time, but as you learn more about C, you will see some examples in which it is very valuable.

EXAMPLES

1. The following program assigns **val** a value using multiple indirection. It displays the value first directly, then through the use of multiple indirection.

```
#include <stdio.h>

int main(void)
{
  float *fp, **mfp, val;

  fp = &val;
  mfp = &fp;

  **mfp = 123.903;
  printf("%f %f", val, **mfp);

  return 0;
}
```

2. This program shows how you can input a string using **gets( )** by using a pointer to a pointer to the string.

```c
#include <stdio.h>

int main(void)
{
  char *p, **mp, str[80];

  p = str;
  mp = &p;

  printf("Enter your name: ");
  gets(*mp);
  printf("Hi %s", *mp);

  return 0;
}
```

Notice that when **mp** is used as an argument to both **gets( )** and **printf( )**, only one * is used. This is because both of these functions require a pointer to a string for their operation. Remember, ****mp** is a pointer to **p**. However, **p** is a pointer to the string **str**. Therefore, ***mp** is a pointer to **str**. If you are a little confused, don't worry. Over time, you will develop a clearer concept of pointers to pointers.

EXERCISE

1. To help you understand multiple indirection better, write a program that assigns an integer a value using a pointer to a pointer. Before the program ends, display the addresses of the integer variable, the pointer, and the pointer to the pointer. (Remember, use **%p** to display a pointer value.)

6.7	***U**SE POINTERS AS PARAMETERS*

Pointers may be passed to functions. For example, when you call a function like **strlen( )** with the name of a string, you are actually passing a pointer to a function. When you pass a pointer to a function, the function must be declared as receiving a pointer of the same type. In the case of **strlen( )**, this is a character pointer. A complete discussion of using pointers as parameters is presented in the next chapter. However, some basic concepts are discussed here.

When you pass a pointer to a function, the code inside that function has access to the variable pointed to by the parameter. This means that the function can change the variable used to call the function. This is why functions like **strcpy( )**, for example, can work. Because it is passed a pointer, the function is able to modify the array that receives the string.

Now you can understand why you need to precede a variable's name with an **&** when using **scanf( )**. In order for **scanf( )** to modify the value of one of its arguments, it must be passed a pointer to that argument.

EXAMPLES

1. Another of C's standard library functions is called **puts( )**; it writes its string argument to the screen followed by a newline. The program that follows creates its own version of **puts( )** called **myputs( )**.

```
#include <stdio.h>

void myputs(char *p);

int main(void)
{
  myputs("this is a test");
```

```
      return 0;
}

void myputs(char *p)
{
  while(*p) { /* loop as long as p does not point to the
                  null that terminates the string */
    printf("%c", *p);
    p++;          /* go to next character */
  }
  printf("\n");
}
```

This program illustrates a very important point that was mentioned earlier in this chapter. When the compiler encounters a string constant, it places it into the program's string table and generates a pointer to it. Therefore, the **myputs( )** function is actually called with a character pointer, and the parameter **p** must be declared as a character pointer in order to receive it.

2. The following program shows one way to implement the **strcpy( )** function, called **mystrcpy( )**.

```
#include <stdio.h>

void mystrcpy(char *to, char *from);

int main(void)
{
  char str[80];

  mystrcpy(str, "this is a test");
  printf(str);

  return 0;
}

void mystrcpy(char *to, char *from)
{
  while(*from) *to++ = *from++;
    *to = '\0'; /* null terminates the string */
}
```

EXERCISES

1. Write your own version of **strcat( )** called **mystrcat( )**, and write a short program that demonstrates it.

2. Write a program that passes a pointer to an integer variable to a function. Inside that function, assign the variable the value –1. After the function has returned, demonstrate that the variable does, indeed, contain –1 by printing its value.

Mastery Skills Check

At this point you should be able to perform these exercises and answer these questions:

1. Show how to declare a pointer to a **double**.

2. Write a program that assigns a value to a variable indirectly by using a pointer to that variable.

3. Is this fragment correct? If not, why not?

```
int main(void)
{
  char *p;

  printf("Enter a string: ");
  gets(p);

  return 0;
}
```

4. How do pointers and arrays relate to each other?

5. Given this fragment:

```
char *p, str[80] = "this is a test";

p = str;
```

show two ways to access the 'i' in "this."

6. Assume that **p** is declared as a pointer to a **double** and contains the address 100. Further, assume that **double**s are 8 bytes long. After **p** is incremented, what will its value be?

Cumulative Skills Check

This section checks how well you have integrated the material in this chapter with that from earlier chapters.

1. What is the advantage of using pointers over array indexing?

2. Below is a program that counts the number of spaces in a string entered by the user. Rewrite the program so that it uses pointer arithmetic rather than array indexing.

```c
#include <stdio.h>

int main(void)
{
  char str[80];
  int i, spaces;

  printf("Enter a string: ");
  gets(str);

  spaces = 0;
  for(i=0; str[i]; i++)
    if(str[i]==' ') spaces++;

  printf("Number of spaces: %d", spaces);

  return 0;
}
```

3. Rewrite the following array reference using pointer arithmetic.

```c
int count[100][10];

count[44][8] = 99;
```

7

A Closer Look
at Functions

chapter objectives

7.1 Understand function prototypes

7.2 Understand recursion

7.3 Take a closer look at parameters

7.4 Pass arguments to **main( )**

7.5 Compare old-style to modern function parameter declarations

A T the very foundation of C is the function. All action statements must appear within one and an understanding of its operation is crucial to successful C programming. This chapter takes a close look at several important topics related to functions.

Review
Skills Check

Before proceeding you should be able to answer these questions and perform these exercises:

1. What does this fragment do?

```
int i, *p;

p = &i;
*p = 19;
```

2. What is generated when you use an array name without an index?

3. Is this fragment correct? If it is correct, explain why it works.

```
char *p = "this is a string";
```

4. Write a short program that assigns a floating-point value to a variable indirectly using a pointer to the variable.

5. Write your own version of **strlen( )**, called **mystrlen( )**, and demonstrate it in a program.

6. Is this fragment correct? If it is, what does the program display?

```
char str[8];

strcpy(str, "ABCDEFG");
printf("%c", *(str+2));
```

7.1 — UNDERSTAND FUNCTION PROTOTYPES

In Chapter 1 you were briefly introduced to the function prototype. Now it is time for you to understand precisely what a prototype does and why it is important to C programming. Function prototypes were not supported by the original version of C. They were added when C was standardized in 1989. Many consider prototypes to be the single most important addition made to the C language since its creation. Prototypes are not technically necessary. However, for reasons that will become self-evident, they should be used in all programs that you write.

The general form of a function prototype is shown here:

type function-name(type parameter-name1,
                    type parameter-name2,

                           .

                           .

                    type parameter-nameN);

A prototype declares three attributes associated with a function:

1. Its return type.
2. The number of its parameters.
3. The type of its parameters.

Prototypes provide several benefits. They inform the compiler about the return type of a function. They allow the compiler to find and report illegal type conversions between the type of arguments used to call a function and the type definition of its parameters. Prototypes also enable the compiler to report when the number of arguments passed to a function is not the same as the number of parameters declared by the function. Let's look at each of these.

When you call a function, the compiler needs to know the type of data returned by that function so that it can generate the proper code to handle that data. The reason for this is easy to understand: different data types have different sizes. The code that handles an integer return type will be different from that which handles a **double**, for example. If you use a function that is not prototyped, then the compiler will simply assume that it is returning an integer. However, if it is actually returning some other type, an error will occur. If the function is in the same file as the rest of your program, then the compiler will catch this error. But if the function is in another file or a library, then the error will go uncaught—and this will lead to trouble when your program is executed.

In the absence of a function prototype, it is not syntactically wrong to call a function with incompatible arguments or with more or less arguments than the function has parameters. Of course, doing either of these is obviously incorrect even though the compiler may accept your program without complaint. The use of a function prototype prevents these errors by enabling the compiler to find them. It is important to understand, however, that not all kinds of type conversions are illegal in a function call. In fact, C automatically converts most types of arguments into the type of data specified by the parameter. But a few type conversions are inherently wrong. For example, you cannot convert an integer into a pointer. A function prototype allows the compiler to catch and return this type of error.

As mentioned, as important as prototypes are, they are not currently required. Because of the need to maintain compatibility with older code, all C compilers still support non-prototyped programs. Of course, at some point in the future, this situation may change.

In early versions of C, before prototypes were invented, it was still necessary to tell the compiler about the return type of a function (unless it returned type **int**) for the reasons explained earlier. This was done using a forerunner of the prototype, called a *forward declaration* or a *forward reference.* A forward declaration is essentially a truncated form of a prototype that declares only the return type of a function—not the type and number of its parameters. Although forward declarations are obsolete, they are still allowed for compatibility with older code.

The following program demonstrates an old-style forward declaration. It uses it to inform the compiler of **volume( )**'s return type.

```
#include <stdio.h>

double volume(); /* old-style forward declaration for
                    volume() */

int main(void)
{
  double vol;

  vol = volume(12.2, 5.67, 9.03);
  printf("Volume: %f", vol);

  return 0;
}

/* Compute the volume of a cube. */
```

```
double volume(double s1, double s2, double s3)
{
  return s1 * s2 * s3;
}
```

Since the old-style declaration does not inform the compiler about any of **volume( )**'s parameters it is not a function prototype. Instead, it simply states **volume( )**'s return type. The trouble is that the lack of a full prototype will allow **volume( )** to be called using an incorrect type and/or number of arguments. For example, given the preceding program, the following will not generate a compiler error message even though it is wrong.

```
volume(120.2, 99.3); /* missing last arg */
```

Since the compiler has not been given information about **volume( )**'s parameters it won't catch the fact that this call is wrong.

Although the old-style forward declaration is no longer used in new code, you will still find it quite frequently in older programs. If you will be updating older programs, you should consider adding prototypes to be your first job.

When function prototypes were added to C, two minor compatibility problems between the old version of C and the ANSI version of C had to be resolved. The first issue was how to handle the old-style forward declaration, which does not use a parameter list. To do so, the ANSI C standard specifies that when a function declaration occurs without a parameter list, nothing whatsoever is being said about the parameters to the function. It might have parameters, it might not. This allows old-style declarations to coexist with prototypes. But it also leads to a question: how do you prototype a function that takes no arguments? For example, this function simply outputs a line of periods:

```
void line()
{
  int i;

  for(i=0; i<80; i++) printf(".");
}
```

If you try to use the following as a prototype, it won't work because the compiler will think that you are simply using the old-style declaration method.

```
void line();
```

The solution to this problem is through the use of the **void** keyword. When a function has no parameters, its prototype uses **void** inside the parentheses. For example, here is **line( )**'s proper prototype:

```
void line(void);
```

This explicitly tells the compiler that the function has no parameters, and any call to that function that has parameters is an error. You must make sure to also use **void** when the function is defined. For example, **line( )** must look like this:

```
void line(void)
{
  int i;

  for(i=0; i<80; i++) printf(".");
}
```

Since we have been using **void** to specify empty parameter lists since Chapter 1, this mechanism is already familiar to you.

The second issue related to prototyping is the way it affects C's automatic type promotions. Because of some features of the environment in which C was developed, when a non-prototyped function is called, all integral promotions take place (for example, characters are converted to integers) and all **float**s are converted to **double**s. However, these type promotions seem to violate the purpose of the prototype. The resolution to this problem is that when a prototype exists, the types specified in the prototype are maintained, and no type promotions will occur.

There is one other special case that relates to prototypes: variable length argument lists. We won't be creating any functions in this book that use a variable number of arguments because they require the use of some advanced techniques. But it is possible to do so, and it is sometimes quite useful. For example, both **printf( )** and **scanf( )** accept a variable number of arguments. To specify a variable number of arguments, use **...** in the prototype. For example,

```
int myfunc(int a, ...);
```

specifies a function that has one integer parameter and a variable number of other parameters.

In C programming there has been a long-standing confusion about the usage of two terms: *declaration* and *definition*. A declaration specifies the type of an object. A definition causes storage for an object to be created. As these terms relate to functions, a prototype is a *declaration*. The function, itself, which contains the body of the function is a *definition*.

In C, it is also legal to fully define a function prior to its first use, thus eliminating the need for a separate prototype. However, this works only in very small programs. In real-world applications, this option is not feasible. For all practical purposes, function prototypes must exist for all functions that your program will use.

Remember that if a function does not return a value, then its return type should be specified as **void**—both in its definition and in its prototype.

Function prototypes enable you to write better, more reliable programs because they help ensure that the functions in your programs are being called with correct types and numbers of arguments. Fully prototyped programs are the norm and represent the current state of the art of C programming. Frankly, no professional C programmer today would write programs without them. Also, future versions of the ANSI C standard may mandate function prototypes and C++ requires them now. Although prototypes are still technically optional, their use is nearly universal. You should use them in all of the programs you write.

EXAMPLES

1. To see how a function prototype can catch an error, try compiling this version of the volume program, which includes **volume( )**'s full prototype:

```
#include <stdio.h>

/* this is volume()'s full prototype */
double volume(double s1, double s2, double s3);

int main(void)
{
```

```
   double vol;

   vol = volume(12.2, 5.67, 9.03, 10.2); /* error */
   printf("Volume: %f", vol);

   return 0;
}

/* Compute the volume of a cube. */
double volume(double s1, double s2, double s3)
{
   return s1 * s2 * s3;
}
```

As you will see, this program will not compile because the compiler knows that **volume( )** is declared as having only three parameters, but the program is attempting to call it with four parameters.

2. As explained, if a function is defined before it is called, it does not require a separate prototype. For example, the following program is perfectly valid:

```
#include <stdio.h>

/* define getnum() prior to its first use */
float getnum(void)
{
   float x;

   printf("Enter a number: ");
   scanf("%f", &x);
   return x;
}

int main(void)
{
   float i;

   i = getnum();
   printf("%f", i);

   return 0;
}
```

Since **getnum( )** is defined before it is used, the compiler knows what type of data it returns and that it has no parameters. A separate prototype is not needed. The reason that you will seldom use this method is that large programs are typically spread across several files. Since you can't define a function more than once, prototypes are the only way to inform all files about a function. (Multi-file programs are explained in Chapter 11.)

3. As you know, the standard library function **sqrt( )** returns a **double** value. You might be wondering how the compiler knows this. The answer is that **sqrt( )** is prototyped in its header file MATH.H. To see the importance of using the header file, try this program:

```
#include <stdio.h>
/* math.h is intentionally not included */

int main(void)
{
  double answer;

  answer = sqrt(9.0);
  printf("%f", answer);

  return 0;
}
```

When you run this program, it displays something other than **3** because the compiler generates code that copies only two bytes (assuming two-byte integers) into **answer** and not the 8 bytes that typically comprise a **double**. If you include MATH.H, the program will work correctly.

In general, each of C's standard library functions has its prototype specified in a header file. For example, **printf( )** and **scanf( )** have their prototypes in STDIO.H. This is one of the reasons that it is important to include the appropriate header file for each library function you use.

4. There is one situation that you will encounter quite frequently that is, at first, unsettling. Some "character-based" functions have a return type of **int** rather than **char**. For example, the

getchar( ) function's return type is **int**, not **char**. The reason for this is found in the fact that C very cleanly handles the conversion of characters to integers and integers back to characters. There is no loss of information. For example, the following program is perfectly valid:

```
#include <stdio.h>

int get_a_char(void);

int main(void)
{
  char ch;

  ch = get_a_char();
  printf("%c", ch);

  return 0;
}

int get_a_char(void)
{
  return 'a';
}
```

When **get_a_char( )** returns, it elevates the character 'a' to an integer by adding a high-order byte (or bytes) containing zeros. When this value is assigned to **ch** in **main( )**, the high-order byte (or bytes) is removed. One reason to declare functions like **get_a_char( )** as returning an integer instead of a character is to allow various error values to be returned that are intentionally outside the range of a **char**.

5. When a function returns a pointer, both the function and its prototype must declare the same pointer return type. For example, consider this short program:

```
#include <stdio.h>

int *init(int x);
int count;

int main(void)
{
```

```
    int *p;

    p = init(110); /* return pointer */

    printf("count (through p) is %d", *p);

    return 0;
}

int *init(int x)
{
  count = x;

  return &count; /* return a pointer */
}
```

As you can see, the function **init( )** returns a pointer to the global variable **count**. Notice the way that the return type for **init( )** is specified. This same general form is used for any sort of pointer return type. Although this example is trivial, functions that return pointers are quite valuable in many programming situations. One other thing: if a function returns a pointer, then it must make sure that the object being pointed to does not go out-of-scope when the function returns. This means that you must not return pointers to local variables.

6. The **main( )** function does not have (nor does it require) a prototype. This allows you to define **main( )** any way that is supported by your compiler. This book uses

```
int main(void) { ...
```

because it is one of the most common forms. Another frequently used form of **main( )** is shown here:

```
void main(void) { ...
```

This form is used when no value is returned by **main( )**. Later in this chapter, you will see another form of **main( )** that has parameters.

The reason **main( )** does not have a prototype is to allow C to be used in the widest variety of environments. Since the precise conditions present at program start-up and what actions must occur at program termination may differ widely from one operating system to the next, C allows the acceptable forms of **main( )** to be determined by the compiler. However, nearly all compilers will accept **int main(void)** and **void main(void)**.

EXERCISES

1. Write a program that creates a function, called **avg( )**, that reads ten floating-point numbers entered by the user and returns their average. Use an old-style forward reference and not a function prototype.

2. Rewrite the program from Exercise 1 so that it uses a function prototype.

3. Is the following program correct? If not, why not? If it is, can it be made better?

```c
#include <stdio.h>

double myfunc();

int main(void)
{
  printf("%f", myfunc(10.2));

  return 0;
}

double myfunc(double num)
{
  return num / 2.0;
}
```

4. Show the prototype for a function called **Purge( )** that has no parameters and returns a pointer to a **double**.

5. On your own, experiment with the concepts presented in this section.

*U*NDERSTAND RECURSION

Recursion is the process by which something is defined in terms of itself. When applied to computer languages, recursion means that a function can call itself. Not all computer languages support recursive functions, but C does. A very simple example of recursion is shown in this program:

```
#include <stdio.h>

void recurse(int i);

int main(void)
{
  recurse(0);

  return 0;
}

void recurse(int i)
{
  if(i<10) {
    recurse(i+1); /* recursive call */
    printf("%d ", i);
  }
}
```

This program prints

9 8 7 6 5 4 3 2 1 0

on the screen. Let's see why.

The **recurse( )** function is first called with 0. This is **recurse( )**'s first activation. Since 0 is less than 10, **recurse( )** then calls itself with the value of **i** (in this case 0) plus 1. This is the second activation of **recurse( )**, and **i** equals 1. This causes **recurse( )** to be called again using the value 2. This process repeats until **recurse( )** is called with the value 10. This causes **recurse( )** to return. Since it returns to the point of its call, it will execute the **printf( )** statement in its previous activation, print **9**, and return. This, then, returns to the point of its call in the previous activation, which causes **8** to be displayed. The process continues until all the calls return, and the program terminates.

It is important to understand that there are not multiple copies of a recursive function. Instead, only one copy exists. When a function is called, storage for its parameters and local data are allocated on the stack. Thus, when a function is called recursively, the function begins executing with a new set of parameters and local variables, but the code that constitutes the function remains the same.

If you think about the preceding program, you will see that recursion is essentially a new type of program control mechanism. This is why every recursive function you write will have a conditional statement that controls whether the function will call itself again or return. Without such a statement, a recursive function will simply run wild, using up all the memory allocated to the stack and then crashing the program.

Recursion is generally employed sparingly. However, it can be quite useful in simplifying certain algorithms. For example, the Quicksort sorting algorithm is difficult to implement without the use of recursion. If you are new to programming in general, you might find yourself uncomfortable with recursion. Don't worry; as you become more experienced, the use of recursive functions will become more natural.

EXAMPLES

1. The recursive program described above can be altered to print the numbers **0** through **9** on the screen. To accomplish this, only the position of the **printf( )** statement needs to be changed, as shown here:

```
#include <stdio.h>

void recurse(int i);

int main(void)
{
  recurse(0);

  return 0;
}

void recurse(int i)
```

```
{
  if(i<10) {
    printf("%d ", i);
    recurse(i+1);
  }
}
```

Because the call to **printf( )** now precedes the recursive call to
recurse( ), the numbers are printed in ascending order.

2. The following program demonstrates how recursion can be used
   to copy one string to another.

```
#include <stdio.h>

void rcopy(char *s1, char *s2);

int main(void)
{
  char str[80];

  rcopy(str, "this is a test");
  printf(str);

  return 0;
}

/* Copy s2 to s1 using recursion. */
void rcopy(char *s1, char *s2)
{
  if(*s2) { /* if not at end of s2 */
    *s1++ = *s2++;
    rcopy(s1, s2);
  }
  else *s1 = '\0'; /* null terminate the string */
}
```

The program works by assigning the character currently pointed
to by **s2** to the one pointed to by **s1**, and then incrementing both
pointers. These pointers are then used in a recursive call to
rcopy( ), until **s2** points to the null that terminates the string.
   Although this program makes an interesting example of
recursion, no professional C programmer would actually code a
function like this for one simple reason: efficiency. It takes
more time to execute a function call than it does to execute a

loop. Therefore, tasks like this will almost always be coded using an iterative approach.

3. It is possible to have a program in which two or more functions are *mutually recursive*. Mutual recursion occurs when one function calls another, which in turn calls the first. For example, study this short program:

```c
#include <stdio.h>

void f2(int b);
void f1(int a);

int main(void)
{
    f1(30);

    return 0;
}

void f1(int a)
{
    if(a) f2(a-1);
    printf("%d ", a);
}

void f2(int b)
{
    printf(".");
    if(b) f1(b-1);
}
```

This program displays

..............0 2 4 6 8 10 12 14 16 18 20 22 24 26 28 30

on the screen. Its output is caused by the way the two functions **f1( )** and **f2( )** call each other. Each time **f1( )** is called, it checks to see if **a** is zero. If not, it calls **f2( )** with **a-1**. The **f2( )** function first prints a period and then checks to see if **b** is zero. If not, it calls **f1( )** with **b-1**, and the process repeats. Eventually, **b** is zero and the function calls start unraveling, causing **f1( )** to display the numbers **0** to **30** counting by twos.

EXERCISES

1. One of the best known examples of recursion is the recursive version of a function that computes the factorial of a number. The factorial of a number is obtained by multiplying the original number by all integers less than it and greater than 1. Therefore, 4 factorial is 4x3x2, or 24. Write a function, called **fact( )**, that uses recursion to compute the factorial of its integer argument. Have it return the result. Also, demonstrate its use in a program.

2. What is wrong with this recursive function?

```
void f(void)
{
  int i;

  printf("in f() \n");

  /* call f() 10 times */
  for(i=0; i<10; i++) f( );
}
```

3. Write a program that displays a string on the screen, one character at a time, using a recursive function.

7.3   **T**AKE A CLOSER LOOK AT PARAMETERS

For computer languages in general, a subroutine can be passed arguments in one of two ways. The first is called *call by value*. This method copies the *value* of an argument into the formal parameter of the subroutine. Therefore, changes made to a parameter of the subroutine *have no effect* on the argument used to call it. The second way a subroutine can have arguments passed to it is through *call by reference*. In this method, the *address* of an argument is copied into the parameter. Inside the subroutine, the address is used to access the actual argument. This means that changes made to the parameter *will affect* the argument.

By default, C uses call by value to pass arguments. This means that you cannot alter the arguments used in a call to a function. What occurs to a parameter inside the function will have no effect on the argument outside the function. However, as you saw in Chapter 6 , it is possible to manually construct a call by reference by passing a pointer to an argument. Since this causes the address of the argument to be passed, it then is possible to change the value of the argument outside the function.

The classic example of a call-by-reference function is **swap( )**, shown here. It exchanges the value of its two integer arguments.

```c
#include <stdio.h>

void swap(int *i, int *j);

int main(void)
{
  int num1, num2;

  num1 = 100;
  num2 = 800;

  printf("num1: %d num2: %d\n", num1, num2);
  swap(&num1, &num2);
  printf("num1: %d num2: %d\n", num1, num2);

  return 0;
}

/* Exchange the values pointed to by two integer pointers. */
void swap(int *i, int *j)
{
  int temp;

  temp = *i;
  *i = *j;
  *j = temp;
}
```

Since pointers to the two integers are passed to the function, the actual values pointed to by the arguments are exchanged.

As you know, when an array is used as an argument to a function, only the address of the array is passed, not a copy of the entire array, which implies call-by-reference. This means that the parameter declaration must be of a compatible pointer type. There are three ways to declare a parameter that is to receive a pointer to an array. First, the parameter may be declared as an array of the same type and size as that used to call the function. Second, it may be specified as an unsized array. Finally, and most commonly, it may be specified as a pointer to the base type of the array. The following program demonstrates all three methods:

```c
#include <stdio.h>

void f1(int num[5]), f2(int num[]), f3(int *num);

int main(void)
{
  int count[5] = {1, 2, 3, 4, 5};

  f1(count);
  f2(count);
  f3(count);

  return 0;
}

/* parameter specified as array */
void f1(int num[5])
{
  int i;

  for(i=0; i<5; i++) printf("%d ", num[i]);
}

/* parameter specified as unsized array */
void f2(int num[])
{
  int i;

  for(i=0; i<5; i++) printf("%d ", num[i]);
}

/* parameter specified as pointer */
void f3(int *num)
{
  int i;
```

```
      for(i=0; i<5; i++) printf("%d ", num[i]);
}
```

Even though the three methods of declaring a parameter that will receive a pointer to an array look different, they all result in a pointer parameter being created.

1. Some computer languages, such as BASIC, provide an input function that allows you to specify a prompting message. C has no counterpart for this type of function. However, you can easily create one. The program shown here uses the function **prompt( )** to display a prompting message and then to read a number entered by the user.

```
#include <stdio.h>

void prompt(char *msg, int *num);

int main(void)
{
   int i;
   prompt("Enter a num: ", &i);
   printf("Your number is: %d", i);

   return 0;
}

void prompt(char *msg, int *num)
{
   printf(msg);
   scanf("%d", num);
}
```

Because the parameter **num** is already a pointer, you do not need to precede it with an **&** in the call to **scanf( )**. (In fact, it would be an error to do so.)

EXERCISES

1. Is this program correct? If not, why not?

    ```c
    #include <stdio.h>

    myfunc(int num, int min, int max);

    int main(void)
    {
        int i;

        printf("Enter a number between 1 and 10: ");
        myfunc(&i, 1, 10);

        return 0;
    }

    void myfunc(int num, int min, int max)
    {
      do {
        scanf("%d", num);
      } while(*num<min || *num>max);
    }
    ```

2. Write a program that creates an input function similar to **prompt( )** described earlier in this section. Have it input a string rather than an integer.

3. Explain the difference between call by value and call by reference.

---

*P*ASS ARGUMENTS TO main( )

Many programs allow command-line arguments to be specified when they are run. A *command-line argument* is the information that follows the program's name on the command line of the operating system. Command-line arguments are used to pass information into a program. For example, when you use a text editor, you probably specify the name of the file you want to edit after the name of the text editor.

Assuming you use a text editor called EDTEXT, then this line causes the file TEST to be edited.

```
EDTEXT TEST
```

Here, TEST is a command-line argument.

Your C programs may also utilize command-line arguments. These are passed to a C program through two arguments to the **main( )** function. The parameters are called **argc** and **argv**. As you probably guessed, these parameters are optional and are not present when no command-line arguments are being used. Let's look at **argc** and **argv** more closely.

The **argc** parameter holds the number of arguments on the command-line and is an integer. It will always be at least 1 because the name of the program qualifies as the first argument.

The **argv** parameter is an array of string pointers. The most common method for declaring **argv** is shown here:

```
char *argv[];
```

The empty brackets indicate that it is an array of undetermined length. All command-line arguments are passed to **main( )** as strings. To access an individual string, index **argv**. For example, **argv[0]** points to the program's name and **argv[1]** points to the first argument. This program displays all the command-line arguments that are present when it is executed.

```
#include <stdio.h>

int main(int argc, char *argv[])
{
  int i;

  for(i=1; i<argc; i++) printf("%s ", argv[i]);

  return 0;
}
```

C does not specify what constitutes a command-line argument, because operating systems vary considerably on this point. However, the most common convention is as follows: Each command-line argument must be separated by a space or a tab character. Commas, semicolons, and the like are not considered separators. For example,

```
This is a test
```

is made up of four strings, but

```
this,that,and,another
```

is one string.

If you need to pass a command-line argument that does, in fact, contain spaces, you must place it between quotes, as shown in this example:

```
"this is a test"
```

The names of **argv** and **argc** are arbitrary—you can use any names you like. However, **argc** and **argv** are traditional and have been used since C's origin. It is a good idea to use these names so that anyone reading your program can quickly identify them as the command-line parameters.

One last point: the ANSI C standard only defines the **argc** and **argv** parameters. However, your compiler may allow additional parameters to **main( )**. For example, some DOS or Windows compatible compilers allow access to environmental information through a command-line argument. Check your compiler's user manual.

EXAMPLES

1. When you pass numeric data to a program, that data will be received in its string form. Your program will need to convert it into the proper internal format using one or another of C's standard library functions. The most common conversion functions are shown here, using their prototypes:

```
int atoi(char *str);

double atof(char *str);

long atol(char *str);
```

These functions use the STDLIB.H header file. The **atoi( )** function returns the **int** equivalent of its string argument. The atof( ) returns the **double** equivalent of its string argument, and the **atol( )** returns the **long** equivalent of its string argument. If you call one of these functions with a string that is not a valid number, zero will be returned. The following program demonstrates these functions. To use it, enter an integer, a long integer, and a floating-point number on the command line. It will then redisplay them on the screen.

```c
#include <stdio.h>
#include <stdlib.h>

int main(int argc, char *argv[])
{
  int i;
  double d;
  long l;

  i = atoi(argv[1]);
  l = atol(argv[2]);
  d = atof(argv[3]);

  printf("%d %ld %f", i, l, d);

  return 0;
}
```

2. This program coverts ounces to pounds. To use it, specify the number of ounces on the command line.

```c
#include <stdio.h>
#include <stdlib.h>

int main(int argc, char *argv[])
{
  double pounds;

  pounds = atof(argv[1]) / 16.0;
  printf("%f pounds", pounds);

  return 0;
}
```

3. Although the examples up to this point haven't done so, you should verify in real programs, that the right number of

command-line arguments have been supplied by the user. The way to do this is to test the value of **argc**. For example, the ounces-to-pounds program can be improved as shown here:

```
#include <stdio.h>
#include <stdlib.h>

int main(int argc, char *argv[])
{
  double pounds;

  if(argc!=2) {
    printf("Usage: CONVERT <ounces>\n");
    printf("Try Again");
  }
  else {
    pounds = atof(argv[1]) / 16.0;
    printf("%f pounds", pounds);
  }

  return 0;
}
```

This way the program will perform a conversion only if a command-line argument is present. (Of course, you may prompt the user for any missing information, if you choose.)

Generally, the preceding program will be written by a professional C programmer like this:

```
#include <stdio.h>
#include <stdlib.h>

int main(int argc, char *argv[])
{
  double pounds;

  if(argc!=2) {
    printf("Usage: CONVERT <ounces>\n");
    printf("Try Again");
    exit(1); /* stop the program */
  }

  pounds = atof(argv[1]) / 16.0;
  printf("%f pounds", pounds);
```

```
    return 0;
}
```

When some condition necessary for a program's execution has not been met, most C programmers call the standard library function **exit( )** to terminate the program. The **exit( )** function has this prototype:

> void exit(int *return-code*);

and uses the STDLIB.H header file. When **exit( )** terminates the program, it returns the value of *return-code* to the operating system. By convention, most operating systems use a return code of zero to mean that a program has terminated normally. Nonzero values indicate abnormal termination.

EXERCISES

1. Write a program that accepts two command-line arguments. Have the program compare them and report which is lexicographically greater than the other.

2. Write a program that takes two numeric arguments and displays their sum.

3. Expand the program in Exercise 2 so that it takes three arguments. The first argument must be one of these words: add, subtract, multiply, or divide. Based on the value of the first argument, perform the requested operation on the remaining two numeric arguments.

  7.5   *C*OMPARE OLD-STYLE TO MODERN
FUNCTION PARAMETER DECLARATIONS

Early versions of C used a different parameter declaration method than has been shown in this book. This original declaration method is now called the *old-style* or *classic form*. The form used in this book is the *modern form*. It was introduced when the ANSI C standard was created. While the modern form should be used for all new programs, you will still find examples of old-style parameter declarations in older programs and you need to be familiar with it.

The general form of the old-style parameter declaration is shown here:

```
type function-name(parameter1, parameter2,...parameterN)
type parameter1;
type parameter2;
         .
         .
         .
type parameterN;
{
  function-code
}
```

Notice that the declaration is divided into two parts. Within the parentheses, only the names of the parameters are specified. Outside the parentheses, the types and names are specified. For example, given the following modern declaration

```
float f(char ch, long size, double max)
{
         .
         .
         .
}
```

the equivalent old-style declaration is

```
float f(ch, size, max)
char ch;
long size;
double max;
{
         .
         .
         .
}
```

One other aspect of the old-style declaration is that you can specify more than one parameter after the type name. For example, this is perfectly valid:

```
myfunc(i, j, k)
int i, j, k;
{
   .
   .
   .
```

The ANSI C standard specifies that either the old-style or the modern declaration form may be used. The reason for this is to maintain compatibility with older C programs. (There are literally millions of lines of C code still in existence that use the old-style form.) So, if you see programs in books or magazines that use the classic form, don't worry; your compiler will be able to compile them. However for all new programs, you should definitely use the modern form.

EXAMPLE

1. This program uses the old declaration form:

```
#include <stdio.h>

int area(int l, int w);

int main(void)
{
  printf("area is %d", area(10, 13));
  return 0;
}

int area(l, w)
int l, w;
{
  return l * w;
}
```

Notice that even though the old form of parameter declaration is used to define the function, it is still possible to prototype the function.

EXERCISE

---

1. Convert this program so that **f_to_m( )** uses the old-style declaration form.

```
#include <stdio.h>

double f_to_m(double f);

int main(void)
{
  double feet;

  printf("Enter feet: ");
  scanf("%lf", &feet);
  printf("Meters: %f", f_to_m(feet));

  return 0;
}

double f_to_m(double f)
{
  return f / 3.28;
}
```

Mastery
Skills Check

At this point you should be able to answer these questions and perform these exercises:

1. How do you prototype a function that does not have parameters?

2. What is a function prototype, and what are the benefits of it?

3. How do command-line arguments get passed to a C program?

4. Write a program that uses a recursive function to display the letters of the alphabet.

5. Write a program that takes a string as a command-line argument. Have it output the string in coded form. To code the string, add 1 to each character.

6. What is the prototype for this function?

```
double myfunc(int x, int y, char ch)
{
    .
    .
    .
}
```

7. Show how the function in Exercise 6 would be coded using the old-style function declaration.

8. What does the **exit( )** function do?

9. What does the **atoi( )** function do?

Cumulative Skills Check

This section checks how well you have integrated the material in this chapter with that from earlier chapters.

1. Write a program that allows access only if the user enters the correct password as a command-line parameter. If the user enters the right word, print **Access Permitted**; otherwise print **Access Denied**.

2. Create a function called **string_up( )** that transforms the string it is called with into uppercase characters. Demonstrate its use in a program. (Hint, use the **toupper( )** function to convert lowercase characters into uppercase.)

3. Write a function called **avg( )** that averages a list of floating-point values. The function will have two arguments. The first is a pointer to the array containing the numbers; the second is an integer value, which specifies the size of the array. Demonstrate its use in a program.

4. Explain how pointers allow C to construct a call-by-reference parameter.

8

Console I/O

chapter objectives

8.1 Learn another preprocessor directive

8.2 Examine character and string input and output

8.3 Examine some non-standard console functions

8.4 Take a closer look at **gets( )** and **puts( )**

8.5 Master **printf( )**

8.6 Master **scanf( )**

N this chapter you will learn about C's console I/O functions. These are the functions that read or write information to and from the console. You have already been using some of these functions. Here we will look at them in detail. This chapter begins with a short but necessary digression that introduces another of C's preprocessor directives: **#define**.

Review
Skills Check

Before proceeding, you should be able to answer these questions and perform these exercises:

1. What must you do to enable the compiler to check that a function is being called correctly?

2. What are the principal advantages of using function prototypes?

3. Write a program that uses a function called **hypot( )** that returns the length of the hypotenuse of a right triangle when passed the length of the two opposing sides. Have the function return a **double** value. The type of the parameters must be **double** as well. Demonstrate the function in a program. (The Pythagorean theorem states that the sum of the squares of the two opposing sides equals the square of the hypotenuse.)

4. What return type should you use for a function that returns no value?

5. Write a recursive function called **rstrlen( )** that uses recursion to compute the length of a string. Demonstrate it in a program.

6. Write a program that reports how many command line arguments it has been called with. Also, have it display the contents of the last one.

7. How is this declaration coded using the old-style function declaration form?

```
void func(int a, char ch, double d)
{
    .
    .
    .
```

*L*EARN ANOTHER PREPROCESSOR DIRECTIVE

As you recall, the C preprocessor performs various manipulations on the source code of your program before it is actually compiled. A preprocessor directive is simply an instruction to the preprocessor. Up to this point, you have learned about and have used one preprocessor directive, **#include**. Before proceeding, you need to learn about another: **#define**.

The **#define** directive tells the preprocessor to perform a text substitution throughout your entire program. That is, it causes one sequence of characters to be replaced by another. This process is generally referred to as *macro substitution*. The general form of the **#define** statement is shown here:

#define *macro-name character-sequence*

Notice that this line does not end in a semicolon. Each time the *macro-name* is encountered in the program, the associated *character-sequence* is substituted for it. For example, consider this program:

```
#include <stdio.h>

#define MAX 100

int main(void)
{
  int i;

  for(i=0; i<MAX; i++) printf("%d ", i);

  return 0;
}
```

When the identifier **MAX** is encountered by the preprocessor, **100** is automatically substituted. Thus, the **for** loop will actually look like this to the compiler:

```
for(i=0; i<100; i++) printf("%d ", i);
```

Keep one thing clearly in mind: At the time of the substitution, **100** is simply a string of characters composed of a 1 and two 0s. The preprocessor does not convert a numeric string into its internal binary format. This is left to the compiler.

The macro name can be any valid C identifier. Thus, macro names must follow the same naming rules as do variables. Although macro names can appear in either upper- or lowercase letters, most programmers have adopted the convention of using uppercase for macro names. This makes it easy for anyone reading your program to know when a macro name is being used.

There must be one or more spaces between the macro name and the character sequence. The character sequence can contain any type of character, including spaces. It is terminated by the end of the line.

Preprocessor directives in general and **#define** in particular are not affected by C's code blocks. That is, whether you define a macro name outside of all functions or within a function, once it is defined, all code after that point may have access to it. For example, this program prints **186000** on the screen.

```c
#include <stdio.h>

void f(void);

int main(void)
{
  #define LIGHTSPEED 186000

  f();

  return 0;
}

void f(void)
{
  printf("%ld", LIGHTSPEED);
}
```

There is one important point you must remember: Each preprocessor directive must appear on its own line.

Macro substitutions are useful for two main reasons. First, many C library functions use certain predefined values to indicate special conditions or results. Your programs will need access to these values when they use one of these functions. However, many times the actual value will vary between programming environments. For this reason, these values are usually specified using macro names. The macro names are defined inside the header file that relates to each specific function. You will see an example of this in the next section.

The second reason macro substitution is important is that it can help make it easier to maintain programs. For example, if you know that a value, such as an array size, is going to be used several places in your program, it is better to create a macro for this value. Then if you ever need to change this value, you simply change the macro definition. All references to it will be changed automatically when the program is recompiled.

EXAMPLES

1. Since a macro substitution is simply a text replacement, you can use a macro name in place of a quoted string. For example, the following program prints **Macro Substitutions are Fun**.

```
#include <stdio.h>

#define FUN "Macro Substitutions are Fun"

int main(void)
{
  printf(FUN);

  return 0;
}
```

To the compiler, the **printf( )** statement looks like this:

```
printf("Macro Substitutions are Fun");
```

2. Once a macro name has been defined, it can be used to help define another macro name. For example, consider this program:

```
#include <stdio.h>

#define SMALL 1
#define MEDIUM SMALL+1
#define LARGE MEDIUM+1

int main(void)
{
  printf("%d %d %d", SMALL, MEDIUM, LARGE);
```

```
   return 0;
}
```

As you might expect, it prints **1 2 3** on the screen.

3. If a macro name appears inside a quoted string, no substitution will take place. For example, given this definition

```
#define ERROR "catastrophic error occurred"
```

the following statement will not be affected.

```
printf("ERROR: Try again");
```

EXERCISES

1. Create a program that defines two macro names, **MAX** and **COUNTBY**. Have the program count from zero to **MAX-1** by whatever value **COUNTBY** is defined as. (Give **COUNTBY** the value 3 for demonstration purposes.)

2. Is this fragment correct?

```
#define MAX MIN+100
#define MIN 10
```

3. Is this fragment correct?

```
#define STR this is a test
   .
   .
   .
printf(STR);
```

4. Is this program correct?

```
#define STDIO <stdio.h>
#include STDIO

int main(void)
{
   printf("This is a test.");

   return 0;
}
```

8.2

*E*XAMINE CHARACTER AND STRING INPUT AND OUTPUT

Although you have already learned how to input and output characters and strings, this section looks at these processes more formally.

The ANSI C standard defines these two functions that perform character input and output, respectively:

```
int getchar(void);
int putchar(int ch);
```

They both use the header file STDIO.H. As mentioned earlier in this book, many compilers implement **getchar( )** in a line-buffered manner, which makes its use limited in an interactive environment. Most compilers contain a non-standard function called **getche( )**, which operates like **getchar( )**, except that it is interactive. Discussion of **getche( )** and other non-standard functions will occur in a later section.

The **getchar( )** function returns the next character typed on the keyboard. This character is read as an **unsigned char** converted to an **int**. However, most commonly, your program will assign this value to a **char** variable, even though **getchar( )** is declared as returning an **int**. If you do this, the high-order byte(s) of the integer is simply discarded.

The reason that **getchar( )** returns an integer is that when an error occurs while reading input, **getchar( )** returns the macro **EOF**, which is a negative integer (usually –1). The **EOF** macro, defined in STDIO.H, stands for end-of-file. Since **EOF** is an integer value, to allow it to be returned, **getchar( )** must return an integer. In the vast majority of circumstances, if an error occurs when reading from the keyboard, it means that the computer has ceased to function. Therefore, most programmers don't usually bother checking for **EOF** when using **getchar( )**. They just assume a valid character has been returned. Of course, there are circumstances in which this is not appropriate—for example, when I/O is redirected, as explained in Chapter 9. But most of the time you will not need to worry about **getchar( )** encountering an error.

The **putchar( )** function outputs a single character to the screen. Although its parameter is declared to be of type **int**, this value is converted into an **unsigned char** by the function. Thus, only the low-order byte of *ch* is actually displayed. If the output operation is successful, **putchar( )** returns the character written. If an output error occurs, **EOF** is returned. For reasons similar to those given for **getchar( )**, if output to the screen fails, the computer has probably crashed anyway, so most programmers don't bother checking the return value of **putchar( )** for errors.

The reason you might want to use **putchar( )** rather than **printf( )** with the **%c** specifier to output a character is that **putchar( )** is faster and more efficient. Because **printf( )** is more powerful and flexible, a call to **printf( )** generates greater overhead than a call to **putchar( )**.

EXAMPLES

1. As stated earlier, **getchar( )** is generally implemented using line buffering. When input is line buffered, no characters are actually passed back to the calling program until the user presses ENTER. The following program demonstrates this:

```
#include <stdio.h>

int main(void)
{
  char ch;
  do {
    ch = getchar();
    putchar('.');
  } while(ch != '\n');

  return 0;
}
```

Instead of printing a period between each character, what you will see on the screen is all the letters you typed before pressing ENTER, followed by a string of periods.

One other point: When entering characters using **getchar( )**, pressing ENTER will cause the newline character (**\n**) to be returned. However, when using one of the alternative non-standard functions, pressing ENTER will cause the carriage return character (**\r**) to be returned. Keep this difference in mind.

2. The following program illustrates the fact that you can use C's backslash character constants with **putchar( )**.

```
#include <stdio.h>

int main(void)
{
  putchar('A');
  putchar('\n');
  putchar('B');

  return 0;
}
```

This program displays

```
A
B
```

on the screen.

1. Rewrite the program shown in the first example so that it checks for errors on both input and output operations.

2. What is wrong with this fragment?

```
char str[80] = "this is a test";
  .
  .
  .
putchar(str);
```

8.3 EXAMINE SOME NON-STANDARD CONSOLE FUNCTIONS

Because character input using **getchar( )** is usually line-buffered, many compilers supply additional input routines that provide interactive character input. You have already been introduced to one of these: **getche( )**. Here is its prototype and that of its close relative **getch( )**:

```
int getche(void);
int getch(void);
```

Both functions use the header file CONIO.H. The **getche( )** function waits until the next keystroke is entered at the keyboard. When a key is pressed, **getche( )** echoes it to the screen and then immediately returns the character. The character is read as an **unsigned char** and elevated to **int**. However, your routines can simply assign this value to a **char** value. The **getch( )** function is the same as **getche( )**, except that the keystroke is not echoed to the screen.

Another very useful non-ANSI-standard function commonly supplied with a C compiler is **kbhit( )**. It has this prototype:

```
int kbhit(void);
```

The **kbhit( )** function also requires the header file CONIO.H. This function is used to determine whether a key has been pressed or not. If the user has pressed a key, this function returns true (nonzero), but does not read the character. If a keystroke is waiting, you may read it with **getche( )** or **getch( )**. If no keystroke is pending, **kbhit( )** returns false (zero).

For some compilers, the non-standard I/O functions such as **getche( )** are not compatible with the standard I/O functions such as **printf( )** or **scanf( )**. When this is the case, mixing the two can cause unusual program behavior. Most troubles caused by this incompatibility occur when inputting information (although problems could occur on output). If the standard and non-standard I/O functions are not compatible in your compiler, you may need to use non-standard versions of **scanf( )** and/or **printf( )**, too. These are called **cprintf( )** and **cscanf( )**.

The **cprintf( )** function works like **printf( )** except that it does not translate the newline character (**\n**) into the carriage return, linefeed pair as does the **printf( )** function. Therefore, it is necessary to explicitly output the carriage return (**\r**) where desired. The **cscanf( )** function works like the **scanf( )** function. Both **cprintf( )** and **cscanf( )** use the CONIO.H header file. The **cprintf( )** and **cscanf( )** functions are expressly designed to be compatible with **getch( )** and **getche( )**, as well as other non-standard I/O functions.

*Microsoft C++ supports the functions just described. In addition, it provides alternative names for the functions that begin with an underscore. For example, when using Visual C++, you can specify **getche( )** as **_getche( )**, too.*

One last point: Even for compilers that have incompatibilities between the standard and non-standard I/O functions, such incompatibilities sometimes only apply in one case and not another. If you encounter a problem, just try substituting a different function.

EXAMPLES

1. The **getch( )** function lets you take greater control of the screen because you can determine what is displayed each time a key is struck. For example, this program reads characters until a 'q' is typed. All characters are displayed in uppercase using the **cprintf( )** function.

```
#include <stdio.h>
#include <conio.h>
#include <ctype.h>

int main(void)
{
  char ch;

  do {
    ch = getch();
    cprintf("%c", toupper(ch));
  } while(ch != 'q');

  return 0;
}
```

2. The **kbhit( )** function is very useful when you want to let a user interrupt a routine without actually forcing the user to continually respond to a prompt like "Continue?". For example, this program prints a 5-percent sales-tax table in increments of 20 cents. The program continues to print the table until either the user strikes a key or the maximum value is printed.

```
#include <stdio.h>
#include <conio.h>

int main(void)
{
  double amount;
```

```
amount = 0.20;

cprintf("Printing 5-percent tax table\n\r");
cprintf("Press a key to stop.\n\n\r");
do {
  cprintf("amount: %f, tax: %f\n\r", amount,
          amount*0.05);
  if(kbhit()) break;
  amount = amount + 0.20;
} while(amount < 100.0);

return 0;
}
```

In the calls to **cprintf( )**, notice how both the carriage return (**\r**) and the newline (**\n**) must be output. As explained, **cprintf( )** does not automatically convert newlines into carriage return, linefeed pairs.

EXERCISES

1. Write a program that displays the ASCII code of each character typed. Do not display the actual character, however.

2. Write a program that prints periods on the screen until you press a key.

8.4 ***T*AKE A CLOSER LOOK AT gets( ) AND puts( )**

Although both **gets( )** and **puts( )** were introduced earlier, let's take a closer look at them now. Their function prototypes are

```
char *gets(char *str);
int puts(char *str);
```

These functions use the header file STDIO.H. The **gets( )** function reads characters entered at the keyboard until a carriage return is read (i.e., until the user presses ENTER). It stores the characters in the array pointed to by *str*. The carriage return is not added to the string. Instead, it is converted into the null terminator. If successful, **gets( )** returns a pointer to the start of *str*. If an error occurs, a null pointer is returned.

The **puts( )** function outputs the string pointed to by *str* to the screen. It automatically appends a carriage return, line-feed sequence. If successful, **puts( )** returns a non-negative value. If an error occurs, **EOF** is returned.

The main reason you may want to use **puts( )** instead of **printf( )** to output a string is that **puts( )** is much smaller and faster. While this is not important in the example programs shown in this book, it may be in some applications.

EXAMPLES

1. This program shows how you can use the return value of **gets( )** to access the string holding the input information. Notice that this program also confirms that no error has occurred before attempting to use the string.

```
#include <stdio.h>

int main(void)
{
  char *p, str[80];

  printf("Enter a string: ");
  p = gets(str);
  if(p) /* if not null */
    printf("%s %s", p, str);

  return 0;
}
```

2. If you simply want to make sure that **gets( )** did not encounter an error before proceeding, you can place **gets( )** directly inside an **if** statement, as illustrated by the following program:

```
#include <stdio.h>

int main(void)
{
  char str[80];
```

```
      printf("Enter a string: ");
      if(gets(str))   /* if not null */
        printf("Here is your string: %s", str);

      return 0;
    }
```

Because a null pointer is false, there is no need for the intermediary variable **p**, and the **gets( )** statement can be put directly inside the **if**.

3. It is important to understand that even though **gets( )** returns a pointer to the start of the string, it still must be called with a pointer to an actual array. For example, the following is wrong:

```
char *p;

p = gets(p); /* wrong!!! */
```

Here, there is no array defined into which **gets( )** can put the string. This will result in a program failure.

4. This program outputs the words **one**, **two**, and **three** on three separate lines, using **puts( )**.

```
#include <stdio.h>

int main(void)
{
  puts("one");
  puts("two");
  puts("three");

  return 0;
}
```

EXERCISES

1. Compile the program shown in Example 2, above. Note the size of the compiled code. Next, convert it so that it uses **printf( )** statements, instead of **puts( )**. You will find that the **printf( )** version is several bytes larger.

2. Is this program correct? If not, why not?

```
#include <stdio.h>

int main(void)
{
  char *p, *q;

  printf("Enter a string: ");
  p = gets(q);
  printf(p);

  return 0;
}
```

*M*ASTER printf( )

Although you already know many things about **printf( )**, you will be surprised by how many more features it has. In this section you will learn about some more of them. To begin, let's review what you know so far.

The **printf( )** function has this prototype:

int printf(char *control-string, ...);

The periods indicate a variable-length argument list. The **printf( )** function returns the number of characters output. If an error occurs, it returns a negative number. Frankly, few programmers bother with the return value of **printf( )** because, as mentioned earlier, if the console is not working, the computer is probably not functional anyway.

The control string may contain two types of items: characters to be output and format specifiers. All format specifiers begin with **%**. A *format specifier*, also referred to as a *format code*, determines how its matching argument will be displayed. Format specifiers and their arguments are matched from left to right, and there must be as many arguments as there are specifiers.

The format specifiers accepted by **printf( )** are shown in Table 8-1. You have already learned about the **%c**, **%d**, **%s**, **%u**, **%p**, and **%f** specifiers. The others will be examined now.

Code	Format
%c	Character
%d	Signed decimal integers
%i	Signed decimal integers
%e	Scientific notation (lowercase 'e')
%E	Scientific notation (uppercase 'E')
%f	Decimal floating point
%g	Uses %e or %f, whichever is shorter
%G	Uses %E or %f, whichever is shorter
%o	Unsigned octal
%s	String of characters
%u	Unsigned decimal integers
%x	Unsigned hexadecimal (lowercase letters)
%X	Unsigned hexadecimal (uppercase letters)
%p	Displays a pointer
%n	The associated argument is a pointer to an integer into which the number of characters written so far is placed.
%%	Prints a % sign

TABLE 8-1   *The* **printf( )** *Format Specifiers* ▼

The **%i** command is the same as **%d** and is redundant.

You can display numbers of type **float** or **double** using scientific notation by using either **%e** or **%E**. The only difference between the two is that **%e** uses a lowercase 'e' and **%E** uses an uppercase 'E'. These specifiers may have the **L** modifier applied to them to allow them to display values of type **long double**.

The **%g** and **%G** specifiers cause output to be in either normal or scientific notation, depending upon which is shorter. The difference between the **%g** and the **%G** is whether a lower- or uppercase 'e' is used in cases where scientific notation is shorter. These specifiers may have the **L** modifier applied to them to allow them to display values of type **long double**.

You can display an integer in octal format using **%o** or in hexadecimal using **%x** or **%X**. Using **%x** causes the letters 'a' through 'f' to be displayed in lowercase. Using **%X** causes them to be displayed in uppercase. These specifiers may have the **h** and **l** modifiers applied to allow them to display **short** and **long** data types, respectively.

The argument that matches the **%n** specifier must be a pointer to an integer. When the **%n** is encountered, **printf( )** assigns the integer pointed to by the associated argument the number of characters output so far.

Since all format commands begin with a percent sign, you must use **%%** to output a percent sign.

All but the **%%**, **%p**, and **%c** specifiers may have a minimum-field-width specifier and/or a precision specifier associated with them. Both of these are integer quantities. If the item to output is shorter than the specified minimum field width, the output is padded with spaces, so that it equals the minimum width. However, if the output is longer than the minimum, output is *not* truncated. The minimum-field-width specifier is placed after the **%** sign and before the format specifier.

The precision specifier follows the minimum-field-width specifier. The two are separated by a period. The precision specifier affects different types of format specifiers differently. If it is applied to the **%d**, **%i**, **%o**, **%u** or **%x** specifiers, it determines how many digits are to be shown. Leading zeros are added if needed. When applied to **%f**, **%e**, or **%E**, it determines how many digits will be displayed after the decimal point. For **%g** or **%G**, it determines the number of significant digits. When applied to the **%s**, it specifies a maximum field width. If a string is longer than the maximum-field-width specifier, it will be truncated.

By default, all numeric output is right justified. To left justify output, put a minus sign directly after the **%** sign.

The general form of a format specifier is shown here. Optional items are shown between brackets.

%[-][*minimum-field-width*][.][*precision*] *format-specifier*

For example, this format specifier tells **printf( )** to output a **double** value using a field width of 15, with 2 digits after the decimal point.

```
%15.2f
```

EXAMPLES

1. If you don't want to specify a minimum field width, you can still specify the precision. Simply put a period in front of the precision value, as illustrated by the following program:

```
#include <stdio.h>

int main(void)
{
  printf("%.5d\n", 10);
  printf("$%.2f\n", 99.95);
  printf("%.10s", "Not all of this will be printed\n");

  return 0;
}
```

The output from this program looks like this:

```
00010
$99.95
Not all of
```

Notice the effect of the precision specifier as applied to each data type.

2. The minimum-field-width specifier is especially useful for creating tables that contain columns of numbers that must line up. For example, this program prints 1000 random numbers in three columns. It uses another of C's standard library functions, **rand( )**, to generate the random numbers. The **rand( )** function returns a random integer value each time it is called. It uses the header STDLIB.H.

```
#include <stdio.h>
#include <stdlib.h>

int main(void)
{
  int i;

  for(i=0; i<1000; i++)
    printf("%10d %10d %10d\n", rand(), rand(), rand());

  return 0;
}
```

Part of the output from this program is shown here. Notice how the columns are aligned. (Remember, if you try the program, you will probably see different numbers.)

```
10982        130        346
 7117      11656       1090
22948       6415      17595
14558       9004      31126
18492      22879       3571
26721       5412       1360
27119      25047      22463
13985       7190      31441
30252      27509      31214
19816      14779      26571
17995      19651      21681
13310       3734      23593
15561      21995       3979
11288      18489      16092
 5892       8664      28466
 5364      22766      13863
20427      21151      17639
 8812      25795        100
12347      12666      15108
```

3. This program prints the value 90 four different ways: decimal, octal, lowercase hexadecimal, and uppercase hexadecimal. It also prints a floating-point number using scientific notation with a lowercase 'e' and an uppercase 'E'.

```c
#include <stdio.h>

int main(void)
{
  printf("%d %o %x %X\n", 90, 90, 90, 90);
  printf("%e %E\n", 99.231, 99.231);

  return 0;
}
```

The output from this program is shown here:

```
90 132 5a 5A
9.92310e+01 9.92310E+01
```

4. The following program demonstrates the **%n** specifier:

```c
#include <stdio.h>

int main(void)
{
```

```
      int i;

      printf("%d %f\n%n", 100, 123.23, &i);
      printf("%d characters output so far", i);

      return 0;
}
```

Its output looks like this:

100 123.230000
15 characters output so far

The fifteenth character is the newline.

1. Write a program that prints a table of numbers, each line consisting of a number, its square, and its cube. Have the table begin at 2 and end at 100. Make the columns line up, and left justify each column.

2. How would you output this line using **printf( )**?

   Clearance price: 40% off as marked

3. Show how to display **1023.03** so that only two decimal places are printed.

8.6   *M*ASTER scanf( )

Like **printf( )**, **scanf( )** has many more features than we have used so far. In this section, several of these additional features are explored. Let's begin by reviewing what you have already learned.

The prototype for **scanf( )** is shown here:

int scanf(char *control-string, ...);

The *control-string* consists mostly of format specifiers. However, it can contain other characters. (You will learn about the effect of other characters in the control string soon.) The format specifiers determine how **scanf( )** reads information into the variables pointed to by the arguments that follow the control string. The specifiers are matched in order, from left to right, with the arguments. There must be as many arguments as there are specifiers. The format specifiers are shown in Table 8-2. As you can see, the **scanf( )** specifiers are very much like the **printf( )** specifiers.

The **scanf( )** function returns the number of fields assigned values. If an error occurs before any assignments are made, **EOF** is returned.

The specifiers **%x** and **%o** are used to read an unsigned integer using hexadecimal and octal number bases, respectively.

The specifiers **%d**, **%i**, **%u**, **%x**, and **%o** may be modified by the **h** when inputting into a **short** variable and by **l** when inputting into a **long** variable.

The specifiers **%e**, **%f**, and **%g** are equivalent. They all read floating-point numbers represented in either scientific notation or standard decimal notation. Unmodified, they input information into a **float** variable. You can modify them using an **l** when inputting into a **double**. To read a **long double**, modify them with an **L**.

You can use **scanf( )** to read a string using the **%s** specifier, but you probably won't want to. Here's why: When **scanf( )** inputs a string, it stops reading that string when the first whitespace character is encountered. A whitespace character is either a space, a tab, or a

Code	Meaning
%c	Read a single character
%d	Read a decimal integer
%i	Read a decimal integer
%e	Read a floating-point number
%f	Read a floating-point number
%g	Read a floating-point number
%o	Read an octal number
%s	Read a string
%x	Read a hexadecimal number
%p	Read a pointer
%n	Receives an integer value equal to the number of characters read so far
%u	Read an unsigned integer
%[ ]	Scan for a set of characters

TABLE 8-2 *The* **scanf( )** *Format Specifiers* ▼

newline. This means that you cannot easily use **scanf( )** to read input like this into a string:

```
this is one string
```

Because there is a space after "this," **scanf( )** will stop inputting the string at that point. This is why **gets( )** is generally used to input strings.

The **%p** specifier inputs a memory address using the format determined by the host environment. The **%n** specifier assigns the number of characters input up to the point the **%n** is encountered to the integer variable pointed to by its matching argument. The **%n** may be modified by either **l** or **h** so that it may assign its value to either a **long** or **short** variable.

A very interesting feature of **scanf( )** is called a *scanset*. A scanset specifier is created by putting a list of characters inside square brackets. For example, here is a scanset specifier containing the letters 'ABC.'

```
%[ABC]
```

When **scanf( )** encounters a scanset, it begins reading input into the character array pointed to by the scanset's matching argument. It will only continue reading characters as long as the next character is part of the scanset. As soon as a character that is not part of the scanset is found, **scanf( )** stops reading input for this specifier and moves on to any others in the control string.

You can specify a range in a scanset using the - (hyphen). For example, this scanset specifies the characters 'A' through 'Z'.

```
%[A-Z]
```

Technically, the use of the hyphen to specify a range is not specified by the ANSI C standard, but it is nearly universally accepted.

When the scanset is very large, sometimes it is easier to specify what is *not* part of a scanset. To do this, precede the set with a ^. For example,

```
%[^0123456789]
```

When **scanf( )** encounters this scanset, it will read any characters *except* the digits 0 through 9.

You can suppress the assignment of a field by putting an asterisk immediately after the **%** sign. This can be very useful when inputting information that contains needless characters. For example, given this **scanf( )** statement

```
int first, second;
scanf("%d%*c%d", &first, &second);
```

this input

```
555-2345
```

will cause **scanf( )** to assign **555** to **first**, discard the **-**, and assign **2345** to **second**. Since the hyphen is not needed, there is no reason to assign it to anything. Hence, no associated argument is supplied.

You can specify a maximum field width for all specifiers except **%c**, for which a field is always one character, and **%n**, to which the concept does not apply. The maximum field width is specified as an unsigned integer, and it immediately precedes the format specifier character. For example, this limits the maximum length of a string assigned to **str** to 20 characters:

```
scanf("%20s", str);
```

If a space appears in the control string, then **scanf( )** will begin reading and discarding whitespace characters until the first non-whitespace character is encountered. If any other character appears in the control string, **scanf( )** reads and discards all matching characters until it reads the first character that does not match that character.

One other point: As **scanf( )** is generally implemented, it line-buffers input in the same way that **getchar( )** often does. While this makes little difference when inputting numbers, its lack of interactivity tends to make **scanf( )** of limited value for other types of input.

EXAMPLES

1. To see the effect of the **%s** specifier, try this program. When prompted, type **this is a test** and press ENTER. You will see only **this** redisplayed on the screen. This is because, when reading strings, **scanf( )** stops when it encounters the first whitespace character.

```
#include <stdio.h>

int main(void)
{
  char str[80];

  /* Enter "this is a test" */
  printf("Enter a string: ");
  scanf("%s", str);
  printf(str);

  return 0;
}
```

2. Here's an example of a scanset that accepts both the upper- and lowercase characters. Try entering some letters, then any other character, and then some more letters. After you press ENTER, only the letters that you entered before pressing the non-letter key will be contained in **str**.

```
#include <stdio.h>

int main(void)
{
  char str[80];

  printf("Enter letters, anything else to stop\n");
  scanf("%[a-zA-Z]", str);

  printf(str);

  return 0;
}
```

3. If you want to read a string containing spaces using **scanf( )**, you can do so using the scanset shown in this slight variation of the previous program.

```
#include <stdio.h>

int main(void)
{
  char str[80];

  printf("Enter letters and spaces\n");
```

```
scanf("%[a-zA-Z ]", str);
printf(str);

return 0;
}
```

You could also specify punctuation symbols and digits, so that you can read virtually any type of string. However, this is a fairly cumbersome way of doing things.

4. This program lets the user enter a number followed by an operator followed by a second number, such as $12 + 4$. It then performs the specified operation on the two numbers and displays the results.

```
#include <stdio.h>

int main(void)
{
  int i, j;
  char op;

  printf("Enter operation: ");
  scanf("%d%c%d", &i, &op, &j);

  switch(op) {
    case '+': printf("%d", i+j);
      break;
    case '-': printf("%d", i-j);
      break;
    case '/': if(j) printf("%d", i/j);
      break;
    case '*': printf("%d", i*j);
  }

  return 0;
}
```

Notice that the format for entering the information is somewhat restricted because no spaces are allowed between the first number and the operator. It is possible to remove this restriction. As you know, **scanf( )** automatically discards leading whitespace characters except when you use the **%c** specifier. However, since you know that the operator will not be a whitespace character, you can modify the **scanf( )** command to look like this:

```
scanf("%d %c%d", &i, &op, &j);
```

Whenever there is a space in the control string, **scanf( )** will match and discard whitespace characters until the first non-whitespace character is found. This includes matching zero whitespace characters. With this change in place, you can enter the information into the program using one or more spaces between the first number and the operator.

5. This program illustrates the maximum-field-width specifier:

```
#include <stdio.h>

int main(void)
{
  int i, j;

  printf("Enter an integer: ");
  scanf("%3d%d", &i, &j);
  printf("%d %d", i, j);

  return 0;
}
```

If you run this program and enter the number **12345**, **i** will be assigned 123, and **j** will have the value 45. The reason for this is that **scanf( )** is told that **i**'s field is only three characters long. The remainder of the input is then sent to **j**.

6. This program illustrates the effect of having non-whitespace characters in the control string. It allows you to enter a decimal value, but it assigns the digits to the left of the decimal point to one integer and those to the right of the decimal to another. The decimal point between the two **%d** specifiers causes the decimal point in the number to be matched and discarded.

```
#include <stdio.h>

int main(void)
{
  int i, j;

  printf("Enter a decimal number: ");
```

```
scanf("%d.%d", &i, &j);
printf("left part: %d, right part: %d", i, j);

return 0;
}
```

EXERCISES

1. Write a program that prompts for your name and then inputs your first, middle, and last names. Have the program read no more than 20 characters for each part of your name. Finally, have the program redisplay your name.

2. Write a program that reads a floating-point number as a string using a scanset.

3. Is this fragment correct? If not why not?

```
char ch;

scanf("%2c", &ch);
```

4. Write a program that inputs a string, a **double**, and an integer. After these items have been read, have the program display how many characters were input. (Hint: use the **%n** specifier.)

5. Write a program that converts a hexadecimal number entered by the user into its corresponding decimal and octal equivalents.

Mastery Skills Check

Before proceeding you should be able to answer these questions and perform these exercises:

1. What is the difference between **getchar( )**, **getche( )**, and **getch( )**?

2. What is the difference between the **%e** and the **%E printf( )** format specifiers?

3. What is a scanset?

4. Write a program, using **scanf( )**, that inputs your first name, birth date (using the format mm/dd/yy), and telephone number. Redisplay the information on the screen to verify that it was input correctly.

5. What is one advantage to using **puts( )** over **printf( )** when you only need to output a string? What is one disadvantage to **puts( )**?

6. Write a program that defines a macro called **COUNT** as the value 100. Have the program then use this macro to control a **for** loop that displays the numbers 0 through 99.

7. What is **EOF**, and where is it defined?

**Cumulative
Skills Check**

This section checks how well you have integrated the material in this chapter with that from earlier chapters.

1. Write a program that allows you to enter the batting averages for the players on a little league team. (Assume there are exactly 9 players.) Have the user enter the first name and batting average of each player. Use a two-dimensional character array to hold the names and a one-dimensional **double** array to hold the batting averages. Once all the names are entered, have the program report the name and average of the players with the highest and lowest averages. Also, have the program display the team average.

2. Write a program that is a simple electronic library card catalog. Have the program display this menu:

   Card Catalog:
     1. Enter
     2. Search by Author
     3. Search by Title
     4. Quit
   Choose your selection:

If you choose Enter, have the program repeatedly input the name, author, and publisher of a book. Have this process continue until the user enters a blank line for the name of the book.

For searches, prompt the user for the specified author or title and then, if a match is found, display the rest of the information. After you finish this program, keep your file, because in the next chapter you will learn how to save the catalog to a disk file.

9

File I/O

chapter objectives

A LTHOUGH C does not define any keywords that perform file I/O, the C standard library contains a very rich set of I/O functions. As you will see in this chapter, C's approach to I/O is efficient, powerful, and flexible.

Note

Most C compilers supply two complete sets of file I/O functions. One is called the ANSI file system (sometimes called the buffered file system). This file system is defined by the ANSI C standard. The second file system is based on the original UNIX operating environment and is called the UNIX-like file system (sometimes called the unbuffered file system). This file system is not defined by the ANSI C standard. The ANSI standard only defines one file system because the two file systems are redundant. Further, not all environments may be able to adapt to the UNIX-like system. For these reasons, this book only discusses the ANSI file system. For a discussion of the UNIX-like file system, see my book C: The Complete Reference (Berkeley, CA, Osborne/McGraw-Hill).

Review

Skills Check

Before proceeding you should be able to perform these exercises and answer these questions:

1. What is the difference between **getchar( )** and **getche( )**?

2. Give one reason why you probably won't use **scanf( )**'s **%s** option to read strings from the keyboard.

3. Write a program that prints a four-column table of the prime numbers between 2 and 1000. Make sure that the columns are aligned.

4. Write a program that inputs a **double**, a character, and a string not longer than 20 characters. Redisplay the values to confirm that they were input correctly.

5. Write a program that reads and discards leading digits and then reads a string. (Hint: Use a scanset to read past any leading digits.)

9.1 *U*NDERSTAND STREAMS

Before we can begin our discussion of file I/O, you must understand two very important concepts: the *stream* and the *file*. The C I/O system supplies a consistent interface to the programmer, independent of the actual I/O device being used. To accomplish this, C provides a level of abstraction between the programmer and the hardware. This abstraction is called a stream. The actual device providing I/O is called a file. Thus, a stream is a logical interface to a file. As C defines the term file, it can refer to a disk file, the screen, the keyboard, memory, a port, a file on tape, and various other types of I/O devices. The most common form of file is, of course, the disk file. Although files differ in form and capabilities, all streams are the same. The advantage to this approach is that to you, the programmer, one hardware device will look much like any other. The stream automatically handles the differences.

A stream is linked to a file using an *open operation*. A stream is disassociated from a file using a *close operation*.

There are two types of streams: text and binary. A *text stream* contains ASCII characters. When a text stream is being used, some character translations may take place. For example, when the newline character is output, it is usually converted into a carriage return, linefeed pair. For this reason, there may not be a one-to-one correspondence between what is sent to the stream and what is written to the file. A *binary stream* may be used with any type of data. No character translations will occur, and there is a one-to-one correspondence between what is sent to the stream and what is actually contained in the file.

One final concept you need to understand is that of the *current location*. The current location, also referred to as the *current position*, is the location in a file where the next file access will occur. For example, if a file is 100 bytes long and half the file has been read, the next read operation will occur at byte 50, which is the current location.

To summarize: In C, disk I/O (like certain other types of I/O) is performed through a logical interface called a stream. All streams have similar properties, and all are operated on by the same I/O functions, no matter what type of file the stream is associated with. A file is the actual physical entity that receives or supplies the data. Even though files differ, streams do not. (Of course, some devices may not support random-access operations, for example, so their associated streams will not support such operations either.)

Now that you are familiar with the theory behind C's file system, it is time to begin learning about it in practice.

9.2 **M**ASTER FILE-SYSTEM BASICS

In this section you will learn how to open and close a file. You will also learn how to read characters from and write characters to a file.

To open a file and associate it with a stream, use **fopen( )**. Its prototype is shown here:

```
FILE *fopen(char *fname, char *mode);
```

The **fopen( )** function, like all the file-system functions, uses the header STDIO.H. The name of the file to open is pointed to by *fname*. It must be a valid file name, as defined by the operating system. The string pointed to by *mode* determines how the file may be accessed. The legal values for *mode* as defined by the ANSI C standard are shown in Table 9-1. Your compiler may allow additional modes.

If the open operation is successful, **fopen( )** returns a valid file pointer. The type **FILE** is defined in STDIO.H. It is a structure that holds various kinds of information about the file, such as its size, the current location of the file, and its access modes. It essentially identifies the file. (A structure is a group of variables accessed under one name. You will learn about structures in the next chapter, but you do not need to know anything about them to learn and fully use C's file system.) The **fopen( )** function returns a pointer to the structure associated with the file by the open process. You will use this pointer with all other functions that operate on the file. However, you must never alter it or the object it points to.

If the **fopen( )** function fails, it returns a null pointer. The header STDIO.H defines the macro **NULL**, which is defined to be a null pointer. It is very important to ensure that a valid file pointer has been returned. To do so, check the value returned by **fopen( )** to make sure that it is not **NULL**. For example, the proper way to open a file called **myfile** for text input is shown in this fragment:

```
FILE *fp;

if((fp = fopen("myfile", "r")) == NULL) {
  printf("Error opening file.\n");
  exit(1); /* or substitute your own error handler */
}
```

Although most of the file modes are self-explanatory, a few comments are in order. If, when opening a file for read-only operations, the file does not exist, **fopen( )** will fail. When opening a file using append mode, if the file does not exist, it will be created. Further, when a file is opened for append all new data written to the file will be written to the end of the file. The original contents will remain unchanged. If, when a file is opened for writing, the file does not exist, it will be created. If it does exist, the contents of the original file will be destroyed and a new file created. The difference between modes **r +** and **w +** is that **r +** will not create a file if it does not exist; however, **w +** will. Further, if the file already exists, opening it with **w +** destroys its contents; opening it with **r +** does not.

Mode	Meaning
"r"	Open a text file for reading.
"w"	Create a text file for writing.
"a"	Append to a text file.
"rb"	Open a binary file for reading.
"wb"	Create a binary file for writing.
"ab"	Append to a binary file.
"r+"	Open a text file for read/write.
"w+"	Create a text file for read/write.
"a+"	Append or create a text file for read/write.
"r+b"	Open a binary file for read/write. You may also use "rb+".
"w+b"	Create a binary file for read/write. You may also use "wb+".
"a+b"	Append or create a binary file for read/write. You may also use "ab+".

TABLE 9-1   *The Legal Values for Mode*   ▼

To close a file, use **fclose( )**, whose prototype is

int fclose(FILE *fp*);

The **fclose( )** function closes the file associated with *fp*, which must be a valid file pointer previously obtained using **fopen( )**, and disassociates the stream from the file. In order to improve efficiency, most file system implementations write data to disk one sector at a time. Therefore, data is buffered until a sector's worth of information has been output before the buffer is physically written to disk. When you call **fclose( )**, it automatically writes any information remaining in a partially full buffer to disk. This is often referred to as *flushing the buffer*.

You must never call **fclose( )** with an invalid argument. Doing so will damage the file system and possibly cause irretrievable data loss.

The **fclose( )** function returns zero if successful. If an error occurs, **EOF** is returned.

Once a file has been opened, depending upon its mode, you may read and/or write bytes (i.e., characters) using these two functions:

int fgetc(FILE *fp*);

int fputc(int *ch*, FILE *fp*);

The **fgetc( )** function reads the next byte from the file described by *fp* as an **unsigned char** and returns it as an integer. (The character is returned in the low-order byte.) If an error occurs, **fgetc( )** returns **EOF**. As you should recall from Chapter 8, **EOF** is a negative integer (usually –1). The **fgetc( )** function also returns **EOF** when the end of the file is reached. Although **fgetc( )** returns an integer value, your program can assign it to a **char** variable since the low-order byte contains the character read from the file.

The **fputc( )** function writes the byte contained in the low-order byte of *ch* to the file associated with *fp* as an **unsigned char**. Although *ch* is defined as an **int**, you may call it using a **char**, which is the common procedure. The **fputc( )** function returns the character written if successful or **EOF** if an error occurs.

Historical note: The traditional names for **fgetc( )** and **fputc( )** are **getc( )** and **putc( )**. The ANSI C standard still defines these names, and they are essentially interchangeable with **fgetc( )** and **fputc( )**. One reason the new names were added was for consistency. All other ANSI file system function names begin with 'f,' so 'f' was added to

getc( ) and **putc( )**. The ANSI standard still supports the traditional names, however, because there are so many existing programs that use them. If you see programs that use **getc( )** and **putc( )**, don't worry. They are essentially different names for **fgetc( )** and **fputc( )**.

EXAMPLES

1. This program demonstrates the four file-system functions you have learned about so far. First, it opens a file called MYFILE for output. Next, it writes the string "This is a file system test." to the file. Then, it closes the file and reopens it for read operations. Finally, it displays the contents of the file on the screen and closes the file.

```c
#include <stdio.h>
#include <stdlib.h>

int main(void)
{
  char str[80] = "This is a file system test.\n";
  FILE *fp;
  char *p;
  int i;

  /* open myfile for output */
  if((fp = fopen("myfile", "w"))==NULL) {
    printf("Cannot open file.\n");
    exit(1);
  }

  /* write str to disk */
  p = str;
  while(*p) {
    if(fputc(*p, fp)==EOF) {
      printf("Error writing file.\n");
      exit(1);
    }
    p++;
  }
  fclose(fp);
```

```
/* open myfile for input */
if((fp = fopen("myfile", "r"))==NULL) {
  printf("Cannot open file.\n");
  exit(1);
}

/* read back the file */
for(;;) {
    i = fgetc(fp);
    if(i == EOF) break;
    putchar(i);
}
fclose(fp);

return 0;
}
```

In this version, when reading from the file, the return value of
fgetc( ) is assigned to an integer variable called **i**. The value of
this integer is then checked to see if the end of the file has been
reached. For most compilers, however, you can simply assign
the value returned by **fgetc( )** to a **char** and still check for **EOF**,
as is shown in the following version:

```
#include <stdio.h>
#include <stdlib.h>

int main(void)
{
  char str[80] = "This is a file system test.\n";
  FILE *fp;
  char ch, *p;

  /* open myfile for output */
  if((fp = fopen("myfile", "w"))==NULL) {
    printf("Cannot open file.\n");
    exit(1);
  }

  /* write str to disk */
  p = str;
  while(*p) {
    if(fputc(*p, fp)==EOF) {
      printf("Error writing file.\n");
      exit(1);
```

```
    }
    p++ ;
  }
  fclose(fp);

  /* open myfile for input */
  if((fp = fopen("myfile", "r"))==NULL) {
    printf("Cannot open file.\n");
    exit(1);
  }

  /* read back the file */
  for(;;) {
    ch = fgetc(fp);
    if(ch == EOF) break;
    putchar(ch);
  }
  fclose(fp);

  return 0;
}
```

The reason this approach works is that when a **char** is being compared to an **int**, the **char** value is automatically elevated to an equivalent **int** value.

There is, however, an even better way to code this program. For example, there is no need for a separate comparison step because the assignment and the comparison can be performed at the same time, within the **if**, as shown here:

```
#include <stdio.h>
#include <stdlib.h>

int main(void)
{
  char str[80] = "This is a file system test.\n";
  FILE *fp;
  char ch, *p;

  /* open myfile for output */
  if((fp = fopen("myfile", "w"))==NULL) {
    printf("Cannot open file.\n");
    exit(1);
  }
```

```
                        /* write str to disk */
                        p = str;
                        while(*p) {
                          if(fputc(*p, fp)==EOF) {
                            printf("Error writing file.\n");
                            exit(1);
                          }
                          p++ ;
                        }
                        fclose(fp);

                        /* open myfile for input */
                        if((fp = fopen("myfile", "r"))==NULL) {
                          printf("Cannot open file.\n");
                          exit(1);
                        }

                        /* read back the file */
                        for(;;) {
                          if((ch = fgetc(fp)) == EOF) break;
                          putchar(ch);
                        }
                        fclose(fp);

                        return 0;
                      }
```

Don't let the statement

```
if((ch = fgetc(fp)) == EOF) break;
```

fool you. Here's what is happening. First, inside the **if**, the
return value of **fgetc( )** is assigned to **ch**. As you may recall, the
assignment operation in C is an expression. The entire value of
(ch = fgetc(fp)) is equal to the return value of **fgetc( )**.
Therefore, it is this integer value that is tested against **EOF**.

Expanding upon this approach, you will normally see this
program written by a professional C programmer as follows:

```
#include <stdio.h>
#include <stdlib.h>

int main(void)
{
  char str[80] = "This is a file system test.\n";
```

```
FILE *fp;
char ch, *p;

/* open myfile for output */
if((fp = fopen("myfile", "w"))==NULL) {
  printf("Cannot open file.\n");
  exit(1);
}

/* write str to disk */
p = str;
while(*p)
  if(fputc(*p++, fp)==EOF) {
    printf("Error writing file.\n");
    exit(1);
  }

fclose(fp);

/* open myfile for input */
if((fp = fopen("myfile", "r"))==NULL) {
  printf("Cannot open file.\n");
  exit(1);
}

/* read back the file */
while((ch = fgetc(fp)) != EOF) putchar(ch);
fclose(fp);

return 0;
}
```

Notice that now, each character is read, assigned to **ch**, and tested against **EOF**, all within the expression of the **while** loop that controls the input process. If you compare this with the original version, you can see how much more efficient this one is. In fact, the ability to integrate such operations is one reason C is so powerful. It is important that you get used to the kind of approach just shown. Later on in this book we will explore such assignment statements more fully.

2. The following program takes two command-line arguments. The first is the name of a file, the second is a character. The program searches the specified file, looking for the character. If the file

contains at least one of these characters, it reports this fact.
Notice how it uses **argv** to access the file name and the
character for which to search.

```c
/* Search specified file for specified character. */
#include <stdio.h>
#include <stdlib.h>

int main(int argc, char *argv[])
{
  FILE *fp;
  char ch;

  /* see if correct number of command line arguments */
  if(argc!=3) {
    printf("Usage: find <file name> <ch>\n");
    exit(1);
  }

  /* open file for input */
  if((fp = fopen(argv[1], "r"))==NULL) {
    printf("Cannot open file.\n");
    exit(1);
  }

  /* look for character */
  while((ch = fgetc(fp)) != EOF)
    if(ch==*argv[2]) {
      printf("%c found", ch);
      break;
    }
  fclose(fp);

  return 0;
}
```

EXERCISES

1. Write a program that displays the contents of the text file
   specified on the command line.

2. Write a program that reads a text file and counts how many times each letter from 'A' to 'Z' occurs. Have it display the results. (Do not differentiate between upper- and lowercase letters.)

3. Write a program that copies the contents of one text file to another. Have the program accept three command-line arguments. The first is the name of the source file, the second is the name of the destination file, the third is optional. If present and if it equals "watch," have the program display each character as it copies the files; otherwise, do not have the program display any screen output. If the destination file does not exist, create it.

9.3   *U*NDERSTAND feof( ) *AND* ferror( )

As you know, when **fgetc( )** returns **EOF**, either an error has occurred or the end of the file has been reached, but how do you know which event has taken place? Further if you are operating on a binary file, all values are valid. This means it is possible that a byte will have the same value (when elevated to an **int**) as **EOF**, so how do you know if valid data has been returned or if the end of the file has been reached? The solution to these problems are the functions **feof( )** and **ferror( )**, whose prototypes are shown here:

```
int feof(FILE *fp);
```

```
int ferror(FILE *fp);
```

The **feof( )** function returns nonzero if the file associated with *fp* has reached the end of the file. Otherwise it returns zero. This function works for both binary files and text files. The **ferror( )** function returns nonzero if the file associated with *fp* has experienced an error; otherwise, it returns zero.

Using the **feof( )** function, this code fragment shows how to read to the end of a file:

```
FILE *fp;
  .
  .
  .
while(!feof(fp)) ch = fgetc(fp);
```

This code works for any type of file and is better in general than checking for **EOF**. However, it still does not provide any error checking. Error checking is added here:

```
FILE *fp;
 .
 .
 .
while(!feof(fp)) {
  ch = fgetc(fp);
  if(ferror(fp)) {
    printf("File Error\n");
    break;
  }
}
```

Keep in mind that **ferror( )** only reports the status of the file system relative to the last file access. Therefore, to provide the fullest error checking, you must call it after each file operation.

The most damaging file errors occur at the operating-system level. Frequently, it is the operating system that intercepts these errors and displays its own error messages. For example, if a bad sector is found on the disk, most operating systems will, themselves, stop the execution of the program and report the error. Often the only types of errors that actually get passed back to your program are those caused by mistakes on your part, such as accessing a file in a way inconsistent with the mode used to open it or when you cause an out-of-range condition. Usually these types of errors can be trapped by checking the return type of the other file system functions rather than by calling **ferror( )**. For this reason, you will frequently see examples of C code in which there are relatively few (if any) calls to **ferror( )**. One last point: Not all of the file system examples in this book will provide full error checking, mostly in the interest of keeping the programs short and easy to understand. However, if you are writing programs for actual use, you should pay special attention to error checking.

EXAMPLES

1. This program copies any type of file, binary or text. It takes two command-line arguments. The first is the name of the source file, the second is the name of the destination file. If the destination file does not exist, it is created. It includes full error checking. (You might want to compare this version with the copy program you wrote for text files in the preceding section.)

```c
/* Copy a file. */
#include <stdio.h>
#include <stdlib.h>

int main(int argc, char *argv[])
{
  FILE *from, *to;
  char ch;

  /* see if correct number of command line arguments */
  if(argc!=3) {
    printf("Usage: copy <source> <destination>\n");
    exit(1);
  }

  /* open source file */
  if((from = fopen(argv[1], "rb"))==NULL) {
    printf("Cannot open source file.\n");
    exit(1);
  }

  /* open destination file */
  if((to = fopen(argv[2], "wb"))==NULL) {
    printf("Cannot open destination file.\n");
    exit(1);
  }

  /* copy the file */
```

```
   while(!feof(from)) {
     ch = fgetc(from);
     if(ferror(from)) {
       printf("Error reading source file.\n");
       exit(1);
     }
     if(!feof(from)) fputc(ch, to);
     if(ferror(to)) {
       printf("Error writing destination file.\n");
       exit(1);
     }
   }

   if(fclose(from)==EOF) {
     printf("Error closing source file.\n");
     exit(1);
   }

   if(fclose(to)==EOF) {
     printf("Error closing destination file.\n");
     exit(1);
   }

   return 0;
}
```

2. This program compares the two files whose names are specified on the command line. It either prints **Files are the same**, or it displays the byte of the first mismatch. It also uses full error checking.

```
/* Compare files. */
#include <stdio.h>
#include <stdlib.h>

int main(int argc, char *argv[])
{
  FILE *fp1, *fp2;
  char ch1, ch2, same;
  unsigned long l;

  /* see if correct number of command line arguments */
  if(argc!=3) {
    printf("Usage: compare <file 1> <file 2>\n");
    exit(1);
```

```
}

/* open first file */
if((fp1 = fopen(argv[1], "rb"))==NULL) {
  printf("Cannot open first file.\n");
  exit(1);
}

/* open second file */
if((fp2 = fopen(argv [2], "rb"))==NULL) {
  printf("Cannot open second file.\n");
  exit(1);
}

l = 0;
same = 1;
/* compare the files */
while(!feof(fp1)) {
  ch1 = fgetc(fp1);
  if(ferror(fp1)) {
    printf("Error reading first file.\n");
    exit(1);
  }
  ch2 = fgetc(fp2);
  if(ferror(fp2)) {
    printf("Error reading second file.\n");
    exit(1);
  }
  if(ch1!=ch2) {
    printf("Files differ at byte number %lu", l);
    same = 0;
    break;
  }
  l++;
}
if(same) printf("Files are the same.\n");

if(fclose(fp1)==EOF) {
  printf("Error closing first file.\n");
  exit(1);
}

if(fclose(fp2)==EOF) {
  printf("Error closing second file.\n");
  exit(1);
```

```
          }

          return 0;
      }
```

1. Write a program that counts the number of bytes in a file (text or binary) and displays the result. Have the user specify the file to count on the command line.

2. Write a program that exchanges the contents of the two files whose names are specified on the command line. That is, given two files called FILE1 and FILE2, after the program has run, FILE1 will contain the contents that originally were in FILE2, and FILE2 will contain FILE1's original contents. (Hint: Use a temporary file to aid in the exchange process.)

9.4 *L*EARN SOME HIGHER-LEVEL TEXT FUNCTIONS

When working with text files, C provides four functions that make file operations easier. The first two are called **fputs( )** and **fgets( )**, which write a string to and read a string from a file, respectively. Their prototypes are

int fputs(char *str, FILE *fp);

char *fgets(char *str, int num, FILE *fp);

The **fputs( )** function writes the string pointed to by str to the file associated with fp. It returns **EOF** if an error occurs and a non-negative value if successful. The null that terminates str is not written. Also, unlike its related function **puts( )** it does not automatically append a carriage return, linefeed pair.

The **fgets( )** function reads characters from the file associated with *fp* into the string pointed to by *str* until *num*–1 characters have been read, a newline character is encountered, or the end of the file is reached. In any case, the string is null-terminated. Unlike its related function **gets( )**, the newline character is retained. The function returns *str* if successful and a null pointer if an error occurs.

The C file system contains two very powerful functions similar to two you already know. They are **fprintf( )** and **fscanf( )**. These functions operate exactly like **printf( )** and **scanf( )** except that they work with files. Their prototypes are:

```
int fprintf(FILE *fp, char *control-string, ...);

int fscanf(FILE *fp, char *control-string, ...);
```

Instead of directing their I/O operations to the console, these functions operate on the file specified by *fp*. Otherwise their operations are the same as their console-based relatives. The advantage to **fprintf( )** and **fscanf( )** is that they make it very easy to write a wide variety of data to a file using a text format.

EXAMPLES

1. This program demonstrates **fputs( )** and **fgets( )**. It reads lines entered by the user and writes them to the file specified on the command line. When the user enters a blank line, the input phase terminates, and the file is closed. Next, the file is reopened for input, and the program uses **fgets( )** to display the contents of the file.

```c
#include <stdio.h>
#include <stdlib.h>
#include <string.h>

int main(int argc, char *argv[])
{
  FILE *fp;
  char str[80];

  /* check for command line arg */
```

```
if(argc!=2) {
  printf("Specify file name.\n");
  exit(1);
}

/* open file for output */
if((fp = fopen(argv[1], "w"))==NULL) {
  printf("Cannot open file.\n");
  exit(1);
}

printf("Enter a blank line to stop.\n");
do {
  printf(": ");
  gets(str);
  strcat(str, "\n"); /* add newline */
  if(*str != '\n') fputs(str, fp);
} while(*str != '\n');
fclose(fp);

/* open file for input */
if((fp = fopen(argv[1], "r"))==NULL) {
  printf("Cannot open file.\n");
  exit(1);
}

/* read back the file */
do {
  fgets(str, 79, fp);
  if(!feof(fp)) printf(str);
} while(!feof(fp));
fclose(fp);

return 0;
}
```

2. This program demonstrates **fprintf( )** and **fscanf( )**. It first writes a **double**, an **int**, and a string to the file specified on the command line. Next, it reads them back and displays their values as verification. If you examine the file created by this program, you will see that it contains human-readable text. This

is because **fprintf( )** writes to a disk file what **printf( )** would write to the screen. No internal data formats are used.

```c
#include <stdio.h>
#include <stdlib.h>
#include <string.h>

int main(int argc, char *argv[])
{
  FILE *fp;
  double ld;
  int d;
  char str[80];

  /* check for command line arg */
  if(argc!=2) {
    printf("Specify file name.\n");
    exit(1);
  }

  /* open file for output */
  if((fp = fopen(argv[1], "w"))==NULL) {
    printf("Cannot open file.\n");
    exit(1);
  }

  fprintf(fp, "%f %d %s", 12345.342, 1908, "hello");
  fclose(fp);

  /* open file for input */
  if((fp = fopen(argv[1], "r"))==NULL) {
    printf("Cannot open file.\n");
    exit(1);
  }

  fscanf(fp, "%lf%d%s", &ld, &d, str);
  printf("%f %d %s", ld, d, str);
  fclose(fp);

  return 0;
}
```

1. In Chapter 6 you wrote a very simple telephone-directory program. Write a program that expands on this concept by allowing the directory to be saved to a disk file. Have the program present a menu that looks like this:

   1. Enter the names and numbers
   2. Find numbers
   3. Save directory to disk
   4. Load directory from disk
   5. Quit

   The program should be capable of storing 100 names and numbers. (Use only first names if you like.) Use **fprintf( )** to save the directory to disk and **fscanf( )** to read it back into memory.

2. Write a program that uses **fgets( )** to display the contents of a text file, one screenful at a time. After each screen is displayed, have the program prompt the user for more.

3. Write a program that copies a text file. Specify both the source and destination file names on the command line. Use **fgets( )** and **fputs( )** to copy the file. Include full error checking.

9.5 *L*EARN TO READ AND WRITE BINARY DATA

As useful and convenient as **fprintf( )** and **fscanf( )** are, they are not necessarily the most efficient way to read and write numeric data. The reason for this is that both functions perform conversions on the data. For example, when you output a number using **fprintf( )** the number is converted from its binary format into ASCII text. Conversely, when you read a number using **fscanf( )**, it must be converted back into its binary representation. For many applications, this conversion time will not be meaningful; for others, it will be a severe limitation. Further, for some types of data, a file created by **fprintf( )** will also be larger than one that contains a mirror image of the data using its binary format. For these reasons, the C file system includes two important functions: **fread( )** and **fwrite( )**. These functions can read and write any type of data, using its binary representation. Their prototypes are

size_t fread(void *buffer, size_t size, size_t num, FILE *fp);

size_t fwrite(void *buffer, size_t size, size_t num, FILE *fp);

As you can see, these prototypes introduce some unfamiliar elements. However, before discussing them, a brief description of each function is necessary.

The **fread( )** function reads from the file associated with *fp, num* number of objects, each object *size* bytes long, into the buffer pointed to by *buffer*. It returns the number of objects actually read. If this value is less than *num*, either the end of the file has been encountered or an error has occurred. You can use **feof( )** or **ferror( )** to find out which.

The **fwrite( )** function is the opposite of **fread( )**. It writes to the file associated with *fp, num* number of objects, each object *size* bytes long, from the buffer pointed to by *buffer*. It returns the number of objects written. This value will be less than *num* only if an output error has occurred.

Before looking at any examples, let's examine the new concepts introduced by the functions' prototypes.

The first concept is that of the **void** pointer. A **void** pointer is a pointer that can point to any type of data without the use of a type cast. This is generally referred to as a *generic pointer*. In C, **void** pointers are used for two primary purposes. First, as illustrated by **fread( )** and **fwrite( )**, they are a way for a function to receive a pointer to any type of data without causing a type mismatch error. As stated earlier, **fread( )** and **fwrite( )** can be used to read or write any type of data. Therefore, the functions must be capable of receiving any sort of data pointed to by *buffer*. **void** pointers make this possible. A second purpose they serve is to allow a function to return a generic pointer. You will see an example of this later in this book.

The second new item is the type **size_t**. This type is defined in the STDIO.H header file. (You will learn how to define types later in this book.) A variable of this type is defined by the ANSI C standard as being able to hold a value equal to the size of the largest object supported by the compiler. For our purposes, you can think of **size_t** as being the same as **unsigned** or **unsigned long**. The reason that **size_t** is used instead of its equivalent built-in type is to allow C compilers running in different environments to accommodate the needs and confines of those environments.

When using **fread( )** or **fwrite( )** to input or output binary data, the file must be opened for binary operations. Forgetting this can cause hard-to-find problems.

To understand the operation of **fread( )** and **fwrite( )**, let's begin with a simple example. The following program writes an integer to a file called MYFILE using its internal, binary representation and then reads it back. (The program assumes that integers are 2 bytes long.)

```c
#include <stdio.h>
#include <stdlib.h>

int main(void)
{
  FILE *fp;
  int i;

  /* open file for output */
  if((fp = fopen("myfile", "wb"))==NULL) {
    printf("Cannot open file.\n");
    exit(1);
  }

  i = 100;

  if(fwrite(&i, 2, 1, fp) != 1) {
    printf("Write error occurred.\n");
    exit(1);
  }
  fclose(fp);

  /* open file for input */
  if((fp = fopen("myfile", "rb"))==NULL) {
    printf("Cannot open file.\n");
    exit(1);
  }

  if(fread(&i, 2, 1, fp) != 1) {
    printf("Read error occurred.\n");
    exit(1);
  }
  printf("i is %d", i);
  fclose(fp);
```

```
    return 0;
}
```

Notice how error checking is easily performed in this program by simply comparing the number of items written or read with that requested. In some situations, however, you will still need to use **feof( ) or ferror( )** to determine if the end of the file has been reached or if an error has occurred.

One thing wrong with the preceding example is that an assumption about the size of an integer has been made and this size is hardcoded into the program. Therefore, the program will not work properly with compilers that use 4-byte integers, for example. More generally, the size of many types of data changes between systems or is difficult to determine manually. For this reason, C includes the keyword **sizeof**, which is a compile-time operator that returns the size, in bytes, of a data type or variable. It takes the general forms

sizeof(*type*)

or

sizeof *var_name*;

For example, if **float**s are four bytes long and **f** is a **float** variable, both of the following expressions evaluate to 4:

```
sizeof f
sizeof(float)
```

When using **sizeof** with a type, the type must be enclosed between parentheses. No parentheses are needed when using a variable name, although the use of parentheses in this context is not an error.

By using **sizeof**, not only do you save yourself the drudgery of computing the size of some object by hand, but you also ensure the portability of your code to new environments. An improved version of the preceding program is shown here, using **sizeof**.

```
#include <stdio.h>
#include <stdlib.h>

int main(void)
{
  FILE *fp;
```

```
int i;

/* open file for output */
if((fp = fopen("myfile", "wb"))==NULL) {
  printf("Cannot open file.\n");
  exit(1);
}

i = 100;

if(fwrite(&i, sizeof(int), 1, fp) != 1) {
  printf("Write error occurred.\n");
  exit(1);
}
fclose(fp);

/* open file for input */
if((fp = fopen("myfile", "rb"))==NULL) {
  printf("Cannot open file.\n");
  exit(1);
}

if(fread(&i, sizeof i, 1, fp) != 1) {
  printf("Read error occurred.\n");
  exit(1);
}
printf("i is %d",i);
fclose(fp);

return 0;
}
```

EXAMPLES

1. This program fills a ten-element array with floating-point numbers, writes them to a file, and then reads them back. This program writes each element of the array separately. Because binary data is being written using its internal format, the file must be opened for binary I/O operations.

```
#include <stdio.h>
#include <stdlib.h>
```

```
double d[10] = {
  10.23, 19.87, 1002.23, 12.9, 0.897,
  11.45, 75.34, 0.0, 1.01, 875.875
};

int main(void)
{
  int i;
  FILE *fp;

  if((fp = fopen("myfile", "wb"))==NULL) {
    printf("Cannot open file.\n");
    exit(1);
  }

  for(i=0; i<10; i++)
    if(fwrite(&d[i], sizeof(double), 1, fp) != 1) {
      printf("Write error.\n");
      exit(1);
    }
  fclose(fp);

  if((fp = fopen("myfile", "rb"))==NULL) {
    printf("Cannot open file.\n");
    exit(1);
  }

  /* clear the array */
  for(i=0; i<10; i++) d[i] = -1.0;

  for(i=0; i<10; i++)
    if(fread(&d[i], sizeof(double), 1, fp) != 1) {
      printf("Read error.\n");
      exit(1);
    }
  fclose(fp);

  /* display the array */
  for(i=0; i<10; i++) printf("%f ", d[i]);

  return 0;
}
```

The array is cleared between the write and read operations only to "prove" that it is being filled by the **fread( )** statement.

2. The following program does the same thing as the first, but here only one call to **fwrite( )** and **fread( )** is used because the entire array is written in one step, which is much more efficient. This example helps illustrate how powerful these functions are.

```c
#include <stdio.h>
#include <stdlib.h>

double d[10] = {
  10.23, 19.87, 1002.23, 12.9, 0.897,
  11.45, 75.34, 0.0, 1.01, 875.875
};

int main(void)
{
  int i;
  FILE *fp;

  if((fp = fopen("myfile", "wb"))==NULL) {
    printf("Cannot open file.\n");
    exit(1);
  }

  /* write the entire array in one step */
  if(fwrite(d, sizeof d, 1, fp) != 1) {
    printf("Write error.\n");
    exit(1);
  }
  fclose(fp);

  if((fp = fopen("myfile", "rb"))==NULL) {
    printf("Cannot open file.\n");
    exit(1);
  }

  /* clear the array */
  for(i=0; i<10; i++) d[i] = -1.0;

  /* read the entire array in one step */
  if(fread(d, sizeof d, 1, fp) != 1) {
    printf("Read error.\n");
```

```
    exit(1);
  }
  fclose(fp);

  /* display the array */
  for(i=0; i<10; i++) printf("%f ", d[i]);

  return 0;
}
```

EXERCISES

1. Write a program that allows a user to input as many **double** values as desired (up to 32,767) and writes them to a disk file as they are entered. Call this file VALUES. Keep a count of the number of values entered, and write this number to a file called COUNT.

2. Using the file you created in Exercise 1, write a program that first reads the number of items in VALUES from COUNT. Next, read the values in VALUES and display them.

9.6   *U*NDERSTAND RANDOM ACCESS

So far, the examples have either written or read a file sequentially from its beginning to its end. However, using another of C's file system functions, you can access any point in a file at any time. The function that lets you do this is called **fseek( )**, and its prototype is

int fseek(FILE *fp, long offset, int origin);

Here, *fp* is associated with the file being accessed. The value of *offset* determines the number of bytes from *origin* to make the new current position. *origin* must be one of these macros, shown here with their meanings:

Origin	Meaning
SEEK_SET	Seek from start of file
SEEK_CUR	Seek from current location
SEEK_END	Seek from end of file

These macros are defined in STDIO.H. For example, if you wanted to set the current location 100 bytes from the start of the file, then *origin* will be **SEEK_SET** and *offset* will be 100.

The **fseek( )** function returns zero when successful and nonzero if a failure occurs. In most implementations, you may seek past the end of the file, but you may never seek to a point before the start of the file.

You can determine the current location of a file using **ftell( )**, another of C's file system functions. Its prototype is

long ftell(FILE *fp);

It returns the location of the current position of the file associated with *fp*. If a failure occurs, it returns –1.

In general, you will want to use random access only on binary files. The reason for this is simple. Because text files may have character translations performed on them, there may not be a direct correspondence between what is in the file and the byte to which it would appear that you want to seek. The only time you should use **fseek( )** with a text file is when seeking to a position previously determined by **ftell( )**, using **SEEK_SET** as the origin.

Remember one important point: Even a file that contains only text can be opened as a binary file, if you like. There is no inherent restriction about random access on files containing text. The restriction applies only to files opened *as* text files.

EXAMPLES

1. The following program uses **fseek( )** to report the value of any byte within the file specified on the command line.

```
#include <stdio.h>
#include <stdlib.h>

int main(int argc, char *argv[])
{
  long loc;
  FILE *fp;

  /* see if file name is specified */
  if(argc!=2) {
    printf("File name missing.\n");
    exit(1);
  }

  if((fp = fopen(argv[1] , "rb"))==NULL) {
    printf("Cannot open file.\n");
    exit(1);
  }

  printf("Enter byte to seek to: ");
  scanf("%ld", &loc);
  if(fseek(fp, loc, SEEK_SET)) {
    printf("Seek error.\n");
    exit(1);
  }

  printf("Value at loc %ld is %d", loc, getc(fp));
  fclose(fp);

  return 0;
}
```

2. The following program uses **ftell( )** and **fseek( )** to copy the contents of one file into another in reverse order. Pay special attention to how the end of the input file is found. Since the program has sought to the end of the file, the program backs up one byte so that the current location of the file associated with **in** is at the last actual character in the file.

```
/* Copy a file in reverse order */
#include <stdio.h>
#include <stdlib.h>

int main(int argc, char *argv[])
{
```

```
    long loc;
    FILE *in, *out;
    char ch;

    /* see if correct number of command line arguments */
    if(argc!=3) {
      printf("Usage: revcopy <source> <destination>.\n");
      exit(1);
    }

    if((in = fopen(argv[1], "rb"))==NULL) {
      printf("Cannot open input file.\n");
      exit(1);
    }
    if((out = fopen(argv[2], "wb"))==NULL) {
      printf("Cannot open output file.\n");
      exit(1);
    }

    /* find end of source file */
    fseek(in, 0L, SEEK_END);
    loc = ftell(in);

    /* copy file in reverse order */
    loc = loc-1; /* back up past end-of-file mark */
    while(loc >= 0L) {
      fseek(in, loc, SEEK_SET);
      ch = fgetc(in);
      fputc(ch, out);
      loc--;
    }
    fclose(in);
    fclose(out);

    return 0;
}
```

3. This program writes ten **double** values to disk. It then asks you which one you want to see. This example shows how you can randomly access data of any type. You simply need to multiply the size of the base data type by its index in the file.

```
#include <stdio.h>
#include <stdlib.h>
```

```c
double d[10] = {
  10.23, 19.87, 1002.23, 12.9, 0.897,
  11.45, 75.34, 0.0, 1.01, 875.875
};

int main(void)
{
  long loc;
  double value;
  FILE *fp;

  if((fp = fopen("myfile", "wb"))==NULL) {
    printf("Cannot open file.\n");
    exit(1);
  }

  /* write the entire array in one step */
  if(fwrite(d, sizeof d, 1, fp) != 1) {
    printf("Write error.\n");
    exit(1);
  }
  fclose(fp);

  if((fp = fopen("myfile", "rb"))==NULL) {
    printf("Cannot open file.\n");
    exit(1);
  }

  printf("Which element? ");
  scanf("%ld", &loc);
  if(fseek(fp, loc*sizeof(double), SEEK_SET)) {
    printf("Seek error.\n");
    exit(1);
  }

  fread(&value, sizeof(double), 1, fp);
  printf("Element %ld is %f", loc, value);

  fclose(fp);

  return 0;
}
```

EXERCISES

1. Write a program that uses **fseek( )** to display every other byte in a text file. (Remember, you must open the text file as a binary file in order for **fseek( )** to work properly.) Have the user specify the file on the command line.

2. Write a program that searches a file, specified on the command line, for a specific integer value (also specified on the command line). If this value is found, have the program display its location, in bytes, relative to the start of the file.

9.7 *LEARN ABOUT VARIOUS FILE-SYSTEM FUNCTIONS*

You can rename a file using **rename( )**, shown here:

    int rename(char *oldname, char *newname);

Here, *oldname* points to the original name of the file and *newname* points to its new name. The function returns zero if successful and nonzero if an error occurs.

You can erase a file using **remove( )**. Its prototype is

    int remove(char *file-name);

This function will erase the file whose name matches that pointed to by *file-name*. It returns zero if successful and nonzero if an error occurs.

You can position a file's current location to the start of the file using **rewind( )**. Its prototype is

    void rewind(FILE *fp);

It rewinds the file associated with *fp*. The **rewind( )** function has no return value, because any file that has been successfully opened can be rewound.

Although seldom necessary because of the way C's file system works, you can cause a file's disk buffer to be flushed using **fflush( )**. Its prototype is

```
int fflush(FILE *fp);
```

It flushes the buffer of the file associated with *fp*. The function returns zero if successful, **EOF** if a failure occurs. If you call **fflush( )** using a **NULL** for *fp*, all existing disk buffers are flushed.

EXAMPLES

1. This program demonstrates **remove( )**. It prompts the user for the file to erase and also provides a safety check in case the user entered the wrong name.

```c
#include <stdio.h>
#include <stdlib.h>
#include <ctype.h>

int main(void)
{
  char fname[80];

  printf("Enter name of file to erase: ");
  gets(fname);
  printf("Are you sure? (Y/N) ");
  if(toupper(getchar())=='Y') remove(fname);

  return 0;
}
```

2. The following program demonstrates **rewind( )** by displaying the contents of the file specified on the command line twice.

```c
#include <stdio.h>
#include <stdlib.h>

int main(int argc, char *argv[])
```

```
    {
      FILE *fp;

      /* see if file name is specified */
      if(argc!=2) {
        printf("File name missing.\n");
        exit(1);
      }

      if((fp = fopen(argv[1], "r"))==NULL) {
        printf("Cannot open file.\n");
        exit(1);
      }

      /* show it once */
      while(!feof(fp))
        putchar(getc(fp));

      rewind(fp);

      /* show it twice */
      while(!feof(fp))
        putchar(getc(fp));

      fclose(fp);

      return 0;
    }
```

3. This fragment causes the buffer associated with **fp** to be flushed to disk.

```
    FILE *fp;
      .
      .
      .
    fflush(fp);
```

4. This program renames a file called MYFILE.TXT to YOURFILE.TXT.

```
    #include <stdio.h>

    int main(void)
    {
      if(rename("myfile.txt", "yourfile.txt"))
```

```
      printf("Rename failed.\n");
    else
      printf("Rename successful.\n");

    return 0;
}
```

1. Improve the erase program so that it notifies the user if he or she tries to remove a nonexistent file.

2. On your own, think of ways that **rewind( )** and **fflush( )** could be useful in real applications.

9.8 *L EARN ABOUT THE STANDARD STREAMS*

When a C program begins execution, three streams are automatically opened and available for use. These streams are called *standard input* (**stdin**), *standard output* (**stdout**), and *standard error* (**stderr**). By default, they refer to the console, but in environments that support redirectable I/O, they can be redirected by the operating system to some other device.

Normally, **stdin** inputs from the keyboard; **stdout** and **stderr** write to the screen. These standard streams are **FILE** pointers and may be used with any function that requires a variable of type **FILE** *. For example, you can use **fprintf( )** to print formatted output to the screen by specifying **stdout** as its output stream. The following two statements are functionally the same:

```
fprintf(stdout, "%d %c %s", 100, 'c', "this is a string");
printf("%d %c %s", 100, 'c', "this is a string");
```

In actuality, C makes little distinction between console I/O and file I/O. As just shown, it is possible to perform console I/O using several of the file-system functions. Although it may come as a bit of a surprise, it is also possible to perform disk file I/O using console I/O functions, such as **printf( )**. Here's why.

All of the functions described in Chapter 8 and referred to as "console I/O functions" are actually special-case file-system functions that automatically operate on **stdin** and **stdout**. Thus, the console I/O functions are just conveniences for you, the programmer. As far as C is concerned, the console is simply another hardware device. You don't actually need the console functions to access the console. Any file-system function can access it. (Of course, non-standard I/O functions like **getche( )** are differentiated from the standard file-system functions and do, in fact, operate only on the console.) In environments that allow redirection of I/O, **stdin** and **stdout** could refer to devices other than the keyboard and screen. Since the console functions operate on **stdin** and **stdout**, if these streams are redirected, the "console" functions can be made to operate on other devices. For example, by redirecting the **stdout** to a disk file, you can use a "console" I/O function to write to a disk file.

One important point: **stdin**, **stdout**, and **stderr** are not variables. They may not be assigned a value using **fopen( )**, nor should you attempt to close them using **fclose( )**. These streams are maintained internally by the compiler. You are free to use them, but not to change them.

EXAMPLES

1. Consider this program:

```
#include <stdio.h>

int main(void)
{
  printf("This is an example of redirection.\n");

  return 0;
}
```

Assume that this program is called TEST. If you execute TEST normally, it displays the string on the screen. However, if an environment supports redirection of I/O, **stdout** can be redirected to a file. For example, in a DOS, OS/2, Windows, or UNIX environment, executing TEST like this

```
TEST > OUTPUT
```

causes the output of TEST to be written to a file called OUTPUT. You might want to try this now for yourself.

2. Input can also be redirected. For example, consider the following program:

```
#include <stdio.h>

int main(void)
{
  int i;

  scanf("%d", &i);
  printf("%d", i);

  return 0;
}
```

Assuming it is called TEST, executing it as

```
TEST < INPUT
```

causes **stdin** to be directed to the file called INPUT. Assuming that INPUT contained the ASCII representation for an integer, the value of this integer will be read from the file and printed on the screen.

3. As mentioned earlier in this book, when using **gets( )** it is possible to overrun the array that is being used to receive the characters entered by the user because **gets( )** provides no bounds checking. One way around this problem is to use **fgets( )**, specifying **stdin** for the input stream. Since **fgets( )** requires you to specify a maximum length, it is possible to prevent an array overrun. The only trouble is that **fgets( )** does not remove the newline character and **gets( )** does. This means that you will have to manually remove it, as shown in the following program:

```
#include <stdio.h>
#include <string.h>
```

```
int main(void)
{
  char str[10];
  int i;

  printf("Enter a string: ");
  fgets(str, 10, stdin);

  /* remove newline, if present */
  i = strlen(str)-1;
  if(str[i]=='\n') str[i] = '\0';

  printf("This is your string: %s", str);

  return 0;
}
```

EXERCISES

1. Write a program that copies the contents of one text file to another. However, use only "console" I/O functions and redirection to accomplish the file copy.

2. On your own, experiment using **fgets( )** to read strings entered from the keyboard.

**Mastery
Skills Check**

Before continuing, you should be able to answer these questions and complete these exercises:

1. Write a program that displays the contents of a text file (specified on the command line), one line at a time. After each line is displayed, ask the user if he or she wants to see another line.

2. Write a program that copies a text file. Have the user specify both file names on the command line. Have the copy program convert all lowercase letters into uppercase ones.

3. What do **fprintf( )** and **fscanf( )** do?

4. Write a program that uses **fwrite( )** to write 100 randomly generated integers to a file called RAND.

5. Write a program that uses **fread( )** to display the integers stored in the file called RAND, created in Exercise 4.

6. Using the file called RAND, write a program that uses **fseek( )** to allow the user to access and display the value of any integer in the file.

7. How do the "console" I/O functions relate to the file system?

**Cumulative
Skills Check**

This section checks how well you have integrated the material in this chapter with that from earlier chapters.

1. Enhance the card-catalog program you wrote in Chapter 8 so that it stores its information in a disk file called CATALOG. When the program begins, have it read the catalog into memory. Also, add an option to save the information to disk.

2. Write a program that copies a file. Have the user specify both the source and destination files on the command line. Have the program remove tab characters, substituting the appropriate number of spaces.

3. On your own, create a small database to keep track of anything you desire—your CD collection, for example.

10

Structures and Unions

chapter objectives

I N this chapter you will learn about two of C's most important user-defined types: the structure and the union.

Review
Skills Check

Before proceeding you should be able to answer these questions and perform these exercises:

1. Write a program that copies a file. Have the user specify both the source and destination file names on the command line. Include full error checking.

2. Write a program using **fprintf( )** to create a file that contains this information:

   ```
   this is a string 1230.23 1FFF A
   ```

   Use a string, a **double**, a hexadecimal integer, and character format specifiers and values.

3. Write a program that contains a 20-element integer array. Initialize the array so that it contains the numbers 1 through 20. Using only one **fwrite( )** statement, save this array to a file called TEMP.

4. Write a program that reads the TEMP file created in Exercise 3 into an integer array using only one **fread( )** statement. Display the contents of the array.

5. What are **stdin**, **stdout**, and **stderr**?

6. How do functions like **printf( )** and **scanf( )** relate to the C file system?

<hr>

10.1 ◼ _M_ _ASTER STRUCTURE BASICS_

A *structure* is an *aggregate* (or *conglomerate*) data type that is composed of two or more related variables called *members*. Unlike an array in which each element is of the same type, each member of a structure can have its own type, which may differ from the types of the other members. Structures are defined in C using this general form:

struct *tag-name* {
  type member1;
  type member2;
  type member3;

  .

  .

  .

  type memberN;
} *variable-list;*

The keyword **struct** tells the compiler that a structure type is being defined. Each *type* is a valid C type. The *tag-name* is essentially the type name of the structure, and the *variable-list* is where actual instances of the structure are declared. Either the *tag-name* or the *variable-list* is optional, but one must be present (you will see why shortly). The members of a structure are also commonly referred to as *fields* or *elements*. This book will use these terms interchangeably.

Generally, the information contained in a structure is logically related. For example, you might use a structure to hold a person's address. Another structure might be used to support an inventory program in which each item's name, retail and wholesale cost, and the quantity on hand are stored. The structure shown here defines fields that can hold card-catalog information:

```
struct catalog  {
   char name[40];    /* author name */
   char title[40];   /* title */
   char pub[40];      /* publisher */
   unsigned date;     /* copyright date */
   unsigned char ed; /* edition */
} card;
```

Here, **catalog** is the type name of the structure. It is not the name of a variable. The only variable defined by this fragment is **card**. It is important to understand that a structure declaration defines only a logical entity, which is a new data type. It is not until variables of that type are declared than an object of that type actually exists. Thus, **catalog** is a logical template; **card** has physical reality. Figure 10-1

name	40 bytes
title	40 bytes
pub	40 bytes
date	2 bytes
ed	1 byte

shows how this structure will appear in memory (using 2-byte integers).

To access a member of a structure, you must specify both the structure variable name and the member name, separated by a period. For example, using **card**, the following statement assigns the **date** field the value 1776:

```
card.date = 1776;
```

C programmers often refer to the period as the *dot operator*. To print the copyright date, you can use a statement such as:

```
printf("Copyright date: %u", card.date);
```

To input the date, use a **scanf( )** statement such as:

```
scanf("%u", &card.date);
```

Notice that the **&** goes before the structure name, not before the member name. In a similar fashion, these statements input the author's name and output the title:

```
gets(card.name);
printf("%s", card.title);
```

To access an individual character in the **title** field, simply index **title**. For example, the following statement prints the third letter:

```
printf("%c", card.title[2]);
```

Once you have defined a structure type, you can create additional variables of that type using this general form:

struct *tag_name var_list*;

Assuming, for example, that **catalog** has been defined as shown earlier in this section, this statement declares three variables of type **struct catalog**:

```
struct catalog var1, var2, var3;
```

This is why it is not necessary to declare any variables when the structure type is defined. You can declare them separately, as needed.

A key concept to understand is that each instance of a structure contains its own copy of the members of the structure. For example, given the preceding declaration, the **title** field of **var1** is completely separate from the **title** field of **var2**. In fact, the only relationship that **var1**, **var2**, and **var3** have with one another is that they are all variables of the same type of structure. There is no other linkage among the three.

If you know you only need a fixed number of structure variables, you do not need to specify the tag name. For example, this code creates two structure variables, but the structure itself is unnamed:

```
struct {
  int a;
  char ch;
} var1, var2;
```

In actual practice, however, you will usually want to specify the tag name.

Structures can be arrayed in the same fashion as other data types. For example, the following structure definition creates a 100-element array of structures of type **catalog**:

```
struct catalog cat[100];
```

To access an individual structure of the array, you must index the array name. For example, the following accesses the first structure:

```
cat[0]
```

To access a member within a specified structure, follow the index with a period and the name of the member you want. For example, the following statement loads the **ed** field of structure 33 with the value of 2:

```
cat[33].ed = 2;
```

Structures may be passed as parameters to functions just like any other type of value. A function may also return a structure.

You may assign the contents of one instance of a structure to another as long as they are both of the same type. For example, this fragment is perfectly valid:

```
struct s_type {
  int a;
  float f;
} var1, var2;

var1.a = 10;
var1.f = 100.23;

var2 = var1;
```

After this fragment executes, **var2** will contain exactly the same thing as **var1**.

EXAMPLES

1. This program demonstrates some ways to access structure members:

```
#include <stdio.h>

struct s_type {
  int i;
  char ch;
  double d;
  char str[80];
} s;

int main(void)
{
  printf("Enter an integer: ");
  scanf("%d:", &s.i);
  printf("Enter a character: ");
  scanf(" %c", &s.ch);
  printf("Enter a floating point number: ");
  scanf("%lf", &s.d);
  printf("Enter a string: ");
```

```
   scanf("%s", s.str);

   printf("%d %c %f %s", s.i, s.ch, s.d, s.str);

   return 0;
}
```

2. When you need to know the size of a structure, you should use
   the **sizeof** compile-time operator. Do not try to manually add up
   the number of bytes in each field. There are three good reasons
   for this. First, as you learned in the preceding chapter, using
   sizeof ensures that your code is portable to different
   environments. Second, in some situations, the compiler may
   need to align certain types of data on even word boundaries. In
   this case, the size of the structure will be larger than the sum of
   its individual elements. Finally, for computers based on the
   8086 family of CPUs (such as the 80486 or the Pentium), there
   are several different ways the compiler can organize memory.
   Some of these ways cause pointers to take up twice the space
   they do when memory is arranged differently.

   When using **sizeof** with a structure type, you must precede
   the tag name with the keyword **struct**, as shown in this program:

```
#include <stdio.h>

struct s_type {
  int i;
  char ch;
  int *p;
  double d;
} s;

int main(void)
{
  printf("s_type is %d bytes long", sizeof(struct s_type));

  return 0;
}
```

3. To see how useful arrays of structures are, examine an
   improved version of the card-catalog program developed in the
   preceding two chapters. Notice how using a structure makes it
   easier to organize the information about each book. Also notice

how the entire structure array is written and read from disk in a single operation.

```c
/* An electronic card catalog. */
#include <stdio.h>
#include <string.h>
#include <stdlib.h>

#define MAX 100

int menu(void);
void display(int i);
void author_search(void);
void title_search(void);
void enter(void);
void save(void);
void load(void);

struct catalog {
  char name[80];      /* author name */
  char title[80];     /* title */
  char pub[80];       /* publisher */
  unsigned date;      /* copyright date */
  unsigned char ed;   /* edition */
} cat[MAX];

int top = 0; /* last location used */

int main(void)
{
  int choice;

  load(); /* read in catalog */

  do {
    choice = menu();
    switch(choice) {
      case 1: enter(); /* enter books */
        break;
      case 2: author_search(); /* search by author */
        break;
      case 3: title_search(); /* search by title */
        break;
      case 4: save();
    }
```

```
  } while(choice!=5);

  return 0;
}

/* Return a menu selection. */
menu(void)
{
  int i;
  char str[80];

  printf("Card catalog:\n");
  printf("  1. Enter\n");
  printf("  2. Search by Author\n");
  printf("  3. Search by Title\n");
  printf("  4. Save catalog\n");
  printf("  5. Quit\n");

  do {
    printf("Choose your selection: ");
    gets(str);
    i = atoi(str);
    printf("\n");
  } while(i<1 || i>5);

  return i;
}

/* Enter books into database. */
void enter(void)
{
  int i;
  char temp[80];

  for(i=top; i<MAX; i++) {
    printf("Enter author name (ENTER to quit): ");
    gets(cat[i].name);
    if(!*cat[i].name) break;
    printf("Enter title: ");
    gets(cat[i].title);
    printf("Enter publisher: ");
    gets(cat[i].pub);
    printf("Enter copyright date: ");
    gets(temp);
    cat[i].date = (unsigned) atoi(temp);
```

```c
      printf("Enter edition: ");
      gets(temp);
      cat[i].ed = (unsigned char) atoi(temp);
    }
  top = i;
}

/* Search by author. */
void author_search(void)
{
  char name[80];
  int i, found;

  printf("Name: ");
  gets(name);

  found = 0;
  for(i=0; i<top; i++)
    if(!strcmp(name, cat[i].name)) {
      display(i);
      found = 1;
      printf("\n");
    }

  if(!found) printf("Not Found\n");
}

/* Search by title. */
void title_search(void)
{
  char title[80];
  int i, found;

  printf("Title: ");
  gets(title);

  found = 0;
  for(i=0; i<top; i++)
    if(!strcmp(title, cat[i].title)) {
      display(i);
      found = 1;
      printf("\n");
    }
  if(!found) printf("Not Found\n");
}
```

```
/* Display catalog entry. */
void display(int i)
{
  printf("%s\n", cat[i].title);
  printf("by %s\n", cat[i].name);
  printf("Published by %s\n", cat[i].pub);
  printf("Copyright: %u, %u edition\n", cat[i].date,
         cat[i].ed);
}

/* Load the catalog file. */
void load(void)
{
  FILE *fp;

  if((fp = fopen("catalog", "rb"))==NULL) {
    printf("Catalog file not on disk.\n");
    return;
  }

  if(fread(&top, sizeof top, 1, fp) != 1) {  /* read count */
    printf("Error reading count.\n");
    exit(1);
  }
  if(fread(cat, sizeof cat, 1, fp) != 1) { /* read data */
    printf("Error reading catalog data.\n");
    exit(1);

  }

  fclose(fp);
}

/* Save the catalog file. */
void save(void)
{
  FILE *fp;

  if((fp = fopen("catalog", "wb"))==NULL) {
    printf("Cannot open catalog file.\n");
    exit(1);
  }
```

```
      if(fwrite(&top, sizeof top, 1, fp) != 1) {  /* write count */
        printf("Error writing count.\n");
        exit(1);
      }
      if(fwrite(cat, sizeof cat, 1, fp) != 1) { /* write data */
        printf("Error writing catalog data.\n");
        exit(1);
      }

      fclose(fp);
    }
```

4. In the preceding example, the entire catalog array is stored on disk, even if the array is not full. If you like, you can change the **load( )** and **save( )** routines as follows, so that only structures actually holding data are stored on disk:

```
/* Load the catalog file. */
void load(void)
{
  FILE *fp;
  int i;

  if((fp = fopen("catalog", "rb"))==NULL) {
    printf("Catalog file not on disk.\n");
    return;
  }

  if(fread(&top, sizeof top, 1, fp) != 1) {  /* read count */
    printf("Error reading count.\n");
    exit(1);
  }
  for(i=0; i<=top; i++) /* read data */
    if(fread(&cat[i], sizeof(struct catalog), 1, fp)!= 1) {
      printf("Error reading catalog data.\n");
      exit(1);
    }

  fclose(fp);
}
```

```
/* Save the catalog file. */
void save(void)
{
  FILE *fp;
  int i;

  if((fp = fopen("catalog", "wb"))==NULL) {
    printf("Cannot open catalog file.\n");
    exit(1);
  }

  if(fwrite(&top, sizeof top, 1, fp) != 1) {  /* write count */
    printf("Error writing count.\n");
    exit(1);
  }
  for(i=0; i<=top; i++) /* write data */
    if(fwrite(&cat[i], sizeof(struct catalog), 1, fp)!= 1) {
      printf("Error writing catalog data.\n");
      exit(1);
    }

  fclose(fp);
}
```

5. The names of structure members will not conflict with other variables using the same names. Because the member name is linked with the structure name, it is separate from other variables of the same name. For example, this program prints **10 100 101** on the screen.

```
#include <stdio.h>

int main(void)
{
  struct s_type {
    int i;
    int j;
  } s;

  int i;

  i = 10;
```

```
        s.i = 100;
        s.j = 101;

        printf("%d %d %d", i, s.i, s.j);

        return 0;
}
```

The variable **i** and the structure member **i** have no relationship to each other.

6. As stated earlier, a function may return a structure to the calling procedure. The following program, for example, loads the members of **var1** with the values **100** and **123.23** and then displays them on the screen:

```
#include <stdio.h>

struct s_type {
  int i;
  double d;
};

struct s_type f(void);

int main(void)
{
  struct s_type var1;

  var1 = f();
  printf("%d %f", var1.i, var1.d);

  return 0;
}

struct s_type f(void)
{
  struct s_type temp;

  temp.i = 100;
  temp.d = 123.23;

  return temp;
}
```

7. This program passes a structure to a function:

```
#include <stdio.h>

struct s_type {
  int i;
  double d;
};

void f(struct s_type temp);

int main(void)
{
  struct s_type var1;

  var1.i = 99;
  var1.d = 98.6;
  f(var1);

  return 0;
}

void f(struct s_type temp)
{
  printf("%d %f", temp.i, temp.d);
}
```

EXERCISES

1. In Chapter 9, you wrote a program that created a telephone directory that was stored on disk. Improve the program so that it uses an array of structures, each containing a person's name, area code, and telephone number. Store the area code as an integer. Store the name and telephone number as strings. Make the array **MAX** elements long, where **MAX** is any convenient value that you choose.

2. What is wrong with this fragment?

```
struct s_type {
  int i;
```

```
    long l;
    char str[80];
} s;
    .

    .

    .

i = 10;
```

3. On your own, examine the header file STDIO.H and look at how the **FILE** structure is defined.

 ## ECLARE POINTERS TO STRUCTURES

It is very common to access a structure through a pointer. You declare a pointer to a structure in the same way that you declare a pointer to any other type of variable. For example, the following fragment defines a structure called **s_type** and declares two variables. The first, **s**, is an actual structure variable. The second, **p**, is a pointer to structures of type **s_type**.

```
struct s_type {
  int i;
  char str[80];
} s, *p;
```

Given this definition, the following statement assigns to **p** the address of **s**:

```
p = &s:
```

Now that **p** points to **s** you can access **s** through **p**. However, to access an individual element of **s** using **p** you cannot use the dot operator. Instead, you must use the *arrow operator*, as shown in the following example:

```
p->i = 1;
```

This statement assigns the value 1 to element **i** of **s** through **p**. The arrow operator is formed using a minus sign followed by a greater-than sign. There must be no spaces between the two.

   C passes structures to functions in their entirety. However, if the structure is very large, the passing of a structure can cause a considerable reduction in a program's execution speed. For this reason, when working with large structures, you might want to pass a pointer to a structure in situations that allow it instead of passing the structure itself.

When accessing a member using a structure variable, use the dot operator. When accessing a member using a pointer, use the arrow operator.

EXAMPLES

1. The following program illustrates how to use a pointer to a structure:

```
#include <stdio.h>
#include <string.h>

struct s_type {
  int i;
  char str[80];
} s, *p;

int main(void)
{
  p = &s;

  s.i = 10;  /* this is functionally the same */
  p->i = 10; /* as this */
  strcpy(p->str, "I like structures.");

  printf("%d %d %s", s.i, p->i, p->str);

  return 0;
}
```

2. One very useful application of structure pointers is found in C's time and date functions. Several of these functions use a pointer to the current time and date of the system. The time and date functions require the header file TIME.H, in which a structure called **tm** is defined. This structure can hold the date and time broken down into its elements. This is called the *broken-down time*. The **tm** structure is defined as follows:

```
struct tm {
    int tm_sec;   /* seconds, 0-61 */
    int tm_min;   /* minutes, 0-59; */
    int tm_hour;  /* hours, 0-23 */
    int tm_mday;  /* day of the month, 1-31*/;
    int tm_mon;   /* months since Jan, 0-11 */
    int tm_year;  /* years from 1900 */
    int tm_wday;  /* days since Sunday, 0-6*/
    int tm_yday;  /* days since Jan 1,  0-365 */
    int tm_isdst; /* Daylight Saving Time indicator */
};
```

The value of **tm_isdst** will be positive if Daylight Saving Time is in effect, zero if it is not in effect, and negative if there is no information available. Also defined in TIME.H is the type **time_t**. It is essentially a **long** integer capable of representing the time and date of the system in an encoded implementation-specific internal format. This is referred to as the *calendar time*. To obtain the calendar time of the system, you must use the **time( )** function, whose prototype is:

time_t time(time_t *systime) ;

The **time( )** function returns the encoded calendar time of the system or –1 if no system time is available. It also places this encoded form of the time into the variable pointed to by *systime*. However, if *systime* is null, the argument is ignored.

Since the calendar time is represented using an implementation-specified internal format, you must use another of C's time and date functions to convert it into a form that is easier to use. One of these functions is called **localtime( )**. Its prototype is

struct tm *localtime(time_t *systime) ;

The **localtime( )** function returns a pointer to the broken-down form of *systime*. The structure that holds the broken-down time is internally allocated by the compiler and will be overwritten by each subsequent call.

This program demonstrates **time( )** and **localtime( )** by displaying the current time of the system:

```
#include <stdio.h>
#include <time.h>

int main(void)
{
  struct tm *systime;
  time_t t;

  t = time(NULL);
  systime = localtime(&t);

  printf("Time is %.2d:%.2d:%.2d\n", systime->tm_hour,
         systime->tm_min, systime->tm_sec);
  printf("Date: %.2d/%.2d/%.2d", systime->tm_mon+1,
         systime->tm_mday, systime->tm_year);

  return 0;
}
```

Here is sample output produced by this program:

```
Time is 10:32:49
Date: 03/15/97
```

EXERCISES

1. Is this program fragment correct?

```
struct s_type {
  int a;
  int b;
} s, *p
```

```
int main(void)
{
  p = &s;

  p.a = 100;
  .
  .
  .
```

2. Another of C's time and date functions is called **gmtime( )**. Its prototype is

    struct tm *gmtime(time_t **time*);

    The **gmtime( )** function works exactly like **localtime( )**, except that it returns the Coordinated Universal Time (which is, essentially, Greenwich Mean Time) of the system. Change the program in Example 2 so that it displays both local time and Coordinated Universal Time. (Note: Coordinated Universal Time may not be available on your system.)

10.3   **W**ORK WITH NESTED STRUCTURES

So far, we have only been working with structures whose members consist solely of C's basic types. However, members can also be other structures. These are referred to as *nested structures*. Here is an example that uses nested structures to hold information on the performance of two assembly lines, each with ten workers:

```
#define NUM_ON_LINE 10

struct worker {
  char name[80];
  int avg_units_per_hour;
  int avg_errs_per_hour;
};

struct asm_line {
  int product_code;
  double material_cost;
```

```
   struct worker wkers[NUM_ON_LINE];
} line1, line2;
```

To assign the value 12 to the **avg_units_per_hour** of the second **wkers** structure of **line1**, use this statement:

```
line1.wkers[1].avg_units_per_hour = 12;
```

As you see, the structures are accessed from the outer to the inner. This is also the general case. Whenever you have nested structures, you begin with the outermost and end with the innermost.

EXAMPLE

1. A nested structure can be used to improve the card catalog program. Here, the mechanical information about each book is stored in its own structure, which, in turn, is part of the **catalog** structure. The entire catalog program using this approach is shown here. Notice how the program now stores the length of the book in pages.

```c
/* An electronic card catalog--3rd Improvement. */
#include <stdio.h>
#include <string.h>
#include <stdlib.h>

#define MAX 100

int menu(void);
void display(int i);
void author_search(void);
void title_search(void);
void enter(void);
void save(void);
void load(void);

struct book_type {
  unsigned date;    /* copyright date */
  unsigned char ed; /* edition */
  unsigned pages;   /* length of book */
} ;
```

```
struct catalog {
  char name[80];  /* author name */
  char title[80]; /* title */
  char pub[80];   /* publisher */
  struct book_type book; /* mechanical info */
} cat[MAX];

int top = 0; /* last location used */

int main(void)
{
  int choice;

  load(); /* read in catalog */

  do {
    choice = menu();
    switch(choice) {
      case 1: enter(); /* enter books */
        break;
      case 2: author_search(); /* search by author */
        break;
      case 3: title_search(); /* search by title */
        break;
      case 4: save();
    }
  } while(choice!=5);

  return 0;
}

/* Return a menu selection. */
menu(void)
{
  int i;
  char str[80];

  printf("Card catalog:\n");
  printf("  1. Enter\n");
  printf("  2. Search by Author\n");
  printf("  3. Search by Title\n");
  printf("  4. Save catalog\n");
  printf("  5. Quit\n");

  do {
```

```
      printf("Choose your selection: ");
      gets(str);
      i = atoi(str);
      printf("\n");
   } while(i<1 || i>5);

   return i;
}

/* Enter books into database. */
void enter(void)
{
   int i;
   char temp[80];

   for(i=top; i<MAX; i++) {
     printf("Enter author name (ENTER to quit): ");
     gets(cat[i].name);
     if(!*cat[i].name) break;
     printf("Enter title: ");
     gets(cat[i].title);
     printf("Enter publisher: ");
     gets(cat[i].pub);
     printf("Enter copyright date: ");
     gets(temp);
     cat[i].book.date = (unsigned) atoi(temp);
     printf("Enter edition: ");
     gets(temp);
     cat[i].book.ed = (unsigned char) atoi(temp);
     printf("Enter number of pages: ");
     gets(temp);
     cat[i].book.pages = (unsigned) atoi(temp);
   }
   top = i;
}

/* Search by author. */
void author_search(void)
{
   char name[80];
   int i, found;

   printf("Name: ");
   gets(name);
```

```
  found = 0;
  for(i=0; i<top; i++)
    if(!strcmp(name, cat[i].name)) {
    display(i);
    found = 1;
    printf("\n");
  }

  if(!found) printf("Not Found\n");
}

/* Search by title. */
void title_search(void)
{
  char title[80];
  int i, found;

  printf("Title: ");
  gets(title);

  found = 0;

  for(i=0; i<top; i++)
    if(!strcmp(title, cat[i].title)) {
      display(i);
      found = 1;
      printf("\n");
    }
  if(!found) printf("Not Found\n");
}

/* Display catalog entry. */
void display(int i)
{
  printf("%s\n", cat[i].title);
  printf("by %s\n", cat[i].name);
  printf("Published by %s\n", cat[i].pub);
  printf("Copyright: %u, edition: %u\n",
         cat[i].book.date, cat[i].book.ed);
  printf("Pages: %u\n", cat[i].book.pages);
}

/* Load the catalog file. */
```

```c
void load(void)
{
  FILE *fp;

  if((fp = fopen("catalog", "rb"))==NULL) {
    printf("Catalog file not on disk.\n");

    return;
  }

  if(fread(&top, sizeof top, 1, fp) != 1) {  /* read count */
    printf("Error reading count.\n");
    exit(1);
  }
  if(fread(cat, sizeof cat, 1, fp) != 1) { /* read data */
    printf("Error reading catalog data.\n");
    exit(1);
  }

  fclose(fp);
}

/* Save the catalog file. */
void save(void)
{
  FILE *fp;

  if((fp = fopen("catalog", "wb"))==NULL) {
    printf("Cannot open catalog file.\n");
    exit(1);
  }

  if(fwrite(&top, sizeof top, 1, fp) != 1) {  /* write count */
    printf("Error writing count.\n");
    exit(1);
  }
  if(fwrite(cat, sizeof cat, 1, fp) != 1) { /* write data */
    printf("Error writing catalog data.\n");
    exit(1);
```

```
        }

        fclose(fp);
    }
```

---

1. Improve the telephone-directory program you wrote earlier in this chapter so that it includes each person's mailing address. Store the address in its own structure, called **address**, which is nested inside the directory structure.

10.4 *U*NDERSTAND BIT-FIELDS

C allows a variation on a structure member called a *bit-field*. A *bit-field* is composed of one or more bits. Using a bit-field, you can access by name one or more bits within a byte or word. To define a bit-field, use this general form:

type name : size;

Here, *type* is either **int** or **unsigned**. If you specify a signed bit-field, then the high-order bit is treated as a sign bit, if possible. The number of bits in the field is specified by *size*. Notice that a colon separates the name of the bit-field from its size in bits.

Bit-fields are useful when you want to pack information into the smallest possible space. For example, here is a structure that uses bit-fields to hold inventory information.

```
struct b_type {
    unsigned department: 3;   /* up to 7 departments */
    unsigned instock: 1;      /* 1 if in stock, 0 if out */
    unsigned backordered: 1;  /* 1 if backordered, 0 if not */
```

```
  unsigned lead_time: 3;    /* order lead time in months */
} inv[MAX_ITEM];
```

In this case one byte can be used to store information on an inventory item that would normally have taken four bytes without the use of bit-fields. You refer to a bit-field just like any other member of a structure. The following statement, for example, assigns the value 3 to the **department** field of item 10:

```
inv[9].department = 3;
```

The following statement determines whether item 5 is out of stock:

```
if(!inv[4].instock) printf("Out of Stock");
else printf("In Stock");
```

It is not necessary to completely define all bits within a byte or word. For example, this is perfectly valid:

```
struct b_type {
  int a: 2;
  int b: 3;
} ;
```

The C compiler is free to store bit-fields as it sees fit. However, usually the compiler will automatically store bit-fields in the smallest unit of memory that will hold them. Whether the bit-fields are stored high-order to low-order or the other way around is implementation-dependent. However, many compilers use high-order to low-order.

You can mix bit-fields with other types of members in a structure's definition. For example, this version of the inventory structure also includes room for the name of each item:

```
struct b_type {
  char name[40];            /* name of item */
  unsigned department: 3;   /* up to 7 departments */
  unsigned instock: 1;      /* 1 if in stock, 0 if not */
  unsigned backordered: 1;  /* 1 if backordered, 0 if not */
  unsigned lead_time: 3;    /* order lead time in months */
} inv[MAX_ITEM];
```

Because the smallest addressable unit of memory is a byte, you cannot obtain the address of a bit-field variable.

Bit-fields are often used to store Boolean (true/false) data because they allow the efficient use of memory—remember, you can pack eight Boolean values into a single byte.

1. It is not necessary to name every bit when using bit-fields. Here, for example, is a structure that uses bit-fields to access the first and last bit in a byte.

```
struct b_type {
  unsigned first: 1;
  int : 6;
  unsigned last: 1;
};
```

The use of unnamed bit-fields makes it easy to reach the bits you are interested in.

2. To see how useful bit-fields can be when working with Boolean data, here is a crude simulation of a spaceship flight recorder. By packing all the relevant information into one byte, comparatively little disk space is used to record a flight.

```
/* Simulation of a 100 minute spaceship
   flight recorder.
*/
#include <stdlib.h>
#include <stdio.h>

/* all fields indicate OK if 1,
   malfunctioning or low if 0 */
struct telemetry {
  unsigned fuel: 1;
  unsigned radio: 1;
  unsigned tv: 1;
  unsigned water: 1;
  unsigned food: 1;
  unsigned waste: 1;
} flt_recd;

void display(struct telemetry i);
```

```
int main(void)
{
  FILE *fp;
  int i;

  if((fp = fopen("flight", "wb"))==NULL) {
    printf("Cannot open file.\n");
    exit(1);
  }

  /* Imagine that each minute a status report of
     the spaceship is recorded on disk.
  */
  for(i=0; i<100; i++) {
    flt_recd.fuel = rand()%2;
    flt_recd.radio = rand()%2;
    flt_recd.tv = rand()%2;
    flt_recd.water = rand()%2;
    flt_recd.food = rand()%2;
    flt_recd.waste = rand()%2;

    display(flt_recd);
    fwrite(&flt_recd, sizeof flt_recd, 1, fp);
  }

  fclose(fp);

  return 0;
}

void display(struct telemetry i)
{
  if(i.fuel) printf("Fuel OK\n");
  else printf("Fuel low\n");
  if(i.radio) printf("Radio OK\n");
  else printf("Radio failure\n");
  if(i.tv) printf("TV system OK\n");
  else printf("TV malfunction\n");
  if(i.water) printf("Water supply OK\n");
  else printf("Water supply low\n");
  if(i.food) printf("Food supply OK\n");
  else printf("Food supply low\n");
  if(i.waste) printf("Waste containment OK\n");
```

```
    else printf("Waste containment failure\n");
    printf("\n");
}
```

Depending on how your compiler packs the bit-fields, after you run this program, the file on disk may be as short as 100 bytes long. Now try the program after modifying the **telemetry** structure as shown here:

```
struct telemetry {
    char fuel;
    char radio;
    char tv;
    char water;
    char food;
    char waste;
} flt_recd;
```

In this version, no bit-fields are used and the resulting file is at least 600 bytes long. As you can see, using bit-fields can provide substantial space savings.

EXERCISES

1. Write a program that creates a structure that contains three bit-fields called **a**, **b**, and **c**. Make **a** and **b** three bits long and make **c** two bits long. Next, assign each a value and display the values.

2. Many compilers supply library functions that return the status of various hardware devices, such as a serial port or the keyboard, by encoding information in a bit-by-bit fashion. On your own, consult the user's manual for your compiler to see if it supports such functions. If it does, write some programs that read and decode the status of one or more devices.

| 10.5 | # CREATE UNIONS |

In C, a *union* is a single piece of memory that is shared by two or more variables. The variables that share the memory may be of different types. However, only one variable may be in use at any one time. A union is defined much like a structure. Its general form is

> union *tag-name* {
>   *type member1*;
>   *type member2*;
>   *type member3*;
>
>   .
>
>   .
>
>   .
>
>   *type memberN*;
> } *variable-names*;

Like a structure, either the *tag-name* or the *variable-names* may be missing. Members may be of any valid C data type. For example, here is a union that contains three elements: an integer, a character array, and a **double**:

```
union u_type {
  int i;
  char c[2];
  double d;
} sample;
```

This union will appear in memory as shown in Figure 10-2.

| FIGURE 10-2 | |

How an instance of the union **u_type** *appears in memory (assuming 2-byte* **int***s and 8-byte* **double***s)*
▼

To access a member of a union, use the dot and arrow operators just as you do for structures. For example, this statement assigns **123.098** to **d** of **sample**:

```
sample.d = 123.098;
```

If you are accessing a union through a pointer, you must use the arrow operator. For example, assume that **p** points to **sample**. The following statement assigns **i** the value **101**:

```
p->i = 101;
```

It is important to understand that the size of a union is fixed at compile time and is large enough to accommodate the largest member of the union. Assuming 8-byte **double**s, this means that **sample** will be 8 bytes long. Even if **sample** is currently used to hold an **int** value, it will still occupy 8 bytes of memory. As is the case with structures, you should use the **sizeof** compile-time operator to determine the size of a union. You should not simply assume that it will be the size of the largest element, because in some environments, the compiler may pad the union so that it aligns on a word boundary.

EXAMPLES

1. Unions are very useful when you need to interpret data in two or more different ways. For example, the **encode( )** function shown below uses a union to encode an integer by swapping its two low-order bytes. The same function can also be used to decode an encoded integer by swapping the already exchanged bytes back to their original positions.

```
#include <stdio.h>

int encode(int i);

int main(void)
{
  int i;

  i = encode(10); /* encode it */
```

```
    printf("10 encoded is %d\n", i);
    i = encode(i); /* decode it */
    printf("i decoded is %d", i);

    return 0;
}

/* Encode an integer, decode an encoded integer. */
int encode(int i)
{
    union crypt_type {
        int num;
        char c[2];
    } crypt;
    unsigned char ch;

    crypt.num = i;

    /* swap bytes */
    ch = crypt.c[0];
    crypt.c[0] = crypt.c[1];
    crypt.c[1] = ch;

    /* return encoded integer */
    return crypt.num;
}
```

The program displays the following:

10 encoded is 2560
i decoded is 10

2. The following program uses the union of a structure containing bit-fields and a character to display the binary representation of a character typed at the keyboard:

```
/* This program displays the binary code for a
   character entered at the keyboard.
*/
#include <stdio.h>
#include <conio.h>

struct sample {
    unsigned a: 1;
    unsigned b: 1;
```

```
    unsigned c: 1;
    unsigned d: 1;
    unsigned e: 1;
    unsigned f: 1;
    unsigned g: 1;
    unsigned h: 1;
};

union key_type {
    char ch;
    struct sample bits;
} key;

int main(void)
{
    printf("Strike a key: ");

    key.ch = getche();
    printf("\nBinary code is: ");

    if(key.bits.h) printf("1 ");
    else printf("0 ");
    if(key.bits.g) printf("1 ");
    else printf("0 ");
    if(key.bits.f) printf("1 ");
    else printf("0 ");
    if(key.bits.e) printf("1 ");
    else printf("0 ");
    if(key.bits.d) printf("1 ");
    else printf("0 ");
    if(key.bits.c) printf("1 ");
    else printf("0 ");
    if(key.bits.b) printf("1 ");
    else printf("0 ");
    if(key.bits.a) printf("1 ");
    else printf("0 ");

    return 0;
}
```

When a key is pressed, its ASCII code is assigned to **key.ch**,
which is a **char**. This data is reinterpreted as a series of bit-fields,
which allow the binary representation of the key to be
displayed. Sample output is shown here:

Strike a key: X
Binary code is: 0 1 0 1 1 0 0 0

EXERCISES

1. Using a union composed of a **double** and an 8-byte character array, write a function that writes a **double** to a disk file, a character at a time. Write another function that reads this value from the file and reconstructs the value using the same union. (Note: If the length of a **double** for your compiler is not 8 bytes, use an appropriately sized character array.)

2. Write a program that uses a union to convert an **int** into a **long**. Demonstrate that it works.

Mastery Skills Check

At this point you should be able to answer these questions and perform these exercises:

1. In general terms what is a structure, and what is a union?

2. Show how to create a structure type called **s_type** that contains these five members:

```
char ch;
float d;
int i;
char str[80];
double balance;
```

Also, define one variable called **s_var** using this structure.

3. What is wrong with this fragment?

```
struct s_type {
  int a;
```

```
    char b;
    float bal;
} myvar, *p;

p = &myvar;

p.a = 10;
```

4. Write a program that uses an array of structures to store employee names, telephone numbers, hours worked, and hourly wages. Allow for 10 employees. Have the program input the information and save it to a disk file. Call the file EMP.

5. Write a program that reads the EMP file created in Exercise 4 and displays the information on the screen.

6. What is a bit-field?

7. Write a program that displays individually the values of the high- and low-order bytes of a short integer. (Hint: Use a union that contains as its two elements a short integer and a two-byte character array.)

**Cumulative
Skills Check**

This section checks how well you have integrated the material in this chapter with that from earlier chapters.

1. Write a program that contains two structure variables defined as:

```
struct s_type {
  int i;
  char ch;
  double d;
} var1, var2;
```

Have the program give each member of both structures initial values, but make sure that the values differ between the two structures. Using a function called **struct_swap( )**, have the program swap the contents of **var1** and **var2**.

2. As you know from Chapter 9, **fgetc( )** returns an integer value, even though it only reads a character from a file. Write a

program that copies one file to another. Assign the return value of **fgetc( )** to a union that contains an integer and character member. Use the integer element to check for **EOF**. Write the character element to the destination file. Have the user specify both the source and destination file names on the command line.

3. What is wrong with this fragment?

```
struct s_type {
   int a;
   int b: 2;
   int c: 6;
} var;
   .
   .
   .
scanf("%d", &var);
```

4. In C, as you know, you cannot pass an array to a function as a parameter. (Only a pointer to an array can be passed.) However, there is one way around this restriction. If you enclose the array within a structure, the array is passed using the standard call-by-value convention. Write a program that demonstrates this by passing a string inside a structure to a function, altering its contents inside the function and demonstrating that the original string is not altered after the function returns.

11

Advanced Data Types and Operators

337
▼

T
H E C language includes a rich set of data type modifiers that allow you to better fit the type of a variable to the information it will be storing. Also, C includes a number of special operators that permit the creation of very efficient routines. Both of these items are the subject of this chapter.

Review
Skills Check

Before proceeding, you should be able to answer these questions and perform these exercises:

1. Write a program that uses an array of structures to hold the squares and cubes of the numbers 1 through 10. Display the contents of the array.

2. Write a program that uses a **union** to display as a character the individual bytes that make up a short integer entered by the user.

3. What does this fragment display? (Assume two-byte **int**s and eight-byte **double**s.)

```
union {
  int i;
  double d;
} uvar;

printf("%d", sizeof uvar);
```

4. What is wrong with this fragment?

```
struct {
  int i;
  char str[80];
  double balance;
} svar;

svar->i = 100;
```

5. What is a bit-field?

11.1   USE THE STORAGE CLASS SPECIFIERS

C defines four type modifiers that affect how a variable is stored. They are

```
auto
extern
register
static
```

These specifiers precede the type name. Let's look at each now.

The specifier **auto** is completely unnecessary. It is provided in C to allow compatibility with its predecessor, B. Its use is to declare *automatic variables*. Automatic variables are simply local variables, which are **auto** by default. You will almost never see **auto** used in any C program.

Although the programs we have been working with in this book are fairly short, programs in the real world tend to be quite long. As the size of a program grows, it takes longer to compile. For this reason, C allows you to break a program into two or more files. You can separately compile these files and then link them together. This saves compilation time and makes your projects easier to work with. (The actual method of separate compilation and linking will be explained in the instructions that accompany your compiler.) When working with multiple source files there is, however, one issue that needs to be addressed. As a general rule, global data can only be defined once. However, global data may need to be accessed by two or more files that form a program. In this case, each source file must inform the compiler about the global data it uses. To accomplish this you will need to use the keyword **extern**. To understand why, consider the following program, which is split between two files:

FILE #1:

```c
#include <stdio.h>

int count;

void f1(void);

int main(void)
{
  int i;
```

```
  f1(); /* set count's value */

  for(i=0; i<count; i++)
    printf("%d ", i);

  return 0;
}
```

FILE #2:

```
#include <stdlib.h>

void f1(void)
{
  count = rand();
}
```

If you try to compile the second file, an error will be reported because **count** is not defined. However, you *cannot* change FILE #2 as follows:

```
#include <stdlib.h>

int count;

void f1(void)
{
  count = rand();
}
```

If you declare **count** a second time, many linkers will report a duplicate-symbol error, which means that **count** is defined twice, and the linker doesn't know which to use.

The solution to this problem is C's **extern** specifier. By placing **extern** in front of **count**'s declaration in FILE #2, you are telling the compiler that **count** is an integer defined elsewhere. In other words, using **extern** informs the compiler about the existence and the type of the variable it precedes, but it does not cause storage for that variable to be allocated. The correct version of FILE #2 is

```
#include <stdlib.h>

extern int count;

void f1(void)
```

```
{
  count = rand();
}
```

Although rarely done, it is not incorrect to use **extern** inside a function to declare a global variable defined elsewhere in the same file. For example, the following is valid:

```
#include <stdio.h>

int count;

int main(void)
{
  extern int count; /* this refers to global count */

  count = 10;
  printf("%d", count);

  return 0;
}
```

The reason you will rarely see this use of **extern** is that it is redundant. Whenever the compiler encounters a variable name not defined by the function as a local variable, it assumes that it is global.

One very important storage-class specifier is **register**. When you specify a **register** variable you are telling the compiler that you want access to that variable to be as fast as possible. In early versions of C, **register** could only be applied to local variables (including formal parameters) of types **int** or **char**, or to a pointer type. It caused the variables to be held in a register of the CPU. (This is how the name **register** came about.) By using a register of the CPU, extremely fast access times are achieved. In modern versions of C, the definition of **register** has been broadened to include all types of variables and the requirement that **register** variables must be held in a CPU register was removed. Instead, the ANSI C standard stipulates that a **register** variable will be stored in such a way as to minimize access time. In practice, however, this means that **register** variables of type **int** and **char** continue to be held in a CPU register—this is still the fastest way to access them.

No matter what storage method is used, only so many variables can be granted the fastest possible access time. For example, the CPU has a limited number of registers. When fast-access locations are exhausted, the compiler is free to make **register** variables into regular variables. For this reason, you must choose carefully which variables you modify with **register**.

One good choice is to make a frequently used variable, such as the variable that controls a loop, into a **register** variable. The more times a variable is accessed, the greater the increase in performance when its access time is decreased. Generally, you can assume that at least two variables per function can be truly optimized for access speed.

Important: Because a **register** variable may be stored in a register of the CPU, it may not have a memory address. This means that you *cannot* use the **&** to find the address of a register variable.

When you use the **static** modifier, you cause the contents of a local variable to be preserved between function calls. Also, unlike normal local variables, which are initialized each time a function is entered, a **static** local variable is initialized only once. For example, take a look at
this program,

```
#include <stdio.h>

void f(void);

int main(void)
{
  int i;

  for(i=0; i<10; i++) f();

  return 0;
}

void f(void)
{
  static int count = 0;

  count++;
  printf("count is %d\n", count);
}
```

which displays the following output:

```
count is 1
count is 2
```

```
count is 3
count is 4
count is 5
count is 6
count is 7
count is 8
count is 9
count is 10
```

As you can see, **count** retains its value between function calls. The advantage to using a **static** local variable over a global one is that the **static** local variable is still known to and accessible by only the function in which it is declared.

The **static** modifier may also be used on global variables. When it is, it causes the global variable to be known to and accessible by only the functions in the same file in which it is declared. Not only is a function not declared in the same file as a **static** global variable unable to access that global variable, it does not even know its name. This means that there are no name conflicts if a **static** global variable in one file has the same name as another global variable in a different file of the same program. For example, consider these two fragments, which are parts of the same program:

FILE #1	**FILE #2**
`int count;`	`static int count;`
`.`	`.`
`.`	`.`
`.`	`.`
`count = 10;`	`count = 5;`
`printf("%d", count);`	`printf("%d", count);`

Because **count** is declared as **static** in FILE #2, no name conflicts arise. The **printf( )** statement in FILE #1 displays **10** and the **printf( )** statement in FILE #2 displays **5** because the two **count**s are different variables.

EXAMPLES

1. To get an idea about how much faster access to a **register** variable is, try the following program. It makes use of another of C's standard library functions called **clock( )**, which returns the

number of system clock ticks since the program began execution. It has this prototype:

clock_t clock(void);

It uses the TIME.H header. TIME.H also defines the **clock_t** type, which is more or less the same as **long**. To time an event using **clock( )**, call it immediately before the event you wish to time and save its return value. Next, call it a second time after the event finishes and subtract the starting value from the ending value. This is the approach used by the program to time how long it takes two loops to execute. One set of loops is controlled by a **register** variable, the other is controlled by a non-**register** variable.

```c
#include <stdio.h>
#include <time.h>

int i;  /* This will not be transformed into a
                register variable because it is global.*/

int main(void)
{
  register int j;

  int k;
  clock_t start, finish;

  start = clock();
  for(k=0; k<100; k++)
    for(i=0; i<32000; i++) ;
  finish = clock();
  printf("Non-register loop: %ld ticks\n", finish - start);

  start = clock();
  for(k=0; k<100; k++)
    for(j=0; j<32000; j++);
  finish = clock();
  printf("Register loop: %ld ticks\n", finish - start);

  return 0;
}
```

For most compilers, the **register**-controlled loop will execute about twice as fast as the non-**register** controlled loop.

The non-**register** variable is global because, when feasible, virtually all compilers will automatically convert local variables not specified as **register** types into **register** types as an automatic optimization. If you do not see the predicted results, it may mean that the compiler has automatically optimized **i** into a register variable, too. Although you can't declare global variables as **register**, there is nothing that prevents a compiler from optimizing your program to this effect. If you don't see much difference between the two loops, try creating extra global variables prior to **i** so that it will not be automatically optimized.

2. As you know, the compiler can optimize access speed for only a limited number of **register** variables in any one function (perhaps as few as two). However, this does not mean that your program can only have a few **register** variables. Because of the way a C program executes, each function may utilize the maximum number of **register** variables. For example, for the average compiler, all the variables shown in the next program will be optimized for speed:

```c
#include <stdio.h>

void f2(void);
void f(void);

int main(void)
{
  register int a, b;
  .
  .
  .

}

void f(void)
{
  register int i, j;
  .
  .
  .

}
```

```
void f2(void)
{
  register int j, k;
  .
  .
  .
}
```

3. Local **static** variables have several uses. One is to allow a function to perform various initializations only once, when it is first called. For example, consider this function:

```
void myfunc(void)
{
  static int first = 1;

  if(first) {  /* initialize the system */
    rewind(fp);
    a = 0;
    loc = 0;
    fprintf("System Initialized");
    first = 0;
  }
  .
  .
  .
}
```

Because **first** is **static**, it will hold its value between calls. Thus, the initialization code will be executed only the first time the function is called.

4. Another interesting use for a local **static** variable is to control a recursive function. For example, this program prints the numbers **1** through **9** on the screen:

```
#include <stdio.h>

void f(void);

int main(void)
{
  f();

  return 0;
}
```

```
void f(void)
{
  static int stop=0;

  stop++;

  if(stop==10) return;
  printf("%d ", stop);
  f(); /* recursive call */
}
```

Notice how **stop** is used to prevent a recursive call to **f( )** when it equals 10.

5. Here is another example of using **extern** to allow global data to be accessed by two files:

FILE #1:

```
#include <stdio.h>

char str[80];

void getname(void);

int main(void)
{
  getname();
  printf("Hello %s", str);

  return 0;
}
```

FILE #2:

```
#include <stdio.h>

extern char str[80];

void getname(void)
{
  printf("Enter your first name: ");
  gets(str);
}
```

1. Assume that your compiler will actually optimize access time of only two **register** variables per function. In this program, which two variables are the best ones to be made into **register** variables?

```c
#include <stdio.h>
#include <conio.h>

int main(void)
{
  int i, j, k, m;

  do {
    printf("Enter a value: ");
    scanf("%d", &i);

    m = 0;
    for(j=0; j<i; j++)
      for(k=0; k<100; k++)
        m = k + m;
  } while(i>0);

  return 0;
}
```

2. Write a program that contains a function called **sum_it( )** that has this prototype:

```c
void sum_it (int value);
```

Have this function use a local **static** integer variable to maintain and display a running total of the values of the parameters it is called with. For example, if **sum_it( )** is called three times with the values 3, 6, 4, then **sum_it( )** will display 3, 9, and 13.

3. Try the program described in Example 5. Be sure to actually use two files. If you are unsure how to compile and link a program consisting of two files, check your compiler's user manual.

4. What is wrong with this fragment?

```c
register int i;
int *p;

p = &i;
```

11.2   # USE THE ACCESS MODIFIERS

C includes two type modifiers that affect the way variables are accessed by both your program and the compiler. These modifiers are **const** and **volatile**. This section examines these type modifiers.

If you precede a variable's type with **const**, you prevent that variable from being modified by your program. The variable may be given an initial value, however, through the use of an initialization when it is declared. The compiler is free to locate **const** variables in ROM (read-only memory) in environments that support it. A **const** variable may also have its value changed by hardware-dependent means.

The **const** modifier has a second use. It can prevent a function from modifying the object that a parameter points to. That is, when a pointer parameter is preceded by **const**, no statement in the function can modify the variable pointed to by that parameter.

When you precede a variable's type with **volatile**, you are telling the compiler that the value of the variable may be changed in ways not explicitly defined in the program. For example, a variable's address might be given to an interrupt service routine, and its value changed each time an interrupt occurs. The reason that **volatile** is important is that most C compilers apply complex and sophisticated optimizations to your program to create faster and more efficient executable programs. If the compiler does not know that the contents of a variable may change in ways not explicitly specified by the program, it may not actually examine the contents of the variable each time it is referenced. (Unless it occurs on the left side of an assignment statement, of course.)

EXAMPLES

1. The following short program shows how a **const** variable can be given an initial value and be used in the program, as long as it is not on the left side of an assignment statement.

```
#include <stdio.h>

int main(void)
{
  const int i = 10;
```

```
  printf("%d", i); /* this is OK */

  return 0;
}
```

The following program tries to assign **i** another value. This program will not compile because **i** cannot be modified by the program.

```
#include <stdio.h>

int main(void)
{
  const int i = 10;

  i = 20; /* this is wrong */

  printf("%d", i);

  return 0;
}
```

2. The next program shows how a pointer parameter can be declared as **const** to prevent the object it points to from being modified.

```
#include <stdio.h>

void pr_str(const char *p);

int main(void)
{
  char str[80];

  printf("Enter a string: ");
  gets(str);

  pr_str(str);

  return 0;
}

void pr_str(const char *p)
{
  while(*p) putchar(*p++); /* this is ok */
}
```

If you change the program as shown below, it will not compile because this version attempts to alter the string pointed to by **p**.

```c
#include <stdio.h>
#include <ctype.h>

void pr_str(const char *p);

int main(void)
{
  char str[80];

  printf("Enter a string: ");
  gets(str);
  pr_str(str);

  return 0;
}

void pr_str(const char *p)
{
  while(*p) {
    *p = toupper(*p); /* this will not compile */
    putchar(*p++);
  }
}
```

3. Perhaps the most important feature of **const** pointer parameters is that they guarantee that many standard library functions will not modify the variables pointed to by their parameters. For example, here is the actual prototype to **strlen( )** specified by the ANSI standard:

size_t strlen(const char *str);

Since *str* is specified as **const**, the string it points to cannot be changed.

4. While short examples of **volatile** are hard to find, the following fragment gives you the flavor of its use:

```c
volatile unsigned u;

give_address_to_some_interrupt(&u);
```

```
for(;;) { /* watch value of u */
  printf("%d", u);
    .
    .
    .
```

In this example, if **u** had not been declared as **volatile**, the compiler could have optimized the repeated calls to **printf( )** in such a way that **u** was not reexamined each time. The use of **volatile** forces the compiler to actually obtain the value of **u** whenever it is used.

EXERCISES

1. One good time to use **const** is when you want to embed a version control number into a program. By using a **const** variable to hold the version, you prevent it from accidentally being changed. Write a short program that illustrates how this can be done. Use 6.01 as the version number.

2. Write your own version of **strcpy( )** called **mystrcpy( )**, which has the prototype

   char *mystrcpy (char *to, const char *from);

   The function returns a pointer to *to*. Demonstrate your version of **mystrcpy( )** in a program.

3. On your own, see if you can think of any ways to use **volatile**.

11.3 *D*EFINE ENUMERATIONS

In C you can define a list of named integer constants called an *enumeration*. These constants can then be used any place an integer can. To define an enumeration, use this general form:

   enum *tag-name* { *enumeration list* } *variable-list;*

Either the *tag-name* or the *variable-list* is optional. The *tag-name* is essentially the type name of the enumeration. For example,

```
enum color_type {red, green, yellow} color;
```

Here, an enumeration consisting of the constants **red**, **green**, and **yellow** is created. The enumeration tag is **color_type** and one variable, called **color**, has been created.

By default, the compiler assigns integer values to enumeration constants, beginning with 0 at the far left side of the list. Each constant to the right is one greater than the constant that precedes it. Therefore, in the color enumeration, **red** is 0, **green** is 1, and **yellow** is 2. However, you can override the compiler's default values by explicitly giving a constant a value. For example, in this statement

```
enum color_type {red, green=9, yellow} color;
```

red is still 0, but **green** is 9, and **yellow** is 10.

Once you have defined an enumeration, you can use its tag name to declare enumeration variables at other points in the program. For example, assuming the **color_type** enumeration, this statement is perfectly valid and declares **mycolor** as a **color_type** variable:

```
enum color_type mycolor;
```

An enumeration is essentially an integer type and an enumeration variable can hold any integer value—not just those defined by the enumeration. But for clarity and structure, you should use enumeration variables to hold only values that are defined by their enumeration type.

Two of the main uses of an enumeration are to help provide self-documenting code and to clarify the structure of your program.

EXAMPLES

1. This short program creates an enumeration consisting of the parts of a computer. It assigns **comp** the value **CPU** and then displays its value (which is 1). Notice how the enumeration tag name is used to declare **comp** as an enumeration variable separately from the actual declaration of **computer**.

```
#include <stdio.h>

enum computer {keyboard, CPU, screen, printer};

int main(void)
{
  enum computer comp;
```

```
    comp = CPU;

    printf("%d", comp);

    return 0;
}
```

2. It takes a little work to display the string equivalent of an enumerated constant. Remember, enumerated constants are not strings; they are named integer constants. The following program uses a **switch** statement to output the string equivalent of an enumerated value. The program uses C's random-number generator to choose a means of transportation. It then displays the means on the screen. (This program is for people who can't make up their minds!)

```
#include <stdio.h>
#include <stdlib.h>
#include <conio.h>

enum transport {car, train, airplane, bus} tp;

int main(void)
{
  printf("Press a key to select transport: ");

  /* generate a new random number each time
     the program is run
  */
  while(!kbhit()) rand();
  getch(); /* read and discard character */

  tp = rand() % 4;
  switch(tp) {
    case car: printf("car");
      break;
    case train: printf("train");
      break;
    case airplane: printf("airplane");
      break;
    case bus: printf("bus");
  }

  return 0;
}
```

In some cases, there is an easier way to obtain a string equivalent of an enumerated value. As long as you do not initialize any of the constants, you can create a two-dimensional string array that contains the string equivalents of the enumerated values in the same order that the constants appear in the enumeration. You can then index the array using an enumeration value to obtain its corresponding string. The following version of the transportation-choosing program, for example, uses this approach:

```c
#include <stdio.h>
#include <stdlib.h>
#include <conio.h>

enum transport {car, train, airplane, bus} tp;

char trans[][20] = {
  "car", "train", "airplane", "bus"
};

int main(void)
{
  printf("Press a key to select transport: ");

  /* Generate a new random number each time
     the program is run
  */
  while(!kbhit()) rand();
  getch(); /* read and discard character */

  tp = rand() % 4;
  printf("%s", trans[tp]);

  return 0;
}
```

3. Remember, the names of enumerated constants are known only to the program, not to any library functions. For example, given the fragment

```c
enum numbers {zero, one, two, three} num;

printf("Enter a number: ");
scanf("%d", &num);
```

you cannot respond to **scanf( )** by entering **one**.

1. Compile and run the example programs.

2. Create an enumeration of the coins of the U.S. from penny to dollar.

3. Is this fragment correct? If not, why not?

```
enum cars {Ford, Chrysler, GM} make;

make = GM;
printf("car is %s", make);
```

11.4 UNDERSTAND typedef

In C you can create a new name for an existing type using **typedef**. The general form of **typedef** is

typedef *old-name new-name;*

This new name can be used to declare variables. For example, in the following program, **smallint** is a new name for a **signed char** and is used to declare **i**.

```
#include <stdio.h>

typedef signed char smallint;

int main(void)
{
  smallint i;

  for(i=0; i<10; i++)
    printf("%d ", i);

  return 0;
}
```

Keep two points firmly in mind: First, a **typedef** does not cause the original name to be deactivated. For example, in the program, **signed char** is still a valid type. Second, you can use several **typedef** statements to create many different, new names for the same type.

There are basically two reasons to use **typedef**. The first is to create portable programs. For example, if you know that you will be writing a program that will be executed on computers using 16-bit integers as well as on computers using 32-bit integers, and you want to ensure that certain variables are 16 bits long in both environments, you might want to use a **typedef** when compiling the program for the 16-bit machines as follows:

```
typedef int myint;
```

Then, before compiling the code for a 32-bit computer, you can change the **typedef** statement like this:

```
typedef short int myint;
```

This works because on computers using 32-bit integers, a **short int** will be 16 bits long. Assuming that you used **myint** to declare all integer values that you wanted to be 16 bits long, you need change only one statement to change the type of all variables declared using **myint**.

The second reason you might want to use **typedef** is to help provide self-documenting code. For example, if you are writing an inventory program, you might use this **typedef** statement.

```
typedef double subtotal;
```

Now, when anyone reading your program sees a variable declared as **subtotal**, he or she will know that it is used to hold a subtotal.

EXAMPLES

1. The new name created by one **typedef** can be used in a subsequent **typedef** to create another name. For example, consider this fragment:

   ```
   typedef int height;
   typedef height length;
   typedef length depth;

   depth d;
   ```

   Here, **d** is still an integer.

2. In addition to the the basic types, you can use **typedef** on more complicated types. For example, the following is perfectly valid:

```
enum e_type {one, two, three } ;

typedef enum e_type mynums;

mynums num; /* declare a variable */
```

Here, **num** is a variable of type **e_type**.

---

1. Show how to make **UL** a new name for **unsigned long**.
   Show that it works by writing a short program that declares a
   variable using **UL**, assigns it a value, and displays the value
   on the screen.

2. What is wrong with this fragment?

   ```
   typedef balance float;
   ```

11.5 USE C'S BITWISE OPERATORS

C contains four special operators that perform their operations on a
bit-by-bit level. These operators are

&	bitwise AND
|	bitwise OR
^	bitwise XOR (eXclusive OR)
~	1's complement

These operators work with character and integer types; they cannot be
used with floating-point types.

The AND, OR, and XOR operators produce a result based on a
comparison of corresponding bits in each operand. The AND operator
sets a bit if both bits being compared are set. The OR sets a bit if either
of the bits being compared is set. The XOR operation sets a bit when
either of the two bits involved is 1, but not when both are 1 or both are
0. Here is an example of a bitwise AND:

```
  1010 0110
& 0011 1011
-----------
  0010 0010
```

Notice how the resulting bit is set, based on the outcome of the operation being applied to the corresponding bits in each operand.

The 1's complement operator is a unary operator that reverses the state of each bit within an integer or character.

EXAMPLES

1. The XOR operation has one interesting property. Given two values A and B, when the outcome of A XOR B is XORed with B a second time, A is produced. For example, this output

   ```
   initial value of i: 100
   i after first XOR: 21895
   i after second XOR: 100
   ```

   is produced by the following program:

   ```c
   #include <stdio.h>

   int main(void)
   {
     int i;

     i = 100;
     printf("initial value of i: %d\n", i);

     i = i ^ 21987;
     printf("i after first XOR: %d\n", i);

     i = i ^ 21987;
     printf("i after second XOR: %d\n", i);

     return 0;
   }
   ```

2. The following program uses a bitwise AND to display, in binary, the ASCII value of a character typed at the keyboard:

   ```c
   #include <stdio.h>
   #include <conio.h>
   ```

```
int main(void)
{
  char ch;
  int i;

  printf("Enter a character: ");
  ch = getche();
  printf("\n");

  /* display binary representation */
  for(i=128; i>0; i=i/2)
    if(i & ch) printf("1 ");
    else printf("0 ");

  return 0;
}
```

The program works by adjusting the value of **i** so that only one bit is set each time a comparison is made. Since the high-order bit in a byte represents 128, this value is used as a starting point. Each time through the loop, **i** is halved. This causes the next bit position to be set and all others cleared. Thus, each time through the loop, a bit in **ch** is tested. If it is 1, the comparison produces a true result and a **1** is output. Otherwise a **0** is displayed. This process continues until all bits have been tested.

3. By modifying the program from Example 2, it can be used to show the effect of the 1's complement operator.

```
#include <stdio.h>
#include <conio.h>

int main(void)
{
  char ch;
  int i;

  ch = 'a';

  /* display binary representation */
  for(i=128; i>0; i=i/2)
    if(i & ch) printf("1 ");
    else printf("0 ");

  /* reverse bit pattern */
```

```
  ch = ~ch;
  printf("\n");

  /* display binary representation */
  for(i=128; i>0; i=i/2)
    if(i & ch) printf("1 ");
    else printf("0 ");

  return 0;
}
```

When you run this program, you will see that the state of bits in **ch** are reversed after the ~ operation has occurred.

4. The following program shows how to use the *&* operator to determine if a signed integer is positive or negative. (The program assumes short integers are 16 bits long.) Since negative numbers are represented with their high-order bit set, the comparison will be true only if **i** is negative. (The value 32768 is the value of an unsigned short integer when only its high-order bit is set. This value is 1000 0000 in binary.)

```
#include <stdio.h>

int main(void)
{
  short i;

  printf("Enter a number: ");
  scanf("%hd", &i);

  if(i & 32768) printf("Number is negative.\n");

  return 0;
}
```

5. The following program makes **i** into a negative number by setting its high-order bit. (Again, 16-bit short integers are assumed.)

```
#include <stdio.h>

int main(void)
{
  short i;
```

```
    i = 1;
    i = i | 32768;
    printf("%hd", i);

    return 0;
}
```

It displays **−32,767.**

---

1. One very easy way to encode a file is to reverse the state of each bit using the ~ operator. Write a program that encodes a file using this method. (To decode the file, simply run the program a second time.) Have the user specify the name of the file on the command line.

2. A better method of coding a file uses the XOR operation combined with a user-defined key. Write a program that encodes a file using this method. Have the user specify the file to code as well as a single character key on the command line. (To decode the file, run the program a second time using the same key.)

3. What is the outcome of these operations?

   A. 1010 0011 & 0101 1101

   B. 0101 1101 | 1111 1011

   C. 0101 0110 ^ 1010 1011

4. Sometimes, the high-order bit of a byte is used as a *parity bit* by modem programs. It is used to verify the integrity of each byte transferred. There are two types of parity: even and odd. If even parity is used, the parity bit is used to ensure that each byte has an even number of 1 bits. If odd parity is used, the parity bit is used to ensure that each byte has an odd number of 1 bits. Since the parity bit is not part of the information being transferred, show how you can clear the high-order bit of a character value.

11.6 ***M*ASTER THE SHIFT OPERATORS**

C includes two operators not commonly found in other computer languages: the left and right bit-shift operators. The left shift operator is <<, and the right shift operator is >>. These operators may be applied only to character or integer operands. They take these general forms:

value << *number-of-bits*

value >> *number-of-bits*

The integer expression specified by *number-of-bits* determines how many places to the left or right the bits within *value* are shifted. Each left-shift causes all bits within the specified value to be shifted left one position and a zero is brought in on the right. A right-shift shifts all bits to the right one position and brings a zero in on the left. (Unless the number is negative, in which case a one is brought in.) When bits are shifted off an end, they are lost.

A right shift is equivalent to dividing a number by 2, and a left shift is the same as multiplying the number by 2. Because of the internal operation of virtually all CPUs, shift operations are usually faster than their equivalent arithmetic operations.

EXAMPLES

1. This program demonstrates the right and left shift operators:

```
#include <stdio.h>

void show_binary(unsigned u);

int main(void)
{
  unsigned short u;

  u = 45678;

  show_binary(u);
  u = u << 1;
  show_binary(u);
  u = u >> 1;
  show_binary(u);
```

```
     return 0;
}

void show_binary(unsigned u)
{
  unsigned n;

  for(n=32768; n>0; n=n/2)
    if(u & n) printf("1 ");
    else printf("0 ");

  printf("\n");
}
```

The output from this program is

1 0 1 1 0 0 1 0 0 1 1 0 1 1 1 0
0 1 1 0 0 1 0 0 1 1 0 1 1 1 0 0
0 0 1 1 0 0 1 0 0 1 1 0 1 1 1 0

Notice that after the left shift, a bit of information has been lost. When the right shift occurs, a zero is brought in. As stated earlier, bits that are shifted off one end are lost.

2. Since a right shift is the same as a division by two, but faster, the **show_binary( )** function can be made more efficient as shown here:

```
void show_binary(unsigned u)
{
  unsigned n;

  for(n=32768; n; n=n>>1)
    if(u & n) printf("1 ");
    else printf("0 ");

  printf("\n");
}
```

EXERCISES

1. Write a program that uses the shift operators to multiply and divide an integer. Have the user enter the initial value. Display the result of each operation.

2. C does not have a rotate operator. A *rotate* is similar to a shift, except that the bit shifted off one end is inserted onto the other. For example, 1010 0000 rotated left one place is 0100 0001. Write a function called **rotate( )** that rotates a byte left one position each time it is called. (Hint, you will need to use a union so that you can have access to the bit shifted off the end of the byte.) Demonstrate the function in a program.

11.7 UNDERSTAND THE ? OPERATOR

C contains one ternary operator: the **?**. A *ternary operator* requires three operands. The **?** operator is used to replace statements such as:

```
if(condition) var = exp1;
else var = exp2;
```

The general form of the **?** operator is

> *var = condition ? exp1: exp2 ;*

Here, *condition* is an expression that evaluates to true or false. If it is true, *var* is assigned the value of *exp1*. If it is false, *var* is assigned the value of *exp2*. The reason for the **?** operator is that a C compiler can produce more efficient code using it instead of the equivalent **if/else** statement.

EXAMPLES

1. The following program illustrates the **?** operator. It inputs a number and then converts the number into 1 if the number is positive and –1 if it is negative.

```
#include <stdio.h>

int main(void)
{
  int i;

  printf("Enter a number: ");
  scanf("%d", &i);

  i = i>0 ? 1: -1;

  printf("Outcome: %d", i);

  return 0;
}
```

2. The next program is a computerized coin toss. It waits for you to press a key and then prints either **Heads** or **Tails**.

```
#include <stdio.h>
#include <stdlib.h>
#include <conio.h>

int main(void)
{
  int i;

  while(!kbhit()) rand();

  i = rand() %2 ? 1: 0;

  if(i) printf("Heads");
  else printf("Tails");

  return 0;
}
```

The coin-toss program can be written in a more efficient way. There is no technical reason that the **?** operator need assign its value to any variable. Therefore, the coin toss program can be written as:

```
#include <stdio.h>
#include <stdlib.h>
#include <conio.h>
```

```
int main(void)
{
  while(!kbhit()) rand();

  rand()%2 ? printf("Heads") : printf("Tails");

  return 0;
}
```

Remember, since a call to a function is a valid C expression, it is perfectly valid to call **printf( )** in the **?** statement.

EXERCISES

---

1. One particularly good use for the **?** operator is to provide a means of preventing a division-by-zero error. Write a program that inputs two integers from the user and displays the result of dividing the first by the second. Use **?** to avoid division by zero.

2. Convert the following statement into its equivalent **?** statement.

```
if(a>b) count = 100;
else count = 0;
```

11.8 ***D**O MORE WITH THE ASSIGNMENT OPERATOR*

The assignment operator is more powerful in C than in most other computer languages. In this section, you will learn some new things about it.

You can assign several variables the same value using the general form

var1 = var2 = var3 = ... = varN = value;

For example, this statement

```
i = j = k = 100;
```

assigns **i**, **j**, and **k** the value 100. In professionally written C code, it is common to see such multiple-variable assignments.

Another variation on the assignment statement is sometimes called C *shorthand*. In C, you can transform a statement like

```
a = a + 3;
```

into a statement like

```
a += 3;
```

In general, any time you have a statement of the form

var = var *op* expression;

you can write it in shorthand form as

var *op*= expression;

Here, *op* is one of the following operators.

$$+ \ - \ * \ / \ \% \ \ll \ \gg \ \& \ | \ \wedge$$

There must be no space between the operator and the equal sign. The reason you will want to use the shorthand form is not that it saves you a little typing effort, but because the C compiler can create more efficient executable code.

EXAMPLES

1. The following program illustrates the multiple-assignment statement:

```c
#include <stdio.h>

int main(void)
{
  int i, j, k;

  i = j = k = 99;

  printf("%d %d %d", i, j, k);

  return 0;
}
```

2. The next program counts to 98 by twos. Notice that it uses C shorthand to increment the loop-control variable by two each iteration.

```c
#include <stdio.h>

int main(void)
{
  int i;

  /* count by 2s */
  for(i=0; i<100; i+=2)
    printf("%d ", i);

  return 0;
}
```

3. The following program uses the left-shift operator in shorthand form to multiply the value of **i** by 2, three times. (The resulting value is 8.)

```c
#include <stdio.h>

int main(void)
{
  int i = 1;

  i <<= 3;   /* multiply by 2, 3 times */

  printf("%d", i);

  return 0;
}
```

EXERCISES

1. Compile and run the program in Example 1 to prove to yourself that the multiple-assignment statement works.

2. How is the following statement written using C shorthand?

```c
x = x & y;
```

3. Write a program that displays all the even multiples of 17 from 17 to 1000. Use C shorthand.

| 11.9 | # UNDERSTAND THE COMMA OPERATOR |

The last operator we will examine is the comma. It has a very unique function: it tells the compiler to "do this and this and this." That is, the comma is used to string together several operations. The most common use of the comma is in the **for** loop. In the following loop, the comma is used in the initialization portion to initialize two loop-control variables, and in the increment portion to increment **i** and **j**.

```
for(i=0, j=0; i+j<count; i++, j++) . . .
```

The value of a comma-separated list of expressions is the rightmost expression. For example, the following statement assigns 100 to **value**:

```
value = (count, 99, 33, 100);
```

The parentheses are necessary because the comma operator is lower in precedence than the assignment operator.

EXAMPLES

---

1. This program displays the numbers 0 through 49. It uses the comma operator to maintain two loop-control variables.

```c
#include <stdio.h>

int main(void)
{
  int i, j;

  /* count to 49 */
  for(i=0, j=100; i<j; i++, j--)
    printf("%d ", i);

  return 0;
}
```

2. In many places in C, it is actually syntactically correct to use the comma in place of the semicolon. For example, examine the following short program:

```
#include <stdio.h>

int main(void)
{
  char ch;

  ch = getchar(), /* notice the comma here */
  putchar(ch+1);

  return 0;
}
```

Because the comma tells the compiler to "do this and this," the program runs the same with the comma after **getchar( )** as it would had a semicolon been used. Using a comma in this way is considered extremely bad form, however. It is possible that an unwanted side effect could occur. (This use of the comma operator *does* make interesting coffee-break conversation, however! Many C programmers are not aware of this interesting twist in the C syntax.)

EXERCISES

1. Write a program that uses the comma operator to maintain three **for** loop-control variables. Have one variable run from 0 to 99, the second run from –50 to 49, and have the third set to the sum of the first two, both initially and each time the loop iterates. Have the loop stop when the first variable reaches 100. Have the program display the value of the third variable each time the loop repeats.

2. What is the value of **i** after the following statement executes?

```
i = (1, 2, 3);
```

11.10 KNOW THE PRECEDENCE SUMMARY

The following table shows the precedence of all the C operators.

Highest	( ) [ ] -> .
	! ~ + - ++ - - (type cast) * & sizeof
	* / %
	+ -
	<< >>
	< <= > >=
	== !=
	&
	^
	|
	&&
	||
	?:
	= += -= *= /= etc.
Lowest	,

Mastery Skills Check

At this point you should be able to answer these questions and perform these exercises:

1. What does the **register** specifier do?

2. What do the **const** and **volatile** modifiers do?

3. Write a program that sums the numbers 1 to 100. Make the program execute as fast as possible.

4. Is this statement valid? If so, what does it do?

   ```
   typedef long double bigfloat;
   ```

5. Write a program that inputs two characters and compares corresponding bits. Have the program display the number of each bit in which a match occurs. For example, if the two integers are

```
1001 0110
1110 1010
```

the program will report that bits 7, 1, and 0 match. (Use the bitwise operators to solve this problem.)

6. What do the `<<` and `>>` operators do?

7. Show how this statement can be rewritten:

```
c = c + 10;
```

8. Rewrite this statement using the **?** operator:

```
if(!done) count = 100;
else count = 0;
```

9. What is an enumeration? Show an example that enumerates the planets.

Cumulative Skills Check

This section checks how well you have integrated the material in this chapter with that from earlier chapters.

1. Write a program that swaps the low-order four bits of a byte with the high-order four bits. Demonstrate that your routine works by displaying the contents of the byte before and after, using the **show_binary( )** function developed earlier. (Change **show_binary( )** so that it works on an eight-bit quantity, however.)

2. Earlier you wrote a program that encoded files using the 1's complement operator. Write a program that reads a text file encoded using this method and displays its decoded contents. Leave the actual file encoded, however.

3. Is this fragment correct?

```
register FILE *fp;
```

4. Using the program you developed for Chapter 10, Section 10.3, Exercise 1, optimize the program by selecting appropriate local variables to become **register** types.

12

The C Preprocessor and Some Advanced Topics

chapter objectives

12.1 Learn more about **#define** and **#include**

12.2 Understand conditional compilation

12.3 Learn about **#error**, **#undef**, **#line**, and **#pragma**

12.4 Examine C's built-in macros

12.5 Use the **#** and **##** operators

12.6 Understand function pointers

12.7 Master dynamic allocation

ONGRATULATIONS! If you have worked your way through all the preceding chapters, you can definitely call yourself a C programmer. This chapter examines three topics: the C preprocessor, pointers to functions, and C's dynamic allocation system. All of the features discussed in this chapter are important, and you need to be aware of their existence. However, you won't use many of them right away. This is not because any of the features discussed in this chapter are particularly difficult, but because some features are more applicable to large programming efforts and the management of sophisticated systems. As your proficiency in C increases, however, you will find these features quite valuable.

Review
Skills Check

Before proceeding you should be able to answer these questions and perform these exercises:

1. What is the major advantage gained when a variable is declared using **register**?

2. What is wrong with this function?

```
void myfunc(const int *i)
{
    *i = *i / 2;
}
```

3. What is the outcome of these operations?

   a. 1101 1101 & 1110 0110

   b. 1101 1101 | 1110 0110

   c. 1101 1101 ^ 1110 0110

4. Write a program that uses the left and right shift operators to double and halve a number entered by the user.

5. How can these statements be written differently?

```
a = 1;
b = 1;
c = 1;
```

```
if(a<b) max = 100;
else max = 0;

i = i * 2;
```

6. What is the **extern** type specifier for?

12.1   *L*EARN MORE ABOUT #define AND
#include

Although you have been using **#define** and **#include** for some time,
both have more features than you've read about so far. Each is
examined here in detail.

In addition to using **#define** to define a macro name that will be
substituted by the character sequence associated with that macro, you
can use **#define** to create *function-like macros*. In a function-like
macro, arguments can be passed to the macro when it is expanded by
the preprocessor. For example, consider this program:

```
#include <stdio.h>

#define SUM(i, j) i+j

int main(void)
{
  int sum;

  sum = SUM(10, 20);
  printf("%d", sum);

  return 0;
}
```

The line

```
sum = SUM(10, 20);
```

is transformed into

```
sum = 10+20;
```

by the preprocessor. As you can see, the values 10 and 20 are
automatically substituted for the parameters **i** and **j**.

A more practical example is **RANGE( )**, illustrated in the following simple program. It is used to confirm that parameter **i** is within the range specified by parameters **min** and **max**. You can imagine how useful a macro like **RANGE( )** can be in programs that must perform several range checks. This program uses it to display random numbers between 1 and 100.

```c
#include <stdio.h>
#include <conio.h>
#include <stdlib.h>

#define RANGE(i, min, max) (i<min) || (i>max) ? 1 : 0

int main(void)
{
  int r;

  /* print random numbers between 1 and 100 */
  do {
    do {
      r = rand();
    } while(RANGE(r, 1, 100));
    printf("%d ", r);
  } while(!kbhit());

  return 0;
}
```

The advantage to using function-like macros instead of functions is that in-line code is generated by the macro, thus avoiding the time it takes to call and return from a function. Of course, only relatively simple operations can be made into function-like macros. Also, because code is duplicated, the resulting program might be longer than it would be if a function were used.

The **#include** directive has these two general forms:

#include <*filename*>
#include "*filename*"

So far, all the example programs have used the first form. The reason for this will become apparent after you read the following descriptions.

   If you specify the file name between angle brackets, you are
instructing the compiler to search for the file in some implementation-
defined manner. For most compilers, this means searching a special
directory devoted to the standard header files. This is why the sample
programs have been using this form to include the header files
required by the standard library functions. If you enclose the file
name between quotation marks, the compiler searches for the file in
another implementation-defined manner. If that search fails, the
search is restarted as if you had specified the file name between angle
brackets. For the majority of compilers, enclosing the name between
quotation marks causes the current working directory to be searched
first. Typically, you will use quotation marks to include header files
that you create.

EXAMPLES

1. Here is a program that uses the function-like macro **MAX( )** to
    compute which argument is larger. Pay close attention to the
    last **printf( )** statement.

    ```
    #include <stdio.h>

    #define MAX(i, j) i>j ? i : j

    int main(void)
    {
      printf("%d\n", MAX(1, 2));
      printf("%d\n", MAX(1, -1));

      /* this statement does not work correctly */
      printf("%d\n", MAX(100 && -1, 0));

      return 0;
    }
    ```

    When the preprocessor expands the final **printf( )** statement,
    the **MAX( )** macro is transformed into this expression:

    ```
    100 && -1 > 0 ? 100 && -1 : 0
    ```

Because of C's precedence rules, however, this expression is executed as if parentheses had been added like this:

```
100 && (-1 > 0) ? 100 && -1 : 0
```

As you can see, this causes the wrong answer to be computed. To fix this problem, the macro needs to be rewritten as:

```
#define MAX(i, j) ((i)>(j)) ? (i) : (j)
```

Now the macro works in all possible situations. In general, you will need to fully parenthesize all parameters to a function-like macro.

*The **RANGE( )** macro discussed earlier will need similar parenthesization as well if it is to work in all possible situations. This is left as an exercise.*

2. The next program uses quotes in the **#include** directive.

```
#include "stdio.h"

int main(void)
{
  printf("This is a test");

  return 0;
}
```

While not as efficient as using the angle brackets, the **#include** statement will still find and include the STDIO.H header file.

3. It is permissible to use both forms of the **#include** directive in the same program. For example,

```
#include <stdio.h>
#include "stdlib.h"

int main(void)
{
  printf("This is a random number: %d", rand());

  return 0;
}
```

EXERCISES

1. Correct the **RANGE( )** macro by adding parentheses in the proper locations.

2. Write a program that uses a parameterized macro to compute the absolute value of an integer, and demonstrate its use in a program.

3. Compile Example 2. If your compiler does not find STDIO.H, recheck the installation instructions that came with your compiler.

12.2   *U*NDERSTAND CONDITIONAL COMPILATION

The C preprocessor includes several directives that allow parts of the source code of a program to be selectively compiled. This is called *conditional compilation*. These directives are

```
#if
#else
#elif
#endif
#ifdef
#ifndef
```

This section examines these directives.

The general form of **#if** is shown here:

```
#if constant-expression
   statement-sequence
#endif
```

If the value of the *constant-expression* is true, the statement or statements between **#if** and **#endif** are compiled. If the *constant-expression* is false, the compiler skips the statement or statements. Keep in mind that the preprocessing stage is the first stage of compilation, so the *constant-expression* means exactly that. No variables may be used.

You can use the **#else** to form an alternative to the **#if**. Its general form is shown here:

```
#if constant-expression
    statement-sequence
#else
    statement-sequence
#endif
```

Notice that there is only one **#endif**. The **#else** automatically terminates the **#if** block of statements. If the *constant-expression* is false, the statement or statements associated with the **#else** are compiled.

You can create an if-else-if ladder using the **#elif** directive, as shown here:

```
#if constant-expression-1
    statement-sequence
#elif constant-expression-2
    statement-sequence
#elif constant-expression-3
    statement-sequence
    .
    .
    .
#endif
```

As soon as the first expression is true, the lines of code associated with that expression are compiled, and the rest of the code is skipped.

Another approach to conditional compilation is the **#ifdef** directive. It has this general form:

```
#ifdef macro-name
    statement-sequence
#endif
```

If the *macro-name* is currently defined, then the *statement-sequence* associated with the **#ifdef** directive will be compiled. Otherwise, it is skipped. The **#else** may also be used with **#ifdef** to provide an alternative.

The complement of **#ifdef** is **#ifndef**. It has the same general form as **#ifdef**. The only difference is that the statement sequence associated with an **#ifndef** directive is compiled only if the *macro-name* is *not* defined.

In addition to **#ifdef**, there is a second way to determine if a macro name is defined. You can use the **#if** directive in conjunction with the **defined** compile-time operator. The **defined** operator has this general form:

defined *macro-name*

If *macro-name* is defined, then the outcome is true. Otherwise, it is false. For example, the following two preprocessor directives are equivalent:

```
#ifdef WIN32
#if defined WIN32
```

You can also apply the **!** operator to **defined** to reverse the condition.

EXAMPLES

1. Sometimes you will want a program's behavior to depend on a value defined within the program. Although examples that are both short and meaningful are hard to find, the following program gives the flavor of it. This program can be compiled to display either the ASCII character set by itself, or the full extended set, depending on the value of **CHAR_SET**. As you know, the ASCII character set defines characters for the values 0 through 127. However, most computers reserve the values 128 through 255 for foreign-language characters and mathematical and other special symbols. (You might want to try this program with **CHAR_SET** set to 256. You will see some very interesting characters!)

```
#include <stdio.h>

/* define CHAR_SET as either 256 or 128 */
```

```
#define CHAR_SET 256

int main(void)
{
  int i;
#if CHAR_SET ==256
  printf("Displaying ASCII character set plus extensions.\n");
#else
  printf("Displaying only ASCII character set.\n");
#endif

  for(i=0; i<CHAR_SET; i++)
    printf("%c", i);

  return 0;
}
```

2. A good use of **#ifdef** is for imbedding debugging information into your programs. For example, here is a program that copies the contents of one file into another:

```
/* Copy a file. */
#include <stdio.h>
#include <stdlib.h>

#define DEBUG

int main(int argc, char *argv[])
{
  FILE *from, *to;
  char ch;

  /* see if correct number of command line arguments */
  if(argc!=3) {
    printf("Usage: copy <source> <destination>\n");
    exit(1);
  }

  /* open source file */
  if((from = fopen(argv[1], "rb"))==NULL) {
    printf("Cannot open source file.\n");
    exit(1);
  }
```

```
/*open destination file */
if((to = fopen (argv[2], "wb")) ==NULL) {
  printf("Cannot open destination file.\n");
  exit(1);
}

/* copy the file */
while(!feof(from)) {
  ch = fgetc(from);
  if(ferror(from)) {
    printf("Error reading source file.\n");
    exit(1);
  }
  if(!feof(from)) {
    fputc(ch, to);
#ifdef DEBUG
    putchar(ch);
#endif
  }
  if(ferror(to)) {
    printf("Error writing destination file.\n");
    exit(1);
  }
}
fclose(from);
fclose(to);

return 0;
}
```

If **DEBUG** is defined, the program displays each byte as it is transferred. This can be helpful during the development phase. Once the program is finished, the statement defining **DEBUG** is removed, and the output is not displayed. However, if the program ever misbehaves in the future, **DEBUG** can be defined again, and output will again be shown on the screen. While this might seem like a lot of work for such a simple program, in actual practice programs may have many debugging statements, and this procedure can greatly facilitate the development and testing cycle.

As shown in this program, to simply define a macro name, you do not have to associate any character sequence with it.

3. Continuing with the debugging theme, it is possible to use the **#if** to allow several levels of debugging code to be easily managed. For example, here is one of the encryption programs from the answers to Chapter 11 that supports three debugging levels:

```c
#include <stdio.h>
#include <stdlib.h>

/* DEBUG levels:
            0: no debug
            1: display byte read from source file
            2. display byte written to destination file
            3: display bytes read and bytes written
*/
#define DEBUG 2

int main(int argc, char *argv[])
{
  FILE *in, *out;
  unsigned char ch;

  /* see if correct number of command line arguments */
  if(argc!=4) {
    printf("Usage: code <in> <out> <key>");
    exit(1);
  }

  /* open input file */
  if((in = fopen(argv[1], "rb"))==NULL) {
    printf("Cannot open input file.\n");
    exit(1);
  }

  /* open output file */
  if((out = fopen(argv[2], "wb"))==NULL) {
    printf("Cannot open output file.\n");
    exit(1);
  }

  while(!feof(in)) {
```

```
      ch = fgetc(in);
#if DEBUG == 1 || DEBUG == 3
      putchar(ch);
#endif
      ch = *argv[3] ^ ch;
#if DEBUG >= 2
      putchar(ch);
#endif
      if(!feof(in)) fputc(ch, out);
  }

  fclose(in);
  fclose(out);

  return 0;
}
```

4. The following fragment illustrates the **#elif**. It displays **NUM is 2** on the screen.

```
#define NUM 2
 .
 .
 .
#if NUM == 1
  printf("NUM is 1");
#elif NUM == 2
  printf("NUM is 2");
#elif NUM == 3
  printf("NUM is 3");
#elif NUM == 4
  printf("NUM is 4");
#endif
```

5. Here, the **defined** operator is used to determine if **TESTPROJECT** is defined.

```
#include <stdio.h>

#define TESTPROJECT 29

#if defined TESTPROJECT
int main(void)
{
  printf("This is a test.\n");
```

```
        return 0;
    }
#endif
```

---

1. Write a program that defines three macros called **INT**, **FLOAT**, and **PWR_TYPE**. Define **INT** as 0, **FLOAT** as 1, and **PWR_TYPE** as either **INT** or **FLOAT**. Have the program request two numbers from the user and display the result of the first number raised to the second number. Using **#if** and depending upon the value of **PWR_TYPE**, have both numbers be integers, or allow the first number to be a **double**.

2. Is this fragment correct? If not, show one way to fix it.

```
#define MIKE

#ifdef !MIKE
   .
   .
   .
#endif
```

12.3   *L EARN ABOUT* #error, #undef, #line, *AND* #pragma

C's preprocessor supports four special-use directives: **#error**, **#undef**, **#line**, and **#pragma**. Each will be examined in turn here.

The **#error** directive has this general form:

#error *error-message*

It causes the compiler to stop compilation and issue the *error-message* along with other implementation-specific information, which will generally include the number of the line the **#error** directive is in and the name of the file. Note that the *error-message* is not enclosed between quotes. The principal use of the **#error** directive is in debugging.

The **#undef** directive undefines a macro name. Its general form is

#undef *macro-name*

If the *macro-name* is currently undefined, **#undef** has no effect. The principal use for **#undef** is to localize macro names.

When a C compiler compiles a source file, it maintains two pieces of information: the number of the line currently being compiled and the name of the source file currently being compiled. The **#line** directive is used to change these values. Its general form is

#line *line-num* "*filename*"

Here, *line-num* becomes the number of the next line of source code, and *filename* becomes the name the compiler will associate with the source file. The value of *line-num* must be between 1 and 32,767. The *filename* may be a string consisting of any valid file name. The principal use for **#line** is for debugging and for managing large projects.

The **#pragma** directive allows a compiler's implementor to define other preprocessing instructions to be given to the compiler. It has this general form:

#pragma *instructions*

If a compiler encounters a **#pragma** statement that it does not recognize, it ignores it. Whether your compiler supports any **#pragma**s depends on how your compiler was implemented.

EXAMPLES

1. This program demonstrates the **#error** directive.

```
#include <stdio.h>
```

```
int main(void)
{
  int i;

  i = 10;
#error This is an error message.
  printf("%d", i); /* this line will not be compiled */

  return 0;
}
```

As soon as the **#error** directive is encountered, compilation stops.

2. The next program demonstrates the **#undef** directive. As the program states, only the first **printf( )** statement is compiled.

```
#include <stdio.h>

#define DOG

int main(void)
{
#ifdef DOG
  printf("DOG is defined.\n");
#endif

#undef DOG

#ifdef DOG
  printf("This line is not compiled.\n");
#endif

  return 0;
}
```

3. The following program demonstrates the **#line** directive. Since virtually all implementations of **#error** display the line number and name of the file, it is used here to verify that **#line** did, in fact, perform its function correctly. (In the next section, you will see how a C program can directly access the line number and file name).

```
#include <stdio.h>

int main(void)
```

```
{
  int i;

/* reset line number to 1000 and file name to
     myprog.c
*/
#line 1000 "myprog.c"
#error Check the line number and file name.

  return 0;
}
```

4. Although the ANSI C standard does not specify any **#pragma** directives, on your own check your compiler's user manual and learn about any supported by your system.

EXERCISE

1. Try the example programs. See how these directives work on your system.

12.4   *E*XAMINE C'S BUILT-IN MACROS

If your C compiler complies with the ANSI C standard, it will have at least five predefined macro names that your program may use. They are

```
__LINE__
__FILE__
__DATE__
__TIME__
__STDC__
```

Each of these is explained here.

The _ _**LINE**_ _ macro defines an integer value that is equivalent to the line number of the source line currently being compiled.

The _ _**FILE**_ _ macro defines a string that is the name of the file currently being compiled.

The _ _**DATE**_ _ macro defines a string that holds the current system date. The string has this general form:

month/day/year

The _ _**TIME**_ _ macro defines a string that contains the time the compilation of a program began. The string has this general form:

hours:minutes:seconds

The _ _**STDC**_ _macro is defined as the value 1 if the compiler conforms to the ANSI standard.

EXAMPLES

1. This program demonstrates the macros _ _**LINE**_ _, _ _**FILE**_ _, _ _**DATE**_ _, and _ _**TIME**_ _.

```
#include <stdio.h>

int main(void)
{
  printf("Compiling %s, line: %d, on %s, at %s",
         __FILE__, __LINE__, __DATE__,
         __TIME__);

  return 0;
}
```

It is important to understand that the values of the macros are fixed at compile time. For example, if the above program is called T.C, and it is compiled on March 18, 1997, at 10 A.M., it will always display this output no matter when the program is run.

Compiling T.C. line: 6, on Mar 18 1997, at 10:00:00

The main use of these macros is to create a *time and date stamp*, which shows when the program was compiled.

2. As you learned in the previous section, you can use the **#line** directive to change the number of the current line of source code and the name of the file. When you do this, you are actually changing the values of _ _**LINE**_ _ and _ _**FILE**_ _. For example, this program sets _ _**LINE**_ _ to **100** and _ _**FILE**_ _ to **myprog.c**:

```
#include <stdio.h>

int main(void)
{
#line 100 "myprog.c"
  printf("Compiling %s, line: %d, on %s, at %s",
          __FILE__, __LINE__, __DATE__,
          __TIME__);

  return 0;
}
```

The program displays the following output, assuming it was compiled on March 18, 1997, at 10 A.M.

Compiling myprog.c, line: 101, on Mar 18 1997, at 10:00:00

EXERCISE

1. Compile and run the example programs.

12.5   *U SE THE # AND ## OPERATORS*

The C preprocessor contains two little-used but potentially valuable operators: **#** and **##**. The **#** operator turns the argument of a function-like macro into a quoted string. The **##** operator concatenates two identifiers.

EXAMPLES

1. This program demonstrates the **#** operator.

```
#include <stdio.h>

#define MKSTRING(str) # str

int main(void)
{
  int value;

  value = 10;

  printf("%s is %d", MKSTRING(value), value);

  return 0;
}
```

The program displays **value is 10**. This output occurs because **MKSTRING( )** causes the identifier **value** to be made into a quoted string.

2. The following program demonstrates the **##** operator. It creates the **output( )** macro, which translates into a call to **printf( )**. The value of two variables, which end in 1 or 2, is displayed.

```
#include <stdio.h>

#define output(i) printf("%d %d\n", i ## 1, i ## 2)

int main(void)
{
  int count1, count2;
  int i1, i2;

  count1 = 10;
  count2 = 20;
  i1 = 99;
  i2 = -10;
```

```
        output(count);
        output(i);

        return 0;
    }
```

The program displays **10 20 99 –10**. In the calls to **output( )**, **count** and **i** are concatenated with 1 and 2 to form the variable names **count1**, **count2**, **i1** and **i2** in the **printf( )** statements.

EXERCISES

1. Compile and run the example programs.

2. What does this program display?

```
#include <stdio.h>

#define JOIN(a, b) a ## b

int main(void)
{
    printf(JOIN("one ", "two"));

    return 0;
}
```

3. On your own, experiment with the **#** and **##** operators. Try to think of ways they can be useful to you in your own programming projects.

12.6   UNDERSTAND FUNCTION POINTERS

This section introduces one of C's most important advanced features: the function pointer. Although it is beyond the scope of this book to discuss all the nuances and implications of function pointers, the main issues are covered here.

A *function pointer* is a variable that contains the address of the entry point to a function. When the compiler compiles your program, it creates an entry point for each function in the program. The entry point is the address to which execution transfers when a function is called. Since the entry point has an address, it is possible to have a pointer variable point to it. Once you have a pointer to a function, it is possible to actually call that function using the pointer. You will see shortly why you might want to do this.

To create a variable that can point to a function, declare the pointer as having the same type as the return type of the function, followed by any parameters. For example, the following declares **p** as a pointer to a function that returns an integer and has two integer parameters, **x** and **y**.

```
int (*p) (int x, int y);
```

The parentheses surrounding ***p** are necessary because of C's precedence rules.

To assign the address of a function to a function pointer, simply use its name without any parentheses. For example, assuming that **sum( )** has the prototype

```
int sum(int a, int b);
```

the assignment statement

```
p = sum;
```

is correct. Once this has been done, you can call **sum( )** indirectly through **p** using a statement like

```
result = (*p) (10, 20);
```

Again, because of C's precedence rules, the parentheses are necessary around ***p**. Actually, you can also just use **p** directly, like this:

```
result = p(10, 20);
```

However, the **(*p)** form tips off anyone reading your code that a function pointer is being used to indirectly call a function, instead of calling a function named **p**.

1. As a first example, this program fills in the details and demonstrates the function pointer that was just described.

```c
#include <stdio.h>

int sum(int a, int b);

int main(void)
{
  int (*p) (int x, int y);
  int result;

  p = sum; /* get address of sum() */

  result = (*p) (10, 20);
  printf("%d", result);

  return 0;
}

int sum(int a, int b)
{
  return a+b;
}
```

The program prompts the user for two numbers, calls **sum( )** indirectly using **p**, and displays the result.

2. Although the program in Example 1 illustrates the mechanics of using function pointers, it does not even hint at their power. The following example, however, will give you a taste.

   One of the most important uses of function pointers occurs when a function-pointer array is created. Each element in the array can point to a different function. To call any specific function, the array is simply indexed. A function pointer array allows very efficient code to be written when a variety of different functions need to be called under differing circumstances. Function-pointer arrays are typically used when writing systems software, such as compilers, assemblers, and interpreters. However, they are not limited to these applications. While meaningful and short examples of function-pointer arrays are difficult to find, the program shown next gives you an idea of their value. Like the program in Example 1, this program prompts the user for two numbers. Next, it asks the user to enter the number of the operation to perform. This number is then used to index the function-pointer array to execute the proper function. Finally, the result is displayed.

```c
#include <stdio.h>

int sum(int a, int b);
int subtract(int a, int b);
int mul(int a, int b);
int div(int a, int b);

int (*p[4]) (int x, int y);

int main(void)
{
  int result;
  int i, j, op;

  p[0] = sum; /* get address of sum() */
  p[1] = subtract; /* get address of subtract() */
  p[2] = mul; /* get address of mul() */
  p[3] = div; /* get address of div() */

  printf("Enter two numbers: ");
  scanf("%d%d", &i, &j);
  printf("0: Add, 1: Subtract, 2: Multiply, 3: Divide\n");
  do {
    printf("Enter number of operation: ");
    scanf("%d", &op);
  } while(op<0 || op>3);

  result = (*p[op]) (i, j);
  printf("%d", result);

  return 0;
}

int sum(int a, int b)
{
  return a+b;
}

int subtract(int a, int b)
```

```
{
  return a-b;
}

int mul(int a, int b)
{
  return a*b;
}

int div(int a, int b)
{
  if(b) return a/b;
  else return 0;
}
```

When you study this code, it becomes clear that using a function-pointer array to call the appropriate function is more efficient than using a **switch( )** statement.

Before leaving this example, we can use it to illustrate one more point: function-pointer arrays can be initialized, just like any other array. The following version of the program shows this.

```
#include <stdio.h>

int sum(int a, int b);
int subtract(int a, int b);
int mul(int a, int b);
int div(int a, int b);

/* initialize the pointer array */
int (*p[4]) (int x, int y) = {
  sum, subtract, mul, div
} ;

int main(void)
{
  int result;
  int i, j, op;

  printf("Enter two numbers: ");
  scanf("%d%d", &i, &j);
  printf("0: Add, 1: Subtract, 2: Multiply, 3: Divide\n");
  do {
    printf("Enter number of operation: ");
```

```
      scanf("%d", &op);
    } while(op<0 || op>3);

    result = (*p[op]) (i, j);
    printf("%d", result);

    return 0;
}

int sum(int a, int b)
{
    return a+b;
}

int subtract(int a, int b)
{
    return a-b;
}

int mul(int a, int b)
{
    return a*b;
}

int div(int a, int b)
{
    if(b) return a/b;
    else return 0;
}
```

3. One of the most common uses of a function pointer occurs when utilizing another of C's standard library functions, **qsort( )**. The **qsort( )** function is a generic sort routine that can sort any type of singly dimensioned array, using the Quicksort algorithm. Its prototype is

   void qsort(void *array, size_t number, size_t size,
            int (*comp)(const void *a, const void *b));

   Here, *array* is a pointer to the first element in the array to be sorted. The number of elements in the array is specified by *number*, and the size of each element of the array is specified by *size.* (Remember, **size_t** is defined by the C compiler and is loosely the same as **unsigned**.) The final parameter is a pointer to a function (which you create) that compares two elements of the array and returns the following results:

*a < *b	returns a negative value
*a == *b	returns a zero
*a > *b	returns a positive value

The **qsort( )** function has no return value. It uses the STDLIB.H header file.

The following program loads a 100-element integer array with random numbers, sorts it, and displays the sorted form. Notice the necessary type casts within the **comp( )** function.

```c
#include <stdio.h>
#include <stdlib.h>

int comp(const void *i, const void *j);

int main(void)
{
  int sort[100], i;

  for(i=0; i<100; i++)
    sort[i] = rand();

  qsort(sort, 100, sizeof(int), comp);

  for(i=0; i<100; i++)
    printf("%d\n", sort[i]);

  return 0;
}

int comp(const void *i, const void *j)
{
  return *(int*)i - *(int*)j;
}
```

1. Compile and run all of the example programs. Experiment with them, making minor changes.

2. Another of C's standard library functions is called **bsearch( )**. This function searches a sorted array, given a key. It returns a pointer to the first entry in the array that matches the key. If no match is found, a null pointer is returned. Its prototype is

   void *bsearch(const void *key, const void *array, size_t number, size_t size, int (*comp)(const void *a, const void *b));

   All the parameters to **bsearch( )** are the same as for **qsort( )** except the first, which is a pointer to *key*, the object being sought. The **comp( )** function operates the same for **bsearch( )** as it does for **qsort( )**.

   Modify the program in Example 3 so that after the array is sorted, the user is prompted to enter a number. Next, using **bsearch( )**, search the sorted array and report if a match is found.

3. Add a function called **modulus( )** to the final version of the arithmetic program in Example 2. Have the function return the result of **a % b**. Add this option to the menu and fully integrate it into the program.

12.7 ***M**ASTER DYNAMIC ALLOCATION*

This final section of the book introduces you to C's dynamic-allocation system. *Dynamic allocation* is the process by which memory is allocated as needed during runtime. This allocated memory can be used for a variety of purposes. Most commonly, memory is allocated by applications that need to take full advantage of all the memory in the computer. For example, a word processor will want to let the user edit documents that are as large as possible. However, if the word processor uses a normal character array, it must fix its size at compile time. Thus, it would have to be compiled to run in computers with the minimum amount of memory, not allowing users with more memory to edit larger documents. If memory is allocated dynamically (as needed until memory is exhausted), however, any user may make full use of the memory in the system. Other uses for dynamic allocation include linked lists and binary trees.

The core of C's dynamic-allocation functions are **malloc( )**, which allocates memory, and **free( )**, which releases previously allocated memory. Their prototypes are

void *malloc(size_t *numbytes*);

void free(void *ptr*);

Here, *numbytes* is the number of bytes of memory you wish to allocate. The **malloc( )** function returns a pointer to the start of the allocated piece of memory. If **malloc( )** cannot fulfill the memory request—for example, there may be insufficient memory available—it returns a null pointer. To free memory, call **free( )** with a pointer to the start of the block of memory (previously allocated using **malloc( )**) you wish to free. Both functions use the header file STDLIB.H.

Memory is allocated from a region called the *heap*. Although the actual physical layout of memory may differ, conceptually the heap lies between your program and the stack. Since this is a finite area, an allocation request can fail when memory is exhausted.

When a program terminates, all allocated memory is automatically released.

EXAMPLES

1. You must confirm that a call to **malloc( )** is successful before you use the pointer it returns. If you perform an operation on a null pointer, you could crash your program and maybe even the entire computer. The easiest way to check for a valid pointer is shown in this fragment:

```
p = malloc(SIZE);

if(!p) {
  printf("Allocation Error");
```

```
    exit(1);
}
```

2. The following program allocates 80 bytes and assigns a character pointer to it. This creates a dynamic character array. It then uses the allocated memory to input a string using **gets( )**. Finally, the string is redisplayed and the pointer is freed. (As stated earlier, all memory is freed when the program ends, so the call to **free( )** is included in this program simply to demonstrate its use.)

```c
#include <stdio.h>
#include <stdlib.h>

int main(void)
{
  char *p;

  p = malloc(80);

  if(!p) {
    printf("Allocation Failed");
    exit(1);
  }

  printf("Enter a string: ");
  gets(p);
  printf(p);
  free(p);

  return 0;
}
```

3. The next program tells you approximately how much free memory is available to your program.

```c
#include <stdio.h>
#include <stdlib.h>

int main(void)
{
  char *p;
  long l;

  l = 0;
```

```
do {
  p = malloc(1000);
  if(p) l += 1000;
} while(p);

printf("Approximately %ld bytes of free memory.", l);

return 0;
}
```

The program works by allocating 1000-byte-long chunks of memory until an allocation request fails. When **malloc( )** returns null, the heap is exhausted. Hence, the value of **l** represents (within 1000 bytes) the amount of free memory available to the program.

4. One good use for dynamic allocation is to create buffers for file I/O when you are using **fread( )** and/or **fwrite( )**. Often, you only need a buffer for a short period of time, so it makes sense to allocate it when needed and free it when done. The following program shows how dynamic allocation can be used to create a buffer. The program allocates enough space to hold ten floating-point values. It then assigns ten random numbers to the allocated memory, indexing the pointer as an array. Next, it writes the values to disk and frees the memory. Finally, it reallocates memory, reads the file and displays the random numbers. Although there is no need to free and then reallocate the memory that serves as a file buffer in this short example, it illustrates the basic idea.

```
#include <stdio.h>
#include <stdlib.h>

int main(void)
{

  int i;
  double *p;
  FILE *fp;

  /* get memory */
  p = malloc(10 * sizeof(double));
  if(!p) {
    printf("Allocation Error");
```

```
      exit(1);
    }

    /* generate 10 random numbers */
    for(i=0; i<10; i++)
      p[i] = (double) rand();

    if((fp = fopen("myfile", "wb"))==NULL) {
      printf("Cannot open file.\n");
      exit(1);
    }

    /* write the entire array in one step */
    if(fwrite(p, 10*sizeof(double), 1, fp) != 1) {
      printf("Write Error.\n");
      exit(1);
    }
    fclose(fp);

    free(p); /* memory not needed now */

    /*
      imagine something transpires here
       .
       .
       .
    */

    /* get memory again */
    p = malloc(10 * sizeof(double));
    if(!p) {
      printf("Allocation Error");
      exit(1);
    }

    if((fp = fopen("myfile", "rb"))==NULL) {
      printf("Cannot open file.\n");
      exit(1);
    }
    /* read the entire array in one step */
    if(fread(p, 10*sizeof(double), 1, fp) != 1) {
      printf("Read Error.\n");
```

```
    exit(1);
  }
  fclose(fp);

  /* display the array */
  for(i=0; i<10; i++) printf("%f ", p[i]);
  free(p);

  return 0;
}
```

5. Just as array boundaries can be overrun, so can the boundaries
   of allocated memory. For example, this fragment is syntactically
   valid, but wrong.

```
p = malloc(10);

for(i=0; i<100; i) p[i] = i;
```

EXERCISES

1. Compile and run the example programs.

2. Write a program that creates a ten-element dynamic integer
   array. Next, using pointer arithmetic or array indexing, assign
   the values 1 through 10 to the integers that comprise the array.
   Finally, display the values and free the memory.

3. What's wrong with this fragment?

```
char *p;

*p = malloc(10);

gets(p);
```

Mastery Skills Check

At this point you should be able to answer these questions and perform these exercises:

1. What is the difference between using quotes and angle brackets with the **#include** directive?

2. Using an **#ifdef**, show how to conditionally compile this fragment of code based upon whether **DEBUG** is defined or not.

```
if(!(j%2)) {
  printf("j = %d\n", j);
  j = 0;
}
```

3. Using the fragment from Exercise 2, show how you can conditionally compile the code when **DEBUG** is defined as 1. (Hint: Use **#if**).

4. How do you undefine a macro?

5. What is _ _**FILE**_ _ and what does it represent?

6. What do the **#** and **##** preprocessor operators do?

7. Write a program that sorts the string "this is a test of qsort". Display the sorted output.

8. Write a program that dynamically allocates memory for one **double**. Have the program assign that location the value 99.01, display the value, and then free the memory.

Cumulative Skills Check

This section checks how well you have integrated the material in this chapter with that from earlier chapters.

1. Section 10.1, Example 3, presents a computerized card-catalog program that uses an array of structures to hold information on books. Change this program so that only an array of structure

pointers is created, and use dynamically allocated memory to actually hold the information for each book as it is entered. This way, less memory is used when information on only a few books is stored.

2. Show the macro equivalent of this function:

```
char code_it(char c)
{
   return ~c;
}
```

Demonstrate that your macro version works in a program.

3. On your own, look over the programs that you have written in the course of working through this book. Try to find places where you can:

   ▼   Use conditional compilation.

   ▼   Replace a short function with a function-like macro.

   ▼   Replace statically allocated arrays with dynamic arrays.

   ▼   Use function pointers.

4. On your own, study the user's manual or online documentation for your C compiler, paying special attention to the description of its standard library functions. The C standard library contains several hundred library functions that can make your programming tasks easier. Also, Appendix A in this book discusses some of the most common library functions.

5. Now that you have finished this book, go back and skim through each chapter, thinking about how each aspect of C relates to the rest of it. As you will see, C is a highly integrated language, in which one feature complements another. The connection between pointers and arrays, for example, is pure elegance.

6. C is a language best learned by doing! Continue to write programs in C and to study other programmers' programs. You will be surprised at how quickly C will become second nature!

7. Finally, you now have the necessary foundation in C to allow you to move on to C++, C's object-oriented extension. If C++ programming is in your future, proceed to *Teach Yourself C++*, (Berkeley, CA, Osborne/McGraw-Hill). It picks up where this book leaves off.

A

*Some Common C
Library Functions*

THIS appendix discusses a number of the more frequently used ANSI C library functions. If you have looked through the library section in your C/C++ compiler's documentation, you are no doubt aware that there are a great many library functions. It is far beyond the scope of this book to cover each one. However, the ones you will most commonly need are discussed here. The library functions can be grouped into the following categories:

▼ I/O functions

▼ String and character functions

▼ Mathematics functions

▼ Time and date functions

▼ Dynamic allocation functions

▼ Miscellaneous functions

The I/O functions were thoroughly covered in Chapters 8 and 9 and will not be expanded upon here.

Each function's description begins with the header file required by the function followed by its prototype. The prototype provides you with a quick way of knowing what types of arguments and how many of them the function takes and what type of value it returns.

Keep in mind that ANSI C specifies many data types, which are defined in the header files used by the functions. New type names will be discussed as they are introduced.

A.1 ▮ STRING AND CHARACTER FUNCTIONS

The C standard library has a rich and varied set of string- and character-handling functions. In C, a string is a null-terminated array of characters. The declarations for the string functions are found in the header file STRING.H. The character functions use CTYPE.H as their header file.

Because C has no bounds-checking on array operations, it is the programmer's responsibility to prevent an array overflow.

The character functions are declared with an integer parameter. While this is true, only the low-order byte is used by the function. Generally, you are free to use a character argument because it will automatically be elevated to **int** at the time of the call.

#include <ctype.h>
int isalnum(int ch);

Description The **isalnum( )** function returns nonzero if its argument is either a letter or a digit. If the character is not alphanumeric, then 0 is returned.

Example This program checks each character read from **stdin** and reports all alphanumeric ones:

```
#include <ctype.h>
#include <stdio.h>

int main(void)
{
  char ch;

  for(;;) {
    ch = getchar();
    if(ch==' ') break;
    if(isalnum(ch)) printf("%c is alphanumeric\n", ch);
  }

  return 0;
}
```

#include <ctype.h>
int isalpha(int ch);

Description The **isalpha( )** function returns nonzero if *ch* is a letter of the alphabet; otherwise 0 is returned.

Example This program checks each character read from **stdin** and reports all those that are letters of the alphabet:

```
#include <ctype.h>
#include <stdio.h>

int main(void)
{
  char ch;

  for(;;) {
    ch = getchar();
    if(ch==' ') break;
    if(isalpha(ch)) printf("%c is a letter\n", ch);
  }

  return 0;
}
```

#include <ctype.h>
int iscntrl(int ch);

Description   The **iscntrl( )** function returns nonzero if *ch* is between 0 and 0x1F or is equal to 0x7F (DEL); otherwise 0 is returned.

Example   This program checks each character read from **stdin** and reports all control characters:

```
#include <ctype.h>
#include <stdio.h>

int main(void)
{
  char ch;

  for(;;) {
    ch = getchar();
    if(ch==' ') break;
    if(iscntrl(ch))
      printf("%c is a control character\n", ch);
  }

  return 0;
}
```

#include <ctype.h>
int isdigit(int ch);

Description   The **isdigit( )** function returns nonzero if *ch* is a digit (0 through 9); otherwise 0 is returned.

Example   This program checks each character read from **stdin** and reports all those that are digits:

```
#include <ctype.h>
#include <stdio.h>

int main(void)
{
  char ch;

  for(;;) {
    ch = getchar();
    if(ch==' ') break;
    if(isdigit(ch)) printf("%c is a digit\n", ch);
  }

  return 0;
}
```

#include <ctype.h>
int isgraph(int ch);

Description   The **isgraph( )** function returns nonzero if *ch* is any printable character other than a space; otherwise 0 is returned. Printable characters are in the range 0x21 through 0x7E.

Example   This program checks each character read from **stdin** and reports all printing characters:

```
#include <ctype.h>
#include <stdio.h>

int main(void)
{
  char ch;
```

```
   for(;;) {
     ch = getchar();
     if(ch==' ') break;
     if(isgraph(ch))
       printf("%c is a printing character\n", ch);
   }

   return 0;
}
```

#include <ctype.h>
int islower(int ch);

Description   The **islower( )** function returns nonzero if *ch* is a lowercase letter (a through z); otherwise 0 is returned.

Example   This program checks each character read from **stdin** and reports all those that are lowercase letters:

```
#include <ctype.h>
#include <stdio.h>

int main(void)
{
  char ch;

  for(;;) {
    ch = getchar();
    if(ch==' ') break;
    if(islower(ch)) printf("%c is lowercase\n", ch);
  }

  return 0;
}
```

#include <ctype.h>
int isprint(int ch);

Description   The **isprint( )** function returns nonzero if *ch* is a printable character, including a space; otherwise 0 is returned. Printable characters are often in the range 0x20 through 0x7E.

Example   This program checks each character read from **stdin** and reports all those that are printable:

```c
#include <ctype.h>
#include <stdio.h>

int main(void)
{
  char ch;

  for(;;) {
    ch = getchar();
    if(ch=='Q') break;
    if(isprint(ch)) printf("%c is printable\n", ch);
  }

  return 0;
}
```

#include <ctype.h>
int ispunct(int ch);

Description   The **ispunct( )** function returns nonzero if *ch* is a punctuation character, excluding the space; otherwise 0 is returned. The term "punctuation," as defined by this function, includes all printing characters that are neither alphanumeric nor a space.

Example   This program checks each character read from **stdin** and reports all those that are punctuation:

```c
#include <ctype.h>
#include <stdio.h>

int main(void)
{
  char ch;

  for(;;) {
    ch = getchar();
    if(ch==' ') break;
    if(ispunct(ch)) printf("%c is punctuation\n", ch);
  }
```

```
    return 0;
}
```

#include <ctype.h>
int isspace(int ch);

Description   The **isspace( )** function returns nonzero if *ch* is either a space, tab, vertical tab, form feed, carriage return, or newline character; otherwise 0 is returned.

Example   This program checks each character read from **stdin** and reports all those that are whitespace characters:

```
#include <ctype.h>
#include <stdio.h>

int main(void)
{
  char ch;

  for(;;) {
    ch = getchar();
    if(isspace(ch)) printf("%c is whitespace\n", ch);
    if(ch==' ') break;
  }

  return 0;
}
```

#include <ctype.h>
int isupper(int ch);

Description   The **isupper( )** function returns nonzero if *ch* is an uppercase letter (A through Z); otherwise 0 is returned.

Example   This program checks each character read from **stdin** and reports all those that are uppercase letters:

```
#include <ctype.h>
#include <stdio.h>
```

```
int main(void)
{
  char ch;

  for(;;) {
    ch = getchar();
    if(ch==' ') break;
    if(isupper(ch)) printf("%c is uppercase\n", ch);
  }

  return 0;
}
```

#include <ctype.h>
int isxdigit(int ch);

Description   The **isxdigit( )** function returns nonzero if *ch* is a hexadecimal digit; otherwise 0 is returned. A hexadecimal digit will be in one of these ranges: **A** through **F**, **a** through **f**, or **0** through **9**.

Example   This program checks each character read from **stdin** and reports all those that are hexadecimal digits:

```
#include <ctype.h>
#include <stdio.h>

int main(void)
{
  char ch;

  for(;;) {
    ch = getchar();
    if(ch==' ') break;
    if(isxdigit(ch)) printf("%c is hexadecimal \n", ch);
  }

  return 0;
}
```

#include <string.h>
char *strcat(char *str1, const char *str2);

Description   The **strcat( )** function concatenates a copy of *str2* to *str1* and terminates *str1* with a null. The null terminator originally ending *str1* is overwritten by the first character of *str2*. The string *str2* is untouched by the operation. The **strcat( )** function returns *str1*.

No bounds-checking takes place, so it is the programmer's responsibility to ensure that str1 *is large enough to hold both its original contents and those of* str2.

Example   This program appends the first string read from **stdin** to the second. For example, assuming the user enters **hello** and **there**, the program will print **therehello**.

```
#include <string.h>
#include <stdio.h>

int main(void)
{
  char s1[80], s2[80];

  printf("Enter two strings: ");
  gets(s1);
  gets(s2);

  strcat(s2, s1);
  printf(s2);

  return 0;
}
```

#include <string.h>
char *strchr(const char *str, int ch);

Description   The **strchr( )** function returns a pointer to the first occurrence of the low-order byte of *ch* in the string pointed to by *str*. If no match is found, a null pointer is returned.

Example   This prints the string **is a test**:

```
#include <string.h>
#include <stdio.h>

int main(void)
{
  char *p;

  p = strchr("this is a test", ' ');
  printf(p);

  return 0;
}
```

#include <string.h>
int strcmp(const char *str1, const char *str2);

Description   A **strcmp( )** function lexicographically compares two null-terminated strings and returns an integer based on the outcome, as shown here:

Result	Meaning
less than 0	*str1* is less than *str2*
0	*str1* is equal to *str2*
greater than 0	*str1* is greater than *str2*

Example   The following function can be used as a password verification routine. It will return 0 on failure and 1 on success.

```
#include <string.h>

int password(void)
{
  char s[80];

  printf("Enter password: ");
  gets(s);

  if(strcmp(s,"pass")) {
    printf("Invalid Password\n");
    return 0;
```

```
    }
  return 1;
}
```

#include <string.h>
char *strcpy(char *str1, const char *str2);

Description   The **strcpy( )** function is used to copy the contents of *str2* into *str1*; *str2* must be a pointer to a null-terminated string. The **strcpy( )** function returns a pointer to *str1*.
   If *str1* and *str2* overlap, the behavior of **strcpy( )** is undefined.

Example   The following code fragment will copy "hello" into string **str**:

```
char str[80];
strcpy(str, "hello");
```

#include <string.h>
size_t strlen(const char *str);

Description   The **strlen( )** function returns the length of the null-terminated string pointed to by *str*. The null is not counted. The **size_t** type is defined in STRING.H.

Example   The following code fragment will print **5** on the screen:

```
strcpy(s, "hello");
printf("%d", strlen(s));
```

#include <stdio.h>
char *strstr(const char *str1, const char *str2);

Description   The **strstr( )** function returns a pointer to the first occurrence of the string pointed to by *str2* in the string pointed to by *str1* (except *str2*'s null terminator). It returns a null pointer if no match is found.

Example   This program displays the message **is a test**:

```
#include <string.h>
#include <stdio.h>

int main(void)
{
  char *p;

  p = strstr("this is a test", "is");
  printf(p);

  return 0;
}
```

#include <string.h>
char *strtok(char *str1, const char *str2);

Description   The **strtok( )** function returns a pointer to the next token in the string pointed to by *str1*. The characters making up the string pointed to by *str2* are the delimiters that separate each token. A null pointer is returned when there are no more tokens.

The first time **strtok( )** is called, *str1* is actually used in the call. Subsequent calls use a null pointer for the first argument. In this way the entire string can be reduced to its tokens.

It is possible to use a different set of delimiters for each call to **strtok( )**.

Example   This program tokenizes the string "The summer soldier, the sunshine patriot" with spaces and commas as the delimiters. The output will be **The | summer | soldier | the | sunshine | patriot**.

```
#include <string.h>
#include <stdio.h>

int main(void)
{
  char *p;

  p = strtok("The summer soldier, the sunshine patriot", " ,");

  printf(p);
  do {
   p = strtok('\0', ", ");
   if(p) printf("|%s", p);
```

```
    } while(p);

    return 0;
}
```

#include <ctype.h>
int tolower(int ch);

Description   The **tolower( )** function returns the lowercase equivalent of *ch* if *ch* is a letter; otherwise *ch* is returned unchanged.

Example   This fragment displays **q**:

```
putchar(tolower('Q'));
```

#include <ctype.h>
int toupper(int ch);

Description   The **toupper( )** function returns the uppercase equivalent of *ch* if *ch* is a letter; otherwise *ch* is returned unchanged.

Example   This displays **A**:

```
putchar(toupper('a'));
```

A.2   *T*HE MATHEMATICS FUNCTIONS

ANSI C defines several mathematics functions that take **double** arguments and return **double** values. These functions fall into the following categories:

▼   Trigonometric functions

▼   Hyperbolic functions

▼   Exponential and logarithmic functions

▼   Miscellaneous functions

All the math functions require that the header MATH.H be included in any program that uses them. In addition to declaring the math functions, this header defines a macro called **HUGE_VAL**. If an operation produces a result that is too large to be represented by a **double**, an overflow occurs, which causes the routine to return **HUGE_VAL**. This is called a *range error*. For all the mathematics functions, if the input value is not in the domain for which the function is defined, a *domain error* occurs.

All angles are specified in radians.

#include <math.h>
double acos(double arg);

Description   The **acos( )** function returns the arc cosine of *arg*. The argument to **acos( )** must be in the range –1 through 1; otherwise a domain error will occur.

Example   This program prints the arc cosines, in one-tenth increments, of the values –1 through 1:

```
#include <math.h>
#include <stdio.h>

int main(void)
{
  double val = -1.0;

  do {
    printf("arc cosine of %f is %f\n", val, acos(val));
    val += 0.1;
  } while(val<=1.0);

  return 0;
}
```

#include <math.h>
double asin(double arg);

Description   The **asin( )** function returns the arc sine of *arg*. The argument to **asin( )** must be in the range –1 through 1; otherwise a domain error will occur.

Example   This program prints the arc sines, in one-tenth increments, of the values –1 through 1:

```
#include <math.h>
#include <stdio.h>

int main(void)
{
  double val=-1.0;

  do {
    printf("arc sine of %f is %f\n", val, asin(val));
    val += 0.1;
  } while(val<=1.0);

  return 0;
}
```

#include <math.h>
double atan(double arg);

Description   The **atan( )** function returns the arc tangent of *arg*.

Example   This program prints the arc tangents, in one-tenth increments, of the values –1 through 1:

```
#include <math.h>
#include <stdio.h>

int main(void)
{
  double val=-1.0;

  do {
    printf("arc tangent of %f is %f\n", val, atan(val));
    val += 0.1;
  } while(val<=1.0);

  return 0;
}
```

#include <math.h>
double atan2(double y, double x);

Description   The **atan2( )** function returns the arc tangent of y/x. It uses the signs of its arguments to compute the quadrant of the return value.

Example   This program prints the arc tangents, in one-tenth increments of y, from –1 through 1:

```c
#include <math.h>
#include <stdio.h>

int main(void)
{
  double y=-1.0;

  do {
    printf("atan2 of %f is %f\n", y, atan2(y, 1.0));
    y += 0.1;
  } while(y<=1.0);

  return 0;
}
```

#include <math.h>
double ceil(double num);

Description   The **ceil( )** function returns the smallest integer (represented as a **double**) that is not less than *num*. For example, given 1.02, **ceil( )** would return 2.0; given –1.02, **ceil( )** would return –1.

Example   This fragment prints **10.0** on the screen:

```c
printf("%f", ceil(9.9));
```

#include <math.h>
double cos(double arg);

Description   The **cos( )** function returns the cosine of *arg*. The value of *arg* must be in radians.

Example   This program prints the cosines, in one-tenth increments, of the values −1 through 1:

```
#include <math.h>
#include <stdio.h>

int main(void)
{
  double val=-1.0;

  do {
    printf("cosine of %f is %f\n", val, cos(val));
    val += 0.1;
  } while(val<=1.0);

  return 0;
}
```

#include <math.h>
double cosh(double arg);

Description   The **cosh( )** function returns the hyperbolic cosine of *arg*.

Example   This program prints the hyperbolic cosines, in one-tenth increments, of the values −1 through 1:

```
#include <math.h>
#include <stdio.h>

int main(void)
{
  double val=-1.0;

  do {
    printf("hyperbolic cosine of %f is %f\n", val, cosh(val));
    val += 0.1;
```

```
  } while(val<=1.0);

  return 0;
}
```

#include <math.h>
double exp(double arg);

Description   The **exp( )** function returns the natural logarithm *e* raised to the *arg* power.

Example   This fragment displays the value of *e* (rounded to 2.718282):

```
printf("Value of e to the first: %f", exp(1.0));
```

#include <math.h>
double fabs(double num);

Description   The **fabs( )** function returns the absolute value of *num*.

Example   This program prints the numbers **1.0 1.0** on the screen:

```
#include <math.h>
#include <stdio.h>

int main(void)
{
  printf("%1.1f %1.1f", fabs(1.0), fabs(-1.0));

  return 0;
}
```

#include <math.h>
double floor(double num);

Description   The **floor( )** function returns the largest integer (represented as a **double**) not greater than *num*. For example, given 1.02, **floor( )** would return 1.0; given –1.02, **floor( )** would return –2.0.

Example This fragment prints **10.0** on the screen:

```
printf("%f", floor(10.9));
```

#include <math.h>
double log(double num);

Description The **log( )** function returns the natural logarithm for *num*. A domain error occurs if *num* is negative and a range error occurs if the argument is 0.

Example This program prints the natural logarithms for the numbers 1 through 10:

```
#include <math.h>
#include <stdio.h>

int main(void)
{
  double val=1.0;

  do {
    printf("%f %f\n", val, log(val));
    val++;
  } while(val<11.0);

  return 0;
}
```

#include <math.h>
double log10(double num);

Description The **log10( )** function returns the base 10 logarithm for the variable *num*. A domain error occurs if *num* is negative and a range error occurs if the argument is 0.

Example This program prints the base 10 logarithms for the numbers 1 through 10:

```
#include <math.h>
#include <stdio.h>
```

```
int main(void)
{
  double val=1.0;

  do {
    printf("%f %f\n", val, log10(val));
    val++;
  } while(val<11.0);

  return 0;
}
```

#include <math.h>
double pow(double base, double exp);

Description   The **pow( )** function returns *base* raised to the *exp* power ($base^{exp}$). A domain error may occur if *base* is 0 and *exp* is less than or equal to 0. A domain error will occur if *base* is negative and *exp* is not an integer. An overflow produces a range error.

Example   This program prints the first ten powers of 10:

```
#include <math.h>
#include <stdio.h>

int main(void)
{
  double x=10.0, y=0.0;

  do {
    printf("%f ", pow(x, y));
    y++;
  } while(y<11);

  return 0;
}
```

#include <math.h>
double sin(double arg);

Description   The **sin( )** function returns the sine of *arg*. The value of *arg* must be in radians.

Example This program prints the sines, in one-tenth increments, of the values –1 through 1:

```c
#include <math.h>
#include <stdio.h>

int main(void)
{
  double val=-1.0;

  do {
    printf("sine of %f is %f\n", val, sin(val));
    val += 0.1;
  } while(val<=1.0);

  return 0;
}
```

#include <math.h>
double sinh(double arg);

Description The **sinh( )** function returns the hyperbolic sine of *arg*.

Example The following program prints the hyperbolic sines, in one-tenth increments, of the values –1 through 1:

```c
#include <math.h>
#include <stdio.h>

int main(void)
{
  double val=-1.0;

  do {
    printf("hyperbolic sine of %f is %f\n", val, sinh(val));
    val += 0.1;
  } while(val<=1.0);

  return 0;
}
```

#include <math.h>
double sqrt(double num);

Description   The **sqrt( )** function returns the square root of *num*. If called with a negative argument, a domain error will occur.

Example   This fragment prints **4.0** on the screen:

```
printf("%f", sqrt(16.0));
```

#include <math.h>
double tan(double arg);

Description   The **tan( )** function returns the tangent of *arg*. The value of *arg* must be in radians.

Example   This program prints the tangents, in one-tenth increments, of the values –1 through 1:

```
#include <math.h>
#include <stdio.h>

int main(void)
{
  double val=-1.0;

  do {
    printf("tangent of %f is %f\n", val, tan(val));
    val += 0.1;
  } while(val<=1.0);

  return 0;
}
```

#include <math.h>
double tanh(double arg);

Description   The **tanh( )** function returns the hyperbolic tangent of *arg*.

Example   This program prints the hyperbolic tangents, in one-tenth increments, of the values –1 through 1:

```
#include <math.h>
#include <stdio.h>

int main(void)
{
  double val=-1.0;

  do {
    printf("tanh of %f is %f\n", val, tanh(val));
    val += 0.1;
  } while(val<=1.0);

  return 0;
}
```

A.3   *T*IME AND DATE FUNCTIONS

The time and date functions require the header TIME.H for their prototypes. This header file also defines four types and two macros. The type **time_t** is able to represent the system time and date as a **long** integer. This is called the *calendar time*. The structure type **tm** holds date and time broken down into its elements. The **tm** structure is defined as shown here:

```
struct tm {
  int tm_sec;   /* seconds, 0-61 */
  int tm_min;   /* minutes, 0-59 */
  int tm_hour;  /* hours, 0-23 */
  int tm_mday;  /* day of the month, 1-31*/
  int tm_mon;   /* months since Jan, 0-11 */
  int tm_year;  /* years from 1900 */
  int tm_wday;  /* days since Sunday, 0-6 */
  int tm_yday;  /* days since Jan 1, 0-365 *;
  int tm_isdst; /* Daylight Saving Time indicator */
};
```

The value of **tm_isdst** will be positive if Daylight Saving Time is in effect, 0 if it is not in effect, and negative if there is no information available. When the date and time are represented in this way, they are referred to as *broken-down time*.

The type **clock_t** is defined the same as **time_t**. The header file also defines **size_t**.

The macros defined are **NULL** and **CLOCKS_PER_SEC**.

#include <time.h>
char *asctime(const struct tm *ptr);

Description   The **asctime( )** function returns a pointer to a string that contains the time and date stored in the structure pointed to by *ptr* after it has been converted into the following form:

day month date hours:minutes:seconds year\n\0

For example:

Wed Jun 19 12:05:34 1999

The structure pointer passed to **asctime( )** is generally obtained from either **localtime( )** or **gmtime( )**.

The buffer used by **asctime( )** to hold the formatted output string is a statically allocated character array and is overwritten each time the function is called. If you want to save the contents of the string, you need to copy it elsewhere.

Example   This program displays the local time defined by the system:

```
#include <time.h>
#include <stdio.h>

int main(void)
{
  struct tm *ptr;
  time_t lt;

  lt = time(NULL);
  ptr = localtime(&lt);
  printf(asctime(ptr));

  return 0;
}
```

#include <time.h>
clock_t clock(void);

Description The **clock( )** function returns the number of system clock cycles that have occurred since the program began execution. To compute the number of seconds, divide this value by the **CLOCKS_PER_SEC** macro.

Example The following program displays the number of system clock cycles occurring since it began:

```
#include <stdio.h>
#include <time.h>

int main(void)
{
  int i;

  for(i=0; i<10000; i++);

  printf("%u", clock());

  return 0;
}
```

#include <time.h>
char *ctime(const time_t *time);

Description The **ctime( )** function returns a pointer to a string of the form

day month date hours:minutes:seconds year\n\0

given a pointer to the calendar time. The calendar time is generally obtained through a call to **time( )**. The **ctime( )** function is equivalent to:

```
asctime(localtime(time))
```

The buffer used by **ctime( )** to hold the formatted output string is a statically allocated character array and is overwritten each time the function is called. If you wish to save the contents of the string, you need to copy it elsewhere.

Example   This program displays the local time defined by the system:

```
#include <time.h>
#include <stdio.h>

int main(void)
{
  time_t lt;

  lt = time(NULL);
  printf(ctime(&lt));

  return 0;
}
```

#include <time.h>
double difftime(time_t time2, time_t time1);

Description   The **difftime( )** function returns the difference, in seconds, between *time1* and *time2*. That is, *time2 – time1*.

Example   This program times the number of seconds that it takes for the empty **for** loop to go from 0 to 500000.

```
#include <time.h>
#include <stdio.h>

int main(void)
{
  time_t start, end;
  long unsigned int t;

  start = time(NULL);
  for(t=0; t<500000L; t++);
  end = time(NULL);
  printf("Loop required %f seconds.\n", difftime(end, start));

  return 0;
}
```

#include <time.h>
strut tm *gmtime(const time_t *time);

Description   The **gmtime( )** function returns a pointer to the broken-down form of *time* in the form of a **tm** structure. The time is represented in Coordinated Universal Time (i.e., Greenwich Mean Time). The *time* value is generally obtained through a call to **time( )**.

The structure used by **gmtime( )** to hold the broken-down time is statically allocated and is overwritten each time the function is called. If you wish to save the contents of the structure, you need to copy it elsewhere.

Example   This program prints both the local time and the Coordinated Universal Time of the system:

```
#include <time.h>
#include <stdio.h>

/* print local and Coordinated Universal time */
int main(void)
{
  struct tm *local, *coordinated;
  time_t t;

  t = time(NULL);
  local = localtime(&t);
  printf("Local time and date: %s", asctime(local));
  coordinated = gmtime(&t);
  printf("Coordinated Universal time and date: %s",
         asctime(coordinated));

  return 0;
}
```

#include <time.h>
struct tm *localtime(const time_t *time);

Description   The **localtime( )** function returns a pointer to the broken-down form of *time* in the form of a **tm** structure. The time is represented in local time. The *time* value is generally obtained through a call to the **time( )** function.

The structure used by **localtime( )** to hold the broken-down time is statically allocated and is overwritten each time the function is called. If you wish to save the contents of the structure, you need to copy it elsewhere.

Example This program prints both the local time and the Coordinated Universal time of the system:

```c
#include <time.h>
#include <stdio.h>

/* print local and Coordinated Universal time */
int main(void)
{
  struct tm *local;
  time_t t;

  t = time(NULL);
  local = localtime(&t);
  printf("Local time and date: %s", asctime(local));
  local = gmtime(&t);
  printf("Coordinated Universal time and date: %s",
         asctime(local));

  return 0;
}
```

#include <time.h>
time_t time(time_t *systime);

Description The **time( )** function returns the current calendar time of the system. If the system has no time-keeping mechanism, then –1 is returned.

The **time( )** function can be called either with a null pointer or with a pointer to a variable of type **time_t**. If the latter is used, then the argument will also be assigned the calendar time.

Example This program displays the local time defined by the system:

```c
#include <time.h>
#include <stdio.h>
```

```
int main(void)
{
  struct tm *ptr;
  time_t lt;

  lt = time(NULL);
  ptr = localtime(&lt);
  printf(asctime(ptr));

  return 0;
}
```

A.4 DYNAMIC ALLOCATION

There are two primary ways a C program can store information in the main memory of the computer. The first uses global and local variables—including arrays and structures. In the case of global and static local variables, the storage is fixed throughout the runtime of your program. For dynamic local variables, storage is allocated on the stack. Although these variables are efficiently implemented in C, they require the programmer to know in advance the amount of storage needed for every situation. The second way information can be stored is with C's dynamic allocation system. In this method, storage for information is allocated from the free memory area (called the *heap*) as it is needed.

The ANSI C standard specifies that the header information necessary to the dynamic allocation system is in STDLIB.H. In this file, the type **size_t** is defined. This type is used extensively by the allocation functions and is essentially the equivalent of **unsigned**.

#include <stdlib.h>
void *calloc(size_t num, size_t size);

Description   The **calloc( )** function returns a pointer to the allocated memory. The amount of memory allocated is equal to *num * size*. That is, **calloc( )** allocates sufficient memory for an array of *num* objects of size *size*.

The **calloc( )** function returns a pointer to the first byte of the allocated region. If there is not enough memory to satisfy the request, a null pointer is returned.

It is always important to verify that the return value is not a null pointer before attempting to use it.

Example. This function returns a pointer to a dynamically allocated array of 100 **float**s:

```c
#include <stdlib.h>
#include <stdio.h>

float *get_mem(void)
{
  float *p;

  p = calloc(100, sizeof(float));
  if(!p) {
    printf("Allocation error - aborting.\n");
    exit(1);
  }
  return p;
}
```

#include <stdlib.h>
void free(void *ptr);

Description The **free( )** function deallocates the memory pointed to by *ptr*. This makes the memory available for future allocation.

It is imperative that the **free( )** function be called only with a pointer that was previously allocated using one of the dynamic allocation system's functions, such as **malloc( )** or **calloc( )**. Using an invalid pointer in the call will probably destroy the memory management mechanism and cause a system crash.

Example This program first allocates room for 100 user-entered strings and then frees them:

```c
#include <stdlib.h>
#include <stdio.h>

int main(void)
```

```
{
  char *str[100];
  int i;

  for(i=0; i<100; i++) {
    if((str[i] = malloc(128))==NULL) {
      printf("Allocation error - aborting.\n");
      exit(0);
    }
    gets(str[i]);
  }

  /* now free the memory */
  for(i=0; i<100; i++) free(str[i]);

  return 0;
}
```

#include <stdlib.h>
void *malloc(size_t size);

Description   The **malloc( )** function returns a pointer to the first byte of a region of memory of size *size* that has been allocated from the heap. (Remember, the heap is a region of free memory managed by C's dynamic allocation subsystem.) If there is insufficient memory in the heap to satisfy the request, **malloc( )** returns a null pointer. It is always important to verify that the return value is not a null pointer before attempting to use it. Attempting to use a null pointer will usually result in a system crash.

Example   This function allocates sufficient memory to hold structures of type **addr**:

```
#include <stdlib.h>
#include <stdio.h>

struct addr {
  char name[40];
  char street[40];
  char city[40];
  char state[3];
  char zip[10];
```

```
};
    .

    .

    .
struct addr *get_struct(void)
{
  struct addr *p;

  if((p = malloc(sizeof(struct addr)))==NULL)
  {
    printf("Allocation error - aborting.\n");
    exit(0);
  }
  return p;
}
```

#include <stdlib.h>
void *realloc(void *ptr, size_t size);

Description   The **realloc( )** function changes the size of the allocated memory pointed to by *ptr* to that specified by *size*. The value of *size* may be greater or less than the original. A pointer to the memory block is returned since it may be necessary for **realloc( )** to move the block to increase its size. If this occurs, the contents of the old block are copied into the new block—no information is lost.

If there is not enough free memory in the heap to allocate *size* bytes, a null pointer is returned. This means it is important to verify the success of a call to **realloc( )**.

Example   This program first allocates 17 characters, copies the string "this is 16 chars" into the space, and then uses **realloc( )** to increase the size to 18 in order to place a period at the end.

```
#include <stdlib.h>
#include <stdio.h>
#include <string.h>

int main(void)
{
  char *p;

  p = malloc(17);
```

```
      if(!p) {
        printf("Allocation error - aborting.\n");
        exit(1);
      }

      strcpy(p, "this is 16 chars");

      p = realloc(p,18);
      if(!p) {
        printf("Allocation error - aborting.\n");
        exit(1);
      }

      strcat(p, ".");

      printf(p);

      free(p);

      return 0;
    }
```

A.5 *M*ISCELLANEOUS FUNCTIONS

The functions discussed in this section are all standard functions that don't easily fit in any other category.

#include <stdlib.h>
void abort(void);

Description   The **abort( )** function causes immediate termination of a program. Whether it closes any open files is defined by the implementation, but generally it won't.

Example   In this program, if the user enters **A**, the program will terminate:

```
#include <stdlib.h>
#include <conio.h>
```

```
int main(void)
{
  for(;;)
    if(getche()=='A') abort();

  return 0;
}
```

#include <stdlib.h>
int abs(int num);

Description   The **abs( )** function returns the absolute value of the integer *num*.

Example   This function converts the user-entered numbers into their absolute values:

```
#include <stdlib.h>
#include <stdio.h>

int get_abs(void)
{
  char num[80];

  gets(num);

  return abs(atoi(num));
}
```

#include <stdlib.h>
double atof(const char * str);

Description   The **atof( )** function converts the string pointed to by *str* into a **double** value. The string must contain a valid floating-point number. If this is not the case, the returned value is 0.

The number may be terminated by any character that cannot be part of a valid floating-point number. This includes whitespace characters, punctuation (other than periods), and characters other than 'E' or 'e'. Thus, if **atof( )** is called with "100.00HELLO", the value 100.00 will be returned.

Example This program reads two floating-point numbers and displays their sum:

```
#include <stdlib.h>
#include <stdio.h>

int main(void)
{
  char num1[80], num2[80];

  printf("Enter first: ");
  gets(num1);
  printf("Enter second: ");
  gets(num2);
  printf("The sum is: %f", atof(num1) + atof(num2));

  return 0;
}
```

#include <stdlib.h>
int atoi(const char *str);

Description The **atoi( )** function converts the string pointed to by *str* into an **int** value. The string must contain a valid integer number. If this is not the case, the returned value is 0.

The number may be terminated by any character that cannot be part of a integer number. This includes whitespace characters, punctuation, and other characters. Thus, if **atoi( )** is called with 123.23, the integer value 123 will be returned, and the 0.23 ignored.

Example This program reads two integer numbers and displays their sum:

```
#include <stdlib.h>
#include <stdio.h>

int main(void)
{
  char num1[80], num2[80];

  printf("Enter first: ");
  gets(num1);
  printf("Enter second: ");
```

```
  gets(num2);
  printf("The sum is: %d", atoi(num1) + atoi(num2));

  return 0;
}
```

#include <stdlib.h>
long atol(const char *str);

Description The **atol( )** function converts the string pointed to by *str* into a **long int** value. The string must contain a valid long integer number. If this is not the case, the returned value is 0.

The number may be terminated by any character that cannot be part of an integer number. This includes whitespace characters, punctuation, and other characters. Thus, if **atol( )** is called with 123.23, the integer value 123 will be returned, and the 0.23 ignored.

Example This program reads two long integer numbers and displays their sum:

```
#include <stdlib.h>
#include <stdio.h>

int main(void)
{
  char num1[80], num2[80];

  printf("Enter first: ");
  gets(num1);
  printf("Enter second: ");
  gets(num2);
  printf("The sum is: %ld", atol(num1) + atol(num2));

  return 0;
}
```

#include <stdlib.h>
void *bsearch(const void *key, const void *base,
                   size_t num, size_t size,
                   int(*compare)(const void *, const void *));

Description   The **bsearch( )** function performs a binary search on the
sorted array pointed to by *base* and returns a pointer to the first
member that matches the key pointed to by *key*. The number of
elements in the array is specified by *num* and the size (in bytes) of
each element is described by *size*. (The **size_t** type is defined in
STDLIB.H and is essentially the equivalent of **unsigned**.)

The function pointed to by *compare* is used to compare an element
of the array with the key. The form of *compare* must be

   int *function_name*(const void **arg1*, const void **arg2*)

It must return the following values:

Less than 0	If *arg1* is less than *arg2*
0	If *arg1* is equal to *arg2*
Greater than 0	If *arg1* is greater than *arg2*

The array must be sorted in ascending order, with the lowest
address containing the lowest element.

If the array does not contain the key, then a null pointer is returned.

Example   This program reads characters entered at the keyboard and
determines whether they belong to the alphabet.

```
#include <stdlib.h>
#include <ctype.h>
#include <stdio.h>

char *alpha = "abcdefghijklmnopqrstuvwxyz";

int comp(const void *ch, const void *s);

int main(void)
{
  char ch;
  char *p;
```

```
  do {
    printf("Enter a character: ");
    scanf("%c%*c",&ch);
    ch = tolower(ch);
    p = bsearch(&ch, alpha, 26, 1, comp);
    if(p) printf("is in alphabet.\n");
    else printf("is not in alphabet.\n");
  } while(p);

  return 0;
}

/* compare two characters */
int comp(const void *ch, const void *s)
{
  return *(char *)ch - *(char *)s;
}
```

#include <stdlib.h>
void exit(int status);

Description   The **exit( )** function causes immediate normal termination of a program.

The value of *status* is passed to the calling process, usually the operating system, if the environment supports it. By convention, if the value of *status* is 0, normal program termination is assumed. A nonzero value may be used to indicate an error.

You may also use the predefined macros **EXIT_SUCCESS** and **EXIT_FAILURE** as arguments to **exit( )**.

Example   This function performs menu selection for a mailing list program. If **Q** is selected, the program is terminated.

```
char menu(void)
{
  char ch;

  do {
    printf("Enter names (E)\n");
    printf("Delete name (D)\n");
    printf("Print (P)\n");
```

```
    printf("Quit (Q)\n");
  } while(!strchr("EDPQ",toupper(ch)));
  if(ch=='Q') exit(0);
  return ch;
}
```

#include <stdlib.h>
long labs(long num);

Description   The **labs( )** function returns the absolute value of the **long int** *num*.

Example   This function converts the user-entered numbers into their absolute values:

```
#include <stdlib.h>
#include <stdio.h>

long int get_labs(void)
{
  char num[80];

  gets(num);

  return labs(atol(num));
}
```

#include <setjmp.h>
void longjmp(jmp_buf envbuf, int val);

Description   The **longjmp( )** function causes program execution to resume at the point of the last call to **setjmp( )**. These two functions are the way ANSI C provides for a jump between functions. Notice that the header SETJMP.H is required.

The **longjmp( )** function operates by resetting the stack as described in *envbuf*, which must have been set by a prior call to **setjmp( )**. This causes program execution to resume at the statement following the **setjmp( )** invocation—the computer is "tricked" into thinking that it never left the function that called **setjmp( )**. (As a somewhat graphic explanation, the **longjmp( )** function "warps" across time and (memory) space to a previous point in your program, without having to perform the normal function-return process.)

The buffer *envbuf* is of type **jmp_buf**, which is defined in the header SETJMP.H. The buffer must have been set through a call to **setjmp( )** prior to calling **longjmp( )**.

The value of *val* becomes the return value of **setjmp( )** and may be interrogated to determine where the long jump came from. The only value not allowed is 0.

It is important to understand that the **longjmp( )** function must be called before the function that called **setjmp( )** returns. If not, the result is technically undefined. In actuality, a crash will almost certainly occur.

By far the most common use of **longjmp( )** is to return from a deeply nested set of routines when a catastrophic error occurs.

Example   This program prints **1 2 3**:

```
#include <setjmp.h>
#include <stdio.h>

void f2(void);

jmp_buf ebuf;

int main(void)
{
  char first=1;
  int i;

  printf("1 ");
  i = setjmp(ebuf);
  if(first) {
    first = !first;
    f2();
    printf("this will not be printed");
  }
  printf("%d", i);

  return 0;
}

void f2(void)
{
```

```
    printf("2 ");
    longjmp(ebuf, 3);
}
```

#include <stdlib.h>
void qsort(void *base, size_t num, size_t size,
int(*compare)(const void*, const void*));

Description   The **qsort( )** function sorts the array pointed to by *base* using a Quicksort (which was developed by C.A.R. Hoare). The Quicksort is generally considered the best general-purpose sorting algorithm. Upon termination, the array will be sorted. The number of elements in the array is specified by *num* and the size (in bytes) of each element is described by *size*. (The **size_t** type is defined in STDLIB.H and is essentially the equivalent of **unsigned**.)

The function pointed to by *compare* is used to compare two elements in the array. The form of *compare* must be

int *function_name*(const void *arg1*, const void *arg2*)

It must return the following values:

Less than 0	If *arg1* is less than *arg2*
0	If *arg1* is equal to *arg2*
Greater than 0	If *arg1* is greater than *arg2*

The array is sorted in ascending order, with the lowest address containing the lowest element.

Example   This program sorts a list of integers and displays the results:

```
#include <stdlib.h>
#include <stdio.h>

int comp(const void *i, const void *j);

int num[10]= {
  1,3, 6, 5, 8, 7, 9, 6, 2, 0
};

int main(void)
```

```
{
  int i;

  printf("Original array: ");
  for(i=0; i<10; i++) printf("%d ", num[i]);
  printf("\n");

  qsort(num, 10, sizeof(int), comp);

  printf("Sorted array: ");
  for(i=0; i<10; i++) printf("%d ", num[i]);

  return 0;
}

/* compare the integers */
int comp(const void *i, const void *j)
{
  return *(int *)i - *(int *)j;
}
```

#include <stdlib.h>
int rand(void);

Description   The **rand( )** function generates a sequence of pseudo-random numbers. Each time it is called, an integer between 0 and **RAND_MAX** is returned. **RAND_MAX** is defined in STDLIB.H. The ANSI standard stipulates that the macro **RAND_MAX** will have a value of at least 32,767.

Example   This program displays ten pseudo-random numbers:

```
#include <stdlib.h>
#include <stdio.h>

int main(void)
{
  int i;

  for(i=0; i<10; i++)
    printf("%d ", rand());
```

```
  return 0;
}
```

#include <setjmp.h>
int setjmp(jmp_buf envbuf);

Description The **setjmp( )** function saves the contents of the system stack in the buffer *envbuf* for later use by **longjmp( )**.

The **setjmp( )** function returns 0 upon invocation. However, **longjmp( )** passes an argument to **setjmp( )** when it executes, and it is this value (always nonzero) that will appear to be the value of **setjmp( )** after a call to **longjmp( )**.

See the **longjmp( )** section for more information.

Example This program prints **1 2 3**:

```
#include <setjmp.h>
#include <stdio.h>

void f2(void);

jmp_buf ebuf;

int main(void)
{
  char first=1;
  int i;

  printf("1 ");
  i = setjmp(ebuf);
  if(first) {
    first = !first;
    f2( );
    printf("this will not be printed");
  }
  printf("%d",i);

  return 0;
}

void f2(void)
{
  printf("2 ");
```

```
    longjmp(ebuf, 3);
}
```

#include <stdlib.h>
void srand(unsigned seed);

Description   The **srand( )** function is used to set a starting point for the sequence generated by **rand( )**, which returns pseudo-random numbers.

Generally **srand( )** is used to allow multiple program runs to use different sequences of pseudo-random numbers.

Example   This program uses the system time to randomly initialize the **rand( )** function using **srand( )**:

```
#include <stdio.h>
#include <stdlib.h>
#include <time.h>

/* Seed rand with the system time
   and display the first 100 numbers.
*/
int main(void)
{
  int i, utime;
  long ltime;

  /* get the current calendar time */
  ltime = time(NULL);
  utime = (unsigned int) ltime/2;
  srand(utime);

  for(i=0; i<10; i++) printf("%d ", rand());

  return 0;
}
```

B

C Keyword Summary

THERE are 32 keywords that, when combined with the formal C syntax, form the C language as defined by the ANSI C standard. These keywords are shown in Table B-1.

All C keywords use lowercase letters. In C, uppercase and lowercase are different; for instance, **else** is a keyword, **ELSE** is not.

An alphabetical summary of each of the keywords follows:

auto

auto is used to create temporary variables that are created upon entry into a block and destroyed upon exit. For example:

```
#include <stdio.h>
#include <conio.h>

int main(void)
{
  for(;;) {
    if(getche()=='a') {
      auto int t;
      for(t=0; t<'a'; t++)
        printf("%d ", t);
      break;
    }
  }

  return 0;
}
```

auto	double	int	struct
break	else	long	switch
case	enum	register	typedef
char	extern	return	union
const	float	short	unsigned
continue	for	signed	void
default	goto	sizeof	volatile
do	if	static	while

TABLE B-1 *Keyword List* ▼

In this example, the variable **t** is created only if the user strikes an **a**. Outside the **if** block, **t** is completely unknown; and any reference to it would generate a compile-time syntax error. The use of **auto** is completely optional since all local variables are **auto** by default.

break

break is used to exit from a **do**, **for**, or **while** loop, bypassing the normal loop condition. It is also used to exit from a **switch** statement.

An example of **break** in a loop is shown here:

```
while(x<100) {
  x = get_new_x();
  if(kbhit()) break; /* key hit on keyboard */
  process(x);
}
```

Here, if a key is pressed, the loop will terminate no matter what the value of **x** is.

In a **switch** statement, **break** effectively keeps program execution from "falling through" to the next **case**. (Refer to the **switch** section for details.)

case

case is covered in conjunction with **switch**.

char

char is a data type used to declare character variables. For example, to declare **ch** to be a character type, you would write:

```
char ch;
```

In C, a character is one byte long.

const

The **const** modifier tells the compiler that the contents of a variable cannot be changed. It is also used to prevent a function from modifying the object pointed to by one of its arguments.

continue

continue is used to bypass portions of code in a loop and forces the conditional expression to be evaluated. For example, the following **while** loop will simply read characters from the keyboard until an **s** is typed:

```
while(ch=getche()) {
  if(ch != 's') continue; /* read another char */
  process(ch);
}
```

The call to **process( )** will not occur until **ch** contains the character **s**.

default

default is used in the **switch** statement to signal a default block of code to be executed if no matches are found in the **switch**. See the **switch** section.

do

The **do** loop is one of three loop constructs available in C. The general form of the **do** loop is

```
do {
   statement block
} while(condition);
```

If only one statement is repeated, the braces are not necessary, but they add clarity to the statement. The **do** loop repeats as long as the *condition* is true.

The **do** loop is the only loop in C that will always have at least one iteration because the condition is tested at the bottom of the loop.

A common use of the **do** loop is to read disk files. This code will read a file until an EOF is encountered.

```
do {
  ch = getc(fp);
  if(!feof(fp)) printf("%c", ch);
} while(!feof(fp));
```

double

double is a data type specifier used to declare double-precision floating-point variables. To declare **d** to be of type **double** you would write the following statement:

```
double d;
```

else

See the **if** section.

enum

The **enum** type specifier is used to create enumeration types. An enumeration is simply a list of named integer constants. For example, the following code declares an enumeration called **color** that consists of three constants: **red**, **green**, and **yellow**.

```
#include <stdio.h>

enum color {red, green, yellow};
enum color c;

int main(void)
{
  c = red;
  if(c==red) printf("is red\n");

  return 0;
}
```

extern

The **extern** data type modifier tells the compiler that a variable is defined elsewhere in the program. This is often used in conjunction with separately compiled files that share the same global data and are linked together. In essence, it notifies the compiler of a variable without redefining it.

As an example, if **first** were declared in another file as an integer, the following declaration would be used in subsequent files:

```
extern int first;
```

float

float is a data type specifier used to declare floating-point variables. To declare **f** to be of type **float** you would write:

```
float f;
```

for

The **for** loop allows automatic initialization and incrementation of a counter variable. The general form is

```
for(initialization; condition; increment) {
    statement block
}
```

If the *statement block* is only one statement, the braces are not necessary.

Although the **for** allows a number of variations, generally the *initialization* is used to set a counter variable to its starting value. The *condition* is generally a relational statement that checks the counter variable against a termination value, and the *increment* increments (or decrements) the counter value. The loop repeats until the condition becomes false.

The following code will print **hello** ten times.

```
for(t=0; t<10; t++) printf("Hello\n");
```

goto

The **goto** causes program execution to jump to the *label* specified in the **goto** statement. The general form of the **goto** is

```
goto label ;
    .
    .
    .
label:
```

All *labels* must end in a colon and must not conflict with keywords or function names. Furthermore, a **goto** can branch only within the current function, and not from one function to another.

The following example will print the message **right** but not the message **wrong**:

```
goto lab1;
  printf("wrong");
lab1:
  printf("right");
```

if

The general form of the **if** statement is

```
if(condition) {
  statement block 1
}
else {
  statement block 2
}
```

If single statements are used, the braces are not needed. The **else** is optional.

The *condition* may be any expression. If that expression evaluates to any value other than 0, then *statement block 1* will be executed; otherwise, if it exists, *statement block 2* will be executed.

The following code fragment can be used for keyboard input and to look for a 'q' which signifies "quit."

```
ch = getche();
if(ch=='q') {
  printf("Program Terminated");
  exit(0);
}
else proceed();
```

int

int is the type specifier used to declare integer variables. For example, to declare **count** as an integer you would write

```
int count;
```

long

long is a data type modifier used to declare long integer and long **double** variables. For example, to declare **count** as a long integer you would write

```
long int count;
```

register

The **register** modifier requests that a variable be stored in the way that allows the fastest possible access. In the case of characters or integers, this usually means a register of the CPU. To declare **i** to be a **register** integer, you would write

```
register int i;
```

return

The **return** statement forces a return from a function and can be used to transfer a value back to the calling routine. For example, the following function returns the product of its two integer arguments.

```
int mul(int a, int b)
{
  return a*b;
}
```

Keep in mind that as soon as a **return** is encountered, the function will return, skipping any other code in the function.

short

short is a data type modifier used to declare small integers. For example, to declare **sh** to be a short integer you would write

```
short int sh;
```

signed

The **signed** type modifier is most commonly used to specify a **signed char** data type.

sizeof

The **sizeof** keyword is a compile-time operator that returns the length of the variable or type it precedes. If it precedes a type, the type must be enclosed in parentheses. For example,

```
printf("%d", sizeof(short int));
```

will print **2** for most C implementations.

The **sizeof** statement's principal use is in helping to generate portable code when that code depends on the size of the C built-in data types.

static

The **static** keyword is a data type modifier that causes the compiler to create permanent storage for the local variable that it precedes. This enables the specified variable to maintain its value between function calls. For example, to declare **last_time** as a **static** integer, you would write

```
static int last_time;
```

static can also be used on global variables to limit their scope to the file in which they are declared.

struct

The **struct** statement is used to create aggregate data types, called structures, that are made up of one or more members. The general form of a structure is

```
struct struct-name {
  type member1 ;
  type member2 ;
     .
     .
     .
  type member N ;
} variable-list ;
```

The individual members are referenced using the dot or arrow operators.

switch

The **switch** statement is C's multi-path branch statement. It is used to route execution in one of several ways. The general form of the statement is

```
switch(int-expression) {
  case constant1: statement-set 1;
    break;
  case constant2 : statement-set 2 ;
    break;

     .

     .

     .

  case constantN: statement-set N ;
    break;
  default: default-statements;
}
```

Each *statement-set* may be one or many statements long. The **default** portion is optional. The expression controlling the **switch** and all **case** constants must be of integral or character types.

The **switch** works by checking the value of *int-expression* against the constants. As soon as a match is found, that set of statements is executed. If the **break** statement is omitted, execution will continue into the next **case**. You can think of the **case**s as labels. Execution will continue until a **break** statement is found or the **switch** ends.

The following example can be used to process a menu selection:

```
ch = getche();

switch(ch) {
  case 'e': enter();
   break;
  case 'l': list();
    break;
  case 's': sort();
    break;
  case 'q': exit(0);
    break;
  default: printf("Unknown Command\n");
    printf("Try Again\n");
}
```

typedef

The **typedef** statement allows you to create a new name for an existing data type. The general form of **typedef** is

typedef *type-specifier new-name* ;

For example, to use the word "balance" in place of "float," you would write

```
typedef float balance;
```

union

The **union** keyword creates an aggregate type in which two or more variables share the same memory location. The form of the declaration and the way a member is accessed are the same as for **struct**. The general form is

```
union union-name {
   type member1 ;
   type member2 ;

     .
     .
     .

   type member N ;
} variable-list ;
```

unsigned

The **unsigned** type modifier tells the compiler to create a variable that holds only unsigned (i.e., positive) values. For example, to declare **big** to be an unsigned integer you would write

```
unsigned int big;
```

void

The **void** type specifier is primarily used to declare **void** functions (functions that do not return values). It is also used to create **void** pointers (pointers to **void**) that are generic pointers capable of pointing to any type of object and to specify an empty parameter list.

volatile

The **volatile** modifier tells the compiler that a variable may have its contents altered in ways not explicitly defined by the program. Variables that are changed by the hardware, such as real-time clocks, interrupts, or other inputs are examples.

while

The **while** loop has the general form:

```
while(condition) {
    statement block
}
```

If a single statement is the object of the **while**, the braces may be omitted. The loop will repeat as long as the *condition* is true.

The **while** tests its *condition* at the top of the loop. Therefore, if the *condition* is false to begin with, the loop will not execute at all. The *condition* may be any expression.

An example of a **while** follows. It reads characters until end-of-file is encountered.

```
t = 0;

while(!feof(fp)) {
    s[t] = getc(fp);
    t++;
}
```

C

Building a Windows Skeleton

C is a popular language for Windows programming. As such, it makes sense that some coverage of this important topic be included in this book. But be forewarned: Programming for Windows requires a thorough knowledge of both C and Windows. Frankly, before you can write useful Windows programs, you will need to hone your C programming skills and then invest substantial time in learning the ins and outs of the Windows operating system. Keep in mind that just a description of the functions available within Windows requires approximately 2,000 printed pages!

The preceding notwithstanding, if you will be moving on to Windows programming, you are probably anxious to begin. The purpose of this appendix is to give you a brief overview of Windows programming and to explain a few of its most fundamental elements. In essence, the information presented here is designed to give you a "jump start" into the world of Windows programming.

This appendix discusses in a general way what Windows is, how a program must interact with it, and what rules must be followed by every Windows application. It also develops an application skeleton that you can use as a basis for your own Windows programs. As you will see, all Windows programs share several common traits. It is these shared attributes that will be contained in the application skeleton.

WHICH VERSION OF WINDOWS?

At the time of this writing, there are three versions of the Windows operating system in common use: Windows 3.1, Windows 95, and Windows NT. The skeleton developed in this appendix is designed for 32-bit versions of Windows, such as Windows 95 or Windows NT, since these are the most widely used versions. However, the basic principles apply to all versions of Windows.

WINDOWS PROGRAMMING PERSPECTIVE

The goal of Windows is to enable a person who has basic familiarity with the system to sit down and run virtually any application without prior training. To accomplish this end, Windows provides a consistent interface to the user. In theory, if you can run one Windows-based program, you can run them all. Of course, in actuality, most useful programs will still require some sort of training in order to be used effectively, but at least this instruction can be restricted to *what* the program *does*, not *how* the user must *interact* with it. In fact, much of the code in a Windows application is there just to support the user interface.

Before continuing, it must be stated that not every program that runs under Windows will necessarily present the user with a Windows-style interface. It is possible to write Windows programs that do not take advantage of the Windows interface elements. To create a Windows-style program, you must purposely do so. Only those programs written to take advantage of Windows will look and feel like Windows programs. While you can override the basic Windows design philosophy, you had better have a good reason to do so, because the users of your programs will, most likely, be very disappointed. In general, any application programs you are writing for Windows should utilize the normal Windows interface and conform to the standard Windows design practices.

Windows is graphics-oriented, which means that it provides a Graphical User Interface (GUI). While graphics hardware and video modes are quite diverse, many of the differences are handled by Windows. This means that, for the most part, your program does not need to worry about what type of graphics hardware or video mode is being used.

Let's look at a few of the more important features of Windows.

THE DESKTOP MODEL

With few exceptions, the point of a window-based user interface is to provide the equivalent of a desktop on the screen. On a desk you might find several different pieces of paper, one on top of another, often with fragments of different pages visible beneath the top page. The equivalent of the desktop in Windows is the screen. The pieces of paper are represented by windows on the screen. On a desk you may move pieces of paper about, maybe switching which piece of paper is on top, or how much of another is exposed to view. Windows allows the same type of operations on its windows. By selecting a window, you can make it current, which means putting it on top of all the other open windows. You can enlarge or shrink a window, or move it about on the screen. In short, Windows lets you control the surface of the screen the way you control the items on your desk.

While the desktop model forms the foundation of the Windows user interface, Windows is not limited by it. In fact, several Windows interface elements emulate other types of familiar devices, such as slider controls, spin controls, property sheets, and toolbars. Windows gives you, the programmer, a large array of features from which you may choose those most appropriate to your specific application.

THE MOUSE

Windows allows the use of the mouse for almost all control, selection, and drawing operations. Of course, to say that it *allows* the use of the mouse is an understatement. The fact is that the Windows interface was *designed for the mouse—*it *allows* the use of the keyboard! Although it is certainly possible for an application program to ignore the mouse, it does so only in violation of a basic Windows design principle.

ICONS AND BITMAPS

Windows encourages the use of icons and bitmaps (graphics images). The theory behind the use of icons and bitmaps is found in the old adage "a picture is worth a thousand words."

An icon is a small symbol that represents some operation or program. Generally, the operation or program can be activated by selecting the icon. A bitmap is often used to convey information quickly and simply to the user. However, bitmaps can also be used as menu elements.

MENUS AND DIALOG BOXES

Aside from standard windows, Windows also provides several special-purpose windows. The most common of these are the menu and the dialog box. A *menu* is, as you would expect, a special window that contains choices from which the user makes a selection. The thing that makes menus valuable is that they are largely automated. Instead of having to manage menu selection manually in your program, you simply create a standard menu—Windows will handle the details for you.

A *dialog box* is a special window that allows more complex interaction with the application than that allowed by a menu. For example, your application might use a dialog box to request a file name. With few exceptions, non-menu input is accomplished via a dialog box.

HOW WINDOWS AND YOUR PROGRAM INTERACT

When you write a program for many operating systems, it is your program that initiates interaction with the operating system. For example, in a DOS program, it is the program that requests such things as input and output. Put differently, programs written in the "traditional way" call the operating system. The operating system does not call your program. However, Windows generally works in the opposite way. It is Windows that calls your program. The process works like this: Your program waits until it is sent a *message* by Windows. The message is passed to your program through a special function that is called by Windows. Once a message is received, your program is expected to take an appropriate action. While your program may call Windows when responding to a message, it is still Windows that initiates the activity. More than anything else, it is the message-based interaction with Windows that dictates the general form of all Windows programs.

There are many different types of messages that Windows may send your program. For example, each time the mouse is clicked on a window belonging to your program, a mouse-clicked message will be sent to your program. Another type of message is sent each time a window belonging to your program must be redrawn. Still another message is sent each time the user presses a key when your program is the focus of input. Keep one fact firmly in mind: As far as your program is concerned, messages arrive randomly. This is why Windows programs resemble interrupt-driven programs. You can't know what message will be next.

One final point: Messages sent to your program are stored in a *message queue* associated with your program. Therefore, no message will be lost because your program is busy processing another message. The message will simply wait in the queue until your program is ready for it.

WINDOWS IS MULTITASKING

Since the start, Windows has been a multitasking operating system. This means that it can run two or more programs concurrently. All 32-bit versions of Windows (such as Windows NT and Windows 95) use *preemptive multitasking*. Using this approach, each active application receives a slice of CPU time. It is during its time slice that an application actually executes. When the application's time slice runs out, the next application begins executing. (The previously executing application enters a suspended state in which it awaits another time slice.) In this fashion, each application in the system receives a portion of CPU time. Although the application skeleton developed in this appendix is not concerned with the multitasking aspects of Windows, they will be an important part of any application you create.

Older, 16-bit versions of Windows used a form of multitasking called non-preemptive multitasking. *With this approach, an application retained the CPU until it explicitly released it. This allowed applications to monopolize the CPU and effectively "lock out" other programs. Preemptive multitasking eliminates this problem.*

THE WIN32 API

In general, the Windows environment is accessed through a call-based interface called the Application Program Interface (API). The API consists of several hundred functions that your program calls as needed. The API functions provide all the system services performed by Windows. There is a subset to the API called the Graphics Device Interface (GDI), which is the part of Windows that provides device-independent graphics support. It is the GDI functions that make it possible for a Windows application to run on a variety of hardware.

Programs designed for use by 32-bit versions of Windows, such as Windows 95 and Windows NT, use the Win32 API. For the most part, Win32 is a superset of the older Windows 3.1 API (Win16). Indeed, for the most part, the functions are called by the same name and are used in the same way. However, even though similar in spirit and purpose, the two APIs differ because Win32 supports 32-bit addressing while Win16 supports only the 16-bit, segmented-memory model. Because of this difference, several of the older API functions have been widened to accept 32-bit arguments and return 32-bit values. A few API functions have had to be altered to accommodate the 32-bit architecture. API functions have also been added to support preemptive multitasking, new interface elements, and other enhanced features.

Because modern versions of Windows support 32-bit addressing, it makes sense that integers are also 32 bits long. This means that types **int** and **unsigned** are 32 bits long, not 16 bits, as is the case for Windows 3.1. If you want to use a 16-bit integer, it must be declared as **short**. Windows provides portable **typedef** names for these types, as you will see shortly.

*T*HE COMPONENTS OF A WINDOW

Before moving on to specific aspects of Windows programming, a few important terms need to be defined. Figure C-1 shows a standard window with each of its elements pointed out.

FIGURE C-1

The elements of a standard window

▼

All windows have a border that defines the limits of the window; the borders are also used when resizing the window. At the top of the window are several items. On the far left is the system menu icon (also called the title bar icon). Clicking on this box displays the system menu. To the right of the system menu icon is the window's title. At the far right are the minimize, maximize, and close boxes. The client area is the part of the window in which your program activity takes place. Most windows also have horizontal and vertical scroll bars that are used to move information through the window.

SOME WINDOWS APPLICATION BASICS

Before developing the Windows a pplication skeleton, some basic concepts common to all Windows programs need to be discussed.

WinMain( )

All Windows programs begin execution with a call to **WinMain( )**. (Windows programs do not have a **main( )** function.) **WinMain( )** has some special properties that differentiate it from other functions in your application. First, it must be compiled using the **WINAPI** calling convention. (You will see **APIENTRY** used as well. They both mean the same thing.) By default, functions in your C programs use the C calling convention. However, it is possible to compile a function so that it uses a different calling convention; Pascal is a common alternative. For various technical reasons, the calling convention Windows uses to call **WinMain( )** is **WINAPI**. The return type of **WinMain( )** should be **int**.

THE WINDOW FUNCTION

All Windows programs must contain a special function that is *not* called by your program, but is called by Windows. This function is generally referred to as the *window function* or the *window procedure*. The window function is called by Windows when it needs to pass a message to your program. It is through this function that Windows communicates with your program. The window function receives the message in its parameters. All window functions must be declared as returning type **LRESULT CALLBACK**. The type **LRESULT** is a **typedef** that, at the time of this writing, is another name for a long integer. The **CALLBACK** calling convention is used with those functions that will be called by Windows. In Windows terminology, any function that is called by Windows is referred to as a *callback* function.

In addition to receiving the messages sent by Windows, the window function must initiate any actions indicated by a message. Typically, a window function's body consists of a **switch** statement that links a specific response to each message that the program will respond to. Your program need not respond to every message that Windows sends. For messages that your program doesn't care about, you can let Windows provide default processing. Since there are hundreds of different messages that Windows can generate, it is common for most messages simply to be processed by Windows and not by your program.

All messages are 32-bit integer values. Furthermore, all messages are linked with any additional information that the messages require.

WINDOW CLASSES

When your Windows program first begins execution, it will need to define and register a *window class*. When you register a window class, you are telling Windows about the form and function of the window. However, registering the window class does not cause a window to come into existence. To actually create a window requires additional steps.

THE MESSAGE LOOP

As explained earlier, Windows communicates with your program by sending it messages. All Windows applications must establish a *message loop* inside the **WinMain( )** function. This loop reads any pending message from the application's message queue and dispatches that message back to Windows, which then calls your program's window function with that message as a parameter. This may seem to be an overly complex way of passing messages, but it is, nevertheless, the way all Windows programs must function. (Part of the reason for this scheme is to return control to Windows so that the scheduler can allocate CPU time as it sees fit rather than waiting for your application's time slice to end.)

WINDOWS DATA TYPES

As you will soon see, Windows programs do not make extensive use of standard C data types, such as **int** or **char ***. Instead, all data types used by Windows have been **typedef**ed within the WINDOWS.H file and/or its related files. The WINDOWS.H file is supplied by your Windows-compatible compiler and must be included in all Windows programs. Some of the most common types are **HANDLE, HWND, BYTE, WORD, DWORD, UINT, LONG, BOOL**, **LPSTR**, and **LPCSTR. HANDLE** is a 32-bit integer that is used as a handle. As you will see, there are a number of handle types, but they are all the same size as **HANDLE**. A *handle* is simply a value that identifies some resource. Also, all handle types begin with an H. For example, **HWND** is a 32-bit integer used as a window handle. **BYTE** is an 8-bit unsigned character. **WORD** is a 16-bit unsigned short integer. **DWORD** is an unsigned long integer. **UINT** is a 32-bit unsigned integer. **LONG** is another name for **long. BOOL** is an integer; this type is used to indicate values that are either true or false. **LPSTR** is a pointer to a string, and **LPCSTR** is a **const** pointer to a string.

In addition to the basic types described above, Windows defines several structures. The two that are needed by the skeleton program are **MSG** and **WNDCLASSEX**. The **MSG** structure holds a Windows message, and **WNDCLASSEX** is a structure that defines a window class. These structures will be discussed later in this appendix.

A WINDOWS SKELETON

Now that the necessary background information has been covered, it's time to develop a minimal Windows application. As stated, all Windows programs have certain things in common. This section develops a Windows skeleton that provides these necessary features. In the world of Windows programming, application skeletons are commonly used because there is a substantial "price of admission" when creating a Windows program. For instance, the short example programs shown in this book are designed for a command-line interface (such as DOS), in which a minimal program is about 5 lines long. A minimal Windows program, however, is approximately 50 lines long.

A minimal Windows program contains two functions: **WinMain( )** and the window function. The **WinMain( )** function must perform the following general steps:

1. Define a window class.

2. Register that class with Windows.

3. Create a window of that class.

4. Display the window.

5. Begin running the message loop.

The window function must respond to all relevant messages. Since the skeleton program does nothing but display its window, the only message that it must respond to is the one telling the application that the user has terminated the program.

Before considering the specifics, examine the following program, which is a minimal Windows skeleton. It creates a standard window that includes a title. The window also contains the system menu and is, therefore, capable of being minimized, maximized, moved, resized, and closed. It also contains the standard minimize, maximize, and close boxes.

```
/* A minimal 32-bit Windows skeleton. */

#include <windows.h>

LRESULT CALLBACK WindowFunc(HWND, UINT, WPARAM, LPARAM);

char szWinName[] = "MyWin"; /* name of window class */

int WINAPI WinMain(HINSTANCE hThisInst, HINSTANCE hPrevInst,
                   LPSTR lpszArgs, int nWinMode)
{
  HWND hwnd;
  MSG msg;
  WNDCLASSEX wcl;

  /* Define a window class. */
  wcl.cbSize = sizeof(WNDCLASSEX); /* size of WNDCLASSEX */

  wcl.hInstance = hThisInst; /* handle to this instance */
```

```
wcl.lpszClassName = szWinName; /* window class name */
wcl.lpfnWndProc = WindowFunc; /* window function */
wcl.style = 0; /* default style */

wcl.hIcon = LoadIcon(NULL, IDI_APPLICATION); /* icon style */
wcl.hIconSm = LoadIcon(NULL, IDI_WINLOGO); /* small icon style */

wcl.hCursor = LoadCursor(NULL, IDC_ARROW); /* cursor style */
wcl.lpszMenuName = NULL; /* no menu */

wcl.cbClsExtra = 0; /* no extra */
wcl.cbWndExtra = 0; /* information needed */

/* Make the window background white. */
wcl.hbrBackground = (HBRUSH) GetStockObject(WHITE_BRUSH);

/* Register the window class. */
if(!RegisterClassEx(&wcl)) return 0;

/* Now that a window class has been registered, a window
   can be created. */
hwnd = CreateWindow(
  szWinName, /* name of window class */
  "Windows Skeleton", /* title */
  WS_OVERLAPPEDWINDOW, /* window style - normal */
  CW_USEDEFAULT, /* X coordinate - let Windows decide */
  CW_USEDEFAULT, /* Y coordinate - let Windows decide */
  CW_USEDEFAULT, /* width - let Windows decide */
  CW_USEDEFAULT, /* height - let Windows decide */
  HWND_DESKTOP, /* no parent window */
  NULL, /* no menu */
  hThisInst, /* handle of this instance of the program */
  NULL /* no additional arguments */
);

/* Display the window. */
ShowWindow(hwnd, nWinMode);
UpdateWindow(hwnd);

/* Create the message loop. */
while(GetMessage(&msg, NULL, 0, 0))
{
```

```
    TranslateMessage(&msg); /* translate keyboard messages */
    DispatchMessage(&msg); /* return control to Windows */
  }
  return msg.wParam;
}


/* This function is called by Windows and is passed
   messages from the message queue.
*/
LRESULT CALLBACK WindowFunc(HWND hwnd, UINT message,
                               WPARAM wParam, LPARAM lParam)
{
  switch(message) {
    case WM_DESTROY: /* terminate the program */
      PostQuitMessage(0);
      break;
    default:
      /* Let Windows process any messages not specified in
         the preceding switch statement. */
      return DefWindowProc(hwnd, message, wParam, lParam);
  }
  return 0;
}
```

The window produced by this program is shown in Figure C-2. Now let's go through this program step by step.

First, all Windows programs must include the header file WINDOWS.H. As stated, this file (along with its support files) contains the API function prototypes and various types, macros, and definitions used by Windows. For example, the data types **HWND** and **WNDCLASSEX** are defined in WINDOWS.H.

The window function used by the program is called **WindowFunc( )**. It is declared as a callback function, because this is the function that Windows calls to communicate with the program.

Program execution begins with **WinMain( ),** which is passed four parameters. **hThisInst** and **hPrevInst** are handles. **hThisInst** refers to the current instance of the program. Remember, Windows is a multitasking system, so more than one instance of your program may be running at the same time. **hPrevInst** will always be **NULL**. (In

FIGURE C-2

*The window
produced by the
Windows skeleton*
▼

Windows 3.1 programs, **hPrevInst** would be non-zero if there were other instances of the program currently executing, but this doesn't apply to 32-bit versions of Windows.) The **lpszArgs** parameter is a pointer to a string that holds any command line arguments specified when the application was begun. The **nWinMode** parameter contains a value that determines how the window will be displayed when your program begins execution.

Inside the function, three variables are created. The **hwnd** variable will hold the handle to the program's window. The **msg** structure variable will hold window messages, and the **wcl** structure variable will be used to define the window class.

DEFINING THE WINDOW CLASS

The first two actions that **WinMain( )** takes are to define a window class and then register it. A window class is defined by filling in the fields defined by the **WNDCLASSEX** structure. Its fields are shown here:

```
UINT cbSize; /* size of the WNDCLASSEX structure */
UINT style; /* type of window */
WNDPROC lpfnWndProc; /* address to window func */
```

```
int cbClsExtra; /* extra class info */
int cbWndExtra; /* extra window info */
HINSTANCE hInstance; /* handle of this instance */
HICON hIcon; /* handle of standard icon */
HICON hIconSm; /* handle of small icon */
HCURSOR hCursor; /* handle of mouse cursor */
HBRUSH hbrBackground; /* background color */
LPCSTR lpszMenuName; /* name of main menu */
LPCSTR lpszClassName; /* name of window class */
```

As you can see by looking at the program, **cbSize** is assigned the size of the **WNDCLASSEX** structure. The **hInstance** field is assigned the current instance handle as specified by **hThisInst**. The name of the window class is pointed to by **lpszClassName**, which points to the string "MyWin" in this case. The address of the window function is assigned to **lpfnWndProc**. No default style is specified, and no extra information is needed.

All Windows applications need to define a default shape for the mouse cursor and for the application's icons. An application can define its own custom version of these resources or it may use one of the built-in styles, as the skeleton does. In either case, handles to these resources must be assigned to the appropriate members of the **WNDCLASSEX** structure. To see how this is done, let's begin with icons.

A modern Windows application has at least two icons associated with it: one standard size and one small. The small icon is used when the application is minimized and it is also the icon that is used for the system menu. The standard icon is displayed when you move or copy an application to the desktop. Typically, standard icons are 32 by 32 bitmaps and small icons are 16 by 16 bitmaps. The style of each icon is loaded by the API function **LoadIcon( )**, whose prototype is shown here:

HICON LoadIcon(HINSTANCE *hInst*, LPCSTR *lpszName*);

This function returns a handle to an icon. Here, *hInst* specifies the handle of the module that contains the icon and the icon's name is specified in *lpszName*. However, to use one of the built in icons, you must use **NULL** for the first parameter and specify one of the following macros for the second:

Icon Macro	Shape
IDI_APPLICATION	Default icon
IDI_ASTERISK	Information icon
IDI_EXCLAMATION	Exclamation point icon
IDI_HAND	Stop sign
IDI_QUESTION	Question mark icon
IDI_WINLOGO	Windows Logo

In the skeleton, **IDI_APPLICATION** is used for the standard icon and **IDI_WINLOGO** is used for the small icon.

To load the mouse cursor, use the **LoadCursor( )** API function. This function has the following prototype:

HCURSOR LoadCursor(HINSTANCE *hInst*, LPCSTR *lpszName*);

This function returns a handle to a cursor resource. Here, *hInst* specifies the handle of the module that contains the mouse cursor, and the name of the mouse cursor is specified in *lpszName*. However, to use one of the built-in cursors, you must use **NULL** for the first parameter and specify one of the built-in cursors, using its macro, for the second parameter. Some of the most common built-in cursors are shown here:

Cursor Macro	Shape
IDC_ARROW	Default arrow pointer
IDC_CROSS	Cross hairs
IDC_IBEAM	Vertical I-beam
IDC_WAIT	Hourglass

The background color of the window created by the skeleton is specified as white, and a handle to this *brush* is obtained using the API function **GetStockObject( )**. A brush is a resource that paints the screen using a predetermined size, color, and pattern. The function **GetStockObject( )** is used to obtain a handle to a number of standard display objects, including brushes, pens (which draw lines), and character fonts. It has this prototype:

HGDIOBJ GetStockObject(int *object*);

The function returns a handle to the object specified by *object*. (The type **HGDIOBJ** is a GDI handle.) Here are some of the built-in brushes available to your program:

Brush Macro	Background Type
BLACK_BRUSH	Black
DKGRAY_BRUSH	Dark gray
HOLLOW_BRUSH	See-through window
LTGRAY_BRUSH	Light gray
WHITE_BRUSH	White

You can use these macros as parameters to **GetStockObject( )** to obtain a brush.

Once the window class has been fully specified, it is registered with Windows using the API function **RegisterClassEx( )**, whose prototype is shown here:

ATOM RegisterClassEx(CONST WNDCLASS **lpWClass*);

The function returns a value that identifies the window class. **ATOM** is a **typedef** that means **WORD**. Each window class is given a unique value. *lpWClass* must be the address of the **WNDCLASSEX** structure.

CREATING A WINDOW

Once a window class has been defined and registered, your application can actually create a window of that class using the API function **CreateWindow( )**, whose prototype is shown here:

```
HWND CreateWindow(
    LPCSTR lpClassName, /* name of window class */
    LPCSTR lpWinName, /* title of window */
    DWORD dwStyle, /* type of window */
    int X, int Y, /* upper-left coordinates */
```

```
    int Width, int Height, /* dimensions of window */
    HWND hParent, /* handle of parent window */
    HMENU hMenu, /* handle of main menu */
    HINSTANCE hThisInst, /* handle of creator */
    LPVOID lpszAdditional /* pointer to additional info */
);
```

As you can see by looking at the skeleton program, many of the parameters to **CreateWindow( )** may be defaulted or specified as **NULL**. In fact, most often the *X, Y, Width,* and *Height* parameters will simply use the macro **CW_USEDEFAULT**, which tells Windows to select an appropriate size and location for the window. If the window has no parent, which is the case in the skeleton, then *hParent* must be specified as **HWND_DESKTOP**. (You may also use **NULL** for this parameter.) If the window does not contain a main menu, then *hMenu* must be **NULL**. Also, if no additional information is required, as is most often the case, then *lpszAdditional* is **NULL**. (The type **LPVOID** is **typedef**ed as **void ***. Historically, **LPVOID** stands for "long pointer to **void**.")

The remaining four parameters must be set explicitly by your program. First, *lpszClassName* must point to the name of the window class. (This is the name you gave it when it was registered.) The title of the window is a string pointed to by *lpszWinName.* This can be a null string, but usually a window will be given a title. The style (or type) of window actually created is determined by the value of *dwStyle.* The macro **WS_OVERLAPPEDWINDOW** specifies a standard window that has a system menu, a border, and minimize, maximize, and close boxes. While this style of window is the most common, you can construct one to your own specifications. To accomplish this, simply OR together the various style macros that you want. Some other common styles are shown here:

Style Macros	Window Feature
WS_OVERLAPPED	Overlapped window with border
WS_MAXIMIZEBOX	Maximize box
WS_MINIMIZEBOX	Minimize box
WS_SYSMENU	System menu
WS_HSCROLL	Horizontal scroll bar
WS_VSCROLL	Vertical scroll bar

The *hThisInst* parameter must contain the current instance handle of the application.

The **CreateWindow( )** function returns the handle of the window it creates or **NULL** if the window cannot be created.

Once the window has been created, it still is not displayed on the screen. To cause the window to be displayed, call the **ShowWindow( )** API function. This function has the following prototype:

BOOL ShowWindow(HWND *hwnd*, int *nHow*);

The handle of the window to display is specified in *hwnd*. The display mode is specified in *nHow*. The first time the window is displayed, you will want to pass **WinMain( )**'s **nWinMode** as the *nHow* parameter. Remember, the value of **nWinMode** determines how the window will be displayed when the program begins execution. Subsequent calls can display (or remove) the window as necessary. Some common values for *nHow* are shown here:

Display Macros	Effect
SW_HIDE	Removes the window
SW_MINIMIZE	Minimizes the window into an icon
SW_MAXIMIZE	Maximizes the window
SW_RESTORE	Returns a window to normal size

The **ShowWindow( )** function returns the previous display status of the window. If the window was displayed, then nonzero is returned. If the window was not displayed, zero is returned.

Although not technically necessary for the skeleton, a call to **UpdateWindow( )** is included because it is needed by virtually every Windows application that you will create. It essentially tells Windows to send a message to your application that the main window needs to be updated.

THE MESSAGE LOOP

The final part of the skeletal **WinMain( )** is the *message loop*. The message loop is a part of all Windows applications. Its purpose is to receive and process messages sent by Windows. When an application is running, it is continually being sent messages. These messages are stored in the application's message queue until they can be read and processed. Each time your application is ready to read another message, it must call the API function **GetMessage( )**, which has this prototype:

BOOL GetMessage(LPMSG *msg*, HWND *hwnd*, UINT *min*, UINT *max*);

The message will be received by the structure pointed to by *msg*. All Windows messages are contained in a structure of type **MSG**, shown here:

```
/* Message structure */
typedef struct tagMSG
{
  HWND hwnd;       /* window that message is for */
  UINT message;    /* message */
  WPARAM wParam;   /* message-dependent info */
  LPARAM lParam;   /* more message-dependent info */
  DWORD time;      /* time message posted */
  POINT pt;        /* X,Y location of mouse */
} MSG;
```

In **MSG**, the handle of the window for which the message is intended is contained in **hwnd**. All Win32 messages are 32-bit integers, and the message is contained in **message**. Additional information relating to each message is passed in **wParam** and **lParam**. The type **WPARAM** is a **typedef** for **UINT**, and **LPARAM** is a **typedef** for **LONG**.

The time the message was sent (posted) is specified in milliseconds in the **time** field.

The **pt** member will contain the coordinates of the mouse when the message was sent. The coordinates are held in a **POINT** structure, which is defined like this:

```
typedef struct tagPOINT {
  LONG x, y;
} POINT;
```

If there are no messages in the application's message queue, then a call to **GetMessage( )** will pass control back to Windows.

The *hwnd* parameter to **GetMessage( )** specifies the window for which messages will be obtained. It is possible, and even likely, that an application will contain several windows, but you only want to receive messages for a specific window. If you want to receive all messages directed at your application, this parameter must be **NULL**.

The remaining two parameters to **GetMessage( )** specify a range of messages that will be received. Generally, you want your application to receive all messages. To accomplish this, specify both *min* and *max* as 0, as the skeleton does.

GetMessage( ) returns zero when the user terminates the program, causing the message loop to terminate. Otherwise it returns nonzero.

Inside the message loop, two functions are called. The first is the API function **TranslateMessage( )**. This function translates raw keyboard input into character messages. Although it is not necessary for all applications, most applications call **TranslateMessage( )** because it is needed to allow full integration of the keyboard into your application program.

Once the message has been read and translated, it is dispatched back to Windows using the **DispatchMessage( )** API function. Windows then holds this message until it can be passed to the program's window function.

Once the message loop terminates, the **WinMain( )** function ends by returning the value of **msg.wParam** to Windows. This value contains the return code generated when your program terminates.

*T*HE WINDOW FUNCTION

The second function in the application skeleton is its window function. In this case, the function is called **WindowFunc( ),** but it could have any name you like. The window function is passed the first four members of the **MSG** structure as parameters. For the skeleton, the only parameter used is the message itself. However, actual applications will use the other parameters to this function.

The skeleton's window function responds to only one message explicitly: **WM_DESTROY**. This message is sent when the user terminates the program. When this message is received, your program must execute a call to the API function **PostQuitMessage( )**. The argument to this function is an exit code that is returned in **msg.wParam** inside **WinMain( )**. Calling **PostQuitMessage( )** causes a **WM_QUIT** message to be sent to your application, which causes **GetMessage( )** to return false, thus stopping your program.

Any other messages received by **WindowFunc( )** are passed to Windows, via a call to **DefWindowProc( )**, for default processing. This step is necessary because all messages must be dealt with in one fashion or another.

A SHORT WORD ABOUT DEFINITION FILES

You may have heard or read about *definition files*. For 16-bit versions of Windows, such as 3.1, programs need to have a definition file associated with them. A definition file is simply a text file that specifies certain information and settings required by a Windows 3.1 program. However, because of the 32-bit architecture (and other improvements) of modern versions of Windows, definition files are no longer needed.

NAMING CONVENTIONS

Before concluding this appendix, a short comment on the naming of functions and variables needs to be made. Several of the variable and parameter names in the skeleton program and its description probably seemed rather unusual. This is because they follow a set of naming conventions that was invented for Windows programming by Microsoft. For functions, the name consists of a verb followed by a noun. The first character of the verb and noun is capitalized.

For variable names, Microsoft chose to use a rather complex system of embedding the data type into the name. To accomplish this, a lowercase type prefix is added to the start of the variable's name. The name itself begins with a capital letter. The type prefixes are shown in Table C-1. Frankly, the use of type prefixes is controversial and is not universally supported. Many Windows programmers use this method, but many do not. You are free to use any naming convention you like.

TO LEARN MORE

The foregoing overview of Windows programming just scratches the surface. In order to write Windows programs that are useful, you must learn much more about Windows programming. To learn more about Windows 95 programs you will want to read the following books:

Schildt's Windows 95 Programming in C and C++

Schildt's Advanced Windows 95 Programming in C and C++

Prefix	Data Type
b	Boolean (one byte)
c	Character (one byte)
dw	Long unsigned integer
f	16-bit bit-field (flags)
fn	Function
h	Handle
l	Long integer
lp	Long pointer
n	Short integer
p	Pointer
pt	Long integer holding screen coordinates
w	Short unsigned integer
sz	Pointer to null-terminated string
lpsz	Long pointer to null-terminated string
rgb	Long integer holding RGB color values

TABLE C-1 *Variable Type Prefix Characters* ▼

To learn more about Windows NT programming, you will find

Windows NT 4 Programming From the Ground Up

especially useful. These books are written by Herbert Schildt and published by Osborne/McGraw-Hill.

D

Answers

CHAPTER 1

 1.3   EXERCISES

2. ```c
#include <stdio.h>

int main(void)
{
  int num;

  num = 1000;
  printf("%d is the value of num", num);

  return 0;
}
```

 **1.4**   EXERCISES

2. ```c
#include <stdio.h>

int main(void)
{
  float a, b;

  printf("Enter two numbers: ");
  scanf("%f", &a);
  scanf("%f", &b);
  printf("Their sum is %f.", a+b);

  return 0;
}
```

1.5   EXERCISES

1. ```c
#include <stdio.h>

int main(void)
{
  int len, width, height;

  printf("Enter length: ");
```
```

```
      scanf("%d", &len);

      printf("Enter width: ");
      scanf("%d", &width);

      printf("Enter height: ");
      scanf("%d", &height);

      printf("Volume is %d.", len * width * height);

      return 0;
   }
```

2.
```
#include <stdio.h>

int main(void)
{
   printf("Number of seconds in a year: ");
   printf("%f", 60.0 * 60.0 * 24.0 * 365.0);

   return 0;
}
```

1.6 **E**XERCISES

2. Yes, a comment can contain nothing.

3. Yes, you can temporarily remove a line of code from your program by making it into a comment. This is sometimes called "commenting out" a line of code.

1.7 **E**XERCISES

2.
```
#include <stdio.h>

void one(void);
void two(void);

int main(void)
{
   one();
   two();
```

```
    return 0;
}

void one(void)
{
    printf("The summer soldier, ");
}

void two(void)
{
    printf("the sunshine patriot.");
}
```

3. The compiler will report an error. The prototype is needed in order for the compiler to properly call **func1( )**.

2.
```
#include <stdio.h>

int convert(void);

int main(void)
{
    printf("%d", convert());

    return 0;
}

int convert(void)
{
    int dollars;

    printf("Enter number of dollars: ");
    scanf("%d", &dollars);
    return dollars / 2;
}
```

3. There is nothing technically wrong with the program. However, function **f1( )** returns an integer value, but it is being assigned to a variable of type **double**. This would lead one to suspect that perhaps the programmer has misunderstood the purpose of the **f1( )** function.

4. A function declared with a **void** return type cannot return a value.

1.9 EXERCISES

1.
```c
#include <stdio.h>

void outnum(int num);

int main(void)
{
  outnum(10);

  return 0;
}

void outnum(int num)
{
  printf("%d", num);
}
```

2. The **sqr_it( )** function requires an integer argument, but it is called with a floating-point value.

MASTERY SKILLS CHECK

1.
```c
#include <stdio.h>

int main(void)
{
  float weight;

  printf("Enter your weight: ");
  scanf("%f", &weight);
  printf("Effective moon weight: %f", weight * 0.17);

  return 0;
}
```

2. The comment is not terminated with a */.

3.
```c
#include <stdio.h>
```

```
int o_to_c(int o);

int main(void)
{
  int ounces;
  int cups;

  printf("Enter ounces: ");
  scanf("%d", &ounces);

  cups = o_to_c(ounces);
  printf("%d cups", cups);

  return 0;
}

int o_to_c(int o)
{
  return o / 8;
}
```

4. **char**, **int**, **float**, **double**, and **void**.

5. The variable names are wrong because

 a. A dash may not be used in a variable name.

 b. A dollar sign may not be used in a variable name.

 c. A + sign may not be used in a variable name.

 d. A digit may not begin a variable name.

CHAPTER 2

REVIEW SKILLS CHECK

1. All programs must have a **main( )** function. This is the first function called when your program begins executing.

2. #include <stdio.h>

```
int main(void)
{
  printf("This is the number %d", 100);
```

```
      return 0;
   }
```

3. To include a header file, use the **#include** compiler directive. For example,

```
#include <stdio.h>
```

includes the STDIO.H header.

4. The five basic data types are **char**, **int**, **float**, **double**, and **void**.

5. The invalid variable names are b, c, and e.

6. The **scanf( )** function is used to input information from the keyboard.

7.
```
#include <stdio.h>

int main(void)
{
   int i;

   printf("Enter a number: ");
   scanf("%d", &i);
   printf("%d", i*i);

   return 0;
}
```

8. Comments must be surrounded by the /* and */ comment symbols. For example, this is a valid C comment.

```
/* This is a comment. */
```

9. A function returns a value to the calling routine using **return**.

10. `void Myfunc(int count, float balance, char ch);`

2.1   EXERCISES

1. b, d, and e are true.

2.
```
#include <stdio.h>

int main(void)
{
   int i;
```

```
      printf("Enter a number: ");
      scanf("%d", &i);
      if((i%2)==0) printf("Even");
      if((i%2)==1) printf("Odd");

      return 0;
    }
```

*E*XERCISES

1.
```
#include <stdio.h>

int main(void)
{
  int a, b, op;

  printf("Enter first number: ");
  scanf("%d", &a);

  printf("Enter second number: ");
  scanf("%d", &b);

  printf("Enter 0 to add, 1 to multiply: ");
  scanf("%d", &op);

  if(op==0) printf("%d", a+b);
  else printf("%d", a*b);

  return 0;
}
```

2.
```
#include <stdio.h>

int main(void)
{
  int i;

  printf("Enter a number: ");
  scanf("%d", &i);
  if((i%2)==0) printf("Even");
  else printf("Odd");
```

```
        return 0;
    }
```

2.3 EXERCISES

1.
```c
#include <stdio.h>

int main(void)
{
    int a, b, op;

    printf("Enter 0 to add, 1 to subtract: ");
    scanf("%d", &op);

    if(op==0) { /* add */
        printf("Enter first number: ");
        scanf("%d", &a);
        printf("Enter second number: ");
        scanf("%d", &b);
        printf("%d", a+b);
    }
    else { /* subtract */
        printf("Enter first number: ");
        scanf("%d", &a);
        printf("Enter second number: ");
        scanf("%d", &b);
        printf("%d", a-b);
    }

    return 0;
}
```

2. No, the opening curly brace is missing.

2.4 EXERCISES

1.
```c
#include <stdio.h>

int main(void)
{
    int i;

    for(i=1; i<101; i=i+1) printf("%d ", i);
```

```
      return 0;
    }
```

2. ```c
   #include <stdio.h>

   int main(void)
   {
     int i;

     for(i=17; i<101; i=i+1)
       if((i%17)==0) printf("%d ", i);

     return 0;
   }
   ```

3. ```c
   #include <stdio.h>

   int main(void)
   {
     int num, i;

     printf("Enter the number to test: ");
     scanf("%d", &num);

     for(i=2; i<(num/2)+1; i=i+1)
       if((num%i)==0) printf("%d ", i);

     return 0;
   }
   ```

2.5 EXERCISES

1. ```c
   #include <stdio.h>

   int main(void)
   {
     int i;

     for(i=1; i<101; i++) printf("%d ", i);

     return 0;
   }
   ```
   ```

```
#include <stdio.h>

int main(void)
{
  int i;

  for(i=17; i<101; i++)
    if((i%17)==0) printf("%d ", i);

  return 0;
}
```

```
#include <stdio.h>

int main(void)
{
  int num, i;

  printf("Enter the number to test: ");
  scanf("%d", &num);

  for(i=2; i<(num/2)+1; i++)
    if((num%i)==0) printf("%d ", i);

  return 0;
}
```

2.
```
#include <stdio.h>

int main(void)
{
  int a, b;

  a = 1;
  a++;
  b = a;
  b--;
  printf("%d %d", a, b);

  return 0;
}
```

2.6 **E**XERCISES

1.
```c
#include <stdio.h>

int main(void)
{
  int i;

  for(i=1; i<11; i++)
    printf("%d %d %d\n", i, i*i, i*i*i);

  return 0;
}
```

2.
```c
#include <stdio.h>

int main(void)
{
  int i, j;

  printf("Enter a number: ");
  scanf("%d", &i);

  for(j=i; j>0; j--) printf("%d\n", j);
  printf("\a");

  return 0;
}
```

2.7 **E**XERCISES

1. The loop prints the numbers **0** through **99**.
2. Yes.
3. No, the first is true, the second is false.

MASTERY SKILLS CHECK

1.
```c
#include <stdio.h>

int main(void)
{
  int magic; /* magic number */
```

```
    int guess; /* user's guess */
    int i;

    magic = 1325;
    guess = 0;

    for(i=0; i<10 && guess!=magic; i++) {
      printf("Enter your guess: ");
      scanf("%d", &guess);

      if(guess == magic) {
        printf("RIGHT!");
        printf(" %d is the magic number.\n", magic);
      }
      else {
        printf("...Sorry, you're wrong...");
        if(guess > magic)
          printf(" Your guess is too high.\n");
        else printf(" Your guess is too low.\n");
      }
    }
    return 0;
  }

2. #include <stdio.h>

  int main(void)
  {
    int rooms, len, width, total;
    int i;

    printf("Number of rooms? ");
    scanf("%d", &rooms);

    total = 0;
    for(i=rooms; i>0; i--) {
      printf("Enter length: ");
      scanf("%d", &len);

      printf("Enter width: ");
      scanf("%d", &width);

      total = total + len * width;
    }
    printf("Total square footage: %d", total);
```

```
   return 0;
}
```

3. The increment operator increases a variable by one and the decrement operator decreases a variable by one.

4.
```c
#include <stdio.h>

int main(void)
{
  int answer, count;
  int right, wrong;

  right = 0;
  wrong = 0;

  for(count=1; count < 11; count=count+1) {
    printf("What is %d + %d? ", count, count);
    scanf("%d", &answer);

    if(answer == count+count) {
      printf("Right!  ");
      right++;
    }
    else {
      printf("Sorry, you're wrong. ");
      printf("The answer is %d.  ", count+count);
      wrong++;
    }
  }
  printf("You got %d right and %d wrong.", right, wrong);

  return 0;
}
```

5.
```c
#include <stdio.h>

int main(void)
{
  int i;

  for(i=1; i<=100; i++) {
    printf("%d\t", i);
```

```
        if((i%5)==0) printf("\n");
    }

    return 0;
}
```

CHAPTER 3

REVIEW SKILLS CHECK

1. C's relational and logical operators are <, >, < =, > =, !=, = =, !, &&, and ||.

2. A block of code is a group of logically connected statements. To make a block, surround the statements with curly braces.

3. To output a newline, use the **\n** backslash character code.

4. ```
   #include <stdio.h>

   int main(void)
   {
     int i;

     for(i=-100; i<101; i++) printf("%d ", i);

     return 0;
   }
   ```

5. ```
   #include <stdio.h>

   int main(void)
   {
     int i;

     printf("Enter proverb number: ");
     scanf("%d", &i);

     if(i==1) printf("A bird in the hand...");
     if(i==2) printf("A rolling stone...");
     if(i==3) printf("Once burned, twice shy.");
     if(i==4) printf("Early to bed, early to rise...");
     if(i==5) printf("A penny saved is a penny earned.");
   ```

```
      return 0;
    }
```

6. ```
   count++;
   /* or */
   ++count;
   ```

7. In C, true is any nonzero value. False is zero.

1. ```c
   #include <stdio.h>
   #include <conio.h>

   int main(void)
   {
     int i;
     char ch, smallest;

     printf("Enter 10 letters.\n");

     smallest = 'z' ; /* make largest to begin with */

     for(i=0; i<10; i++) {
       ch = getche();
       if(ch < smallest) smallest = ch;
     }
     printf("\nThe smallest character is %c.", smallest);

     return 0;
   }
   ```

2. ```c
   #include <stdio.h>

   int main(void)
   {
     char ch;

     for(ch='A'; ch<='Z'; ch++)
       printf("%d ", ch);

     printf("\n");

     for(ch='a'; ch<='z'; ch++)
   ```
   ```

```
    printf("%d ", ch);

    return 0;
}
```

The codes differ by 32.

3.2   *EXERCISES*

1. The **else** relates to the first **if**; it is not in the same block as the second.

2.
```
#include <stdio.h>

int main(void)
{
  char ch;
  int s1, s2;
  float radius;

  printf("Compute area of Circle, Square, or Triangle? ");
  ch = getchar();
  printf("\n");

  if(ch=='C') {
    printf("Enter radius of circle: ");
    scanf("%f", &radius);
    printf("Area is: %f", 3.1416*radius*radius);
  }
  else if(ch=='S') {
    printf("Enter length of first side: ");
    scanf("%d", &s1);
    printf("Enter length of second side: ");
    scanf("%d", &s2);
    printf("Area is: %d", s1*s2);
  }
  else if(ch=='T') {
    printf("Enter length of base: ");
    scanf("%d", &s1);
    printf("Enter height: ");
    scanf("%d", &s2);
    printf("Area is: %d", (s1*s2)/2);
  }
```

```
        return 0;
    }
```

3.3 EXERCISES

```
1. #include <stdio.h>

   int main(void)
   {
     float dist, speed;
     int num;

     printf("Enter number of drive time computations: ");
     scanf("%d", &num);

     for(; num; num-- ) {
       printf("\nEnter distance: ");
       scanf("%f", &dist);

       printf("Enter average speed: ");
       scanf("%f", &speed);

       printf("Drive time is %f\n", dist/speed);
     }

     return 0;
   }


2. #include <stdio.h>

   int main(void)
   {
     int i;

     printf("Enter a number: ");

     scanf("%d", &i);

     for( ; i; i--) ;

     printf("\a");
```

```
      return 0;
   }
```

3.
```c
#include <stdio.h>

int main(void)
{
   int i;

   for(i=1; i<1001; i=i+i) printf("%d ", i);

   return 0;
}
```

3.4 EXERCISES

1.
```c
#include <stdio.h>

int main(void)
{
   float dist, speed;
   int num;

   printf("Enter number of drive time computations: ");
   scanf("%d", &num);

   while(num) {
      printf("\nEnter distance: ");
      scanf("%f", &dist);

      printf("Enter average speed: ");
      scanf("%f", &speed);

      printf("Drive time is %f\n", dist/speed);

      num--;
   }

   return 0;
}
```

2.
```c
#include <stdio.h>
#include <conio.h>
```

```
int main(void)
{
  char ch;

  printf("Enter your encoded message.\n");

  ch = getche();
  while(ch!='\r') {
    printf("%c", ch-1);
    ch = getche();
  }

  return 0;
}
```

3.5 EXERCISES

1.
```
#include <stdio.h>

int main(void)
{
  float gallons;

  printf("\nEnter gallons: ");
  scanf("%f", &gallons);

  do {
    printf("Liters: %f\n", gallons*3.7854);

    printf("Enter gallons or 0 to quit. ");
    scanf("%f", &gallons);

  } while(gallons!=0);

  return 0;
}
```

2.
```
#include <stdio.h>

int main(void)
{
  int choice;

  printf("Mailing list menu:\n\n");
```

```
      printf("  1. Enter addresses\n");
      printf("  2. Delete addresses\n");
      printf("  3. Search the list\n");
      printf("  4. Print the list\n");
      printf("  5. Quit\n");

      do {
        printf("Enter the number of the choice (1-5): ");
        scanf("%d", &choice);
      } while(choice<1 || choice>5);

      return 0;
    }
```

3.6   *EXERCISES*

```
1. /* This program finds the prime numbers from
      2 to 1000.
   */

   #include <stdio.h>

   int main(void)
   {
     int i, j, prime;

     for(i=2; i<1000; i++) {
       prime = 1;
       for(j=2; j <= i/2; j++)
         if(!(i%j)) prime=0;
       if(prime) printf("%d is prime.\n", i);
     }

     return 0;
   }

2. #include <stdio.h>
   #include <conio.h>

   int main(void)
   {
     int i;
     char ch;
```

```
      for(i=0; i<10; i++) {
        printf("\nEnter a letter: ");
        ch = getche();
        printf("\n");
        for( ; ch; ch--) printf("%c", '.');
      }

      return 0;
    }
```

 3.7 *E*XERCISES

```
2. #include <stdio.h>
   #include <conio.h>

   int main(void)
   {
     float i;
     char ch;

     printf("Tip Computer\n");

     for(i=1.0; i<101.0; i=i+1.0) {
       printf("%f %f %f %f\n", i, i+i*.1, i+i*.15, i+i*.2);
       printf("More? (Y/N) ");
       ch = getche();
       printf("\n");
       if(ch=='N') break;
     }

     return 0;
   }
```

3.8 *E*XERCISES

```
1. #include <stdio.h>

   int main(void)
   {
     int i;

     for(i=1; i<101; i++) {
       if(!(i%2)) continue;
```

```
        printf("%d ", i);
    }

    return 0;
}
```

***E**XERCISES*

1. Floating point values may not be used to control **switch**.

2.
```
#include <stdio.h>
#include <conio.h>

int main(void)
{
  char ch;
  int digit, punc, letter;

  printf("Enter characters, ENTER to stop.\n");

  digit = 0;
  punc = 0;
  letter = 0;

  do {
    ch = getche();
    switch(ch) {
      case '1':
      case '2':
      case '3':
      case '4':
      case '5':
      case '6':
      case '7':
      case '8':
      case '9':
      case '0':
        digit++;
        break;
      case '.':
      case ',':
      case '?':
      case '!':
      case ':':
```

```
            case ';':
              punc++;
              break;
            default:
              letter++;
        }
      } while(ch!='\r');
      printf("\nDigits: %d\n", digit);
      printf("Punctuation: %d\n", punc);
      printf("Letters: %d\n", letter);

      return 0;
    }
```

  EXERCISES

1.
```
#include <stdio.h>

int main(void)
{
  int i;

  i = 1;

  jump_label:
    if(i>=11) goto done_label;
    printf("%d ", i);
    i++;
    goto jump_label;
  done_label: printf("Done");

  return 0;
}
```

MASTERY SKILLS CHECK

1.
```
#include <stdio.h>
#include <conio.h>

int main(void)
{
  char ch;
```

```c
    printf("Enter lowercase letters. ");
    printf("(Press ENTER to Quit.)\n");
    do {
      ch = getche();
      if(ch!='\r') printf("%c", ch-32);
    } while(ch!='\r');

    return 0;
  }
```

2.
```c
#include <stdio.h>

int main(void)
{
  int i;

  printf("Enter a number: ");
  scanf("%d", &i);

  if(!i) printf("zero");
  else if(i<0) printf("negative");
  else printf("positive");

  return 0;
}
```

3. The **for** loop is valid. C allows any of its expressions to be empty.

4. `for( ; ; ) ...`

5.
```c
/* for */
for(i=1; i<11; i++) printf("%d ", i);

/* do */
i = 1;
do {
  printf("%d ",i);
  i++;
} while(i<11);

/* while */
i=1;
while (i<11) {
  printf("%d ", i);
```

```
      i++;
   }
```

6. The **break** statement causes immediate termination of the loop.

7. Yes.

8. No, the label is missing the colon.

CUMULATIVE SKILLS CHECK

```
1. #include <stdio.h>
   #include <conio.h>

   int main(void)
   {
     char ch;

     printf("Enter characters (q to quit): \n");
     do {
       ch = getche();
       switch(ch) {
         case '\t': printf("tab\n");
           break;
         case '\b': printf("backspace\n");
           break;
         case '\r': printf("Enter\n");
       }
     } while(ch!='q');

     return 0;
   }

2. include <stdio.h>

   int main(void)
   {
     int i, j, k;

     for(k=0; k<10; k++) { /* use increment operator */
       printf("Enter first number: ");
       scanf("%d", &i);

       printf("Enter second number: ");
       scanf("%d", &j);
```

```
          if(j) printf("%d\n", i/j); /* simplify condition */
          else printf("Cannot divide by zero.\n"); /* use else */
        }

        return 0;
      }
```

*C*HAPTER 4

*R*EVIEW SKILLS CHECK

1.
```
int i;
for(i=1; i<11; i++) printf("%d ", i);

i = 1;
do {
  printf("%d ", i);
  i++;
} while(i<11);

i = 1;
while(i<11){
  printf("%d ", i);
  i++;
}
```

2.
```
switch(ch) {
    case 'L': load();
      break;
    case 'S': save();
      break;
    case 'E': enter();
      break;
     case 'D': display();
      break;
     case 'Q': quit();
      break;
}
```

3.
```
#include <stdio.h>
#include <conio.h>
```

```
int main(void)
{
  char ch;

  do {
    ch = getche();
  } while(ch!='\r');

  return 0;
}
```

4. The **break** statement causes immediate termination of the loop that contains it. It also terminates a statement sequence in a **switch**.

5. The **continue** statement causes the next iteration of a loop to occur.

6.
```
#include <stdio.h>

int main(void)
{
  int i;
  float feet, meters, ounces, pounds;

  do {
    printf("Convert\n\n");
    printf("1. feet to meters\n");
    printf("2. meters to feet\n");
    printf("3. ounces to pounds\n");
    printf("4. pounds to ounces\n");
    printf("5. Quit\n\n");
    do {
      printf("Enter the number of your choice: ");
      scanf("%d", &i);
    } while(i<0 || i>5);

    switch(i) {
      case 1:
        printf("Enter feet: ");
        scanf("%f", &feet);
        printf("Meters: %f\n", feet / 3.28);
        break;
      case 2:
        printf("Enter meters: ");
        scanf("%f", &meters);
```

```
                    printf("Feet: %f\n", meters * 3.28);
                    break;
                  case 3:
                    printf("Enter ounces: ");
                    scanf("%f", &ounces);
                    printf("Pounds: %f\n", ounces / 16);
                    break;
                  case 4:
                    printf("Enter pounds: ");
                    scanf("%f", &pounds);
                    printf("ounces: %f\n", pounds * 16);
                    break;
                }
            } while(i!=5);

            return 0;
        }
```

4.1 *E XERCISES*

1. `unsigned short int loc_counter;`

2. ```
   #include <stdio.h>

   int main(void)
   {
     unsigned long int distance;

     printf("Enter distance: ");

     scanf("%lu", &distance);

     printf("%ld seconds", distance / 186000);

     return 0;
   }
   ```

3. The statement can be recoded using C's shorthand as follows:

   `short i;`
   ```

*E*XERCISES

1. Local variables are known only to the function in which they are declared. Global variables are known to and accessible by all functions. Further, local variables are created when the function is entered and destroyed when the function is exited. Thus they cannot maintain their values between function calls. However, global variables stay in existence during the entire lifetime of the program and maintain their values.

2. Here is the non-generalized version.

```c
#include <stdio.h>

void soundspeed(void);

double distance;

int main(void)
{
  printf("Enter distance in feet: ");
  scanf("%lf", &distance);
  soundspeed();

  return 0;
}

void soundspeed(void)
{
  printf("Travel time: %f", distance / 1129);
}
```

Here is the parameterized version.

```c
#include <stdio.h>

void soundspeed(double distance);

int main(void)
{
  double distance;

  printf("Enter distance in feet: ");
  scanf("%lf", &distance);
  soundspeed(distance);
```

```
        return 0;
    }

    void soundspeed(double distance)
    {
        printf("Travel time: %f", distance / 1129);
    }
```

4.3 ▮ ͤXERCISES

1. To cause a constant to be recognized by the compiler explicitly as a **float**, follow the value with an **F**.

2.
```
#include <stdio.h>

int main(void)
{
    long int i;

    printf("Enter a number: ");
    scanf("%ld", &i);
    printf("%ld", i);

    return 0;
}
```

3.
```
#include <stdio.h>

int main(void)
{
    printf("%s %s %s", "I", "like", "C");

    return 0;
}
```

4.4 ▮ ͤXERCISES

1.
```
#include <stdio.h>

int main(void)
{
    int i=100;
```

```
for( ; i>0; i--) printf("%d ", i);

return 0;
}
```

2. No. You cannot initialize a global variable using another variable.

3. Yes. A local variable can be initialized using any expression valid at the time of the initialization.

 EXERCISES

1. The entire expression is **float**.

2. The subexpression is **unsigned long**.

 EXERCISES

1. The program displays **10**.

2. The program displays **3.0**.

4.7 **EXERCISE**

1.
```
#include <stdio.h>

int main(void)
{
  float f;

  for(f=1.0; (int) f<=9; f=f + 0.1)
  printf("%f ", f);

  return 0;
}
```

2. Here is the corrected statement.

```
x = (int)123.23 % 3; /* now fixed */
```

MASTERY SKILLS CHECK

1. The data-type modifiers are

   unsigned
   long
   short
   signed

   They are used to modify the base type so that you can obtain variables that best fit the needs of your program.

2. To define an **unsigned** constant, follow the value with a **U**. To define a **long** constant, follow the value with an **L**. To specify a **long double**, follow the value with an **L**.

3. `float balance = 0.0;`

4. When the C compiler evaluates an expression, it automatically converts all **char**s and **short**s to **int**.

5. A **signed** integer uses the high-order bit as a sign flag. When the bit is set, the number is negative, when it is cleared, the number is positive. An **unsigned** integer uses all bits as part of the number and can represent only positive values.

6. Global variables maintain their values throughout the lifetime of the program. They are also accessible by all functions in the program.

7.
```c
#include <stdio.h>

int series(void);

int num = 21;

int main(void)
{
  int i;

  for(i=0; i<10; i++)
    printf("%d ", series());

  return 0;
}
```

```
int series(void)
{
  num = (num*1468) % 467;
  return num;
}
```

8. A type cast temporarily changes the type of a variable. For example, here the **int i** is temporarily changed into a **double**.

```
(double) i
```

UMULATIVE SKILLS CHECK

1. The fragment is not valid because to C, both 'A' and 65 are the same thing, and no two **case** constants can be the same.

2. The reason that the return value of **getchar( )** or **getche( )** can be assigned to a **char** is because C automatically removes the high-order byte.

3. No. Because **i** is a signed integer, its maximum value is 32,767. Therefore, it will never exceed 33,000.

CHAPTER 5

REVIEW SKILLS CHECK

1. A local variable is known only to the function in which it is declared. Further, it is created when the function is entered and destroyed when the function returns. A global variable is known throughout the entire program and remains in existence the entire time the program is executing.

2. C compiler will assign the following types:

   a. **int**

   b. **int**

   c. **double**

   d. **long**

   e. **long**

3.
```
#include <stdio.h>

int main(void)
{
  long l;
  short s;
  double d;

  printf("Enter a long value: ");
  scanf("%ld", &l);

  printf("Enter a short value: ");
  scanf("%hd", &s);

  printf("Enter a double value: ");
  scanf("%lf", &d);

  printf("%ld\n", l);
  printf("%hd\n", s);
  printf("%f\n", d);

  return 0;
}
```

4. A type cast temporarily changes the type of a value.

5. The **else** is associated with the **if(j)** statement, contrary to what the (incorrect) indentation would have you believe.

6. When **i** is 1, **a** is 2. When **i** is 4, **a** is 5.

5.1 EXERCISES

1. The array **count** is being overrun. It is only 10 elements long, but the program requires one that is 100 elements long.

2.
```
#include <stdio.h>

int main(void)
{
  int i[10], j, k, match;

  printf("Enter 10 numbers:\n");
  for(j=0; j<10; j++) scanf("%d", &i[j]);
```

```
                    /* see if any match */
                    for(j=0; j<10; j++) {
                      match = i[j];
                        for(k=j+1; k<10; k++)
                          if(match==i[k])
                            printf("%d is duplicated\n", match);
                    }

                    return 0;
                  }

          3. #include <stdio.h>

             int main(void)
             {
               float item[100], t;
               int a, b;
               int count;

               /* read in numbers */
               printf("How many numbers? ");
               scanf("%d", &count);
               for(a=0; a<count; a++) scanf("%f", &item[a]);

               /* now sort them using a bubble sort */
               for(a=1; a<count; ++a)
                 for(b=count-1; b>=a; --b) {
                   /* compare adjacent elements */
                   if(item[b-1] > item[b]) {
                     /* exchange elements */
                     t = item[b-1];
                     item[b-1] = item[b];
                     item[b] = t;
                   }
                 }

               /* display sorted list */
               for(a=0; a<count; a++) printf("%f ", item[a]);

               return 0;
             }
```

***E**XERCISES*

1.
```c
/* Reverse a string. */
#include <stdio.h>
#include <string.h>

int main(void)
{
  char str[80];
  int i;

  printf("Enter a string: ");
  gets(str);

  for(i=strlen(str)-1; i>=0; i--)
    printf("%c", str[i]);

  return 0;
}
```

2. The string **str** is not long enough to hold the string "this is a test".

3.
```c
#include <stdio.h>
#include <string.h>

int main(void)
{
  char bigstr[1000] = "", str[80];

  for( ; ; ) {
    printf("Enter a string: ");
    gets(str);
    if(!strcmp(str, "quit")) break;
    strcat(str, "\n");
    /* prevent an array overrun */
    if(strlen(bigstr)+strlen(str) >= 1000) break;
    strcat(bigstr, str);
  }

  printf(bigstr);

  return 0;
}
```

5.3 EXERCISES

1.
```c
#include <stdio.h>

int main(void)
{
  int three_d[3][3][3];
  int i, j, k, x;

  x = 1;
  for(i=0; i<3; i++)
    for(j=0; j<3; j++)
      for(k=0; k<3; k++) {
        three_d[i][j][k] = x;
        x++;
        printf("%d ", three_d[i][j][k]);
      }

  return 0;
}
```

2.
```c
#include <stdio.h>

int main(void)
{
  int three_d[3][3][3];
  int i, j, k, sum;

  for(i=0; i<3; i++)
    for(j=0; j<3; j++)
      for(k=0; k<3; k++) {
        three_d[i][j][k] = (i+1) * (j+1) * (k+1);
        printf("%d ", three_d[i][j][k]);
      }

  /* sum all elements */
  sum = 0;
  for(i=0; i<3; i++)
    for(j=0; j<3; j++)
      for(k=0; k<3; k++)
        sum = sum + three_d[i][j][k];

  printf("\n%d", sum);
```

```
      return 0;
    }
```

5.4   *E*XERCISES

1. No. The list must be enclosed between curly braces.

2. No. The array **name** is only 4 characters long. The attempted call to **strcpy( )** will cause the array to be overrun.

3.
```
#include <stdio.h>

int main(void)
{
  int cube[][3] = {
    1, 1, 1,
    2, 4, 8,
    3, 9, 27,
    4, 16, 64,
    5, 25, 125,
    6, 36, 216,
    7, 49, 343,
    8, 64, 512,
    9, 81, 729,
    10, 100, 1000
  };
  int num, i;

  printf("Enter cube: ");
  scanf("%d", &num);

  for(i=0; i<10; i++)
    if(cube[i][2]==num) {
      printf("Root: %d\n", cube[i][0]);
      printf("Square: %d", cube[i][1]);
      break;
    }

  if(i==10) printf("Cube not found.\n");

  return 0;
}
```

EXERCISES

1.
```c
#include <stdio.h>
#include <conio.h>

int main(void)
{
  char digits[10][10] = {
    "zero", "one", "two", "three",
    "four", "five", "six", "seven",
    "eight", "nine"
  };
  char num;

  printf("Enter number: ");
  num = getche();
  printf("\n");

  num = num - '0';
  if(num>=0 && num<10) printf("%s", digits[num]);

  return 0;
}
```

MASTERY SKILLS CHECK

1. An array is a list of like-type variables.

2. The statement will not generate an error message because C provides no bounds checking on array operations, but it is wrong because it causes **count** to be overrun.

3.
```c
#include <stdio.h>

int main(void)
{
  int stats[20], i, j;
  int mode, count, oldcount, oldmode;

  printf("Enter 20 numbers: \n");
  for(i=0; i<20; i++) scanf("%d", &stats[i]);

  oldcount = 0;
  /* find the mode */
```

```c
      for(i=0; i<20; i++) {
        mode = stats[i];
        count = 1;

        /* count the occurrences of this value */
        for(j=i+1; j<20; j++)
          if(mode==stats[j]) count++;

        /* if count is greater than old count, use new mode */
        if(count>oldcount) {
          oldmode = mode;
          oldcount = count;
        }
      }
      printf("The mode is %d\n", oldmode);

      return 0;
    }
```

4.
```c
int items[] = {1, 2, 3, 4, 5, 6, 7, 8, 9, 10};
```

5.
```c
#include <stdio.h>
#include <string.h>

int main(void)
{
  char str[80];

  do {
    printf("Enter a string: ");
    gets(str);
  } while(strcmp("quit", str));

  return 0;
}
```

6.
```c
/* Computerized dictionary program. */

#include <stdio.h>
#include <string.h>

int main(void)
{
  char dict[][2][40] = {
```

```
      "house", "a place of dwelling",
      "car", "a vehicle",
      "computer", "a thinking machine",
      "program", "a sequence of instructions",
      "", ""
    };
    char word[80];
    int i;

    printf("Enter word: ");
    gets(word);

    /* look up the word */
    i = 0;
    /* search while null string not yet encountered */
    while(strcmp(dict[i][0], "" )) {
      if(!strcmp(word, dict[i][0])) {
        printf("meaning: %s", dict[i][1]);
        break;
      }
      i++;
    }
    if(!strcmp(dict[i][0], ""))
    printf("Not in dictionary\n");

    return 0;
}
```

CUMULATIVE SKILLS CHECK

1.
```
#include <stdio.h>
#include <string.h>

int main(void)
{
  char str[80];
  int i;

  printf("Enter a string: ");
  gets(str);

  /* pad the string if necessary */
  for(i=strlen(str); i<79; i++)
    strcat(str, ".");
```

```
    printf(str);

    return 0;
}
```

2. `/* A simple coding program. */`

```
#include <stdio.h>
#include <string.h>

int main(void)
{
  char str[80];
  int i, j;

  printf("Enter message: ");
  gets(str);

  /* code it */
  i=0; j = strlen(str) - 1;
  while(i<=j) {
    if(i<j) printf("%c%c", str[i], str[j]);
    else printf("%c", str[i]);
    i++; j--;
  }

  return 0;
}
```

3.
```
#include <stdio.h>
#include <string.h>

int main(void)
{
  char str[80];
  int spaces, periods, commas;
  int i;

  printf("Enter a string: ");
  gets(str);

  spaces = 0;
  commas = 0;
  periods = 0;
```

```
      for(i=0; i<strlen(str); i++)
        switch(str[i]) {
          case '.': periods++;
            break;
          case ',': commas++;
            break;
          case ' ': spaces++;
        }

    printf("spaces: %d\n", spaces);
    printf("commas: %d\n", commas);
    printf("periods: %d", periods);

    return 0;
}
```

4. The **getchar( )** function returns a character, not a string. Hence, it cannot be used as shown. You must use **gets( )** to read a string from the keyboard.

5.
```
/* A simple game of Hangman */

#include <stdio.h>
#include <string.h>

int main(void)
{
  char word[] = "concatenation";
  char temp[] = "-------------";
  char ch;
  int i, count;

  count = 0; /* count number of guesses */

  do {
    printf("%s\n", temp);
    printf("Enter your guess: ");
    ch = getchar();
    printf("\n");

    /* see if letter matches any in word */
    for(i=0; i<strlen(word); i++)
      if(ch==word[i]) temp[i] = ch;
      count++;
  } while(strcmp(temp, word));
```

```
      printf("%s\n", temp);
      printf("You guessed the word and used %d guesses", count);

      return 0;
   }
```

CHAPTER 6

REVIEW SKILLS CHECK

1.
```
#include <stdio.h>

int main(void)
{
   int num[10], i, even, odd;

   printf("Enter 10 integers: ");

   for(i=0; i<10; i++) scanf("%d", &num[i]);

   even = 0; odd = 0;
   for(i=0;  i< 10; i++) {
      if(num[i]%2) odd = odd + num[i];
      else even = even + num[i];
   }

   printf("Sum of even numbers: %d\n", even);
   printf("Sum of odd numbers: %d", odd);

   return 0;
}
```

2.
```
#include <stdio.h>
#include <string.h>

int main(void)
{
   char pw[80];
   int i;

   for(i=0; i<3; i++) {
      printf("Password: ");
```

```
      gets(pw);
      if(!strcmp("Tristan", pw)) break;
    }

    if(i==3) printf("Access Denied");
    else printf("Log-on Successful");

    return 0;
}
```

3. The array, **name**, is not big enough to hold the string being assigned to it.

4. A null string is a string that contains only the null character.

5. The **strcpy( )** function copies the contents of one string into another. The **strcmp( )** function compares two strings and returns less than zero if the first string is less than the second, zero if the strings match, or greater than zero if the first string is greater than the second.

6.
```
/* A Simple computerized telephone book. */

#include <stdio.h>
#include <string.h>

char phone[][2][40] = {
  "Fred", "555-1010",
  "Barney", "555-1234",
  "Ralph", "555-2347",
  "Tom", "555-8396",
  "", ""
};

int main(void)
{
  char name[80];
  int i;

  printf("Name? ");
  gets(name);

  for(i=0; phone[i][0][0]; i++)
    if(!strcmp(name, phone[i][0]))
      printf("number: %s", phone[i][1]);
```

```
    return 0;
  }
```

6.1 **E**XERCISES

1. A pointer is a variable that contains the address of another variable.

2. The pointer operators are the * and the **&**. The * operator returns the value of the object pointed to by the pointer it precedes. The **&** operator returns the address of the variable it precedes.

3. The base type of a pointer is important because all pointer arithmetic is done relative to it.

4.
```
#include <stdio.h>

int main(void)
{
  int i, *p;

  p = &i;

  for(i=0; i<10; i++) printf("%d ", *p);

  return 0;
}
```

6.2 **E**XERCISES

1. You cannot multiply a pointer.

2. No, you can only add or subtract integer values.

3. 108

6.3 **E**XERCISES

1. No, you cannot change the value of a pointer that is generated by using an array name without an index.

2. 8

3.
```c
#include <stdio.h>

int main(void)
{
  char str[80], *p;

  printf("Enter a string: ");
  gets(str);

  p = str;

  /* While not at the end of the string and no
     space has been encountered, increment p to
     point to next character.
  */
  while(*p && *p!=' ') p++;

  printf(p);

  return 0;
}
```

6.4 **E**XERCISE

1.
```c
#include <stdio.h>

int main(void)
{
  char *one = "one";
  char *two = "two";
  char *three = "three";

  printf("%s %s %s\n", one, two, three);
  printf("%s %s %s\n", one, three, two);
  printf("%s %s %s\n", two, one, three);
  printf("%s %s %s\n", two, three, one);
  printf("%s %s %s\n", three, one, two);
  printf("%s %s %s\n", three, two, one);

  return 0;
}
```

6.5 **E**XERCISE

```c
1. #include <stdio.h>
   #include <string.h>

   int main(void)
   {
     char *p[3] = {
       "yes", "no",
       "maybe - rephrase the question"
     } ;
     char str[80];

     printf("Enter your question: \n");
     gets(str);

     printf(p[strlen(str) % 3]);

     return 0;
   }
```

6.6 **E**XERCISE

```c
1. #include <stdio.h>

   int main(void)
   {
     int i, *p, **mp;

     p = &i;
     mp = &p;

     **mp = 10;

     printf("%p %p %p", &i, p, mp);

     return 0;
   }
```

EXERCISES

1.
```c
#include <stdio.h>
#include <string.h>

void mystrcat(char *to, char *from);

int main(void)
{
  char str[80];

  strcpy(str, "first part");
  mystrcat(str, " second part");
  printf(str);

  return 0;
}

void mystrcat(char *to, char *from)
{
  /* find the end of to */
  while(*to) to++;

  /* concatenate the string */
  while(*from) *to++ = *from++;

  /* add the null terminator */
  *to = '\0';
}
```

2.
```c
#include <stdio.h>

void f(int *p);

int main(void)
{
  int i;

  f(&i);

  printf("%d", i);

  return 0;
}
```

```
void f(int *p)
{
   *p = -1;
}
```

ASTERY SKILLS CHECK

1. `double *p;`

2. ```
   #include <stdio.h>

   int main(void)
   {
      int i, *p;

      p = &i;

      *p = 100;

      printf("%d", i);

      return 0;
   }
   ```

3. No. The pointer **p** has never been initialized to point to a valid piece of memory that can hold a string.

4. Pointers and arrays are basically two ways of looking at the same thing. They are virtually interchangeable.

5. `str[2]`

   `*(str+2)`

   `*(p+2)`

6. 108

CUMULATIVE SKILLS CHECK

1. Pointers are often more convenient than array indexing and may be faster in some cases.
   ```

2.
```
#include <stdio.h>

int main(void)
{
  char str[80], *p;
  int spaces;

  printf("Enter a string: ");
  gets(str);

  spaces = 0;
  p = str;
  while(*p) {
    if(*p==' ') spaces++;
    p++;
  }

  printf("Number of spaces: %d", spaces);

  return 0;
}
```

3.
```
*((int *)count + (44 * 10) + 8) = 99;
```

CHAPTER 7

REVIEW SKILLS CHECK

1. The fragment assigns to **i** the value 19 indirectly using a pointer.

2. An array name with no index generates a pointer to the start of the array.

3. Yes, the fragment is correct. It works because the compiler creates a string table entry for the string "this is a string" and assigns **p** a pointer to the start of it.

4.
```
#include <stdio.h>

int main(void)
{
```

```
   double d, *p;

   p = &d;

   *p = 100.99;

   printf("%f", d);

   return 0;
}
```

5.
```
#include <stdio.h>

int mystrlen(char *p);

int main(void)
{
  char str[80];

  printf("Enter a string: ");
  gets(str);

  printf("Length is %d", mystrlen(str));

  return 0;
}

int mystrlen(char *p)
{
  int i;

  i = 0;
  while(*p) {
    i++;
    p++;
  }
  return i;
}
```

6. The fragment is correct. It displays **C**.

1.
```c
#include <stdio.h>

double avg();

int main(void)
{
  printf("%f", avg());

  return 0;
}

double avg()
{
  int i;
  double sum, num;

  sum = 0.0;
  for(i=0; i<10; i++) {
    printf("Enter next number: ");
    scanf("%lf", &num);
    sum = sum + num;
  }
  return sum / 10.0;
}
```

2.
```c
#include <stdio.h>

double avg(void);

int main(void)
{
  printf("%f", avg());

  return 0;
}

double avg(void)
{
  int i;
  double sum, num;

  sum = 0.0;
```

```
    for(i=0; i<10; i++) {
      printf("Enter next number: ");
      scanf("%lf", &num);
      sum = sum + num;
    }
    return sum / 10.0;
  }
```

3. The program is correct. However, the program would be better if a full function prototype were used when declaring **myfunc( )**.

4. `double *Purge(void);`

7.2 EXERCISES

1.
```
#include <stdio.h>

int fact(int i);

int main(void)
{
  printf("5 factorial is %d", fact(5));

  return 0;
}

int fact(int i)
{
  if(i==1) return 1;
  else return i * fact(i-1);
}
```

2. The function will call itself repeatedly, until it crashes the program, because there is no condition that prevents a recursive call from occurring.

3.
```
#include <stdio.h>

void display(char *p);

int main(void)
{
  display("this is a test");

  return 0;
```

```
    }

    void display(char *p)
    {
      if(*p) {
        printf("%c", *p);
        display(p+1);
      }
    }
```

7.3 ■ EXERCISES

1. No. The function **myfunc( )** is being called with a pointer to the first parameter instead of the parameter itself.

2.
```
   #include <stdio.h>

   void prompt(char *msg, char *str);

   int main(void)
   {
     char str[80];

     prompt("Enter a string: ", str);
     printf("Your string is: %s", str);

     return 0;
   }

   void prompt(char *msg, char *p)
   {
     printf(msg);
     gets(p);
   }
```

3. In call by value, the value of an argument is passed to a function. In call by reference, the address of an argument is passed to a function.

7.4 ■ EXERCISES

1.
```
   #include <stdio.h>
   #include <string.h>
```

```
#include <stdlib.h>

int main(int argc, char *argv[])
{
  int i;

  if(argc!=3) {
    printf("You must specify two arguments.");
    exit(1);
  }

  i = strcmp(argv[1], argv[2]);
  if(i < 0) printf("%s > %s", argv[2], argv[1]);
  else if(i > 0) printf("%s > %s", argv[1], argv[2]);
  else printf("They are the same");

  return 0;
}
```

2.
```
#include <stdio.h>
#include <string.h>
#include <stdlib.h>

int main(int argc, char *argv[])
{
  if(argc!=3) {
    printf("You must specify two numbers.");
    exit(1);
  }

  printf("%f", atof(argv[1]) + atof(argv[2]));

  return 0;
}
```

3.
```
#include <stdio.h>
#include <string.h>
#include <stdlib.h>

int main(int argc, char *argv[])
{
  if(argc!=4) {

    printf("You must specify the operation ");
    printf("followed by two numbers.");
```

```
      exit(1);
   }

   if(!strcmp("add", argv[1]))
     printf("%f", atof(argv[2]) + atof(argv[3]));
   else if(!strcmp("subtract", argv[1]))
     printf("%f", atof(argv[2]) - atof(argv[3]));
   else if(!strcmp("multiply", argv[1]))
     printf("%f", atof(argv[2]) * atof(argv[3]));
   if(!strcmp("divide", argv[1]))
     printf("%f", atof(argv[2]) / atof(argv[3]));

   return 0;
}
```

7.5 EXERCISE

1.
```
#include <stdio.h>

double f_to_m(double f);

int main(void)
{
  double feet;

  printf("Enter feet: ");
  scanf("%lf", &feet);
  printf("Meters: %f", f_to_m(feet));

  return 0;
}

/* use old-style declaration. */
double f_to_m(f)
double f;
{
  return f / 3.28;
}
```

MASTERY SKILLS CHECK

1. A function that does not have parameters specifies **void** in the
   parameter list of its prototype.

2. A function prototype tells the compiler these three things: the return type of the function, the type of its parameters, and the number of its parameters. It is useful because it allows the compiler to find errors if the function is called incorrectly.

3. Command-line arguments are passed to a C program through the **argc** and **argv** parameters to **main( )**.

4.
```c
#include <stdio.h>

void alpha(char ch);

int main(void)
{
  alpha('A');

  return 0;
}

void alpha(char ch)
{
  printf("%c", ch);
  if(ch < 'Z') alpha(ch+1);
}
```

5.
```c
#include <stdio.h>
#include <stdlib.h>

int main(int argc, char *argv[])
{
  char *p;

  if(argc!=2) {
    printf("You need to specify a string");
    exit(1);
  }

  p = argv[1];

  while(*p) {
    printf("%c", (*p)+1);
    p++;
  }
```

```
      return 0;
}
```

6. The prototype is shown here.

```
double myfunc(int x, int y, char ch);
```

7. Using the old-style function declaration, the function from Exercise 6 looks like this.

```
double myfunc(x, y, ch)
int x, y;
char ch;
{
     .
     .
     .
}
```

8. The **exit( )** function causes immediate program termination. It also returns a value to the operating system.

9. The **atoi( )** function converts its string argument into its equivalent integer form. The string must represent (in string form) a valid integer.

▬▬▬▬ *C*UMULATIVE SKILLS CHECK

```
1. #include <stdio.h>
   #include <string.h>
   #include <stdlib.h>

   int main(int argc, char *argv[])
   {
     if(argc!=2) {
       printf("Specify a password");
       exit(1);
     }
     if(!strcmp(argv[1], "password"))
       printf("Access Permitted");
     else printf("Access Denied");

     return 0;
   }
```

```
2. #include <stdio.h>
   #include <ctype.h>

   void string_up(char *p);

   int main(void)
   {
     char str[] = "this is a test";

     string_up(str);
     printf(str);

     return 0;
   }

   void string_up(char *p)
   {
     while(*p) {
       *p = toupper(*p);
       p++;
     }
   }

3. #include <stdio.h>

   void avg(double *d, int num);

   int main(void)
   {
     double nums[] = {1.0, 2.0, 3.0, 4.0, 5.0,
                      6.0, 7.0, 8.0, 9.0, 10.0};

     avg(nums, 10);

     return 0;
   }

   void avg(double *d, int num)
   {
     double sum;
     int temp;

     temp = num-1;

     for(sum=0; temp>=0; temp--)
```

```
      sum = sum + d[temp];

   printf("Average is %f", sum / (double) num);
}
```

4. A pointer contains the address of another variable. When a pointer is passed to a function, the function may alter the contents of the object pointed to by the pointer. This is the equivalent of call by reference.

CHAPTER 8

REVIEW SKILLS CHECK

1. To allow the compiler to verify that a function is being called correctly, you must include its prototype.

2. Function prototypes enable the compiler to provide stronger type checking between the arguments used to call a function and the parameters of the function. Also, it lets the compiler confirm that the function is called with the proper number of arguments.

3.
```
#include <stdio.h>
#include <math.h>

double hypot(double s1, double s2);

int main(void)
{
  printf("%f", hypot(12.2, 19.2));

  return 0;
}

double hypot(double s1, double s2)
{
  double h;

  h = s1*s1 + s2*s2;
  return sqrt(h);
}
```

4. When a function does not return a value, its return type should be specified as **void**.

5.
```c
#include <stdio.h>

int rstrlen(char *p);

int main(void)
{
  printf("%d", rstrlen("hello there"));

  return 0;
}

int rstrlen(char *p)
{
  if(*p) {
    p++;
    return 1+rstrlen(p);
  }
  else return 0;
}
```

6.
```c
#include <stdio.h>

int main(int argc, char *argv[])
{
  printf("There were %d arguments.\n", argc);
  printf("The last one is %s.", argv[argc-1]);

  return 0;
}
```

7.
```c
func(a, ch, d)
int a;
char ch;
double d;
{
```

1.
```c
#include <stdio.h>

#define MAX 100
```

```
#define COUNTBY 3

int main(void)
{
  int i;

  for(i=0; i<MAX; i++)
    if(!(i%COUNTBY)) printf("%d ", i);

  return 0;
}
```

2. No, the fragment is wrong because a macro cannot be defined in terms of another before the second macro is defined. Stated differently, **MIN** is not defined when **MAX** is being defined.

3. As the macro is used, the fragment is wrong. The string needs to be within double quotes.

4. Yes.

8.2 *E*XERCISES

```
1. #include <stdio.h>

int main(void)
{
  int i;

  do {
    i = getchar();
    if(i==EOF) {
      printf("Error on input.");
      break;
    }
    if(putchar('.')==EOF) {
      printf("Error on output.");
      break;
    }
  } while((char) i != '\n');

  return 0;
}
```

2. The **putchar( )** function outputs a character. It cannot output a string.

8.3   EXERCISES

1.
```c
#include <conio.h>
#include <stdio.h>

int main(void)
{
  char ch;

  ch = getch();
  printf("%d", ch);

  return 0;
}
```

2.
```c
#include <stdio.h>
#include <conio.h>

int main(void)
{
  do {
    printf("%c", '.');
  } while(!kbhit());

  return 0;
}
```

8.4   EXERCISES

2. No. The program is incorrect because **gets( )** must be called with a pointer to an actual array.

8.5   EXERCISES

1.
```c
#include <stdio.h>

int main(void)
{
```

```
    unsigned long i;

    for(i=2; i<=100; i++)
      printf("%-10lu %-10lu %-10lu\n", i, i*i, i*i*i);

    return 0;
}
```

2. `printf("Clearance price: 40% off as marked");`

3. `printf("%.2f", 1023.03);`

▮ 8.6 ▮ EXERCISES

1.
```
#include <stdio.h>

int main(void)
{
  char first[21], middle[21], last[21];

  printf("Enter your entire name: ");
  scanf("%20s%20s%20s", first, middle, last);
  printf("%s %s %s", first, middle, last);

  return 0;
}
```

2.
```
#include <stdio.h>

int main(void)
{
  char num[80];

  printf("Enter a floating point number: ");
  scanf("%[0-9.]", num);
  printf(num);

  return 0;
}
```

3. No, a character can only have a maximum field length of 1.

4.
```
#include <stdio.h>

int main(void)
```

```
    {
      char str[80];
      double d;
      int i, num;

      printf("Enter a string, a double, and an integer: ");
      scanf("%s%lf%d%n", str, &d, &i, &num);
      printf("Number of characters read: %d", num);

      return 0;
    }

5.  #include <stdio.h>

    int main(void)
    {
      unsigned u;

      printf("Enter hexadecimal number: ");
      scanf("%x", &u);
      printf("Decimal equivalent: %u", u);

      return 0;
    }
```

*M*ASTERY SKILLS CHECK

1. All these functions input a character from the keyboard. The **getchar( )** function is often implemented using line-buffered I/O which makes its use in interactive environments undesirable. The **getche( )** is an interactive equivalent to **getchar( )**. The **getch( )** function is the same as **getche( )** except that it does not echo the character typed.

2. The **%e** specifier outputs a number in scientific notation using a lowercase 'e'. The **%E** specifier outputs a number in scientific notation using an 'E'.

3. A scanset is a set of characters that **scanf( )** matches with input. As long as the characters being read are part of the scanset, **scanf( )** continues to input them into the array pointed to by the scanset's corresponding argument.

4.
```c
#include <stdio.h>

int main(void)
{
  char name[80], date[80], phone[80];

  printf("Enter first name, birthdate ");
  printf("and phone number:\n");
  scanf("%s%8s%8s", name, date, phone);
  printf("%s %s %s", name, date, phone);

  return 0;
}
```

5. The **puts( )** function is much smaller and faster than **printf( )**. But, it can only output strings.

6.
```c
#include <stdio.h>

#define COUNT 100

int main(void)
{
  int i;

  for(i=0; i<COUNT;i++)
    printf("%d ", i);

  return 0;
}
```

7. **EOF** is a macro that stands for end-of-file. It is defined in STDIO.H.

CUMULATIVE SKILLS CHECK

1.
```c
#include <stdio.h>

int main(void)
{
  char name[9][80];
  double b_avg[9];
  int i, h, l;
```

```
      double high, low, team_avg;

      for(i=0; i<9; i++) {
        printf("Enter name %d: ", i+1);
        scanf("%s", name[i]);
        printf("Enter batting average: ");
        scanf("%lf", &b_avg[i]);
        printf("\n");
      }

      high = 0.0;
      low = 1000.0;
      team_avg = 0.0;
      for(i=0; i<9; i++) {
        if(b_avg[i]>high) {
          h = i;
          high = b_avg[i];
        }
        if(b_avg[i]<low) {
          l = i;
          low = b_avg[i];
        }
        team_avg = team_avg+b_avg[i];
      }
      printf("The high is %s %f\n", name[h], b_avg[h]);
      printf("The low is %s %f\n", name[l], b_avg[l]);
      printf("The team average is %f", team_avg/9.0);

      return 0;
    }
```

2. Note: There are many ways you could have written this program. This one is simply representative.

```
/* An electronic card catalog. */
#include <stdio.h>
#include <stdlib.h>
#include <string.h>

#define MAX 100

int menu(void);
void display(int i);
void author_search(void);
void title_search(void);
```

```
void enter(void);

char names[MAX][80]; /* author names */
char titles[MAX][80]; /* titles */
char pubs[MAX][80]; /* publisher */

int top = 0; /* last location used */

int main(void)
{
  int choice;

  do {
    choice = menu();
    switch(choice) {
      case 1: enter(); /* enter books */
        break;
      case 2: author_search(); /* search by author */
        break;
      case 3: title_search(); /* search by title */
        break;
    }
  } while(choice!=4);

  return 0;
}

/* Return a menu selection. */
menu(void)
{
  char str[80];
  int i;

  printf("Card Catalog:\n");
  printf("  1. Enter\n");
  printf("  2. Search by Author\n");
  printf("  3. Search by Title\n");
  printf("  4. Quit\n");

  do {
    printf("Choose your selection: ");
    gets(str);
    i = atoi(str);
    printf("\n");
  } while(i<1 || i>4);
```

```
      return i;
    }

    /* Enter books into database. */
    void enter(void)
    {
      int i;

      for(i=top; i<MAX; i++) {
        printf("Enter author name (ENTER to quit): ");
        gets(names[i]);
        if(!*names[i]) break;
        printf("Enter title: ");
        gets(titles[i]);
        printf("Enter publisher: ");
        gets(pubs[i]);
      }
      top = i;
    }

    /* Search by author. */
    void author_search(void)
    {
      char name[80];
      int i, found;

      printf("Name: ");
      gets(name);

      found = 0;
      for(i=0; i<top; i++)
        if(!strcmp(name, names[i])) {
          display(i);
          found = 1;
          printf("\n");
        }

      if(!found) printf("Not Found\n");
    }

    /* Search by title.*/
    void title_search(void)
    {
      char title[80];
```

```
      int i, found;

      printf("Title: ");
      gets(title);

      found = 0;
      for(i=0; i<top; i++)
        if(!strcmp(title, titles[i])) {
          display(i);
          found = 1;
          printf("\n");
        }
      if(!found) printf("Not Found\n");
    }

    /* Display catalog entry. */
    void display(int i)
    {
      printf("%s\n", titles[i]);
      printf("by %s\n", names[i]);
      printf("Published by %s\n", pubs[i]);
    }
```

CHAPTER 9

REVIEW SKILLS CHECK

1. The **getchar( )** function is defined by the ANSI standard and is used to input characters from the keyboard. However, in most implementations, it uses line-buffered I/O, which makes it impractical for interactive use. The **getche( )** function is not defined by the ANSI standard, but it is quite common and is essentially an interactive version of **getchar( )**.

2. When **scanf( )** is reading a string, it stops when it encounters the first whitespace character.

3. #include <stdio.h>

   int isprime(int i);

   int main(void)
   {

```
      int i, count;

      count = 0;
      for(i=2; i<1001; i++)
        if(isprime(i)) {
          printf("%10d", i);
          count++;
          if(count==4) {
            printf("\n");
            count = 0;
          }
        }

      return 0;
    }

    int isprime(int i)
    {
      int j;

      for(j=2; j<=(i/2); j++)
         if(!(i%j)) return  0;
      return 1;
    }
```

4.
```
#include <stdio.h>

int main(void)
{
  double d;
  char ch;
  char str[80];

  printf("Enter a double, a character, and a string\n");
  scanf("%lf%c%20s", &d, &ch, str);
  printf("%f %c %s", d, ch, str);

  return 0;
}
```

5.
```
#include <stdio.h>

int main(void)
{
  char str[80];
```

```
      printf("Enter leading digits followed by a string\n");
      scanf("%*[0-9]%s", str);
      printf("%s", str);

      return 0;
    }
```

▌ 9.2 ▌ ƎXERCISES

```
1. #include <stdio.h>
   #include <stdlib.h>

   int main(int argc, char *argv[])
   {
     FILE *fp;
     char ch;

     /* see if filename is specified */
     if(argc!=2) {
       printf("File name missing.\n");
       exit(1);
     }

     if((fp = fopen(argv[1], "r"))==NULL) {
       printf("Cannot open file.\n");
       exit(1);
     }

     while((ch=fgetc(fp)) != EOF) putchar(ch);

     fclose(fp);

     return 0;
   }

2. #include <stdio.h>
   #include <stdlib.h>
   #include <ctype.h>

   int count[26];

   int main(int argc, char *argv[])
   {
```

```
      FILE *fp;
      char ch;
      int i;

      /* see if file name is specified */
      if(argc!=2) {
        printf("File name missing.\n");
        exit(1);
      }

      if((fp = fopen(argv[1], "r"))==NULL) {
        printf("Cannot open file.\n");
        exit(1);
      }

      while((ch=fgetc(fp))!=EOF) {
        ch = toupper(ch);
        if(ch>='A' && ch<='Z') count[ch-'A']++;
      }

      for(i=0; i<26; i++)
        printf("%c occurred %d times\n", i+'A', count[i]);

      fclose(fp);

      return 0;
    }

3. /* Copy a file. */
   #include <stdio.h>
   #include <stdlib.h>
   #include <string.h>

   int main(int argc, char *argv[])
   {
     FILE *from, *to;
     char ch, watch;

     /* see if correct number of command line arguments */
     if(argc<3) {
       printf("Usage: copy <source> <destination>\n");
       exit(1);
     }

     /* open source file */
```

```
  if(( from = fopen(argv[1], "r"))==NULL){
    printf("Cannot open source file.\n");
    exit(1);
  }

  /* open destination file */
  if((to = fopen(argv[2], "w"))==NULL) {
    printf("Cannot open destination file.\n");
    exit(1);
  }

  if(argc==4 && !strcmp(argv[3], "watch")) watch = 1;
  else watch = 0;

  /* copy the file */
  while((ch=fgetc(from))!=EOF) {
    fputc(ch, to);
    if(watch) putchar(ch);
  }
  fclose(from);
  fclose(to);

  return 0;
}
```

▬▬ 9.3 ▬▬ *E*XERCISES

```
1. #include <stdio.h>
   #include <stdlib.h>

   int main(int argc, char *argv[])
   {
     FILE *fp;

     unsigned count;

     /* see if file name is specified */
     if(argc!=2) {
       printf("File name missing.\n");
       exit(1);
     }

     if((fp = fopen(argv[1], "rb"))==NULL) {
       printf("Cannot open file.\n");
```

```
      exit(1);
    }

    count = 0;
    while(!feof(fp)) {
      fgetc(fp);
      if(ferror(fp)) {
        printf("File error.\n");
        exit(1);
      }
      count++;
    }

    printf("File has %u bytes", count-1);
    fclose(fp);

    return 0;
  }
```

2.
```
  /* Exchange two files. */
  #include <stdio.h>
  #include <stdlib.h>
  #include <string.h>

  int main(int argc, char *argv[])
  {
    FILE *f1, *f2, *temp;
    char ch;

    /* see if correct number of command line arguments */
    if(argc!=3) {
      printf("Usage: exchange<f1> <f2>\n");
      exit(1);
    }

    /* open first file */
    if((f1 = fopen(argv[1], "rb"))==NULL) {
      printf("Cannot open first file.\n");
      exit(1);
    }

    /* open second file */
    if((f2 = fopen(argv[2],"rb"))==NULL) {
      printf("Cannot open second file.\n");
      exit(1);
```

```
}

/* open temporary file */
if((temp = fopen("temp.tmp", "wb"))==NULL) {
  printf("Cannot open temporary file.\n");
  exit(1);
}

/* copy f1 to temp */
while(!feof(f1)) {
  ch = fgetc(f1);
  if(!feof(f1)) fputc(ch, temp);
}

fclose(f1);
/* open first file for output */
if((f1 = fopen(argv[1], "wb"))==NULL) {
  printf("Cannot open first file.\n");
  exit(1);
}

/* copy f2 to f1 */
while(!feof(f2)) {
  ch = fgetc(f2);
  if(!feof(f2)) fputc(ch, f1);
}
fclose(f2);
fclose(temp);

/* open second file for output */
if((f2 = fopen(argv[2], "wb"))==NULL) {
  printf("Cannot open second file.\n");
  exit(1);
}
/* open temp file for input */
if((temp = fopen("temp.tmp", "rb"))==NULL) {
  printf("Cannot open temporary file.\n");
  exit(1);
}

/* copy temp to f2 */
while(!feof(temp)) {
  ch = fgetc(temp);
  if(!feof(temp)) fputc(ch, f2);
}
```

```
        fclose(f1);
        fclose(f2);
        fclose(temp);

        return 0;
      }
```


9.4   **E**XERCISES

```
1. /* A simple computerized telephone book. */
   #include <stdio.h>
   #include <string.h>
   #include <stdlib.h>

   char names[100][40];
   char numbers[100][40];

   int loc=0;

   int menu(void);
   void enter(void);
   void load(void);
   void save(void);
   void find(void);

   int main(void)
   {
     int choice;

     do {
       choice = menu();
       switch(choice) {
         case 1: enter();
           break;
         case 2: find();
           break;
         case 3: save();
           break;
         case 4: load();
       }
     } while(choice!=5);

     return 0;
```

```
}

/* Get menu choice. */
int menu(void)
{
  int i;
  char str[80];

  printf("1. Enter names and numbers\n");
  printf("2. Find numbers\n");
  printf("3. Save directory to disk\n");
  printf("4. Load directory from disk\n");
  printf("5. Quit\n");

  do {
    printf("Enter your choice: ");
    gets(str);
    i = atoi(str);
    printf("\n");
  } while(i<1 || i>5);
  return i;
}

void enter(void)
{

  for(;loc<100; loc++) {
    if(loc<100) {
      printf("Enter name and phone number:\n");
      gets(names[loc]);
      if(!*names[loc]) break;
      gets(numbers[loc]);
    }
  }
}

void find(void)
{
  char name[80];
  int i;

  printf("Enter name: ");
  gets(name);

  for(i=0; i<100; i++)
```

```
         if(!strcmp(name, names[i]))
           printf("%s %s\n", names[i], numbers[i]);
    }

    void load(void)
    {
      FILE *fp;

      if((fp = fopen("phone", "r"))==NULL) {
        printf("Cannot open file.\n");
        exit(1);
      }

      loc = 0;
      while(!feof(fp)) {
        fscanf(fp, "%s%s", names[loc], numbers[loc]);
        loc++;
      }
      fclose(fp);
    }

    void save(void)
    {
      FILE *fp;
      int i;

      if((fp = fopen("phone", "w"))==NULL) {
        printf("Cannot open file.\n");
        exit(1);
      }

      for(i=0; i<loc; i++) {
        fprintf(fp, "%s %s ", names[i], numbers[i]);
      }
      fclose(fp);
    }

2.  #include <stdio.h>
    #include <stdlib.h>
    #include <ctype.h>

    int main(int argc, char *argv[])
    {
      FILE *fp;
      char ch;
```

```
      char str[80];
      int count;

      /* see if correct number of common line arguments */
      if(argc!=2) {
        printf("Usage: display <file>\n");
        exit(1);
      }

      /* open the file */
      if((fp = fopen(argv[1], "r"))==NULL) {
        printf("Cannot open the file.\n");
        exit(1);
      }

      count = 0;
      while(!feof(fp)) {
        fgets(str, 79, fp);
        printf("%s", str);
        count++;

        if(count==23) {
          printf("More? (y/n) ");
          gets(str);
          if(toupper(*str)=='N') break;
          count = 0;
        }
      }

      fclose(fp);

      return 0;
    }

3. /* Copy a file. */
   #include <stdio.h>
   #include <stdlib.h>
   #include <string.h>

   int main(int argc, char *argv[])
   {
     FILE *from, *to;
     char str[128];

     /* see if correct number of command line arguments */
```

```
if(argc<3) {
  printf("Usage: copy <source> <destination>\n");
  exit(1);
}

/* open source file */
if((from = fopen(argv[1], "r"))==NULL) {
  printf("Cannot open source file.\n");
  exit(1);
}

/* open destination file */
if((to = fopen(argv[2], "w"))==NULL) {
  printf("Cannot open destination file.\n");
  exit(1);
}

/* copy the file */
while(!feof(from)) {
  fgets(str, 127, from);
  if(ferror(from)) {
    printf("Error on input.\n");
    break;
  }
  if(!feof(from)) fputs(str, to);
  if(ferror(to)) {
    printf("Error on output.\n");
    break;
  }
}

if(fclose(from)==EOF) {
  printf("Error closing source file.\n");
  exit(1);
}

if(fclose(to)==EOF) {
  printf("Error closing destination file.\n");
  exit(1);
}

return 0;
}
```

9.5 EXERCISES

1.
```c
#include <stdio.h>
#include <stdlib.h>

int main(void)
{
  FILE *fp1, *fp2;
  double d;
  int i;

  if((fp1 = fopen("values", "wb"))==NULL) {
    printf("Cannot open file.\n");
    exit(1);
  }

  if((fp2 = fopen("count", "wb"))==NULL) {
    printf("Cannot open file.\n");
    exit(1);
  }

  d = 1.0;
  for(i=0; d!=0.0 && i<32766; i++) {
    printf("Enter a number (0 to quit): ");
    scanf("%lf", &d);
    fwrite(&d, sizeof d, 1, fp1);
  }

  fwrite(&i, sizeof i, 1, fp2);

  fclose(fp1);
  fclose(fp2);

  return 0;
}
```

2.
```c
#include <stdio.h>
#include <stdlib.h>

int main(void)
{
  FILE *fp1, *fp2;
  double d;
  int i;
```

```
      if((fp1 = fopen("values", "rb"))==NULL) {
        printf("Cannot open file.\n");
        exit(1);
      }

      if((fp2 = fopen("count", "rb"))==NULL) {
        printf("Cannot open file.\n");
        exit(1);
      }

      fread(&i, sizeof i, 1, fp2); /* get count */

      for(; i>0; i--) {
        fread(&d, sizeof d, 1, fp1);
        printf("%f\n", d);
      }

      fclose(fp1);
      fclose(fp2);

      return 0;
    }
```

9.6 EXERCISES

```
1. #include <stdio.h>
   #include <stdlib.h>

   int main(int argc, char *argv[])
   {
     FILE *fp;
     char ch;
     long l;

     if(argc!=2) {
       printf("You must specify the file.\n");
       exit(1);
     }

     if((fp = fopen(argv[1], "rb"))== NULL) {
       printf("Cannot open file.\n");
       exit(1);
     }
```

```
      fseek(fp, 0, SEEK_END); /* find end of file */
      l = ftell(fp);

      /* go back to the start of the file */
      fseek(fp, 0, SEEK_SET);
      for( ; l>=0; l = l - 2L) {
        ch = fgetc(fp);
        putchar(ch);
        fseek(fp, 1L, SEEK_CUR);
      }

      fclose(fp);

      return 0;
    }
```

2.
```
    #include <stdio.h>
    #include <stdlib.h>

    int main(int argc, char *argv[])
    {
      FILE *fp;
      unsigned char ch, val;

      if(argc!=3) {
        printf("Usage: find <filename> <value>");
        exit(1);
      }

      if((fp = fopen(argv[1], "rb"))==NULL) {
        printf("Cannot open file.\n");
        exit(1);
      }

      val = atoi(argv[2]);

      while(!feof(fp)) {
        ch = fgetc(fp);
        if(ch == val)
          printf("Found value at %ld\n", ftell(fp));
      }

      fclose(fp);
```

```
          return 0;
     }
```

9.7   EXERCISES

```
1. #include <stdio.h>
   #include <stdlib.h>
   #include <ctype.h>

   int main(void)
   {
     char fname[80];

     printf("Enter name of file to erase: ");
     gets(fname);
     printf("Are you sure? (Y/N) ");
     if(toupper(getchar())=='Y')
       if(remove(fname))
         printf("\nFile not found or write protected.\n");

     return 0;
   }
```

9.8   EXERCISE

```
1. /* Copy using redirection.

      Execute like this:

      C>NAME < in > out

   */

   #include <stdio.h>

   int main(void)
   {
     char ch;

     while(!feof(stdin)) {
       scanf("%c", &ch);
       if(!feof(stdin)) printf("%c", ch);
     }
```

```
      return 0;
   }
```

```
1. #include <stdio.h>
   #include <stdlib.h>
   #include <ctype.h>

   int main(int argc, char *argv[])
   {
     FILE *fp;
     char str[80];

     /* see if file name is specified */
     if(argc!=2) {
       printf("File name missing.\n");
       exit(1);
     }

     if((fp = fopen(argv[1], "r"))==NULL) {
       printf("Cannot open file.\n");
       exit(1);
     }

     while (!feof(fp)) {
       fgets(str, 79, fp);
       if(!feof(fp)) printf("%s", str);
       printf("...More? (y/n) ");
       if(toupper(getchar())=='N') break;
       printf("\n");
     }

     fclose(fp);

     return 0;
   }

2. /* Copy a file and convert to uppercase. */
   #include <stdio.h>
   #include <stdlib.h>
   #include <ctype.h>
```

```
int main(int argc, char *argv[])
{
  FILE *from, *to;
  char ch;

  /* see if correct number of command line arguments */
  if(argc!=3) {
    printf("Usage: copy <source> <destination>\n");
    exit(1);
  }

  /* open source file */
  if((from = fopen(argv[1], "r"))==NULL) {
    printf("Cannot open source file.\n");
    exit(1);
  }

  /* open destination file */
  if((to = fopen(argv[2], "w"))==NULL) {
    printf("Cannot open destination file.\n");
    exit(1);
  }

  /* copy the file */
  while(!feof(from)) {
    ch = fgetc(from);
    if(!feof(from)) fputc(toupper(ch), to);
  }
  fclose(from);
  fclose(to);

  return 0;
}
```

3. The **fprintf( )** and **fscanf( )** functions operate exactly like **printf( )** and **scanf( )**, except that they work with files.

4.
```
#include <stdio.h>
#include <stdlib.h>

int main(void)
{
  FILE *fp;
  int i, num;
```

```
   if((fp = fopen("rand", "wb"))==NULL) {
     printf("Cannot open file.\n");
     exit(1);
   }

   for(i=0; i<100; i++) {
     num = rand();
     fwrite(&num, sizeof num, 1, fp);
   }

   fclose(fp);

   return 0;
}
```

5.
```
#include <stdio.h>
#include <stdlib.h>

int main(void)
{
   FILE *fp;
   int i, num;

   if((fp = fopen("rand", "rb"))==NULL) {
     printf("Cannot open file.\n");
     exit(1);
   }

   for(i=0; i<100; i++) {
     fread(&num, sizeof num, 1, fp);
     printf("%d\n", num);
   }

   fclose(fp);

   return 0;
}
```

6.
```
#include <stdio.h>
#include <stdlib.h>

int main(void)
{
   FILE *fp;
   long i;
```

```
  int num;

  if((fp = fopen("rand", "rb"))==NULL) {
    printf("Cannot open file.\n");
    exit(1);
  }

  printf("Which number (0-99)? ");
  scanf("%ld", &i);
  fseek(fp, i * sizeof(int), SEEK_SET);
  fread(&num, sizeof num, 1, fp);
  printf("%d\n", num);

  fclose(fp);

  return 0;
}
```

7. The "console" I/O functions are simply special cases of the general file system.

*C*UMULATIVE SKILLS CHECK

```
1. /* An electronic card catalog. */
   #include <stdio.h>
   #include <string.h>
   #include <stdlib.h>

   #define MAX 100

   int menu(void);
   void display(int i);
   void author_search(void);
   void title_search(void);
   void enter(void);
   void save(void);
   void load(void);

   char names[MAX][80]; /* author names */
   char titles[MAX][80]; /* titles */
   char pubs[MAX][80]; /* publisher */

   int top = 0; /* last location used */
```

```c
int main(void)
{
  int choice;

  load(); /* read in catalog */

  do {
    choice = menu();
    switch(choice) {
      case 1: enter(); /* enter books */
        break;
      case 2: author_search(); /* search by author */
        break;
      case 3: title_search(); /* search by title */
        break;
      case 4: save();
    }
  } while(choice!=5);

  return 0;
}

/* Return a menu selection. */
menu(void)
{
  int i;
  char str[80];

  printf("Card Catalog:\n");
  printf("  1. Enter\n");
  printf("  2. Search by author\n");
  printf("  3. Search by Title\n");
  printf("  4. Save catalog\n");
  printf("  5. Quit\n");

  do {
    printf("Choose your selection: ");
    gets(str);
    i = atoi(str);
    printf("\n");
  } while(i<1 || i>5);

  return i;
}
```

```c
/* Enter books into database. */
void enter(void)
{
  int i;

  for(i=top; i<MAX; i++) {
    printf("Enter author name (ENTER to quit) : ");
    gets(names[i]);
    if(!*names[i]) break;
    printf("Enter title: ");
    gets(titles[i]);
    printf("Enter publisher: ");
    gets(pubs[i]);
  }
  top = i;
}

/* Search by author. */
void author_search(void)
{
  char name[80];
  int i, found;

  printf("Name: ");
  gets(name);

  found = 0;
  for(i=0; i<top; i++)
    if(!strcmp(name, names[i])) {
      display(i);
      found = 1;
      printf("\n");
    }

  if(!found) printf("Not Found\n");
}

/* Search by title. */
void title_search(void)
{
  char title[80];
  int i, found;

  printf("Title: ");
  gets(title);
```

```
      found = 0;
      for(i=0; i<top; i++)
        if(!strcmp(title, titles[i])) {
          display(i);
          found = 1;
          printf("\n");
        }
      if(!found) printf("Not Found\n");
}

/* Display catalog entry. */
void display(int i)
{
  printf("%s\n", titles[i]);
  printf("by %s\n", names[i]);
  printf("Published by %s\n", pubs[i]);
}

/* Load the catalog file. */
void load(void)
{
  FILE *fp;

  if((fp = fopen("catalog", "r"))==NULL) {
    printf("Catalog file not on disk.\n");
    return;
  }

  fread(&top, sizeof top, 1, fp); /* read count */
  fread(names, sizeof names, 1, fp);
  fread(titles, sizeof titles, 1, fp);
  fread(pubs, sizeof pubs, 1, fp);

  fclose(fp);
}

/* save the catalog file. */
void save(void)
{
  FILE *fp;

  if((fp = fopen("catalog", "w"))==NULL) {
    printf("Cannot open catalog file.\n");
    exit(1);
```

```
    }

    fwrite(&top, sizeof top, 1, fp);
    fwrite(names, sizeof names, 1, fp);

    fwrite(titles, sizeof titles, 1, fp);
    fwrite(pubs, sizeof pubs, 1, fp);

    fclose(fp);
  }
```

2.
```
   /* Copy a file and remove tabs. */
   #include <stdio.h>
   #include <stdlib.h>
   #include <string.h>

   int main(int argc, char *argv[])
   {
     FILE *from, *to;
     char ch;
     int tab, count;

     /* see if correct number of command line arguments */
     if(argc!=3) {
       printf("Usage: copy <source> <destination>\n");
       exit(1);
     }

     /* open source file */
     if((from = fopen(argv[1], "r"))==NULL) {
       printf("Cannot open source file.\n");
       exit(1);
     }

     /* open destination file */
     if((to = fopen(argv[2], "w"))==NULL) {
       printf("Cannot open destination file.\n");
       exit(1);
     }
     /* copy the file */
     count = 0;
     while(!feof(from)) {
       ch = fgetc(from);
       if(ch=='\t') {
         for(tab = count; tab<8; tab++)
```

```
            fputc(' ', to);
          count = 0;
        }
        else {
          if(!feof(from)) fputc(ch, to);
          count++;
          if(count==8 || ch=='\n') count = 0;
        }
      }
      fclose(from);
      fclose(to);

      return 0;
    }
```

CHAPTER 10

REVIEW SKILLS CHECK

```
1. /* Copy a file. */
   #include <stdio.h>
   #include <stdlib.h>

   int main(int argc, char *argv[])
   {
     FILE *from, *to;
     char ch;

     /* see if correct number of command line arguments */
     if(argc!=3) {
       printf("Usage: copy <source> <destination>\n");
       exit(1);
     }

     /* open source file */
     if((from = fopen(argv[1], "rb"))==NULL) {
       printf("Cannot open source file.\n");
       exit(1);
     }

     /* open destination file */
     if((to = fopen(argv[2], "wb"))==NULL) {
       printf("Cannot open destination file.\n");
```

```
      exit(1);
    }

    /* copy the file */
    while(!feof(from)) {
      ch = fgetc(from);
      if(ferror(from)) {
        printf("Error on input.\n");
        break;
      }
      if(!feof(from)) fputc(ch, to);
      if(ferror(to)) {
        printf("Error on output.\n");
        break;
      }
    }

    if(fclose(from)==EOF) {
      printf("Error closing source file.\n");
      exit(1);
    }

    if(fclose(to)==EOF) {
      printf("Error closing destination file.\n");
      exit(1);
    }

    return 0;
  }

2. #include <stdio.h>
  #include <stdlib.h>

  int main(void)
  {
    FILE *fp;

    /* open file */
    if((fp = fopen("myfile", "w"))==NULL) {
      printf("Cannot open file.\n");
      exit(1);
    }

    fprintf(fp, "%s %.2f %X %c", "this is a string",
            1230.23, 0x1FFF, 'A');
```

```
      fclose(fp);

      return 0;
    }

3. #include <stdio.h>
   #include <stdlib.h>

   int main(void)
   {
     FILE *fp;
     int count[20], i;

     /* open file */
     if((fp = fopen("TEMP", "wb"))==NULL) {
       printf("Cannot open file.\n");
       exit(1);
      }

      for(i=0; i<20; i++) count[i] = i+1;

      fwrite(count, sizeof count, 1, fp);

      fclose(fp);

      return 0;
    }

4. #include <stdio.h>
   #include <stdlib.h>

   int main(void)
   {
     FILE *fp;
     int count[20], i;

     /* open file */
     if((fp = fopen("TEMP", "rb"))==NULL) {
       printf("Cannot open file.\n");
       exit(1);
     }

      fread(count, sizeof count, 1, fp);
```

```
    for(i=0; i<20; i++) printf("%d ", count[i]);

    fclose(fp);

    return 0;
}
```

5. **stdin**, **stdout**, and **stderr** are three streams that are opened automatically when your C program begins executing. By default they refer to the console, but in operating systems that support I/O redirection, they can be redirected to other devices.

6. The **printf( )** and **scanf( )** functions are part of the C file system. They are simply special case functions that automatically use **stdin** and **stdout**.

10.1 *EXERCISES*

1.
```
/* A simple computerized telephone book. */

#include <stdio.h>
#include <string.h>
#include <stdlib.h>

#define MAX 100

struct phone_type {
  char name[40];
  int areacode;
  char number[9];
} phone[MAX];

int loc=0;

int menu(void);
void enter(void);
void load(void);
void save(void);
void find(void);

int main(void)
{
  int choice;
```

```
    do {
      choice = menu();
      switch(choice) {
        case 1: enter();
          break;
        case 2: find();
          break;
        case 3: save();
          break;
        case 4: load();
      }
    } while(choice!=5);

    return 0;
}

/* Get menu choice. */
menu(void)
{
  int i;
  char str[80];

  printf("1. Enter names and numbers\n");
  printf("2. Find numbers\n");
  printf("3. Save directory to disk\n");
  printf("4. Load directory from disk\n");
  printf("5. Quit\n");

  do {
    printf("Enter your choice: ");
    gets(str);
    i = atoi(str);
    printf("\n");
  } while (i<1 || i>5);
  return i;
}

void enter(void)
{
  char temp[80];

  for(;loc<100; loc++) {
    if(loc<100) {
      printf("Enter name: ");
      gets(phone[loc].name);
```

```
          if(!*phone[loc].name) break;
          printf("Enter area code: ");
          gets(temp);
          phone[loc].areacode = atoi(temp);
          printf("Enter number: ");
          gets(phone[loc].number);
      }
   }
}

void find(void)
{
  char name[80];
  int i;

  printf("Enter name: ");
  gets(name);
  if(!*name) return;

  for(i=0; i<100; i++)
    if(!strcmp(name, phone[i].name))
      printf("%s (%d) %s\n", phone[i].name,
             phone[i].areacode, phone[i].number);
}

void load(void)
{
  FILE *fp;

  if((fp = fopen("phone", "r"))==NULL) {
    printf("Cannot open file.\n");
    exit(1);
  }

  loc = 0;
  while(!feof(fp)) {
    fscanf(fp, "%s%d%s", phone[loc].name,
           &phone[loc].areacode, phone[loc].number);
    loc++;
  }
  fclose(fp);
}

void save(void)
{
```

```
        FILE *fp;
        int i;

        if((fp = fopen("phone", "w"))==NULL) {
          printf("Cannot open file.\n");
          exit(1);
        }

        for(i=0; i<loc; i++) {
          fprintf(fp, "%s %d %s ", phone[i].name,
                    phone[i].areacode, phone[i].number);

        }
        fclose(fp);
      }
```

2. The variable **i** is a member of structure **s_type**. Therefore, it cannot be used by itself. Instead, it must be accessed using **s** and the dot operator, as shown here.

```
        s.i = 10;
```

▆ 10.2 ▆ **E**XERCISES

1. No. Since **p** is a pointer to a structure, you must use the arrow operator, not the dot operator, to access a member.

2. ```
   #include <stdio.h>
   #include <time.h>

   int main(void)
   {
     struct tm *systime, *gmt;
     time_t t;

     t = time(NULL);
     systime = localtime(&t);

     printf("Time is %.2d:%.2d:%.2d\n", systime->tm_hour,
             systime->tm_min, systime->tm_sec);
     gmt = gmtime(&t);
     printf("Coordinated Universal Time is %.2d:%.2d:%.2d\n",
             gmt->tm_hour,
             gmt->tm_min, gmt->tm_sec);
   ```
   ```

```
    printf("Date: %.2d/%.2d/%.2d", systime->tm_mon+1,
           systime->tm_mday, systime->tm_year);

    return 0;
}
```

10.3 **E XERCISES**

1.
```
/* A simple computerized telephone book. */

#include <stdio.h>
#include <string.h>
#include <stdlib.h>

#define MAX 100

struct address {
  char street[40];
  char city[40];
  char state[3];
  char zip[12];
};

struct phone_type {
  char name[40];
  int areacode;
  char number[9];
  struct address addr;
} phone[MAX];

int loc=0;

int menu(void);
void enter(void);
void load(void);
void save(void);
void find(void);

int main(void)
{
  int choice;

  do {
    choice = menu( );
```

```
      switch(choice) {
        case 1: enter( );
          break;
        case 2: find( );
          break;
        case 3: save( );
          break;
        case 4: load( );
      }
  } while(choice!=5);

  return 0;
}

/* Get menu choice. */
menu(void)
{
  int i;
  char str[80];

  printf("1. Enter names and numbers\n");
  printf("2. Find numbers\n");
  printf("3. Save directory to disk\n");
  printf("4. Load directory from disk\n");
  printf("5. Quit\n");

  do {
    printf("Enter your choice: ");
    gets(str);
    i = atoi(str);
    printf("\n");
  } while(i<1 || i>5);
  return i;
}

void enter(void)
{
  char temp[80];

  for(;loc<100; loc++) {
    if(loc<100) {
      printf("Enter name: ");
      gets(phone[loc].name);
      if(!*phone[loc].name) break;
      printf("Enter area code: ");
```

```
        gets(temp);
        phone[loc].areacode = atoi(temp);
        printf("Enter number: ");
        gets(phone[loc].number);

        /* input address info */
        printf("Enter street address: ");
        gets(phone[loc].addr.street);
        printf("Enter city: ");
        gets(phone[loc].addr.city);
        printf("Enter State: ");
        gets(phone[loc].addr.state);
        printf("Enter zip code: ");
        gets(phone[loc].addr.zip);
      }
    }
}

void find(void)
{
  char name[80];
  int i;

  printf("Enter name: ");
  gets(name);
  if(!*name) return;

  for(i=0; i<100; i++)
    if(!strcmp(name, phone[i].name)) {
      printf("%s (%d) %s\n", phone[i].name,
             phone[i].areacode, phone[i].number);
      printf("%s\n%s %s %s\n", phone[i].addr.street,
             phone[i].addr.city, phone[i].addr.state,
             phone[i].addr.zip);
  }
}

void load(void)
{
  FILE *fp;

  if((fp = fopen("phone", "rb"))==NULL) {
    printf("Cannot open file.\n");
    exit(1);
  }
```

```
        loc = 0;
        while(!feof(fp)) {
          fread(&phone[loc], sizeof phone[loc], 1, fp);
          loc++;
        }
        fclose(fp);
      }

      void save(void)
      {
        FILE *fp;
        int i;

        if((fp = fopen("phone", "wb"))==NULL) {
          printf("Cannot open file.\n");
          exit(1);
        }

        for(i=0; i<loc; i++) {
          fwrite(&phone[i], sizeof phone[i], 1, fp);
        }
        fclose(fp);
      }
```

■■ 10.4 ■■ *E*XERCISES

```
1. #include <stdio.h>

   int main(void)
   {
     struct b_type {
       int a: 3;
       int b: 3;
       int c: 2;
     } bvar;

     bvar.a = -1;
     bvar.b = 3;
     bvar.c = 1;
     printf("%d %d %d", bvar.a, bvar.b, bvar.c);

     return 0;
   }
```

```
1. #include <stdio.h>
   #include <stdlib.h>

   union u_type {
     double d;
     unsigned char c[8];
   } ;

   double uread(FILE *fp);
   void  uwrite(double num, FILE *fp);

   int main(void)
   {
     FILE *fp;
     double d;

     if((fp = fopen("myfile", "wb+"))==NULL) {
       printf("Cannot open file.\n");
       exit(1);
     }

     uwrite(100.23, fp);
     d = uread(fp);
     printf("%1f", d);

     return 0;
   }

   void uwrite (double num, FILE *fp)
   {
     int i;
     union u_type var;

     var.d = num;
     for(i=0; i<8; i++) fputc(var.c[i], fp);
   }

   double uread(FILE *fp)
   {
     int i;
     union u_type var;
```

```
      rewind(fp);
      for(i=0; i<8; i++) var.c[i] = fgetc(fp);

      return var.d;
   }
```

2.
```
#include <stdio.h>

int main(void)
{
  union t_type {
    long l;
    int i;
  } uvar;

  uvar.l = 0L; /* clear l */
  uvar.i = 100;

  printf("%ld", uvar.l);

  return 0;
}
```

MASTERY SKILLS CHECK

1. A structure is a named group of related variables. A union defines a memory location shared by two or more variables of different types.

2.
```
struct s_type {
    char ch;
    float d;
    int i;
    char str[80];
    double balance;
} s_var;
```

3. Because **p** is a pointer to a structure, you must use the arrow operator to reference an element, not the dot operator.

4.
```
#include <stdio.h>
#include <stdlib.h>

struct s_type {
  char name[40];
```

```
      char phone[14];
      int hours;
      double wage;
    } emp[10];

    int main(void)
    {
      FILE *fp;
      int i;
      char temp[80];

      if((fp = fopen("emp", "wb"))==NULL) {
        printf("Cannot open EMP file.\n");
        exit(1);
      }

      for(i=0; i<10; i++) {
        printf("Enter name: ");
        gets(emp[i].name);
        printf("Enter telephone number: ");
        gets(emp[i].phone);
        printf("Enter hours worked: ");
        gets(temp);
        emp[i].hours = atoi(temp);
        printf("Enter hourly wage: ");
        gets(temp);
        emp[i].wage = atof(temp);
      }

      fwrite(emp, sizeof emp, 1, fp);
      fclose(fp);

      return 0;
    }

 5. #include <stdio.h>
    #include <stdlib.h>

    struct s_type {
      char name[40];
      char phone[14];
      int hours;
      double wage;
    } emp[10];
```

```
int main(void)
{
  FILE *fp;
  int i;

  if((fp = fopen("emp", "rb"))==NULL) {
    printf("Cannot open EMP file.\n");
    exit(1);
  }

  fread(emp, sizeof emp, 1, fp);
  for(i=0; i<10; i++) {
    printf("%s %s\n", emp[i].name, emp[i].phone);
    printf("%d %f\n\n", emp[i].hours, emp[i].wage);
  }

  fclose(fp);

  return 0;
}
```

6. A bit-field is a structure member that specifies its length in bits.

7. ```
#include <stdio.h>

int main(void)
{
  union u_type {
    short int i;
    unsigned char c[2];
  } uvar;

  uvar.i = 99;

  printf("High order byte: %u\n", uvar.c[1]);
  printf("Low order byte: %u\n", uvar.c[0]);

  return 0;
}
```
```

*C*UMULATIVE SKILLS CHECK

1.
```c
#include <stdio.h>

struct s_type {
  int i;
  char ch;
  double d;
} var1, var2;

void struct_swap(struct s_type *i, struct s_type *j);

int main(void)
{
  var1.i = 100;
  var2.i = 99;
  var1.ch = 'a';
  var2.ch = 'b';
  var1.d = 1.0;
  var2.d = 2.0;

  printf("var1: %d %c %f\n", var1.i, var1.ch, var1.d);
  printf("var2: %d %c %f\n", var2.i, var2.ch, var2.d);

  struct_swap(&var1, &var2);

  printf("After swap:\n");
  printf("var1: %d %c %f\n", var1.i, var1.ch, var1.d);
  printf("var2: %d %c %f", var2.i, var2.ch, var2.d);

  return 0;
}

void struct_swap(struct s_type *i, struct s_type *j)
{
  struct s_type temp;

  temp = *i;
  *i = *j;
  *j = temp;
}
```

2.
```c
/* Copy a file. */
#include <stdio.h>
```

```
#include <stdlib.h>

int main(int argc, char *argv[])
{
  FILE *from, *to;
  union u_type {
    int i;
    char ch;
  } uvar;

  /* see if correct number of command line arguments */
  if(argc!=3) {
    printf("Usage: copy <source> <destination>\n");
    exit(1);
  }

  /* open source file */
  if((from = fopen(argv[1], "rb"))==NULL) {
    printf("Cannot open source file.\n");
    exit(1);
  }

  /* open destination file */
  if((to = fopen(argv[2], "wb"))==NULL) {
    printf("Cannot open destination file.\n");
    exit(1);
  }

  /* copy the file */
  for(;;) {
    uvar.i = fgetc(from);
    if(uvar.i==EOF) break;
    fputc(uvar.ch, to);
  }
  fclose(from);
  fclose(to);

  return 0;
}
```

3. You cannot use a structure as an argument to **scanf( )**. However, you can use a structure element as an argument, as shown here.

```
scanf("%d", &var.a);
```

```
4. #include <string.h>
   #include <stdio.h>

   struct s_type {
     char str[80];
   } var;

   void f(struct s_type i);

   int main(void)
   {
     strcpy(var.str, "this is original string");
     f(var);
     printf("%s", var.str);

     return 0;
   }

   void f(struct s_type i)
   {
     strcpy(i.str, "new string");
     printf("%s\n", i.str);
   }
```

 ## CHAPTER 11

REVIEW SKILLS CHECK

```
1. #include <stdio.h>

   struct num_type {
     int i;
     int sqr;
     int cube;
   } nums[10];

   int main(void)
   {
     int i;

     for(i=1; i<11; i++) {
       nums[i-1].i = i;
```

```
      nums[i-1].sqr = i*i;
      nums[i-1].cube = i*i*i;
    }

    for(i=0; i<10; i++) {
      printf("%d ", nums[i].i);
      printf("%d ", nums[i].sqr);
      printf("%d\n", nums[i].cube);
    }

    return 0;
}
```

2.
```
#include <stdio.h>

union i_to_c {
  char c[2];
  short int i;
} ic;

int main(void)
{
  printf("Enter an integer ");
  scanf("%hd", &ic.i);
  printf("Character representation of each byte: %c %c",
         ic.c[0], ic.c[1]);

  return 0;
}
```

3. The fragment displays **8**, the size of the largest element of the union.

4. To access a structure member when actually using a structure variable, you must use the dot operator. The arrow operator is used when accessing a member using a pointer to a structure.

5. A bit-field is a structure element whose size is specified in bits.

11.1 ***E*XERCISES**

1. The best variables to make into **register** types are **k** and **m**, because they are accessed most frequently.

2.
```c
#include <stdio.h>

void sum_it(int value);

int main(void)
{
   sum_it(10);
   sum_it(20);
   sum_it(30);
   sum_it(40);

   return 0;
}

void sum_it(int value)
{
   static int sum=0;

   sum = sum + value;
   printf("Current value: %d\n", sum);
}
```

4. You cannot obtain the address of a **register** variable.

<table>
<tr><td>**11.2**</td><td>*EXERCISES*</td></tr>
</table>

1.
```c
#include <stdio.h>

const double version = 6.01;

int main(void)
{
   printf("Version %.2f", version);

   return 0;
}
```

2.
```c
#include <stdio.h>

char *mystrcpy(char *to, const char *from);

int main(void)
{
```

```
      char *p, str[80];

      p = mystrcpy(str, "testing");

      printf("%s %s", p, str);

      return 0;
}

char *mystrcpy(char *to, const char *from)
{
   char *temp;

   temp = to;

   while(*from) *to++ = *from++;
   *to = '\0' ; /* null terminator */

   return temp;
}
```

11.3 ▮ **E**XERCISES

2. `enum money {penny, nickel, quarter, half_dollar, dollar};`

3. No, you cannot output an enumeration constant as a string as is attempted in the **printf( )** statement.

11.4 ▮ **E**XERCISES

1.
```
#include <stdio.h>

typedef unsigned long UL;

int main(void)
{
   UL count;

   count = 312323;

   printf("%lu", count);
```

```
      return 0;
   }
```

2. The **typedef** statement is out of order. The correct form of **typedef** is

typedef *oldname newname*;

11.5 EXERCISES

```
1. #include <stdio.h>
   #include <stdlib.h>

   int main(int argc, char *argv[])
   {
     FILE *in, *out;
     unsigned char ch;

     if(argc!=3) {
       printf("Usage: code <in> <out>\n");
       exit(1);
     }

     if((in = fopen(argv[1], "rb"))==NULL) {
       printf("Cannot open input file.\n");
       exit(1);
     }

     if((out = fopen(argv[2], "wb"))==NULL) {
       printf("Cannot open output file.\n");
       exit(1);
     }

     while(!feof(in)) {
       ch = fgetc(in);
       if(!feof(in)) fputc(~ch, out);
     }

     fclose(in);
     fclose(out);

     return 0;
   }
```

2.
```c
#include <stdio.h>
#include <stdlib.h>

int main(int argc, char *argv[])
{
  FILE *in, *out;
  unsigned char ch;

  if(argc!=4) {
    printf("Usage: code <in> <out> <key>\n");
    exit(1);
  }

  if(( in = fopen(argv[1], "rb"))==NULL) {
    printf("Cannot open input file.\n");
    exit(1);
  }

  if((out = fopen(argv[2], "wb"))==NULL) {
    printf("Cannot open output file.\n");
    exit(1);
  }

  while(!feof(in)) {
    ch = fgetc(in);
    ch = *argv[3] ^ ch;
    if(!feof(in)) fputc(ch, out);
  }

  fclose(in);
  fclose(out);

  return 0;
}
```

3. a. 0000 0001

   b. 1111 1111

   c. 1111 1101

4. `char ch;`

   .

   .

   .

```
/* To zero high order bit, AND with 127, which
   in binary is 0111 1111. This causes the high-
   order bit to be zeroed and all other bits left
   untouched.
*/
ch = ch & 127;
```

11.6 EXERCISES

1.
```
#include <stdio.h>

int main(void)
{
  int i, j, k;

  printf("Enter a number: ");
  scanf("%d", &i);

  j = i << 1;
  k = i >> 1;
  printf("%d doubled: %d\n", i, j);
  printf("%d halved: %d", i, k);

  return 0;
}
```

2.
```
#include <stdio.h>

void rotate(unsigned char *c);

int main(void)
{
  unsigned char ch;
  int i;

  ch = 1;

  for(i=0; i<16; i++) {
    rotate(&ch);
    printf("%u\n", ch);
  }
```

```
      return 0;
    }

    void rotate(unsigned char *c)
    {
      union {
        unsigned char ch[2];
        unsigned u;
      } rot;

      rot.u = 0; /* clear 16 bits */

      rot.ch[0] = *c;

      /* shift integer left */
      rot.u = rot.u << 1;

      /* See if a bit got shifted into c[1].
         If so, OR it back onto the other end. */
      if(rot.ch[1]) rot.ch[0] = rot.ch[0] | 1;

      *c = rot.ch[0];
    }
```

11.7   EXERCISES

1.
```
#include <stdio.h>

int main(void)
{
  int i, j, answer;

  printf("Enter two integers: ");
  scanf("%d%d", &i, &j);

  answer = j ? i/j: 0;
  printf("%d", answer);

  return 0;
}
```

2. `count = a>b ? 100 : 0;`

11.8 ***E****XERCISES*

2. `x &= y;`

3.
```
#include <stdio.h>

int main(void)
{
  int i;

  for(i=17; i<=1000; i+=17)
    printf("%d\n", i);

  return 0;
}
```

11.9 ***E****XERCISES*

1.
```
#include <stdio.h>

int main(void)
{
  int i, j, k;

  for(i=0, j=-50, k=i+j; i<100; i++, j++, k=i+j)
    printf("k = %d\n", k);

  return 0;
}
```

2. 3

M*ASTERY SKILLS CHECK*

1. The **register** specifier causes the C compiler to provide the fastest access possible for the variable it precedes.

2. The **const** specifier tells the C compiler that no statement in the program may modify a variable declared as **const**. Also, a **const** pointer parameter may not be used to modify the object pointed to by the pointer. The **volatile** specifier tells the compiler that

any variable it precedes may have its value changed in ways not explicitly specified by the program.

3.
```c
#include <stdio.h>

int main(void)
{
  register int i, sum;

  sum = 0;
  for(i=1; i<101; i++)
    sum = sum + i;

  printf("%d", sum);

  return 0;
}
```

4. Yes, the statement is valid. It creates another name for the type **long double**.

5.
```c
#include <stdio.h>
#include <conio.h>

int main(void)
{
  char ch1, ch2;
  char mask, i;

  printf("Enter two characters: ");
  ch1 = getche();
  ch2 = getche();
  printf("\n");

  mask = 1;
  for(i=0; i<8; i++) {
    if((mask & ch1) && (mask & ch2))
      printf("bits %d the same\n", i);
    mask <<= 1;
  }

  return 0;
}
```

6. The << and >> are the left and right shift operators, respectively.

7. c += 10;

8. count = done ? 0 : 100;

9. An enumeration is a list of named integer constants. Here is one that enumerates the planets.

```
enum planets {Mercury, Venus, Earth, Mars, Jupiter,
              Saturn, Neptune, Uranus, Pluto} ;
```

▬▬▬▬ CUMULATIVE SKILLS CHECK

1.
```
#include <stdio.h>

void show_binary(unsigned u);

int main(void)
{
  unsigned char ch, t1, t2;

  ch = 100;
  show_binary(ch);

  t1 = ch;
  t2 = ch;

  t1 <<= 4;
  t2 >>= 4;

  ch = t1 | t2;

  show_binary(ch);

  return 0;
}

void show_binary(unsigned u)
{
  unsigned n;

  for(n=128; n>0; n=n/2)
    if(u & n) printf("1 ");
    else printf("0 ");
```

```
      printf("\n");
    }

2.  #include <stdio.h>
    #include <stdlib.h>

    int main(int argc, char *argv[])
    {
      FILE *in;
      unsigned char ch;

      if(argc!=2) {
        printf("Usage: code <in>\n");
        exit(1);
      }

      if((in = fopen(argv[1], "rb"))==NULL) {
        printf("Cannot open input file.\n");
        exit(1);
      }

      while(!feof(in)) {
        ch = fgetc(in);
        if(!feof(in)) putchar(~ch);
      }

      fclose(in);

      return 0;
    }
```

3. Yes, any type of variable can be specified using **register**. However, on some types, it may have no effect.

4.  ```
    /* A simple computerized telephone book. */

    #include <stdio.h>
    #include <string.h>
    #include <stdlib.h>

    #define MAX 100

    struct address {
      char street[40];
      char city[40];
    ```
    ```

```
      char state[3];
      char zip[12];
};

struct phone_type {
  char name[40];
  int areacode;
  char number[9];
  struct address addr;
} phone[MAX];

int loc =0;

int menu(void);
void enter(void);
void load(void);
void save(void);
void find(void);

int main(void)
{
  register int choice;

  do {
    choice = menu();
    switch(choice) {
      case 1: enter();
        break;
      case 2: find();
        break;
      case 3: save();
        break;
      case 4: load();
    }
  } while(choice!=5);

  return 0;
}

/* Get menu choice. */
menu(void)
{
  register int i;
  char str[80];
```

```c
        printf("1. Enter names and numbers \n");
        printf("2. Find numbers\n");
        printf("3. Save directory to disk\n");
        printf("4. Load directory from disk\n");
        printf("5. Quit\n");

        do {
          printf("Enter your choice: ");
          gets(str);
          i = atoi(str);
          printf("\n");
        } while(i<1 || i>5);
        return i;
      }

void enter(void)
{
  char temp[80];

  for(; loc<100; loc++) {
    if(loc<100) {
      printf("Enter name: ");
      gets(phone[loc].name);
      if(!*phone[loc].name) break;
      printf("Enter area code: ");
      gets(temp);
      phone[loc].areacode = atoi(temp);
      printf("Enter number: ");
      gets(phone[loc].number);

      /* input address info */
      printf("Enter street address: ");
      gets(phone[loc].addr.street);
      printf("Enter city: ");
      gets(phone[loc].addr.city);
      printf("Enter State: ");
      gets(phone[loc].addr.state);
      printf("Enter zip code: ");
      gets(phone[loc].addr.zip);
    }
  }
}

void find(void)
{
```

```
        char name[80];
        register int i;

        printf("Enter name: ");
        gets(name);
        if(!*name) return;

        for(i=0; i<100; i++)
          if(!strcmp(name, phone[i].name)) {
            printf("%s (%d) %s\n", phone[i].name,
                    phone[i].areacode, phone[i].number);
            printf("%s\n%s %s %s\n", phone[i].addr.street,
                    phone[i].addr.city, phone[i].addr.state,
                    phone[i].addr.zip);
          }
      }

      void load(void)
      {
        FILE *fp;

        if((fp = fopen("phone", "rb"))==NULL) {
          printf("Cannot open file.\n");
          exit(1);
        }

        loc = 0;
        while(!feof(fp)) {
          fread(&phone[loc], sizeof phone[loc], 1, fp);
          loc++;
        }
        fclose(fp);
      }

      void save(void)
      {
        FILE *fp;
        register int i;

        if((fp = fopen("phone", "wb"))==NULL) {
          printf("Cannot open file.\n");
          exit(1);
        }

        for(i=0; i<loc; i++) {
```

```
        fwrite(&phone[i], sizeof phone[i], 1, fp);
      }
      fclose(fp);
    }
```

CHAPTER 12

REVIEW SKILLS CHECK

1. Modifying a variable with **register** causes the compiler to store the variable in such a way that access to it is as fast as possible. For integer and character types, this typically means storing it in a register of the CPU.

2. Because **i** is declared as **const** the function cannot modify any object pointed to by it.

3. a. 1100 0100

   b. 1111 1111

   c. 0011 1011

4.
```
#include <stdio.h>

int main(void)
{
  int i;

  printf("Enter a number: ");
  scanf("%d", &i);

  printf("Doubled: %d\n", i << 1);
  printf("Halved: %d\n", i >> 1);

  return 0;
}
```

5.
```
a = b = c = 1;

max = a<b ? 100 : 0;

i *= 2;
```

6. The **extern** modifier is principally used to inform the compiler about global variables defined in a different file. Placing **extern** in front of a variable's declaration tells the compiler that the variable is defined elsewhere, but allows the current file to refer to it.

12.1 EXERCISES

1. ```
#define RANGE(i, min, max) ((i)<(min)) || ((i)>(max)) ? 1 : 0
```

2. ```c
#include <stdio.h>

#define ABS(i) (i)<0 ? -(i) : i

int main(void)
{
   printf("%d %d", ABS(-1), ABS(1));

   return 0;
}
```

12.2 EXERCISES

1. ```c
#include <stdio.h>

#define INT 0
#define FLOAT 1
#define PWR_TYPE INT

int main(void)
{
   int e;
#if PWR_TYPE==FLOAT
   double base, result;
#elif PWR_TYPE==INT
   int base, result;
#endif

#if PWR_TYPE==FLOAT
   printf("Enter floating point base: ");
   scanf("%lf", &base);
```
```

```
#elif PWR_TYPE==INT
  printf("Enter integer base: ");
  scanf("%d", &base);
#endif
  printf("Enter integer exponent (greater than 0): ");
  scanf("%d", &e);

  result = 1;
  for(; e; e--)
    result = result * base;

#if PWR_TYPE==FLOAT
    printf("Result: %f", result);
#elif PWR_TYPE==INT
    printf("Result: %d", result);
#endif

  return 0;
}
```

2. No. You cannot use an expression like **!MIKE** with **#ifdef**. Here are two possible solutions.

```
#ifndef MIKE
.
.
.
#endif

/* or */

#if !defined MIKE
.
.
.
#endif
```

▬ **12.5** ▬ **E**XERCISES

2. The program displays **one two**.

| 12.6 | **E**XERCISES |

2.
```c
#include <stdio.h>
#include <stdlib.h>

int comp(const void *i, const void *j);

int main(void)
{
  int sort[100], i, key;
  int *p;

  for(i=0; i<100; i++)
    sort[i] = rand();

  qsort(sort, 100, sizeof(int), comp);

  for(i=0; i<100; i++)
    printf("%d\n", sort[i]);

  printf("Enter number to find: ");
  scanf("%d", &key);
  p = bsearch(&key, sort, 100, sizeof(int), comp);
  if(p) printf("Number is in array.\n");
  else printf("Number not found.\n");

  return 0;
}

int comp(const void *i, const void *j)
{
  return *(int*)i - *(int*)j;
}
```

3.
```c
#include <stdio.h>

int sum(int a, int b);
int subtract(int a, int b);
int mul(int a, int b);
int div(int a, int b);
int modulus(int a, int b);

/* initialize the pointer array */
int(*p[5]) (int x, int y) = {
```

```
      sum, subtract, mul, div, modulus
} ;

int main(void)
{
  int result;
  int i, j, op;

  printf("Enter two numbers: ");
  scanf("%d%d", &i, &j);
  printf("0: add, 1: subtract, 2: multiply, 3: divide, ");
  printf("4: modulus\n");
  do {
    printf("Enter number of operation: ");
    scanf("%d", &op);
  } while(op<0 || op>4);

  result = (*p[op]) (i, j);
  printf("%d", result);

  return 0;
}

int sum(int a, int b)
{
  return a+b;
}

int subtract(int a, int b)
{
  return a-b;
}

int mul(int a, int b)
{
  return a*b;
}

int div(int a, int b)
{
  if(b) return a/b;
  else return 0;
}
```

```
int modulus(int a, int b)
{
  if(b) return a%b;
  else return 0;
}
```

12.7   EXERCISES

2.
```
#include <stdio.h>
#include <stdlib.h>

int main(void)
{
  int *p, i;

  p = malloc(10*sizeof(int));
  if(!p) {
    printf("Allocation Error");
    exit(1);
  }

  for(i=0; i<10; i++) p[i] = i+1;

  for(i=0; i<10; i++) printf("%d ", *(p+i));

  free(p);

  return 0;
}
```

3. The statement

```
*p = malloc(10);
```

should be

```
p = malloc(10);
```

Also, the value returned by **malloc( )** is not verified as a valid pointer.

1. When you specify the file name within angle brackets, the compiler searches for the file in an implementation-defined manner. When you enclose the file name within double quotes, the compiler first tries some other implementation-defined manner to find the file. If that fails, it restarts the search as if you had enclosed the file name within angle brackets.

2.
```
#ifdef DEBUG
if(!(j%2)) {
  printf("j = %d\n", j);
  j = 0;
}
#endif
```

3.
```
#if DEBUG==1
if(!(j%2)) {
  printf("j = %d\n", j);
  j = 0;
}
#endif
```

4. To undefine a macro name use **#undef**.

5. _ _FILE_ _ is a predefined macro that contains the name of the source file currently being compiled.

6. The **#** operator makes the argument it precedes into a quoted string. The **##** operator concatenates two arguments.

7.
```
#include <stdio.h>
#include <stdlib.h>
#include <string.h>

int comp(const void *i, const void *j);

int main(void)
{
  char str[] = "this is a test of qsort";

  qsort(str, strlen(str), 1, comp);

  printf(str);
```

```
      return 0;
    }

    int comp(const void *i, const void *j)
    {
      return *(char*)i - *(char*)j;
    }

8.  #include <stdio.h>
    #include <stdlib.h>

    int main(void)
    {
      double *p;

      p = malloc(sizeof(double));
      if(!p) {
        printf("Allocation Error");
        exit(1);
      }

      *p = 99.01;
      printf("%f", *p);
      free(p);

      return 0;
    }
```

 CUMULATIVE SKILLS CHECK

```
1.  /* An electronic card catalog. */
    #include <stdio.h>
    #include <string.h>
    #include <stdlib.h>

    #define MAX 100

    int menu(void);
    void display(int i);
    void author_search(void);
    void title_search(void);
    void enter(void);
    void save(void);
    void load(void);
```

```
struct catalog {
  char name[80];     /* author name */
  char title[80];    /* title */
  char pub[80];      /* publisher */
  unsigned date;     /* date of publication */
  unsigned char ed; /* edition */
} *cat[MAX]; /* notice that this declares a pointer array */

int top = 0; /* last location used */

int main(void)
{
  int choice;

  load(); /* read in catalog */

  do {
    choice = menu();
    switch(choice) {
      case 1: enter(); /* enter books */
        break;
      case 2: author_search(); /* search by author */
        break;
      case 3: title_search(); /* search by title */
        break;
      case 4: save();
    }
  } while(choice!=5);

  return 0;
}

/* Return a menu selection. */
int menu(void)
{
  int i;
  char str[80];

  printf("Card Catalog:\n");
  printf(" 1. Enter\n");
  printf(" 2. Search by Author\n");
  printf(" 3. Search by Title\n");
  printf(" 4. Save catalog\n");
  printf(" 5. Quit\n");
```

```
  do {
    printf("Choose your selection: ");
    gets(str);
    i = atoi(str);
    printf("\n");
  } while(i<1 || i>5);

  return i;
}

/* Enter books into database. */
void enter(void)
{
  int i;
  char temp[80];

  for(i=top; i<MAX; i++){
    /* allocate memory for book info */
    cat[i] = malloc(sizeof(struct catalog));
    if(!cat[i]) {
      printf("Out of memory.\n");
      return;
    }

    printf("Enter author name (ENTER to quit): ");
    gets(cat[i]->name);
    if(!*cat[i]->name) break;
    printf("Enter title: ");
    gets(cat[i]->title);
    printf("Enter publisher: ");
    gets(cat[i]->pub);
    printf("Enter copyright date: ");
    gets(temp);
    cat[i]->date = (unsigned) atoi(temp);
    printf("Enter edition: ");
    gets(temp);
    cat[i]->ed = (unsigned char) atoi(temp);
  }
  top = i;
}

/* Search by author. */
void author_search(void)
{
```

```c
  char name[80];
  int i, found;

  printf("Name: ");
  gets(name);
  found = 0;
  for( i=0; i<top; i++)
    if(!strcmp(name, cat[i]->name)) {
      display(i);
      found = 1;
      printf("\n");
    }

  if(!found) printf("Not Found\n");
}

/* Search by title. */
void title_search(void)
{
  char title[80];
  int i, found;

  printf("Title: ");
  gets(title);

  found = 0;
  for(i=0; i<top; i++)
    if(!strcmp(title, cat[i]->title)) {
      display(i);
      found = 1;
      printf("\n");
    }
  if(!found) printf("Not Found\n");
}

/* Display catalog entry. */
void display(int i)
{
  printf("%s\n", cat[i]->title);
  printf("by %s\n", cat[i]->name);
  printf("Published by %s\n", cat[i]->pub);
  printf("Copyright: %u, %u edition\n", cat[i]->date,
         cat[i]->ed);
}
```

```c
/* Load the catalog file. */
void load(void)
{
  FILE *fp;
  int i;

  if((fp = fopen("catalog", "rb"))==NULL) {
    printf("Catalog file not on disk.\n");
    return;
  }


  if(fread(&top, sizeof top, 1, fp) != 1) {  /* read count */
    printf("Error reading count.\n");
    exit(1);
  }

  for(i=0; i<top; i++) {
    cat[i] = malloc(sizeof(struct catalog));
    if(!cat[i]) {
      printf("Out of memory.\n");
      top = i-1;
      break;
    }
    if(fread(cat[i], sizeof(struct catalog), 1, fp)!= 1) {
      printf("Error reading catalog data.\n");
      exit(1);
    }
  }

  fclose(fp);
}

/* Save the catalog file. */
void save(void)
{
  FILE *fp;
  int i;

  if((fp = fopen("catalog", "wb"))==NULL) {
    printf("Cannot open catalog file.\n");
    exit(1);
  }
```

```
      if(fwrite(&top, sizeof top, 1, fp) != 1) {  /* write count */
        printf("Error writing count.\n");
        exit(1);
      }

    for(i=0; i<top; i++)
      if(fwrite(cat[i], sizeof(struct catalog), 1, fp)!= 1) {
        printf("Error writing catalog data.\n");
        exit(1);
      }

    fclose(fp);
  }
```

2. ```
   #include <stdio.h>

   #define CODE_IT(ch) ~ch

   int main(void)
   {
     int ch;
     printf("Enter a character: ");
     ch = getchar();
     printf("%c coded is %c", ch, CODE_IT(ch));

     return 0;
   }
   ```
   ```

Index